VISUAL QUICKSTART GUIDE

PHP

FOR THE WEB
Third Edition

Larry Ullman

Peachpit Press

Visual QuickStart Guide
PHP for the Web, Third Edition
Larry Ullman

Peachpit Press
1249 Eighth Street
Berkeley, CA 94710
510/524-2178
510/524-2221 (fax)

Find us on the Web at www.peachpit.com.
To report errors, please send a note to errata@peachpit.com.
Peachpit Press is a division of Pearson Education.

Editor: Rebecca Gulick
Copy Editor: Bob Campbell
Production Coordinator: Myrna Vladic
Compositor: Debbie Roberti
Indexer: Julie Bess
Cover design: Peachpit Press

ISBN 13: 978-0-321-44249-9
ISBN 10: 0-321-44249-0

9 8 7 6 5 4 3 2 1

Printed and bound in the United States of America

For Jessica, Gina, and Rich,
with gratitude for all of their
love and support.

Special thanks

Many, many thanks to everyone at Peachpit Press for their assistance and hard work, especially:

The best darn editor in the world, Rebecca Gulick. Thanks for, well, just about everything. As always, it's my pleasure to be able to work with you.

Bob Campbell, for his attention to detail.

Deb Roberti and Myrna Vladic, who take a bunch of disparate stuff and turn it into a book. Julie Bess for her excellent indexing.

Everyone at Peachpit for doing what's required to create, publish, distribute, market, sell, and support these books.

My sincerest thanks to the readers of the other editions of this book and my other books. Thanks for your feedback and support and for keeping me in business.

Finally, thanks to: Rasmus Lerdorf (who got the PHP ball rolling); the people at PHP.net and Zend.com; those who frequent the various newsgroups and mailing lists; and the greater PHP and open source communities for developing, improving upon, and supporting such wonderfully useful technology.

TABLE OF CONTENTS

TABLE OF CONTENTS

INTRODUCTION

When I began the first edition of this book, back in the year 2000, PHP was a little-known *open source* project. It was adored by technical people in the know but not yet recognized as the popular choice for Web development that it is today. When I taught myself PHP, very little documentation was available on the language—and that was my motivation for writing this book in the first place.

Today things are different. The Internet has gone through a boom and a bust and has righted itself. Furthermore, PHP is now the reigning king of dynamic Web design tools and has begun to expand beyond the realm of Web development. But despite PHP's popularity and the increase in available documentation, sample code, and examples, a good book discussing the language is still relevant. Particularly as PHP makes its sixth major release, a book such as this—which teaches the language in simple but practical terms—can be your best guide in learning the information you need to know.

This book will teach you PHP, providing both a solid understanding of the fundamentals and a sense of where to look for more advanced information. Although it isn't a comprehensive programming reference, through demonstrations and real-world examples, this book provides the knowledge you need to begin building dynamic Web sites and Web applications using PHP.

What Is PHP?

PHP originally stood for *Personal Home Page*. It was created in 1994 by Rasmus Lerdorf to track the visitors to his online résumé. As its usefulness and capabilities grew (and as it began to be utilized in more professional situations), PHP came to mean *PHP: Hypertext Preprocessor*. (The definition basically means that PHP handles data before it becomes HTML—which stands for Hypertext Markup Language.)

According to the official PHP Web site, found at www.php.net (**Figure i.1**), PHP is an HTML embedded scripting language. I'll explain this definition in more detail.

To say that PHP is *HTML embedded* means that it can be written within your HTML code—HTML being the code with which all Web pages are built. Therefore, programming with PHP starts off as only slightly more complicated than hand-coding HTML.

Also, PHP is a *scripting language*, as opposed to a *programming language*. This means that PHP is designed to do something *only after an event occurs*—for example, when a user submits a form or goes to a URL (Uniform Resource Locator—the technical term for a Web address). Conversely, programming languages such as Java and C can be used to write stand-alone applications, which may or may not involve the Web. The most popular example of a scripting language is JavaScript, which commonly handles events that occur within the Web browser. Another way to refer to the different types of languages is to use the term *interpreted* for languages such as PHP and JavaScript, which can't act on their own, and *compiled* for those like C and Java, which can.

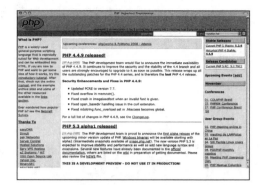

Figure i.1 At the time of this writing, this is the appearance of the official PHP Web site, located at www.php.net. Naturally, this should be the first place you look to address most of your PHP questions and curiosities.

You should also understand that PHP is a *server-side* technology. This refers to the fact that everything PHP does occurs on the server (as opposed to on the *client*, which is the computer being used by the person viewing the Web site). A *server* is just a computer set up to provide the pages you see when you go to a Web address with your browser (for example, Firefox, Microsoft Internet Explorer, or Safari). I'll discuss this process in more detail later (see "How PHP Works").

Finally, PHP is *cross-platform*, meaning that it can be used on machines running Unix, Windows, Macintosh, and other operating systems. Again, we're talking about the *server's* operating system, not the client's. Not only can PHP run on almost any operating system, but, unlike most other programming languages, it enables you to switch your work from one platform to another with few or no modifications.

At the time this book was written, PHP was simultaneously in versions 4.4.9 and 5.2.6. (The 5.*x* branch has not yet been universally adapted, so the older version is still being maintained for any major security concerns.) This book was actually tested using a development version of PHP 6, the next major release of the language (it's release date is not known at the time of this writing). The primary change in PHP 6—and it's a big one—is support for *Unicode*. Unicode, in short, provides a way to represent every character from every language. Thus, in PHP 6, you can handle strings in any language; even variable and function names can be written in any language.

What PHP Is Not

The thing about PHP that confuses most new learners is what PHP *can't do*. Although you can use the language for an amazing array of tasks, its main limitation is that PHP cannot be used for client-side features found in some Web sites.

Using a client-side technology like JavaScript, you can create a new browser window, add mouseovers, make pop-up alerts, resize the browser window, find out the screen size on the user's machine, and dynamically generate and alter forms. None of these tasks can be accomplished using PHP (because PHP is server-side, whereas those are client-side issues). But, you can use PHP to create JavaScript, just as you can use PHP to create HTML.

When it comes time to develop your own PHP projects, remember that you can only use PHP to send information (HTML and such) to the Web browser. You can't do anything else within the Web browser until another request from the server has been made (a form has been submitted or a link has been clicked).

The other significant change in PHP 6 is the removal of several outdated features. Every removed feature has been disabled in PHP's default configuration for some time, and although you could enable it, the recommendation was not to use it at all. In PHP 6, you won't have the choice.

Although this book was written using a development version of PHP 6, all of the code is backward compatible, at least to PHP version 5.x, if not to 4.x. In a couple of situations where you might still have and be using a feature that will be removed in PHP 6, a note in a sidebar or a tip will indicate how you can adjust the code accordingly.

More information can be found at PHP.net and www.zend.com, the minds behind the core of PHP (**Figure i.2**).

Figure i.2 This is the home page of Zend, creators of the programming at the heart of PHP. The site contains much useful software as well as a code gallery and well-written tutorials.

Why Use PHP?

Put simply, PHP is better, faster, and easier to learn than the alternatives. All Web sites must begin with just HTML, so you can create an entire site using a number of static HTML pages. But basic HTML is a limited approach that does not allow for flexibility or responsiveness. Visitors accessing HTML pages see simple pages with no level of customization or dynamic behavior. With PHP, you can create exciting and original pages based on whatever factors you want to consider. PHP can also interact with databases and files, handle email, and do many other things that HTML can't.

Webmasters learned a long time ago that HTML alone won't produce enticing and lasting Web sites. Toward this end, server-side technologies such as PHP have become the norm. These technologies allow Web-page designers to create Web applications that are dynamically generated, taking into account whichever elements the programmer desires. Often database-driven, these advanced sites can be updated and maintained more readily than static HTML pages.

When it comes to choosing a server-side technology, the primary alternatives to PHP are CGI scripts (Common Gateway Interface, commonly, but not necessarily written in Perl), ASP.NET (Active Server Pages), Adobe's ColdFusion, JSP (JavaServer Pages), and Ruby on Rails. JavaScript isn't truly an alternative to PHP (or vice versa) because JavaScript is a client-side technology and can't be used to create HTML pages the same way PHP or these others can.

So the question is, why should a Web designer use PHP instead of CGI, ASP.NET, JSP, or whatever to make a dynamic Web site?

◆ **PHP is much easier to learn and use.** People—perhaps like you—without any formal programming training can write PHP scripts with ease after reading this one book. In comparison, ASP.NET requires an understanding of VBScript, C#, or another language; and CGI requires Perl (or C). These are more complete languages and are much more difficult to learn.

◆ **PHP was written specifically for dynamic Web page creation.** Perl (and VBScript and Java) were not, and this fact suggests that, by its very intent, PHP can do certain tasks faster and more easily than the alternatives. I'd like to make it clear, however, that although I'm suggesting PHP is better for certain things (specifically those it was created to do), PHP isn't a better programming language than Java or Perl—they can do things PHP can't.

◆ **PHP is both free and cross-platform.** So, you can learn and use it on nearly any computer and incur no cost. Furthermore, its open source nature means that PHP's users are driving its development, not some corporate entity.

◆ **PHP is the most popular tool available for developing dynamic Web sites.** At the time of this writing, PHP is in use on over 20 million domain names (**Figure i.3**). By mastering this technology, you'll provide yourself with either a usable hobby or a lucrative skill.

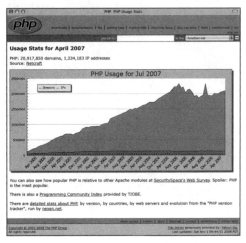

Figure i.3 Netcraft's (`www.netcraft.com`) graphic shows PHP's phenomenal growth since 2000.

WHY USE PHP?

How PHP Works

PHP is a server-side language, which means the code you write in PHP resides on a host computer that serves Web pages to Web browsers. When you go to a Web site (www. DMCinsights.com, for example), your Internet service provider (ISP) directs your request to the server that holds the www.DMCinsights. com information. The server reads the PHP code and processes it according to its scripted directions. In this example, the PHP code tells the server to send the appropriate Web page data to your browser in the form of HTML (**Figure i.4**). In short, PHP creates an HTML page on the fly based on parameters of your choosing.

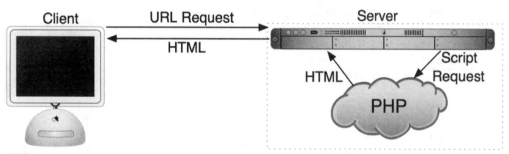

Figure i.4 This graphic demonstrates (albeit in very simplistic terms) how the process works between a client, the server, and a PHP module (an application added to the server to increase its functionality) to send HTML back to the browser. All server-side technologies use a third-party module on the server to process the data that's sent back to the client.

This differs from an HTML-generated site in that when a request is made, the server merely sends the HTML data to the Web browser—no server-side interpretation occurs (**Figure i.5**). Hence, to the end user's browser, there may or may not be an obvious difference between what home.html and home.php look like, but how you arrive at that point is critically altered. The major difference is that by using PHP, you can have the server *dynamically* generate the HTML code. For example, different information could be presented if it's Monday as opposed to Tuesday or if the user has visited the page before. Dynamic Web page creation sets apart the less appealing, static sites from the more interesting and, therefore, more visited, interactive ones.

The central difference between using PHP and using straight HTML is that PHP does everything on the server and then sends the appropriate information to the browser. This book covers how to use PHP to send the right data to the browser.

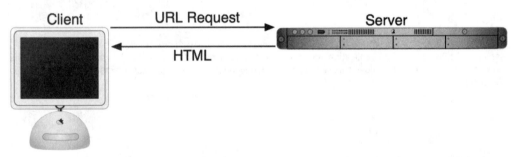

Figure i.5 Compare this direct relationship of how a server works with basic HTML to that of Figure i.4. This is also why HTML pages can be viewed in your browser from your own computer—they don't need to be "served," but dynamically generated pages need to be accessed through a server that handles the processing.

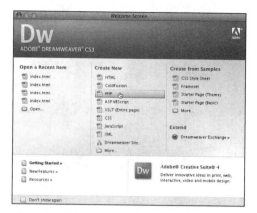

Figure i.6 The popular Dreamweaver IDE supports PHP development, among other server-side technologies.

What You'll Need

The most important requirement for working with PHP—because it's a server-side scripting language—is access to a PHP-enabled server. Considering PHP's popularity, your ISP or Web host most likely has this option available to you on their servers. You'll need to contact them to see what technology they support.

Your other option is to install PHP and a Web server application (like Apache) on your own computer. Users of Windows, Mac OS X, or Linux can easily install and use PHP for no cost. Directions for installing PHP are available in Appendix A, "Installation and Configuration." If you're up to the task of using your own PHP-installed server, you can take some consolation in knowing that PHP is available for free from the PHP Web site (www.php.net) and comes in easy-to-install packages. If you take this approach, and I recommend that you do, then your computer will act as both the client and the server.

The second requirement is almost a given: You must have a text editor on your computer. Crimson Editor, WordPad, TextWrangler, and similar freeware applications are all sufficient for your purposes; and BBEdit, EditPad, TextMate, and other commercial applications offer more features that you may appreciate. If you're accustomed to using a graphical interface (also referred to as WYSIWYG—What You See Is What You Get) like Adobe Dreamweaver (**Figure i.6**), you can consult that application's manual to see how to program within it. For help in finding a good PHP-capable editor, head to http://www.dmcinsights.com/links/1.

Third, you need a method of getting the scripts you write in your text editor to the server. If you've installed PHP on your own computer, you can save the scripts to the appropriate directory. However, if you're using a remote server with your ISP or Web host, you'll need an FTP (File Transfer Protocol) program to send the script to the server. There are plenty of FTP applications available; in Chapter 1, "Getting Started with PHP," I use the free FileZilla (www.filezilla-project.org, **Figure i.7**) for an example.

Finally, if you want to follow the examples in Chapter 12, "Introduction to Databases," you need access to MySQL (www.mysql.com, **Figure i.8**) or another database application. MySQL is available in a free version that you can install on your own computer.

This book assumes only a basic knowledge of HTML, although the more comfortable you are handling raw HTML code *without* the aid of a Web-creation application such as Dreamweaver, the easier the transition to using PHP will be. Every programmer will eventually turn to an HTML reference at some time or other, regardless of how much you know, so I encourage you to keep a good HTML book by your side. One such introduction to HTML coding is Elizabeth Castro's *HTML for the World Wide Web with XHTML and CSS: Visual QuickStart Guide* (Peachpit Press, 2002).

Previous programming experience is certainly not required. However, it may expedite your learning, because you'll quickly see numerous similarities between, for example, Perl and PHP or JavaScript and PHP.

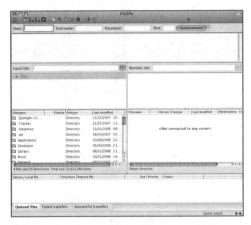

Figure i.7 The FileZilla application can be used on many different operating systems to move PHP scripts and other files to a remote server.

Figure i.8 MySQL's Web site (at the time of this writing).

Script i.1 A sample PHP script, with line numbers and bold emphasis on a specific section of code.

```
     ⊖ ⊖ ⊖                    Script
1    <!DOCTYPE html PUBLIC "-//W3C//DTD XHTML
     1.0 Transitional//EN"
2        "http://www.w3.org/TR/xhtml1/DTD/
         xhtml1-transitional.dtd">
3    <html xmlns="http://www.w3.org/1999/
     xhtml" xml:lang="en" lang="en">
4    <head>
5        <meta http-equiv="Content-Type"
         content="text/html; charset=utf-8"/>
6        <title>Hello, World!</title>
7    </head>
8    <body>
9    <?php print "Hello, World!"; ?>
10   </body>
11   </html>
```

What's New in This Book?

I would consider this third edition to be a relatively light revision of an already solid book. When the second edition was written, PHP was at version 4.*x*, with version 5 in development. Now version 5 is out and version 6 is in development. The most significant changes in PHP 5 affect more advanced topics than are covered here. The most significant changes in PHP 6 are support for Unicode and the removal of some features.

With that in mind, the first wave of alterations in this edition are the removal of a few topics that no longer apply to PHP 6. Second, I updated all the examples to make use of Unicode and the UTF-8 encoding (if you don't know what this means, see Chapter 1). Third, I tweaked some of the examples mostly to satisfy my own drive for perfection.

About This Book

This book attempts to convey the fundamentals of programming with PHP while hinting at some of the more advanced features you may want to consider in the future, without going into overwhelming detail. It uses the following conventions to do so.

The step-by-step instructions indicate what coding you're to add to your scripts and where. The specific text you should type is printed in a unique type style to separate it from the main body text. For example:

```
<?php print "Hello, World!"; ?>
```

The PHP code is also written as its own complete script and is numbered by line for reference (**Script i.1**). You shouldn't insert these numbers yourself, because doing so will render your work inoperable. I recommend using a text editor that automatically displays the line numbers for you—the numbers will help when you're debugging your work. In the scripts you'll sometimes see particular lines highlighted in bold, in order to draw attention to new or relevant material.

Because of the nature of how PHP works, you need to understand that there are essentially three views of every script: the PHP code (e.g., Script i.1), the code that's sent to the browser (primarily HTML), and what the browser displays to the end user. Where appropriate, sections of or all of the browser window are revealed, showing the end result of the exercise (**Figure i.9**). Occasionally, you'll also see an image displaying the HTML source that the browser received (**Figure i.10**). You can normally access this view by choosing View Source or View Page Source from the appropriate Web browser menu. To summarize, Figure i.10 displays the HTML the browser receives, and Figure i.9 demonstrates how the browser interprets that HTML. Using PHP, you'll create the HTML that's sent to the browser.

Because the column in this book is narrower than the common text editor screen, sometimes lines of PHP code printed in the steps have to be broken where they would not otherwise break in your editor. A small gray arrow indicates when this kind of break occurs. For example:

```
print "This is going to be a longer line
→ of code.";
```

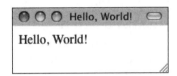

Figure i.9 This is a sample view you'll see of the browser window. For the purposes of this book, it won't make any difference which Web browser or operating system you use.

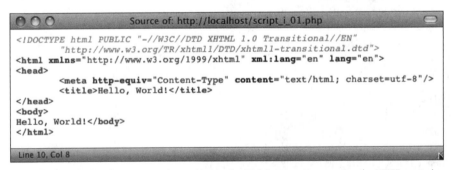

Figure i.10 By viewing the source code received by the Web browser, you can see the HTML created by PHP and sent by the server.

You should continue to use one line in your scripts, or else you'll encounter errors when executing. (The gray arrow isn't used in scripts that are numbered.)

While demonstrating new features and techniques, I'll do my best to explain the why's and how's of them as I go. Between reading about and using a function, you should clearly comprehend it. Should something remain confusing, though, this book contains a number of references where you can find answers to any questions (see Appendix B, "Resources and Next Steps"). If you're confused by a particular function or example, your best bet will be to check the online PHP manual or the book's supporting Web site (and its user support forum).

Which Book Is Right for You?

This is the third edition of my first book on PHP. Like the original, it's written with the beginner or nonprogrammer in mind. If you have little or no programming experience, prefer a gentler pace, or like to learn things in bite-sized pieces, this is the book for you. Make no mistake: This book covers what you need to know to begin develop dynamic Web sites (while using practical examples), but it does so without any in-depth theory or advanced applications.

Conversely, if you pick up new technologies really quickly or already have some experience developing Web sites, you may find this to be too basic. In that case, you should consider my *PHP 6 and MySQL 5 for Dynamic Web Sites: Visual QuickPro Guide* instead (Peachpit Press, 2008). It discusses SQL and MySQL in much greater detail and goes through several more complex examples, but it does so at a quick jog.

ABOUT THIS BOOK

Companion Web Site

While you're reading this book, you may also find it helpful to visit the *PHP for the World Wide Web: Visual QuickStart Guide, 3rd Edition* Web site, located at www. DMCinsights.com/phpvqs3/ (**Figure i.11**). There you'll find every script in this book available in a downloadable form. (However, I strongly encourage you to type the scripts yourself in order to become more familiar with the structure and syntax of PHP.)

The site also includes a more detailed reference section with links to numerous useful Web pages where you can continue learning PHP. In addition, the site provides an errata section listing any mistakes made in this text.

What many users find most helpful, though, is the book's supporting forum, found through the Web site or directly at www. DMCInsights.com/phorum/list.php?23 (**Figure i.12**). Using the forum, you can:

◆ Find answers to problems you're having

◆ Receive advice on how to approach an idea you have

◆ Get debugging help from other readers

◆ See how changes in the technologies have affected the examples in the book

◆ Learn what other people are doing with PHP

◆ See a faster reply from me than if you send me a direct email

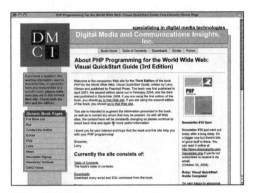

Figure i.11 The book's associated Web site.

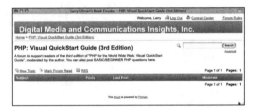

Figure i.12 If you need more assistance, use the book's supporting forum, where readers and I post problems and solutions.

Questions, comments, or suggestions?

If you have a PHP-specific question, there are newsgroups, mailing lists, and question-and-answer sections available on PHP-related Web sites for you to turn to. These are discussed in more detail in Appendix B. Browsing through these references or searching the Internet will almost always provide you with the fastest answer.

You can also direct your questions, comments, and suggestions to me. You'll get the fastest reply using the book's corresponding forum (I always answer those questions first). If you'd rather email me, my contact information is available on the Web site. I do try to answer every email I receive, but it will probably take a couple of weeks (whereas you'll likely get a reply in the forum within a couple of days).

For more tips and an enlightening read, see Eric Steven Raymond's "How to Ask Questions the Smart Way" at www.catb.org/~esr/faqs/smart-questions.html. The 10 minutes you spend on it will save you hours in the future. Those people who will answer your questions, like myself, will be most appreciative!

How to Ask Questions the Smart Way

Whether you're posting a message to the book's supporting forum, sending me an email, or asking a question in a newsgroup, knowing how to most effectively ask a question improves the quality of the response you'll receive as well as the speed with which you'll get your answer. To receive the best answer in the shortest amount of time, follow these steps:

1. Search the Internet, read the manuals, and browse any applicable documentation.

2. Ask your question in the most appropriate forum (newsgroup, mailing list, and so on).

3. Use a clear and concise subject.

4. Describe your problem in detail, show any relevant code, say what went wrong, indicate what version of PHP you're using, and state what operating system you're running.

COMPANION WEB SITE

GETTING STARTED WITH PHP

When you're learning any new programming language, you should always begin with an understanding of the basic syntax, and that's what I'll introduce in this chapter. I'll primarily discuss the fundamentals, but I'll also cover some recommended programming techniques that will improve your work in the long run.

If you've never programmed before, a focused reading of this chapter will start you on the right track. If you have some programming experience, you'll be able to breeze through this section, gaining a reference for the book's remaining material in the meantime. By the end of this chapter you will have successfully written and executed your first PHP scripts and be on your way to developing dynamic Web applications.

New in this edition are two topics. The first is a brief introduction to character encoding, which is more important thanks to changes in PHP 6. The final section of the chapter is a quick introduction to some basic debugging techniques to keep in mind as you work your way through the rest of the book.

Basic XHTML Syntax

As you should know already, all Web pages are made using HTML (Hypertext Markup Language). Every Web browser, be it Microsoft's Internet Explorer, Apple's Safari, or Mozilla's Firefox, turns HTML code into the stylized Web page seen by the user. In this book, I'm using a slight variant of HTML called XHTML, so I want to give it special mention up front.

The World Wide Web Consortium (W3C)— the group responsible for defining HTML and other protocols—created XHTML as a transition between HTML and XML (Extensible Markup Language). XHTML is almost exactly like HTML, with the following differences:

◆ All tags are written in lowercase.

◆ Nested tags must be *well formed*. This rule isn't as complicated as it sounds. It means that you can't write `<div><p>text</div></p>`; instead you would use `<div><p>text</p></div>`.

◆ All tag attributes must be quoted. In HTML, you might write `<table border=2>`, but in XHTML, you must use `<table border="2">`.

◆ All tags must be closed. This rule is the most confusing for most people. Many HTML tags have both an open and a close, like `<div class="someclass">text</div>`. However, a few don't have implicit closing tags. These include `<hr>`, `<br>`, `<img>`, and `<input>`. To make these valid XHTML tags, you need to close them by adding a space and a slash at the end, like this:

```
<hr />
<br />
<img src="image.jpg" width="100"
→ height="42" />
<input type="text" name="age"
→ size="3" />
```

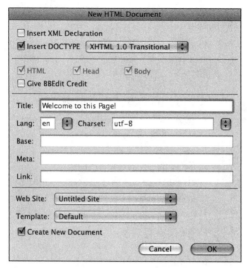

Figure 1.1 BBEdit and most other Web development applications will create the basics of an XHTML document for you.

As a final note, CSS (Cascading Style Sheets) is the recommended way of formatting HTML and XHTML documents. You can do so within style tags:

```
<style type="text/css">
.error { color: red; }
</style>
```

Or inline:

```
<p style="color: red;">text</p>
```

As with the subjects of HTML and XHTML, this book does not (nor cannot) cover CSS in any detail, but you'll only encounter a smattering of CSS in these pages and for the most basic and obvious reasons. In other words, you shouldn't find any of the CSS code to be that complex or puzzling.

Before getting into the syntax of PHP, let's create one simple but valid XHTML document that will act as a template for almost all of this book's examples.

To create an XHTML page:

1. Open your text editor or IDE.

   You can use pretty much any application to create HTML, XHTML, and PHP pages. Popular choices include: Adobe's Dreamweaver (www.adobe.com), which runs on Windows and Mac OS X; EditPlus (www.editplus.com) and Crimson Editor (www.crimsoneditor.com) for Windows; and Bare Bones' BBEdit (www.barebones.com) or MacroMates' TextMate (www.macromates.com) for Mac.

2. Choose File > New to create a new, blank document.

   Some text editors allow you to start by creating a new document of a certain type—for example, a new XHTML file (**Figure 1.1**). If your application has this option, feel free to use it.

continues on next page

3. Start with the XHTML header lines (**Script 1.1**):

```
<!DOCTYPE html PUBLIC "-//W3C//DTD
→ XHTML 1.0 Transitional//EN"
   "http://www.w3.org/TR/xhtml1/DTD/
   → xhtml1-transitional.dtd">
<html xmlns="http://www.w3.org/1999/
→ xhtml" xml:lang="en" lang="en">
```

A valid XHTML document begins with these lines. They tell the Web browser what type of document to expect. For this template, and in this book, I'll be creating *XHTML 1.0 Transitional* pages. This means I'll be adhering to XHTML 1.0 standards. The *Transitional* part means I'll be forgiven for using *deprecated* (no longer recommended) tags (as opposed to *Strict* mode, which isn't forgiving).

4. Create the head section of the page:

```
<head>
   <meta http-equiv="content-type"
   → content="text/html;
   → charset=utf-8" />
   <title>Welcome to this Page!
   → </title>
</head>
```

The head of an XHTML page includes the content-type meta tag (required for valid XHTML) and the title tags. The sidebar "Understanding Encoding" discusses what the *charset* part of the tag means.

JavaScript and CSS references can also be placed here.

Script 1.1 This sample document shows the basics of XHTML code.

```
1   <!DOCTYPE html PUBLIC "-//W3C//DTD XHTML
    1.0 Transitional//EN"
2          "http://www.w3.org/TR/xhtml1/DTD/
           xhtml1-transitional.dtd">
3   <html xmlns="http://www.w3.org/1999/
    xhtml" xml:lang="en" lang="en">
4   <head>
5       <meta http-equiv="content-type"
        content="text/html; charset=utf-8" />
6       <title>Welcome to this Page!</title>
7   </head>
8   <body>
9   <h1>This is a basic XHTML page!</h1>
10  <br />
11  <p>Even with <span style="font-size:
    150%;">some</span> decoration, it's
    still not very exciting.</p>
12  </body>
13  </html>
```

5. Create the body section:

```
<body>
<h1>This is a basic XHTML page!</h1>
<br />
<p>Even with <span style="font-size:
→ 150%;">some</span> decoration,
→ it's still not very exciting.</p>
</body>
```

The page's content—what is seen in the Web browser—goes between opening and closing body tags. Per XHTML rules, the break tag (`<br />`) includes a space before the slash that closes it. All the other tags are similar to their standard HTML counterparts except that they're in lowercase. Some CSS is used to increase the font size for the word *some*.

6. Type `</html>` to complete the HTML page.

7. Choose File > Save As. In the dialog box that appears, choose Text Only (or ASCII) for the format, if you're given the option.

XHTML and PHP documents are just plain text files (unlike, for example, a Microsoft Word document, which is stored in a proprietary format). You may also need to indicate the encoding when you save the file (again, see the sidebar).

8. Navigate to the location where you wish to save the script.

You can place this script anywhere you'd like on your computer, although using one dedicated folder for every script in this book, perhaps with subfolders for each chapter, makes sense.

continues on next page

Understanding Encoding

Encoding is a huge subject, but what you most need to understand is this: *the encoding you use in a file dictates what characters can be represented* (and therefore, what languages can be used). To choose an encoding, you must first confirm that your text editor or IDE can save documents using that encoding. Some applications let you set the encoding in the preferences or options area; others set the encoding when you save the file.

To indicate to the Web browser the encoding being used, there's the corresponding meta tag:

```
<meta http-equiv="content-type"
→ content="text/html;
→ charset=iso-8859-1" />
```

The *charset=iso-8859-1* part says that ISO-8859-1 encoding is being used (and this value needs to match the encoding actually used in the editor). This encoding is the most common for Western European and Latin-derived languages. If a Web page contains characters from other languages, you'll need to choose a different encoding, which is where Unicode comes in.

Unicode is way of reliably representing every symbol in every alphabet. Version 5 of Unicode—the current version at the time of this writing—supports over 99,000 characters! The most commonly used Unicode encoding is called UTF-8. If you want to create a multilingual Web page, UTF-8 is the way to go. I'll be using it in this book's examples (although you don't have to).

9. Save the file as `welcome.html`.

Even though you're coding with XHTML, the page will still use the standard `.html` or `.htm` extension.

10. Test the page by viewing it in your Web browser (**Figure 1.2**).

Unlike with PHP scripts (as you'll soon discover), you can test your XHTML and HTML pages by opening them directly in your Web browser.

Figure 1.2 The XHTML document as interpreted by the Web browser.

✔ Tips

■ To find an HTML and PHP editor or IDE, head to `www.DMCInsights.com/links/1`.

■ I'll be using XHTML throughout the book, but that doesn't mean you have to. If you're more comfortable with HTML, stick with what you know. It won't affect the operability of your PHP scripts.

■ For more information on XHTML, XML, and HTML, check out the W3C's Web page at `www.w3c.org` or Elizabeth Castro's excellent book, *HTML, XHTML, and CSS, Sixth Edition: Visual QuickStart Guide* (Peachpit Press, 2006).

■ For many reasons, including sheer convenience, I'll use the terms *HTML* and *XHTML* interchangeably throughout the book. In fact, you'll probably see just *HTML* the majority of the time, but understand that I mean XHTML as well.

■ The standards committees are currently working on the next versions of HTML and XHMTL, called *X/HTML 5* and *XHTML 2*. Finalizing and adopting standards like these moves at a glacial pace, so it could be years before either is fully implemented.

Basic PHP Syntax

Now that you've seen how the HTML will be handled in this book, it's time to begin PHP scripting. To create your first PHP page, you'll start exactly as you would if you were creating an HTML document from scratch. Understanding the reason for this is vitally important: *PHP is a server-side technology*, which means it doesn't run on the client, which is what a Web browser is. But a Web browser does understand HTML (and JavaScript and CSS), so PHP will be used to generate the HTML that's run in a Web browser (refer back to Figure i.4 for a visual representation of this relationship).

There are three main differences between a standard HTML document and a PHP document. First, PHP scripts should be saved with the .php file extension (for example, index.php). Second, you place PHP code within <?php and ?> tags:

```
...
<body><h1>This is HTML.</h1>
<?php PHP code! ?>
<p>More HTML</p>
...
```

The PHP tags indicate the parts of the page to be run through the PHP executable. This leads me to the third major difference: PHP scripts must be run on a PHP-enabled Web server (whereas HTML pages can be viewed on any computer). This also means that *PHP scripts must always be run through a URL* (i.e., http://something/page.php).

To make this first PHP script do something without too much programming fuss, you'll use the phpinfo() function. This function, when called, sends a table of information to the Web browser. That table lists the specifics of the PHP installation on that particular server. It's a great way to test your PHP installation, and it has a high "bang for your buck" quality.

To create a new PHP script on your computer:

1. Create a new HTML document in your text editor or IDE (**Script 1.2**):

   ```
   <!DOCTYPE html PUBLIC "-//W3C//DTD
   → XHTML 1.0 Transitional//EN"
      "http://www.w3.org/TR/xhtml1/DTD/
      → xhtml1-transitional.dtd">
   <html xmlns="http://www.w3.org/1999/
   → xhtml" xml:lang="en" lang="en">
   <head>
      <meta http-equiv="content-type"
      → content="text/html;
      → charset=utf-8" />
      <title>First PHP Script</title>
   </head>
   <body>
   </body>
   </html>
   ```

   This particular code is largely irrelevant to the overall point of creating a PHP page; but, for consistency's sake, this is the same template as the basic XHTML example (Script 1.1).

2. Create some blank lines between the opening and closing body tags by pressing Return.

3. Type <?php on its own line, just after the opening body tag.

   This initial PHP tag tells the server that the following code is PHP and should be handled as such.

4. Add the following on the next line:

   ```
   phpinfo();
   ```

   I'll explain the syntax in detail later, but in short, this is just a call to an existing PHP function named *phpinfo*.

Script 1.2 This first PHP script takes a typical HTML page, adds the PHP tags, and makes use of a PHP function.

```
1   <!DOCTYPE html PUBLIC "-//W3C//DTD XHTML
    1.0 Transitional//EN"
2        "http://www.w3.org/TR/xhtml1/DTD/
         xhtml1-transitional.dtd">
3   <html xmlns="http://www.w3.org/1999/
    xhtml" xml:lang="en" lang="en">
4   <head>
5      <meta http-equiv="content-type"
       content="text/html; charset=utf-8" />
6      <title>First PHP Script</title>
7   </head>
8   <body>
9   <?php
10  phpinfo();
11  ?>
12  </body>
13  </html>
```

5. Type ?> on its own line, just before the closing body tag.

The closing PHP tag tells the server that the PHP section of the script is over. Any text outside of the PHP tags is immediately sent to the Web browser as HTML and isn't treated as PHP code.

6. Save the script as `phpinfo.php`.

Not to overstate the point, but remember that PHP scripts must use a valid file extension. Most likely you'll have no problems if you save your files as `filename.php`.

✔ Tips

■ Just as a file's extension on your computer tells the operating system what application to open the file in, a Web page's extension tells the server how to process the file: `file.php` goes through the PHP module, `file.aspx` is processed as ASP. NET, and `file.html` is a static HTML document (normally). This is determined by the Web server application's settings.

■ If you're developing PHP scripts for a hosted Web site, check with your hosting company to learn which file extensions you can use for PHP documents. In this book you'll see `.php`, the most common extension.

■ You'll occasionally see PHP's short tags—simply <? and ?>—used in other people's scripts, although it's best to stick with the formal tags as I do in this book.

■ You'll find it handy to have a copy of the `phpinfo.php` file around. You can use it to check the PHP capabilities of a new server or see what features are supported, such as databases, image creation, and so on.

BASIC PHP SYNTAX

Testing Your Script

Unlike HTML, which can be tested on your own computer, PHP scripts needs to be run from a PHP-enabled server in order for you to see what the output will look like. Fortunately, PHP is open-source software (meaning, in part, that it's free) and is generally easy to install. If you need to do so, follow the directions in Appendix A, "Installation and Configuration."

PHP is run through a Web server application, like Apache (`http://httpd.apache.org`), Abyss (`www.aprelium.com`), or Internet Information Server (IIS, `www.iis.net`). If you have installed one of these on your personal computer and enabled support for PHP, then you can test your PHP scripts by saving them in, or moving them to, the Web document root. This is normally

- ◆ `~/Sites` for Mac OS X users (where ~ stands for your home directory)

- ◆ `AbyssDir/htdocs` on any operating system, where *AbyssDir* is the directory in which the Abyss Web Server was installed

- ◆ `C:\Inetpub\wwwroot` for Windows users running IIS

If you're not running PHP on your own computer, you'll need to transfer your PHP scripts to the PHP-enabled server using FTP (File Transfer Protocol). The Web hosting company or server's administrator will provide you with FTP access, which you'll use with an FTP client. There are many available; in this next sequence of steps, I'll use the free FileZilla (`http://filezilla-project.org/`), which runs on many operating systems.

To FTP your script to the server:

1. Open your FTP application.

2. In the application's connect window, enter the information provided by your Web host (**Figure 1.3**).

   FTP access requires a host name, username, and password.

continues on next page

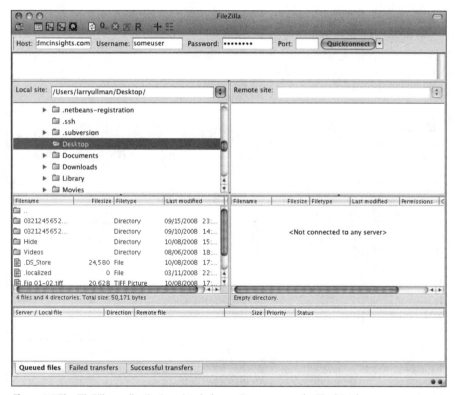

Figure 1.3 The FileZilla application's main window as it appears on the Macintosh.

3. Click Quickconnect (or your FTP client's equivalent).

If you've provided the correct information, you should be able to connect. If not, you'll see error messages at the top of the FileZilla window (**Figure 1.4**).

4. Navigate to the proper directory for your Web pages (for example, `www/` or `htdocs/`).

The FTP application won't necessarily drop you off in the appropriate directory. You may need to do some navigation to get to the *Web document root*. This directory is the location on the server to which a URL points (for example, `www.dmcinsights.com`).

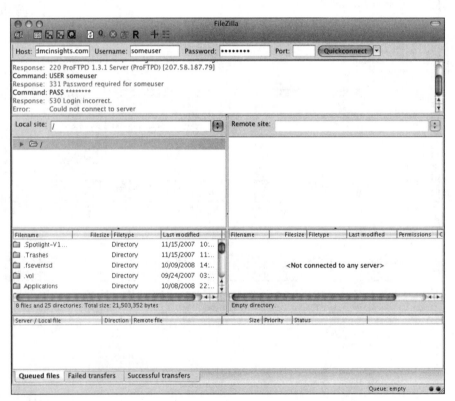

Figure 1.4 The reported error says that the login information is incorrect.

In FileZilla, the right-hand column represents the files and directories on the server; the left-hand column represents the files and directories on your computer (**Figure 1.5**).

5. Upload your script—phpinfo.php—to the server.

To do this in FileZilla, you just need to drag the file from the left column— your computer—to the right column— the server.

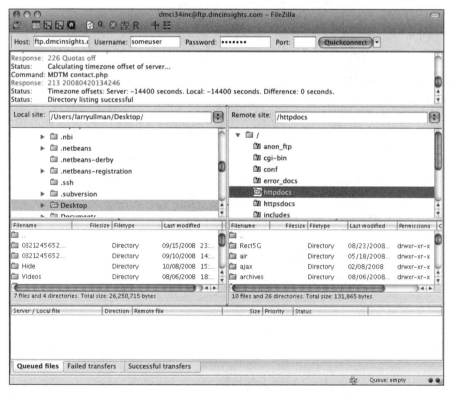

Figure 1.5 I've successfully connected to the remote server and navigated into the httpdocs directory (aka the *Web document root*).

To test your script in the browser:

1. Open your favorite Web browser.

For the most part, PHP doesn't behave differently on different browsers (because PHP runs on the server), so use whichever browser you prefer. In this book, you'll see that I primarily use Firefox (on both Windows and Mac OS X) and Safari (on Mac OS X).

2. In the browser's address bar, enter the URL of the site where your script has been saved.

In my case, this is www.DMCinsights.com, but your URL will certainly be different. If you're running PHP on your own computer, the URL is http://localhost (Windows); or http://localhost/~*username* (Mac OS X), where you should replace *username* with your actual username.

3. Add /phpinfo.php to the URL.

4. Press Return to load the URL.

The page should load in your browser window (**Figure 1.6**). If you see the PHP code (**Figure 1.7**) or a blank page, it most likely means that PHP has not been enabled on the server or you're using an unrecognized file extension.

Figure 1.6 If your script has been executed correctly, your browser should look like this (woohoo!).

Figure 1.7 If you see the raw PHP or HTML code, then either PHP isn't installed correctly or the extension you used (.php) isn't treated as a PHP file by the server.

TESTING YOUR SCRIPT

✔ Tips

- Some text editors and IDEs have built-in FTP capability, allowing you to save your scripts directly to the server. Some, like Dreamweaver and TextMate, can run PHP scripts without leaving the application at all.

- It's very important to remember that you can't open a PHP file directly in your Web browser as you would open HTML pages or files in other applications. PHP scripts must be processed by the Web server, which means you must access them via a URL (an address that starts with http://).

- Even if you aren't a seasoned computer professional, you should consider installing PHP on your computer. Doing so isn't too difficult, and PHP is free. Again, see Appendix A for directions.

- Technically speaking, you don't need to add any HTML to a phpinfo() script. If you don't, the phpinfo() function will still generate a complete HTML page.

Sending Text to the Browser

PHP wouldn't be very useful if all you could do was see that it works. You'll use PHP most frequently to send information to the browser in the form of plain text and HTML tags. To do so, use the print() function:

```
print("Hello, world!");
```

Functions in PHP are followed by parentheses in which *arguments* are passed to the function. Here the argument is the text you want printed. Because this argument is a string of text, you must surround it with quotation marks (in comparison, numbers are not quoted).

Also notice that the line is terminated with a semicolon (;). Every statement in PHP code must end with a semicolon, and forgetting this requirement is a common cause of errors. A *statement* in PHP is an executable line of code, like

```
print("something");
```

or

```
phpinfo();
```

Conversely, comment lines, PHP tags, control structures (conditionals, loops, and so on), and certain other constructs I'll discuss in this book don't merit a semicolon.

Before using this new bit of information in this next example, I have an early clarification to make: print() is not really a function, it's a *language construct*. What this means is that it can be, and often is, called without the parentheses:

```
print "something";
```

But you do still need the semicolon.

Script 1.3 By putting the print statement between the PHP tags, the server will dynamically send the *Hello, world!* greeting to the browser.

```
1    <!DOCTYPE html PUBLIC "-//W3C//DTD XHTML
     1.0 Transitional//EN"
2         "http://www.w3.org/TR/xhtml1/DTD/
          xhtml1-transitional.dtd">
3    <html xmlns="http://www.w3.org/1999/
     xhtml" xml:lang="en" lang="en">
4    <head>
5      <meta http-equiv="content-type"
       content="text/html; charset=utf-8" />
6      <title>Hello, World!</title>
7    </head>
8    <body>
9    <p>The following was created by PHP:
10   <?php
11   print "Hello, world!";
12   ?>
13   </p>
14   </body>
15   </html>
```

To print a simple message:

1. Begin a new HTML document in your text editor or IDE (**Script 1.3**):

   ```
   <!DOCTYPE html PUBLIC "-//W3C//DTD
   → XHTML 1.0 Transitional//EN"
     "http://www.w3.org/TR/xhtml1/DTD/
     → xhtml1-transitional.dtd">
   <html xmlns="http://www.w3.org/1999/
   → xhtml" xml:lang="en" lang="en">
   <head>
     <meta http-equiv="content-type"
     → content="text/html;
     → charset=utf-8" />
     <title>Hello, World!</title>
   </head>
   <body>
   <p>The following was created by PHP:
   ```

   The last line will be used to distinguish between the hard-coded HTML and the PHP-generated HTML.

2. Type <?php to create the initial PHP tag.

3. Add:

   ```
   print "Hello, world!";
   ```

   Printing the phrase *Hello, world!* is the first step most programming references teach. Even though it's a trivial reason to use PHP, you're not really a programmer until you've made at least one *Hello, world!* application.

4. Close the PHP section and the HTML page:

   ```
   ?>
   </p>
   </body>
   </html>
   ```

continues on next page

SENDING TEXT TO THE BROWSER

5. Save your file as hello.php, place it on your PHP-enabled server, and test it in your browser (**Figure 1.8**).

If you're running PHP on your own computer, remember that you can save the file to the proper directory and access the script via http://localhost/.

If you see an error or a blank page instead of the results shown in the figure, see the debugging section at the end of this chapter.

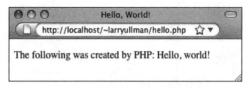

Figure 1.8 A simple *Hello, world!* example: your first foray into PHP programming.

✔ Tips

■ PHP is case-insensitive when it comes to calling functions like phpinfo() and print(): print(), Print(), and PRINT() net the same results. Later in the book (for example, in Chapter 2, "Variables") you'll see examples where case makes a crucial difference.

■ You can use other functions to send text to the browser, including echo() and printf(), but in this book, I'll primarily use print().

■ You can—and commonly will—use the print() function over multiple lines: just follow the closing quotation mark with a semicolon:

```
print "This is a longer
sentence of text.";
```

PHP Functions in the Manual

The PHP manual—accessible online at www.php.net/manual—lists every function available in the language, but using the manual takes a bit of know-how. The manual is organized with general concepts (installation, syntax, variables) discussed first, and ends with the functions by topic (MySQL, string functions, and so on). To quickly look up any function in the PHP manual, go to www.php.net/*functionname* in your Web browser (for example, www.php.net/print).

To understand how functions are described, look at the start of the print() function's page:

```
print
(PHP 4, PHP 5)
print - Output a string
Description
int print ( string $arg )
Outputs arg.
```

The first line is the function itself, followed by the versions of PHP in which it's available. (As the language grows, new functions are added that aren't usable in older versions.) Then there's a textual description of the function along with the function's basic usage. The usage is the most important and confusing part.

In this example, the first value, int, says that the print() function returns an integer value (specifically, print() returns 1 if it worked and 0 if it didn't). Within the parentheses, string $arg says that the function takes one required argument, which should be in the form of a string.

In comparison, the listing for the number_format() function (which formats a number to some decimal places) looks like this:

```
string number_format ( float $number [, int $decimals] )
```

This function, which returns a string, takes a floating-point number as its first argument and an optional integer as its second. Whenever you see the square brackets, that indicates optional arguments, which must be listed last. Whenever a function takes multiple arguments, they are separated by commas. Hence, this function can be called like so:

```
number_format(1.294);
```

```
number_format(1.294, 2);
```

If you're ever confused by a function or how it's properly used, check the PHP manual's reference page for it.

SENDING TEXT TO THE BROWSER

Sending HTML to the Browser

As those who first learned HTML quickly discovered, viewing plain text in a Web browser leaves a lot to be desired. Indeed, HTML was created to make plain text more appealing and useful. Because HTML works by adding tags to text, you can use PHP to send HTML tags to the browser, along with other data:

```
print "<b>Hello, world!</b>";
```

There is one situation where you have to be careful, though. HTML tags that require quotation marks, like `<a href="somepage.php">link</a>`, will cause problems when printed by PHP, because the `print()` function uses quotation marks as well. The fix is to *escape* the quotation marks by preceding them with a backslash (\):

```
print "<span style=\"color: red;\">
→ An error occurred.</span>";
```

By escaping each quotation mark within your `print()` statement, you make PHP print the mark itself instead of interpreting it as either the beginning or end of the string to be printed.

To send HTML to the browser:

1. Open the `hello.php` script (Script 1.3) in your text editor or IDE.

2. Edit the *Hello, world!* text on line 11 by adding HTML tags so that it reads as follows (**Script 1.4**):

   ```
   print "<span style=\"font-weight:
   → bold;\">Hello, world!</span>";
   ```

   To make the PHP-generated part of the message stand out, it'll be made bold by applying some CSS. For this to work, you need to escape the quotation marks within the span tag so that it doesn't conflict with the `print()` statement's quotation mark.

Script 1.4 With the `print()` function, you can send HTML tags along with your text to the browser, where the formatting will be applied.

```
1   <!DOCTYPE html PUBLIC "-//W3C//DTD XHTML
    1.0 Transitional//EN"
2        "http://www.w3.org/TR/xhtml1/DTD/
         xhtml1-transitional.dtd">
3   <html xmlns="http://www.w3.org/1999/
    xhtml" xml:lang="en" lang="en">
4   <head>
5       <meta http-equiv="content-type"
        content="text/html; charset=utf-8" />
6       <title>Hello, World!</title>
7   </head>
8   <body>
9   <p>The following was created by PHP:
10  <?php
11  print "<span style=\"font-weight:
    bold;\">Hello, world!</span>";
12  ?>
13  </p>
14  </body>
15  </html>
```

Hello, World!
http://localhost/~larryullman/hello2.php
The following was created by PHP: **Hello, world!**

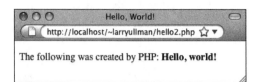

Figure 1.9 The new version of the page (compare with Figure 1.8), with a little more decoration and appeal.

3. Save the script as `hello2.php`, place it on your PHP-enabled server, and run the page in your browser (**Figure 1.9**).

4. View the HTML page source to see the code that was sent to the browser (**Figure 1.10**).

   How you do this depends upon the browser: select View > Page Source in Firefox, View > Source in Internet Explorer, or View > View Source in Safari.

   This is a step you'll want to be in the habit of taking, particularly when problems occur. Remember that PHP is primarily used to generate HTML, sent to and interpreted by the Web browser. Often, confirming what was sent to the Web browser (by viewing the source) will help explain the problem you're seeing in the browser's interpretation (or visible result).

✔ Tips

- Understanding the role of quotation marks and how to escape problematic characters is crucial to programming with PHP. These topics will be covered in more detail in the next two chapters.
- The HTML you send to the Web browser from PHP doesn't need to be this simple. You can create tables, JavaScript, and much, much more.
- Remember that any HTML outside of the PHP tags will automatically go to the browser. Within the PHP tags, `print()` statements are used to send HTML to the Web browser.

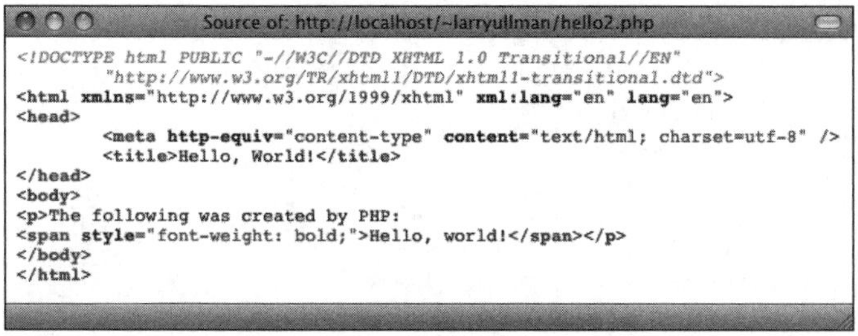

Source of: http://localhost/~larryullman/hello2.php

```
<!DOCTYPE html PUBLIC "-//W3C//DTD XHTML 1.0 Transitional//EN"
        "http://www.w3.org/TR/xhtml1/DTD/xhtml1-transitional.dtd">
<html xmlns="http://www.w3.org/1999/xhtml" xml:lang="en" lang="en">
<head>
        <meta http-equiv="content-type" content="text/html; charset=utf-8" />
        <title>Hello, World!</title>
</head>
<body>
<p>The following was created by PHP:
<span style="font-weight: bold;">Hello, world!</span></p>
</body>
</html>
```

Figure 1.10 The resulting HTML source for `hello2.php` (Script 1.4).

Using White Space

If you've ever hand-coded HTML or done any programming, you've probably noticed that judicious use of white space—blank lines, tabs, and other extra spaces—makes the code easier to write, read, and maintain. Well-written scripts place blank lines between sections of code, nest elements one tab-stop in from their parent element, and generally space out the page nicely. These techniques are not just about aesthetics—they are a trademark of professionally written code.

The content in this book focuses on three areas of Web development: the PHP scripts themselves, the data (HTML) that the PHP scripts send to the Web browser, and how the Web browser interprets or displays that data. I'll briefly address the issue of white space in each of these areas.

When you're programming in PHP, you should understand that white space is generally (but not universally) ignored. Any blank line (just one or several in a row) is irrelevant to the end result. Likewise, tabs and spaces are normally inconsequential to PHP. And as PHP code is not visible in the Web browser (unless there's a problem with the server), white space in your PHP files has no impact on what the end user sees.

The spacing of HTML code shows up in the HTML source of a Web page but has only a minimal effect on what's viewed in the Web browser. For example, all of the source code in Figure 1.10 could be placed on one line without changing the net effect. If you had to find a problem in the HTML source, however, you would not appreciate the long, single line of HTML.

Finally, to adjust the spacing in the rendered Web page—i.e., what the end user will see—you'll use tables and CSS, plus paragraph, div, and break tags, among others.

With all this in mind, let's rewrite the preceding script.

Script 1.5 The script now has three different kinds of white space: blank lines in the PHP, a newline in the HTML source (created by \n), and added space in the browser result (thanks to the <br />).

```
1   <!DOCTYPE html PUBLIC "-//W3C//DTD XHTML
    1.0 Transitional//EN"
2         "http://www.w3.org/TR/xhtml1/DTD/
          xhtml1-transitional.dtd">
3   <html xmlns="http://www.w3.org/1999/
    xhtml" xml:lang="en" lang="en">
4   <head>
5       <meta http-equiv="content-type"
        content="text/html; charset=utf-8" />
6       <title>Hello, World!</title>
7   </head>
8   <body>
9   <p>The following was created by PHP:
    <br />
10  <?php
11
12  print "<span style=\"font-weight:
    bold;\">Hello,
13  world!</span>\n";
14
15  ?>
16  </p>
17  </body>
18  </html>
```

To affect PHP and HTML spacing:

1. Open hello2.php (Script 1.4) in your text editor.

2. Insert new lines before and after the PHP print() function by pressing Return at the appropriate places (**Script 1.5**).

   The new lines within the PHP serve only to add focus and clarity to the script.

3. Make the print() statement extend over two lines by pressing Return with your cursor between *Hello,* and *world!*.

   As I stated earlier, you can print text over multiple lines because the end of the string being printed is marked by the closing quotation mark.

4. At the end of line 9, just before the opening PHP tag, add an HTML break:

   ```
   <p>The following was created by
   → PHP: <br />
   ```

   The <br /> tag will make the next line of text appear on a subsequent line in the rendered HTML page (if you don't quite follow, it should be clear after you run the example).

   continues on next page

23

5. At the end of the `print()` command (now on line 13), add \n within the quotation marks.

The \n character combination sends a command to the Web browser to start a new line in the HTML source. Think of it as the equivalent of pressing the Return key.

The line should now read

```
print "<span style=\"font-weight:
→ bold;\">Hello,
world!</span>\n";
```

6. Save the script as `hello3.php`, place it on your PHP-enabled server, and run it in your browser (**Figure 1.11**).

The break tag, added to the HTML source code, forces the *Hello, world!* message to go on the next line. The added blank lines in the PHP code have no effect on the visible result. Having PHP print the HTML over two lines, and also print a newline character (\n), only impacts the HTML source (**Figure 1.12**).

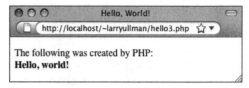

Figure 1.11 The blank lines have not affected the resulting Web page, but the `<br />` tag added some spacing.

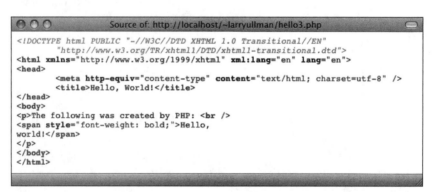

Figure 1.12 The \n in the print statement separates the *Hello, world!* line from the other HTML tags (note the placement of the closing paragraph tag here and in Figure 1.10).

Using White Space

Script 1.6 By putting either // or # in front of a single line of code, that line will no longer be processed by PHP.

```
      ● ● ●              📄 Script
1    <!DOCTYPE html PUBLIC "-//W3C//DTD XHTML
     1.0 Transitional//EN"
2           "http://www.w3.org/TR/xhtml1/DTD/
            xhtml1-transitional.dtd">
3    <html xmlns="http://www.w3.org/1999/
     xhtml" xml:lang="en" lang="en">
4    <head>
5       <meta http-equiv="content-type"
        content="text/html; charset=utf-8" />
6       <title>Hello, World!</title>
7    </head>
8    <body>
9    <p>The following was created by PHP:
     <br />
10   <?php
11   /*
12    * Filename: hello4.php
13    * Book reference: Script 1.6
14    * Created by: Larry Ullman
15    */
16
17   //print "<span style=\"font-weight:
     bold;\">Hello, world!</span>\n";
18
19   ?>
20   <!-- This is an HTML comment. -->
21   </p>
22   </body>
23   </html>
```

Adding Comments to Scripts

Comments are integral to programming not because they do anything but because they help you remember why *you* did something. The computer ignores these comments when it processes the script. Furthermore, PHP comments are never sent to the Web browser and therefore remain your secret.

PHP supports three ways of adding comments. You can comment out one line of code by putting either // or # at the beginning of the line you want ignored. For example:

```
// This is a comment.
```

You can also use // or # to begin a comment at the end of a PHP line, like so:

```
print "Hello"; // Just a greeting.
```

You can comment out multiple lines by using /* to begin the comment and */ to conclude it:

```
/* This is a
multi-line comment. */
```

To add comments to a script:

1. Open the hello3.php (Script 1.5) in your text editor.

2. After the initial PHP tag, add some comments to your script (**Script 1.6**):

   ```
   /*
    * Filename: hello4.php
    * Book reference: Script 1.6
    * Created by: Larry Ullman
    */
   ```

continues on next page

ADDING COMMENTS TO SCRIPTS

This is just a sample of the kind of comments you can write. I highly recommend that you document what the script does, what information it relies upon, who created it, when you created it, and so forth. Stylistically, such comments are often placed at the top of a script (as the first thing within the PHP section, that is), using formatting like this. The extra asterisks aren't required; they just draw attention to the comments.

3. On line 17, before the print() statement, type //.

   By preceding the print() statement with two slashes, you comment out the function, meaning it will never be executed.

4. Delete the Return between lines 17 and 18 so that the print() function is entirely on one line.

   Line 17 should now read

   ```
   //print "<span style=\"font-weight:
   → bold;\">Hello, world!</span>\n";
   ```

   Because the print() statement flows over two lines, you need to either precede each line with // or place it back on one line as you've done here. If you don't do one of those two things, you'll get a parse error when you run the script (**Figure 1.13**).

5. After the closing PHP tag (line 19), add an HTML comment.

   ```
   <!-- This is an HTML comment. -->
   ```

   This line of code just helps you to comprehend the different comments and where they appear. This comment will only appear within the HTML source code.

6. Save the script as hello4.php, place it on your PHP-enabled server, and run the page in your Web browser (**Figure 1.14**).

7. View the source of the page to see the HTML comment (**Figure 1.15**).

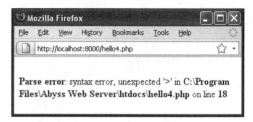

Figure 1.13 Parse errors are frequently caused by an imbalance of quotation marks or parentheses, or by omitting a semicolon.

Figure 1.14 With the print statement commented out, the page looks just as it would if the print() function weren't there.

✔ Tips

■ You can comment out just one line of code or several using the /* and */ method. With // or #, you can negate only one line at a time.

■ Different programmers prefer to comment code in different ways. The important thing is to find a system that works for you and stick to it. Those who also do JavaScript programming will most likely use // and /* */ because these are the same in both languages. Perl and Ruby programmers are more familiar with the # method.

■ Note that you can't use HTML comment characters (<!-- and -->) within PHP to comment out code. You could have PHP print those tags to the browser, but in that case you'd create a comment that appeared in the HTML source code on the client's computer (but not in the browser window). PHP comments never make it as far as a user's computer.

■ Despite my strong belief that you can't over-comment your scripts, the scripts in this book aren't as documented as they should be, in order to save space. But I will begin documenting the script name and number, for cross-reference purposes.

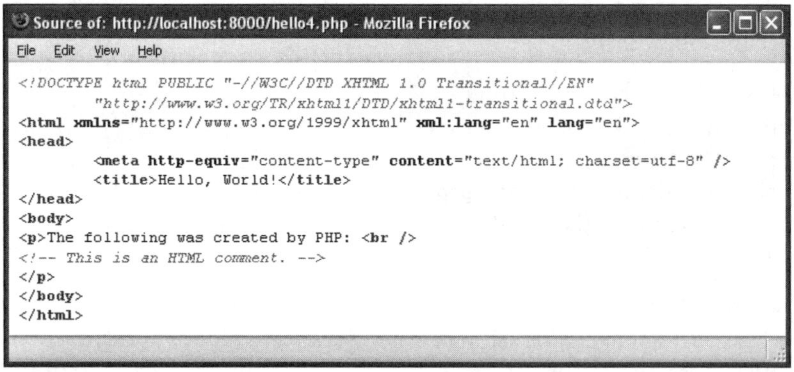

```
Source of: http://localhost:8000/hello4.php - Mozilla Firefox
File   Edit   View   Help

<!DOCTYPE html PUBLIC "-//W3C//DTD XHTML 1.0 Transitional//EN"
        "http://www.w3.org/TR/xhtml1/DTD/xhtml1-transitional.dtd">
<html xmlns="http://www.w3.org/1999/xhtml" xml:lang="en" lang="en">
<head>
        <meta http-equiv="content-type" content="text/html; charset=utf-8" />
        <title>Hello, World!</title>
</head>
<body>
<p>The following was created by PHP: <br />
<!-- This is an HTML comment. -->
</p>
</body>
</html>
```

Figure 1.15 HTML comments don't appear in the Web browser but are in the HTML source. PHP comments remain in the PHP script on the server.

Basic Debugging Steps

Debugging is by no means a simple concept to grasp, and unfortunately, it's one that is only truly mastered by doing. The next 50 pages could be dedicated to the subject and you'd still only be able to pick up a fraction of the debugging skills that you'll eventually acquire.

The reason I introduce debugging in this somewhat harrowing way is that it's important not to enter into programming with delusions. Sometimes code won't work as expected, you'll inevitably create careless errors, and some days you'll want to pull your hair out, even when using a comparatively user-friendly language such as PHP. I've been coding in PHP since 1999, and occasionally I still get stuck in the programming muck. But debugging is a very important skill to have, and one that you will eventually pick up out of necessity and experience. As you begin your PHP programming adventure, I can offer up the following basic but concrete debugging tips.

To debug a PHP script:

◆ Make sure you're always running PHP scripts through a URL (**Figure 1.16**)!

This is perhaps the most common beginner's mistake. PHP code must be run through the Web server application, which means it must be requested through http://something.

◆ Know what version of PHP you're running.

Some problems will arise from the version of PHP in use. Before you ever use any PHP-enabled server, run the phpinfo.php file (Script 1.2) to confirm the version of PHP in use.

◆ Make sure *display_errors* is on.

This is a basic PHP configuration setting (discussed in Appendix A). For security reasons, PHP may not be set to display

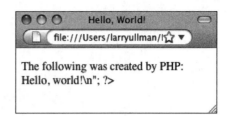

Figure 1.16 Because I loaded this PHP script directly in my Web browser (notice that the address starts with *file://*), the PHP code is not executed.

the errors that occur. If that's the case, you'll end up seeing blank pages when problems occur. To debug the problem, you'll need to see the error, so turn this setting on while you're learning. You'll find instructions for doing so in Appendix A and Chapter 3, "HTML Forms and PHP."

◆ Check the HTML source code.

Sometimes the problem is hidden in the HTML source of the page. In fact, sometimes the PHP error message is hidden there!

◆ Trust the error message!

Another very common beginner's mistake is to not fully read and trust the error that PHP reports. Although the error message can often be cryptic and may seem meaningless, it can't be ignored. At the very least, PHP is normally correct as to the line on which the problem can be found.

◆ Take a break!

So many of the programming problems I've encountered over the years, and the vast majority of the toughest ones, have been solved by walking away from my computer for a while. It's easy to get frustrated and confused, and in such situations, any further steps you take are likely to only make matters worse.

✔ Tip

■ These are just some general debugging techniques, specifically tailored to the beginning PHP programmer. They should suffice for now, though, as the examples in this book are relatively simple. More complex coding requires more advanced debugging techniques, so my *PHP 6 and MySQL 5 for Dynamic Web Sites: Visual QuickPro Guide* (Peachpit Press, 2007) dedicates a whole chapter to this subject.

BASIC DEBUGGING STEPS

VARIABLES 2

In the last chapter, you used PHP to send simple text and HTML code to a Web browser—in other words, something for which you don't need PHP at all! Don't worry, though; this book will teach you how to use the `print( )` function in conjunction with other PHP features to do useful things with your Web site.

To make the leap from creating simple, static pages to dynamic Web applications and interactive Web sites, you need to use variables. Variables are an essential concept in PHP, as well as in any other programming language. Understanding what variables are, the types that a language supports, and how to use them is critical to your work.

This chapter will discuss the fundamentals of variables used in PHP, and later chapters will cover the different types in greater detail. If you've never dealt with variables before, this chapter will be a good introduction. If you're familiar with the concept, then you should be able to work through this section with ease.

What Are Variables?

A *variable* is best thought of as a container for data. Once data has been stored in a variable (or, stated more accurately, once a variable has been assigned a value), that data/variable can be altered, printed to the Web browser, saved to a database, emailed, and so forth.

Variables in PHP are, by their nature, flexible: You can put data into a variable, retrieve that data from it (without affecting the value of the variable), put new data in, and continue this cycle as long as necessary. But variables in PHP are also temporary: They only exist— that is, they only have a value—for the duration of a script. Once a user clicks a link or submits a form, they are taken to a new page and those variables cease to exist, unless you take special measures to alter their longevity.

Before I get too deep into the discussion of variables, let's write a quick script that lists some of PHP's predefined variables. These are variables that you do not need to create, but you can use, because PHP creates them for you. Over the course of the book you'll be introduced to many different predefined variables. For this example, I'll use the predefined $_SERVER variable. It contains lots of information about the computer on which PHP is running. To display the variable's value, I'll turn to the print_r() function. This function is used specifically to print a variable's value in a more readable format.

To print PHP's predefined variables:

1. Create a new PHP script in your text editor or IDE (**Script 2.1**).

Script 2.1 The print_r() function is called in order to see the values stored in the $_SERVER variable.

```
1  <!DOCTYPE html PUBLIC "-//W3C//DTD XHTML
   1.0 Transitional//EN"
2     "http://www.w3.org/TR/xhtml1/DTD/
      xhtml1-transitional.dtd">
3  <html xmlns="http://www.w3.org/1999/
   xhtml" xml:lang="en" lang="en">
4  <head>
5     <meta http-equiv="Content-Type"
      content="text/html; charset=utf-8"/>
6     <title>Using print_r()</title>
7  </head>
8  <body>
9  <pre>
10 <?php // Script 2.1 - print_r.php
11
12 // Show the value of the $_SERVER
   variable:
13 print_r ($_SERVER);
14
15 ?>
16 </pre>
17 </body>
18 </html>
```

2. Create the initial HTML tags:

```
<!DOCTYPE html PUBLIC "-//W3C//DTD
→ XHTML 1.0 Transitional//EN"
    "http://www.w3.org/TR/xhtml1/DTD/
    → xhtml1-transitional.dtd">
<html xmlns="http://www.w3.org/1999/
→ xhtml" xml:lang="en" lang="en">
<head>
    <meta http-equiv="Content-Type"
    → content="text/html;
    → charset=utf-8"/>
    <title>Using print_r()</title>
</head>
<body>
<pre>
```

This code repeats the XHTML template created in the preceding chapter. Within the body of the page, I'm using the <pre> tags to make the generated PHP information more legible. Although these tags are deprecated (it's recommended that you no longer use them), they're fine for this purpose. Without using the <pre> tags, the result generated by the print_r() function will be quite messy.

3. Add the PHP code:

```
<?php // Script 2.1 - print_r.php
print_r ($_SERVER);
?>
```

This PHP code is just one function call, print_r(). The function should be provided with the name of a variable. In this example, the variable is $_SERVER, which is special in PHP. $_SERVER stores all sorts of data about the server: its name and operating system, the name of the current user, information about the Web server application (Apache, Abyss, IIS, etc.), and more. It also reflects the PHP script being executed: its name, where it's stored on the server, and so forth.

Note that you must type $_SERVER exactly as it is here, in all uppercase letters.

continues on next page

4. Complete the HTML page:

```
</pre>
</body>
</html>
```

5. Save the file as `print_r.php`, upload it to your server (or save it to the appropriate directory on your computer), and test it in your Web browser (**Figure 2.1**).

Once again, remember that you must run all PHP scripts through a URL.

6. If possible, save the file on another computer or server running PHP and run the script in your Web browser again (**Figure 2.2**).

Figure 2.1 The `$_SERVER` variable, as printed out by this script, is a master list of values pertaining to the server and the PHP script.

✔ Tips

- Printing out the value of any variable as you've done here is a great debugging tool, because often the problem is that a variable doesn't have the value that you assume it does.

- If you don't use the HTML `<pre></pre>` tags, the result will be like the mess in **Figure 2.3**.

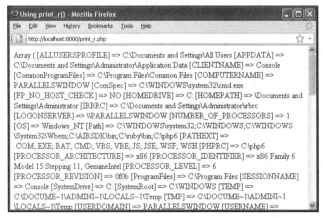

Figure 2.2 With the `print_r.php` page, different servers will generate different results (compare with Figure 2.1).

Figure 2.3 Use the HTML preformatting tags when using `print_r()` to avoid an incomprehensible page like this (compare to Figures 2.1 and 2.2).

Variable Syntax

Now that you've had a quick dip in the variable pool, it's time to investigate the subject further. In the preceding example, PHP's predefined $_SERVER variable was used. You can also create your own variables, once you understand the proper syntax. To create appropriate variable names, you must follow these rules:

◆ All variable names must be preceded by a dollar sign ($).

◆ Following the dollar sign, the variable name must begin with either a letter (A–Z, a–z) or an underscore (_). It can't begin with a number.

◆ The rest of the variable name can contain any combination and quantity of letters, underscores, and numbers.

◆ You may not use spaces within the name of a variable. (Instead, the underscore is commonly used to separate words.)

◆ Variable names are case-sensitive! Consequently, $variable and $Variable are two different constructs, although it would be a bad idea to use two variables with such similar names.

This last point is perhaps the most important: variable names in PHP are case-sensitive. Using the wrong letter case is very common cause of bugs.

Script 2.2 This script shows how one might document the purpose of variables. It's always better to have too many comments than too few.

```
1   <!DOCTYPE html PUBLIC "-//W3C//DTD XHTML
    1.0 Transitional//EN"
2       "http://www.w3.org/TR/xhtml1/DTD/
        xhtml1-transitional.dtd">
3   <html xmlns="http://www.w3.org/1999/
    xhtml" xml:lang="en" lang="en">
4   <head>
5       <meta http-equiv="Content-Type"
        content="text/html; charset=utf-8"/>
6       <title>Variables and Comments</title>
7   </head>
8   <body>
9   <pre>
10  <?php // Script 2.2
11
12  // Define my variables....
13
14  $year = 2009; // The current year.
15  $june_avg = 88; // The average temperature
    for the month of June.
16  $page_title = 'Weather Reports'; // A
    title for the page.
17
18  // ... and so forth.
19
20  ?>
21  </pre>
22  </body>
23  </html>
```

To help minimize bugs, I would recommend the following policies:

◆ Always use all lowercase variable names.

◆ Make your variable names descriptive (e.g., $first_name is better than $fn).

◆ Use comments to indicate the purpose of variables (**Script 2.2**), redundant as that may seem.

◆ Above all, be consistent with whatever naming convention you choose!

✔ Tips

■ Unlike some other languages, PHP generally doesn't require you to declare or initialize a variable prior to use. In other words, you can refer to variables without first defining them. That being said, it's best not to do that; I try to write my scripts so that every variable is defined before use.

■ There are two main variable naming conventions, determined by how you delineate words. These are the so-called *camel-hump* (named because of the way capital letters break up the word—for example, $FirstName) and *underscore* ($first_name) styles. I'll use the latter convention in my examples.

VARIABLE SYNTAX

Types of Variables

In this book, I'll cover three variable types: numbers, strings, and arrays. I'll introduce them quickly here, and later chapters will discuss them in more detail (Chapter 4, "Using Numbers"; Chapter 5, "Using Strings"; and Chapter 7, "Using Arrays"). A fourth variable type, objects, is introduced in Appendix B, "Resources and Next Steps," but isn't covered in this book. That particular subject is just too advanced for this beginner's guide—in fact, basic coverage of the subject in my *PHP 5 Advanced: Visual QuickPro Guide* (Peachpit Press, 2007) requires over 150 pages.

Numbers

Technically speaking, PHP breaks numbers into two types: *integers* and *floating-point* (also known as *double-precision floating-point* or *doubles*). Due to the lax way PHP handles variables, it won't affect your programming to group the two categories of numbers into one all-inclusive membership. Still, I'll briefly discuss the differences between the two, for clarity's sake.

The first type of numbers—integers—are the same as whole numbers. They can be positive or negative but include neither fractions nor decimals. Numbers that use a decimal point (even something like 1.0) are floating-point numbers. You must also use floating-point numbers to refer to fractions, because the only way to express a fraction in PHP is to convert it to its decimal equivalent. Hence 11/4 is written as 1.25. **Table 2.1** lists some sample valid numbers and their formal type; **Table 2.2** lists invalid numbers and the rules they violate.

Table 2.1

Valid Numbers in PHP	
NUMBER	TYPE
1	Integer
1.0	Floating-point
1972	Integer
19.72	Floating-point
−1	Integer
−1.0	Floating-point

Table 2.2

Invalid Numbers in PHP	
NUMBER	REASON
1 1/4	Contains a space and a slash
1972a	Contains a letter
02.23.72	Contains multiple decimals

✔ Tips

- As you'll soon see, you can quote invalid numbers to turn them into valid strings.

- PHP doesn't have a *date* type of variable like that used in database applications and other programming languages. The dates you work with in your PHP scripts will therefore consist of numbers and/or strings.

Strings

A string is any number of characters enclosed within a pair of either single (`'`) or double (`"`) quotation marks. Strings can contain any combination of letters, numbers, symbols, and spaces. Strings can also contain variables.

Examples of valid strings values include:

```
"Hello, world!"
"Hello, $first_name!"
"1 1/4"
'Hello, world! How are you today?'
"02.23.72"
"1972"
''
```

That last one is an *empty string*: a string that contains no characters.

An example of an invalid string would be:

```
"I said, "How are you?""
```

This example can be tricky. I hinted at this problem in Chapter 1, "Getting Started with PHP," with respect to printing HTML code. When PHP hits the second quotation mark, it assumes the string ends there; the continuing text (*How...*) causes an error. As I mentioned previously, to use a quotation mark within a string you can *escape* the quotation mark by putting a backslash (`\`) before it. By changing this string to `"I said, \"How are you?\""`, you tell PHP to treat the two quotation marks as part of the value of the string, rather than using them as the string's opening or closing indicators.

You can similarly circumvent this problem by using different quotation mark types:

```
'I said, "How are you?"'
"I said, 'How are you?'"
```

✔ Tips

- Notice that the `"1972"` example converts an integer into a string by putting it within quotes. Essentially, the string contains the characters *1972*, whereas the number (a non-quoted value) would be equal to 1972. It's a fine distinction, and one that won't matter in your code, because you can perform mathematical calculations with the string *1972* just as you can with the number.

- In Chapter 1, I demonstrated how to create a new line by printing the \n character within double quotation marks. Although escaping a quotation mark prints the quotation mark, escaping an *n* prints a new line, escaping an *r* creates a carriage return, and escaping a *t* inserts a tab into your HTML source code.

- Understanding strings, variables, and the single and double quotation marks is critical to programming with PHP. For this reason, I've dedicated a section at the end of this chapter to the subject.

Arrays

I'll cover arrays more thoroughly in Chapter 7, but I'll introduce them briefly here. Whereas a string or a number contains a single value (both are said to be *scalar*), an array can have more than one value assigned to it. You can think of an array as a list of values. In other words, you can put multiple strings and/or numbers into one array.

Arrays use *keys* to create and retrieve the values they store. The resulting structure—a list of key-value pairs—looks similar to a two-column spreadsheet. Interestingly, the array structure in PHP is so flexible that it can use either numbers or strings for both the keys and the values. The array doesn't even need to be consistent in this respect. (All of this will make more sense in Chapter 7, when you start working with specific examples.)

PHP has two different types of arrays, based on the format of the keys. If the array uses numbers for the keys (**Table 2.3**), it's an *indexed* array. If it uses strings for the keys (**Table 2.4**), it's an *associative* array. In either case, the values in the array can be of any variable type (string, number, and so on).

✔ Tips

- The array's key is also called its *index*. You'll see these two terms used interchangeably.

- An array can, and frequently will, contain other arrays, creating what is called a *multidimensional* array.

- What PHP calls an *associative array* is called a *hash* in Perl and Ruby, among other languages.

Table 2.3

Indexed Array	
KEY	VALUE
0	Don
1	Betty
2	Roger
3	Jane

Table 2.4

Associative Array	
KEY	VALUE
VT	Vermont
NH	New Hampshire
IA	Iowa
PA	Pennsylvania

Assigning Values to Variables

I mentioned at the beginning of this chapter that you don't need to initialize or declare your variables (as a general rule), but you still need to know how to assign a value to one. To assign a value to a variable, regardless of the variable type, you use the equals sign (=). Therefore, the equals sign is called the *assignment operator*, because it assigns the value on the right to the variable on the left. For example:

```
$number = 1;
$floating_number = 1.2;
$string = "Hello, world!";
```

To print out the value of a variable, you can use the print( ) function:

```
print $number;
print $string;
```

If you want to print a variable's value within a context, you can place the variable's name in the printed string, so long as you use double quotation marks:

```
print "Number is $number";
print "String is $string";
```

Using print( ) in this way works for the scalar (single-valued) variable types, which is to say numbers and strings. Arrays and objects use more complex syntax for defining and accessing their values, as you'll later learn.

Because variable types aren't locked in (PHP is referred to as a *weakly typed* language), they can be changed on the fly:

```
$variable = 1;
$variable = "Greetings";
```

If you were to print the value of $variable now, the result would be *Greetings*. The following script better demonstrates the concept of assigning values to variables and then accessing those values.

To assign values to and access variables:

1. Create a new PHP script in your text editor or IDE (**Script 2.3**).

2. Create the initial HTML tags.

   ```
   <!DOCTYPE html PUBLIC "-//W3C//DTD
   → XHTML 1.0 Transitional//EN"
       "http://www.w3.org/TR/xhtml1/DTD/
       → xhtml1-transitional.dtd">
   <html xmlns="http://www.w3.org/1999/
   → xhtml" xml:lang="en" lang="en">
   <head>
       <meta http-equiv="Content-Type"
       → content="text/html;
       → charset=utf-8"/>
       <title>Variables</title>
   </head>
   <body>
   ```

3. Begin the PHP code:

   ```
   <?php // Script 2.3 - variables.php
   ```

4. Define some number and string variables:

   ```
   $street = "100 Main Street";
   $city = "State College";
   $state = "PA";
   $zip = 16801;
   ```

   These lines create some different variables of string and number types. The strings are defined using quotation marks, and each variable name follows the syntactical naming rules.

   Because this is the first true multilined PHP script you've written, I'll remind you to conclude each statement with a semicolon.

Script 2.3 This script defines some basic variables and then prints out their values.

```
1    <!DOCTYPE html PUBLIC "-//W3C//DTD XHTML
     1.0 Transitional//EN"
2        "http://www.w3.org/TR/xhtml1/DTD/
         xhtml1-transitional.dtd">
3    <html xmlns="http://www.w3.org/1999/
     xhtml" xml:lang="en" lang="en">
4    <head>
5        <meta http-equiv="Content-Type"
         content="text/html; charset=utf-8"/>
6        <title>Variables</title>
7    </head>
8    <body>
9    <?php // Script 2.3 - variables.php
10
11   // An address:
12   $street = "100 Main Street";
13   $city = "State College";
14   $state = "PA";
15   $zip = 16801;
16
17   // Print the address.
18   print "<p>The address is:<br />$street
     <br />$city $state $zip</p>";
19
20   ?>
21   </body>
22   </html>
```

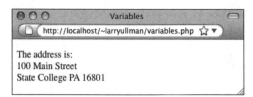

Figure 2.4 Some variables are assigned values, then printed within a context.

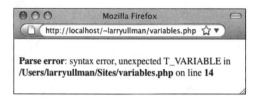

Figure 2.5 Parse errors are the most common type of PHP error, as you'll discover. They're frequently caused by missing semicolons or an imbalance of quotation marks or parentheses.

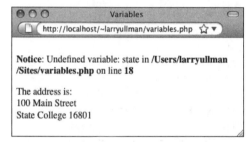

Figure 2.6 The *Undefined variable* error indicates that you used a variable with no value (it hasn't been defined). This can happen with misspellings and capitalization inconsistencies.

5. Print out the variables:

```
print "<p>The address is:
→ <br />$street <br />$city $state
→ $zip</p>";
```

Here you use a single `print()` statement to access all the variables. The entire string to be printed (consisting of text, HTML tags, and variables) is enclosed within double quotation marks. The HTML `<br />` tags make the text flow over multiple lines in the browser window (remember, the extra space and slash in the break tag are there for sake of XHTML compliance).

6. Complete the PHP section and the HTML page:

```
?>
</body>
</html>
```

7. Save the file as `variables.php`, upload it to your server (or save it to the appropriate directory on your computer), and test it in your Web browser (**Figure 2.4**).

✔ Tips

■ If you see a *parse* error (**Figure 2.5**) when you run this script, you probably either omitted a semicolon or have an imbalance in your quotation marks.

■ If one of the variable's values isn't printed out or you see an *Undefined variable* error (**Figure 2.6**), you most likely failed to spell a variable name the same way twice.

■ If you see a blank page, you most likely have an error but PHP's *display_errors* configuration is set to off. See Chapter 3, "HTML Forms and PHP," for details.

Understanding Quotation Marks

Now that you know the basics of variables and how to create them, I'll clarify the important concept of quotation marks. PHP, like most programming languages, allows you to use both double (") and single (') quotation marks—but they give vastly different results. It's critical that you comprehend the distinction, so the next example will run tests using both types.

The rule of thumb is this: Items within single quotation marks are treated literally; items within double quotation marks are extrapolated (that is, a variable's name is replaced with its value, as you saw in Script 2.3). This rule applies anywhere in PHP you might use quotation marks, including the creation of string variables and using the print() function. An example is the best way to explain.

To use quotation marks:

1. Begin a new PHP script in your text editor or IDE (**Script 2.4**).

2. Create the initial HTML tags:

```
<!DOCTYPE html PUBLIC "-//W3C//DTD
→ XHTML 1.0 Transitional//EN"
   "http://www.w3.org/TR/xhtml1/DTD/
   → xhtml1-transitional.dtd">
<html xmlns="http://www.w3.org/1999/
→ xhtml" xml:lang="en" lang="en">
<head>
  <meta http-equiv="content-type"
  → content="text/html;
  → charset=utf-8" />
  <title>Quotes</title>
</head>
<body>
```

Script 2.4 This script simply demonstrates how the type of quotation mark you use with variables affects the end result.

```
1   <!DOCTYPE html PUBLIC "-//W3C//DTD XHTML
    1.0 Transitional//EN"
2      "http://www.w3.org/TR/xhtml1/DTD/
       xhtml1-transitional.dtd">
3   <html xmlns="http://www.w3.org/1999/
    xhtml" xml:lang="en" lang="en">
4   <head>
5      <meta http-equiv="content-type"
       content="text/html; charset=utf-8" />
6      <title>Quotes</title>
7   </head>
8   <body>
9   <?php // Script 2.4 - quotes.php
10
11  // Single or double quotation marks won't
    matter here:
12  $first_name = 'Larry';
13  $last_name = "Ullman";
14
15  // Single or double quotation marks DOES
    matter here:
16  $name1 = '$first_name $last_name';
17  $name2 = "$first_name $last_name";
18
19  // Single or double quotation marks DOES
    matter here:
20  print "<h1>Double Quotes</h1><p>name1 is
    $name1 <br />
21  name2 is $name2</p>";
22
23  print '<h1>Single Quotes</h1><p>name1 is
    $name1 <br />
24  name2 is $name2</p>';
25
26  ?>
27  </body>
28  </html>
```

3. Begin the PHP code:

```
<?php // Script 2.4 - quotes.php
```

4. Create two string variables:

```
$first_name = 'Larry';
$last_name = "Ullman";
```

It doesn't matter whether you use single or double quotation marks for these two variables, as each string should be treated literally. However, if you're using your own name here (and feel free to do so) and it contains an apostrophe, you'll need to either use double quotation marks or escape the apostrophe within single quotation marks:

```
$last_name = "O'Toole";
$last_name = 'O\'Toole';
```

5. Create two different name variables, using the first- and last-name variables:

```
$name1 = '$first_name $last_name';
$name2 = "$first_name $last_name";
```

In these lines it makes a huge difference which quotation marks you use. The $name1 variable is now literally equal to *$first_name $last_name*, because no extrapolation occurs. Conversely, $name2 is equal to *Larry Ullman*, presumably the intended result.

6. Print out the variables using both types of quotation marks:

```
print "<h1>Double Quotes</h1>
→ <p>name1 is $name1 <br />
name2 is $name2</p>";
print '<h1>Single Quotes</h1>
→ <p>name1 is $name1 <br />
name2 is $name2</p>';
```

Again, the quotation marks make all the difference. The first print() statement prints out the values of the $name1 and $name2 variables, whereas the second prints out *$name1* and *$name2*.

continues on next page

UNDERSTANDING QUOTATION MARKS

The HTML in the print() statements makes them more legible in the browser, and each statement is executed over two lines, which is perfectly acceptable.

7. Complete the PHP section and the HTML page:

```
?>
</body>
</html>
```

8. Save the file as quotes.php, upload it to your server (or save it to the appropriate directory on your computer), and test it in your Web browser (**Figure 2.7**).

✔ Tips

■ If you're still confused about the distinction between the two types of quotation marks, stick with double quotation marks and you'll be safe.

■ Arguably, using single quotation marks when you can is preferable, as PHP won't need to search the strings looking for variables. This rule is more of a finesse issue—the performance won't be measurably affected regardless.

■ The shortcuts for creating newlines (\n), carriage returns (\r), and tabs (\t) must also be used within double quotation marks to have the desired effect.

■ Remember that you don't always need to use quotation marks. When assigning a numeric value or when only printing a variable, you can skip them:

```
$num = 2;
print $num;
```

Figure 2.7 The different quotation marks (single versus double) dictate whether the variable's name or value is printed.

HTML FORMS
AND PHP

3

The preceding chapter provides a brief introduction to the topic of variables. Although you'll often create your own variables, you'll also commonly use variables in conjunction with HTML forms. Forms are a fundamental unit of today's Web sites, enabling such features as registration and login systems, search capability, and online shopping. Even the most basic site will find logical reasons to incorporate HTML forms. And with PHP, it's stunningly simple to receive and handle data generated by them.

With that in mind, this chapter will cover the basics of creating HTML forms and how the form data is accessible in a PHP script. Simultaneously, this chapter will introduce several key concepts of real PHP programming, including how to manage errors in your scripts.

Creating a Simple Form

For the HTML form example in this chapter, you'll create a feedback page that takes the user's salutation, name, email address, response, and comment (**Figure 3.1**). You'll need to create the necessary fields with this in mind. The code to generate a form goes between opening and closing form tags:

```
<form>
form elements
</form>
```

The form tags dictate where a form begins and ends. Every element of the form must be entered between these two tags. The opening form tag also contains an *action* attribute. It indicates to which page the form data should be submitted. This is one of the most important considerations when creating a form. In this book, the action attributes will always point to PHP scripts:

```
<form action="somepage.php">
```

Before creating this next form, I want to briefly revisit the topic of XHTML. As stated in the first chapter, XHTML has some rules that result in a significantly different syntax than HTML. For starters, the code needs to be in all lowercase letters, and every tag attribute must be enclosed in quotes. Further, every tag must be closed; those that don't have formal closing tags, like input, are closed by adding a blank space and a slash at the end. Thus, in HTML you might write

```
<INPUT TYPE=TEXT NAME=address SIZE=40>
```

but in XHTML it's

```
<input type="text" name="address"
→ size="40" />
```

I hope this quick explanation will help to avoid confusion with the XHTML in the following script.

Figure 3.1 The HTML form that will be used in this chapter's examples.

Script 3.1 This HTML page has a form with several different types of input.

```
1   <!DOCTYPE html PUBLIC "-//W3C//DTD XHTML
    1.0 Transitional//EN"
2       "http://www.w3.org/TR/xhtml1/DTD/
        xhtml1-transitional.dtd">
3   <html xmlns="http://www.w3.org/1999/
    xhtml" xml:lang="en" lang="en">
4   <head>
5       <meta http-equiv="Content-Type"
        content="text/html; charset=utf-8"/>
6       <title>Feedback Form</title>
7   </head>
8   <body>
9   <!-- Script 3.1 - feedback.html -->
10  <div><p>Please complete this form to
    submit your feedback:</p>
11
12  <form action="handle_form.php">
13
14      <p>Name: <select name="title">
15      <option value="Mr.">Mr.</option>
16      <option value="Mrs.">Mrs.</option>
17      <option value="Ms.">Ms.</option>
18      </select> <input type="text"
        name="name" size="20" /></p>
19
20      <p>Email Address: <input type="text"
        name="email" size="20" /></p>
21
22      <p>Response: This is...
23      <input type="radio" name="response"
        value="excellent" /> excellent
24      <input type="radio" name="response"
        value="okay" /> okay
25      <input type="radio" name="response"
        value="boring" /> boring</p>
26
27      <p>Comments: <textarea name="comments"
        rows="3" cols="30"></textarea></p>
28
29      <input type="submit" name="submit"
        value="Send My Feedback" />
30
31  </form>
32  </div>
33  </body>
34  </html>
```

To create a basic HTML form:

1. Begin a new document in your text editor or IDE (**Script 3.1**):

   ```
   <!DOCTYPE html PUBLIC "-//W3C//DTD
   → XHTML 1.0 Transitional//EN"
       "http://www.w3.org/TR/xhtml1/DTD/
       → xhtml1-transitional.dtd">
   <html xmlns="http://www.w3.org/1999/
   → xhtml" xml:lang="en" lang="en">
   <head>
       <meta http-equiv="Content-Type"
   → content="text/html;
   → charset=utf-8"/>
       <title>Feedback Form</title>
   </head>
   <body>
   <!-- Script 3.1 - feedback.html -->
   <div><p>Please complete this form to
   → submit your feedback:</p>
   ```

2. Add the opening form tag:

   ```
   <form action="handle_form.php">
   ```

   The form tag indicates that this form will be submitted to the page handle_form.php, found within the same directory as this HTML page. You can use a full URL to the PHP script, if you'd prefer to be explicit.

   continues on next page

3. Add a select menu plus a text input for the person's name:

```
<p>Name: <select name="title">
<option value="Mr.">Mr.</option>
<option value="Mrs.">Mrs.</option>
<option value="Ms.">Ms.</option>
</select> <input type="text"
→ name="name" size="20" /></p>
```

The inputs for the person's name will consist of two elements (see Figure 3.1). The first is a drop-down menu of common titles: *Mr.*, *Mrs.*, and *Ms.* Each option listed between the select tags is an answer the user can choose (**Figure 3.2**). The second input is a basic text box for the person's full name.

Stick to a consistent naming convention within the form by giving each form element a logical and descriptive name. Only use letters, numbers, and the underscore (_) when naming elements.

4. Add a text input for the user's email address:

```
<p>Email Address: <input type="text"
→ name="email" size="20" /></p>
```

5. Add radio buttons for a response:

```
<p>Response: This is...
<input type="radio" name="response"
→ value="excellent" /> excellent
<input type="radio" name="response"
→ value="okay" /> okay
<input type="radio" name="response"
→ value="boring" /> boring</p>
```

This HTML code creates three radio buttons (clickable circles; see Figure 3.1). Because they all have the same name value, only one of the three can be selected at a time. Per XHTML rules, the code is in lowercase except for the values, and an extra space and slash are added to the end of each input to close the tag.

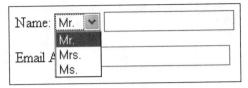

Figure 3.2 The select element creates a drop-down menu of options.

6. Add a textarea to record the comments:

```
<p>Comments: <textarea
→ name="comments" rows="3"
→ cols="30"></textarea></p>
```

A textarea gives the user more space to enter their comments than a text input would. However, the text input lets you limit how much information the user can enter, which you can't do with the textarea (not without using JavaScript, that is). When you're creating a form, choose input types appropriate to the information you wish to retrieve from the user.

Note that a textarea does have a closing tag.

7. Add the submit button:

```
<input type="submit" name="submit"
value="Send My Feedback" />
```

The value attribute of a submit element is what appears on the button in the Web browser (see Figure 3.1). You could also use *Go!* or *Enter*, for example.

8. Close the form:

```
</form>
```

9. Complete the page:

```
</div>
</body>
</html>
```

10. Save the page as feedback.html and view it in your browser.

Because this is an HTML page, not a PHP script, you could view it in your Web browser directly from your computer.

✔ Tips

■ Note that you use the HTML extension (.html) here because it's a standard HTML page (not a PHP page). You could use the .php extension without a problem, even though there's no actual PHP code. (Remember that in a PHP page, anything not within the PHP brackets—<?php and ?>—is assumed to be HTML.)

■ Be certain that your action attribute correctly points to an existing file on the server, or your form won't be processed properly. In this case, you indicate that the form should be submitted to handle_form.php, which is located in the same directory as the feedback.html page.

■ In this example, an HTML form is created by hand-coding the HTML, but you can do this in a Web page application (such as Adobe Dreamweaver) if you're more comfortable with that approach.

CREATING A SIMPLE FORM

Using GET or POST

The experienced HTML developer will notice that the feedback form is missing one thing: The initial form tag has no *method* value. This attribute tells the server how to transmit the data from the form to the handling script.

You have two choices with method: GET and POST. Many HTML coders may not be entirely clear on the distinction and when to use which. The difference between using GET and POST is squarely in how the information is passed from the form to the processing script. The GET method sends all the gathered information along as part of the URL. The POST method transmits the information invisibly to the user. For example, upon submitting a form, if you use the GET method, the resulting URL will be something like this:

```
http://www.example.com/page.php?
→ some_var=some_value&age=20&...
```

Whereas using the POST method, the end user will only see:

```
http://www.example.com/page.php
```

When choosing which method to use, you may want to keep in mind these three factors:

◆ With the GET method, a limited amount of information can be passed.

◆ The GET method sends the input to the handling script publicly (which means, for example, that a password entered in a form can be viewed by anyone within eyesight of the Web browser, creating a larger security risk).

◆ A page generated by a form that used the GET method can be bookmarked, but one based on POST can't be.

This book uses POST almost exclusively for handling forms, although you'll also see a useful technique involving the GET method (see "Manually Sending Data to a Page" at the

Script 3.2 The method attribute with a value of *post* is been added to complete the form.

```
1   <!DOCTYPE html PUBLIC "-//W3C//DTD XHTML
    1.0 Transitional//EN"
2       "http://www.w3.org/TR/xhtml1/DTD/
    xhtml1-transitional.dtd">
3   <html xmlns="http://www.w3.org/1999/
    xhtml" xml:lang="en" lang="en">
4   <head>
5       <meta http-equiv="Content-Type"
    content="text/html; charset=utf-8"/>
6       <title>Feedback Form</title>
7   </head>
8   <body>
9   <!-- Script 3.2 - feedback.html -->
10  <div><p>Please complete this form to
    submit your feedback:</p>
11
12  <form action="handle_form.php"
    method="post">
13
14      <p>Name: <select name="title">
15      <option value="Mr.">Mr.</option>
16      <option value="Mrs.">Mrs.</option>
17      <option value="Ms.">Ms.</option>
18      </select> <input type="text"
    name="name" size="20" /></p>
19
20      <p>Email Address: <input type="text"
    name="email" size="20" /></p>
21
22      <p>Response: This is...
23      <input type="radio" name="response"
    value="excellent" /> excellent
24      <input type="radio" name="response"
    value="okay" /> okay
25      <input type="radio" name="response"
    value="boring" /> boring</p>
26
27      <p>Comments: <textarea name="comments"
    rows="3" cols="30"></textarea></p>
28
29      <input type="submit" name="submit"
    value="Send My Feedback" />
30
31  </form>
32  </div>
33  </body>
34  </html>
```

Figure 3.3 With forms, much of the important information, such as the action and method values or element names, can only be seen within the HTML source code.

Figure 3.4 If a user refreshes a PHP script that data has been sent to via the POST method, they will be asked to confirm the action (the specific message will differ using other browsers).

end of this chapter). The final decision about which method to use should be based on mitigating factors in your form and whether the resulting page should be bookmark-able. Experience will make the distinction clearer, but you can safely use POST most of the time.

To add a method to your script:

1. Open feedback.html (Script 3.1) in your text editor or IDE.

2. Within the initial form tag, add method="post" (**Script 3.2**, line 12).

   The form's method attribute tells the browser how to send the form data to the receiving script. Because there may be a lot of data in the form's submission (including the comments), and because it wouldn't make sense for the user to bookmark the resulting page, POST is the logical method to use.

3. Save the script and reload it in your Web browser.

4. View the source of the page to make sure all the required elements are present and have the right attributes (**Figure 3.3**).

✔ Tips

■ In the discussion of the methods, GET and POST are written in capital letters to make them stand out. However, the form in the script uses *post* for XHTML compliance. Don't worry about this inconsistency (if you caught it at all)—the method will work regardless of case.

■ Another difference between GET and POST is that attempts to reload a page that data has been posted to will result in a confirmation box (**Figure 3.4**). Users will not see such messages for pages loaded via the GET method.

Receiving Form Data in PHP

Now that you've created a basic HTML form, you need to write the PHP script that will receive and process the form data. For this example, the PHP script will simply repeat what the user entered into the form. In later chapters, you'll learn how to take this information and store it in a database, send it in an email, write it to a file, etc.

To access the submitted form data, you need to refer to a particular *predefined variable*. Chapter 2, "Variables," already introduced one predefined variable: $_SERVER. The specific variable the PHP script would refer to for handling form data is either $_GET or $_POST. If an HTML form uses the GET method, the submitted form data will be found in $_GET. If an HTML form uses the POST method, the submitted form data will be found in $_POST.

$_GET and $_POST, besides being predefined variables (i.e., ones you don't need to create), are *arrays*, a special variable type. This means that each variable may contain numerous values. You cannot use arrays like so:

```
print $_POST; // Will not work!
```

Instead, to access a specific value, you must refer to the array's *index* or *key*. Chapter 7, "Using Arrays," goes into this subject in detail, but the premise is actually very simple. Start with a form element whose name attribute has a value of *something*:

```
<input type="text" name="something" />
```

Then, assuming that the form uses the POST method, the value entered into that form element would be available in $_POST['something']:

```
print $_POST['something'];
```

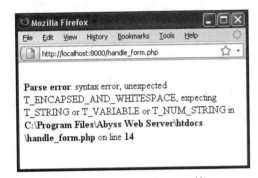

Figure 3.5 This ugly parse error is created by attempting to use $_POST['name'] within double quotation marks.

Script 3.3 This script displays the form data submitted to it by referencing the associated $_POST variables.

```
                          Script
1   <!DOCTYPE html PUBLIC "-//W3C//DTD XHTML
    1.0 Transitional//EN"
2      "http://www.w3.org/TR/xhtml1/DTD/
       xhtml1-transitional.dtd">
3   <html xmlns="http://www.w3.org/1999/
    xhtml" xml:lang="en" lang="en">
4   <head>
5      <meta http-equiv="Content-Type"
       content="text/html; charset=utf-8"/>
6      <title>Your Feedback</title>
7   </head>
8   <body>
9   <?php // Script 3.3 handle_form.php
10
11  // This page receives the data from
    feedback.html.
12  // It will receive: title, name, email,
    response, comments, and submit in $_POST.
13  $title = $_POST['title'];
14  $name = $_POST['name'];
15  $response = $_POST['response'];
16  $comments = $_POST['comments'];
17
18  // Print the received data:
19  print "<p>Thank you, $title $name, for
    your comments.</p>
20  <p>You stated that you found this
    example to be '$response' and added:
    <br />$comments</p>";
21
22  ?>
23  </body>
24  </html>
```

Unfortunately, there is one little hitch here: when used within double quotation marks, the single quotation marks around the key will cause parse errors (**Figure 3.5**):

```
print "Hello $_POST['name'].";
```

There are a couple of ways you can avoid this problem. In this chapter, I'll go with the solution that's syntactically the simplest: just assign the particular $_POST element to another variable first:

```
$name = $_POST['name'];
print "Hello, $name.";
```

Two final notes before implementing this information in a new PHP script. First, $_POST is case-sensitive: it must be typed exactly as you see it here (a dollar sign, one underscore, then all capital letters). Second, the indexes in $_POST—name in the preceding example— must exactly match the name values given to the form elements.

To create the PHP script:

1. Begin a new document in your text editor or IDE (**Script 3.3**):

```
<!DOCTYPE html PUBLIC "-//W3C//DTD
→ XHTML 1.0 Transitional//EN"
   "http://www.w3.org/TR/xhtml1/DTD/
   → xhtml1-transitional.dtd">
<html xmlns="http://www.w3.org/1999/
→ xhtml" xml:lang="en" lang="en">
<head>
   <meta http-equiv="Content-Type"
   → content="text/html;
   → charset=utf-8"/>
   <title>Your Feedback</title>
</head>
<body>
```

continues on next page

2. Add the opening PHP tag and any comments:

```
<?php // Script 3.3 handle_form.php
// This page receives the data from
→ feedback.html.
// It will receive: title, name,
→ email, response, comments, and
→ submit in $_POST.
```

Comments are added to the script to make it clear what its purpose is. Even though the feedback.html page indicates where the data is sent (via the action attribute), a comment here indicates the reverse (where this script is getting its data).

3. Assign the received data to new variables:

```
$title = $_POST['title'];
$name = $_POST['name'];
$response = $_POST['response'];
$comments = $_POST['comments'];
```

Again, since the form uses the POST method, the submitted data can be found in the $_POST array. The individual values are accessed using the syntax $_POST['name']. This works regardless of the form element's type (input, select, checkbox, etc.).

To make it easier to use these values in a print() statement in Step 4, each value is assigned to a new variable here. I am not doing anything with either $_POST['email'] or $_POST['submit'], but you can incorporate them if you'd like.

4. Print out the user information:

```
print "<p>Thank you, $title $name,
→ for your comments.</p>
<p>You stated that you found this
→ example to be '$response' and
→ added:<br />$comments</p>";
```

This one print statement uses the four variables within a context to show the user what data the script received.

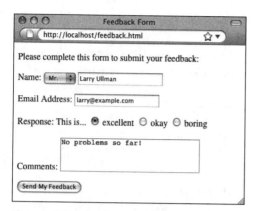

Figure 3.6 Whatever the user enters into the HTML form should be printed out to the Web browser by the handle_form.php script (see Figure 3.7).

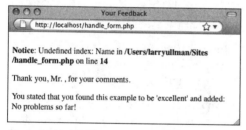

Figure 3.7 This is another application of the print() statement discussed in Chapter 1, but it constitutes your first dynamically generated Web page.

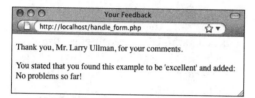

Figure 3.8 Notices like these occur when variables that don't exist are used in some ways. In this particular case, the cause is erroneously referring to $_POST['Name'] when it should be $_POST['name'].

5. Close the PHP section and complete the HTML page:

```
?>
</body>
</html>
```

6. Save the script as handle_form.php.

7. Upload the script to the server (or store it in the proper directory on your computer if you've installed PHP), making sure it's saved in the same directory as feedback.html.

8. Test the script in your Web browser by going to feedback.html and then submitting the form (**Figures 3.6** and **3.7**).

You must load the HTML form through a URL so that when it's submitted to the PHP script, that PHP script is also run through a URL.

If you see a blank page, read the next section of the chapter for how to display the errors that presumably occurred. If you see an error notice (**Figure 3.8**) or see that a variable does not have a value when printed, you likely misspelled either the form element's name value or the $_POST array's index (or you filled out the form incompletely).

✔ Tips

- If you want to pass a preset value along to a PHP script, use the hidden type of input within your HTML form. For example, the line

```
<input type="hidden" name="this_page"
value="feedback.html" />
```

inserted between the form tags will create a variable in the handling script called `$_POST['this_page']` with the value *feedback.html*.

- Notice that the value of radio button and select menu variables is based on the value attribute of the selected item (for example, *excellent* from the radio button). This is also true for check boxes. For text boxes, the value of the variable is what the user typed.

- If the `handle_form.php` script displays extra slashes in submitted strings, see the sidebar "Magic Quotes" for an explanation and solution.

- Some of the changes in PHP 6 are simply the removal of features that were no longer welcome. Among these is *register_globals*. This setting, when enabled, would make the values in $_POST, $_GET, $_SERVER, and other predefined arrays accessible in a different way. Relying upon `register_globals` created less secure scripts, so that setting was turned off as of PHP 4.2 and removed entirely as of PHP 6.

Magic Quotes

Earlier versions of PHP had a feature called *Magic Quotes*, which was removed in PHP 6. Magic Quotes—when enabled—automatically escapes single and double quotation marks found in submitted form data. So the string *I'd like more information* would be turned into *I\'d like more information*.

The escaping of potentially problematic characters can be useful and even necessary in some situations. But if the Magic Quotes feature is enabled on your PHP installation (which means you're using a pre–PHP 6 version), you'll see these backslashes when the PHP script prints out the form data. You can undo its effect using the `stripslashes()` function. To apply it to the `handle_form.php` script, you would do this, for example:

```
$comments = stripslashes($_POST
→['comments']);
```

Instead of just:

```
$comments = $_POST['comments'];
```

This will have the effect of turning an escaped submitted string back to its original, non-escaped value.

If you're using PHP 6 or later, you no longer need to worry about this, as Magic Quotes has been removed (for several good reasons).

Displaying Errors

One of the very first issues when it comes to debugging PHP scripts is that you may or may not even see the errors that occur. After you install PHP on a Web server, it will run under a default configuration with respect to security, how it handles data, performance, and so forth. One of the default settings is to not display any errors that occur. In other words, the *display_errors* setting will be off (**Figure 3.9**). When that's the case, what you might see when a script has an error is a blank page. (This is the norm on fresh installations of PHP; most hosting companies will enable display_errors.)

The reason that errors should not be displayed in a live site is that it's a security risk. Simply put, PHP's errors often give away too much information for the public at large to see. But you, the developer, *do need* to see these errors in order to fix them!

To have PHP display errors, you can

◆ Turn display_errors back on. (See the "Configuring PHP" section of Appendix A, "Installation and Configuration," for more information.)

◆ Turn display_errors back on for an individual script.

continues on next page

phpinfo()		
http://localhost/phpinfo.php		
display_errors	Off	Off
display_startup_errors	Off	Off
doc_root	*no value*	*no value*
docref_ext	*no value*	*no value*
docref_root	*no value*	*no value*
error_append_string	*no value*	*no value*
error_log	*no value*	*no value*
error_prepend_string	*no value*	*no value*
error_reporting	30719	30719

Figure 3.9 Run a phpinfo( ) script (e.g., Script 1.2) to see your server's display_errors setting.

DISPLAYING ERRORS

59

While developing a site, the first option is by far preferred. However, it's only an option for those with administrative control over the server. Anyone can use the second option by including this line in your script:

```
ini_set ('display_errors', 1);
```

The ini_set() function allows a script to temporarily override a setting in PHP's configuration file. In that example, you'll turn the display_errors setting to *on*, which is represented by the number 1.

Although this second method can be implemented by anyone, the downside is that if your script contains certain kinds of errors (discussed next in the chapter), the script cannot be executed. Therefore, this line of code can't be executed, and that particular error—or any that prevents a script from running at all—still results in a blank page.

To display errors:

1. Open handle_form.php in your text editor or IDE.

2. As the first line of PHP code, enter the following (**Script 3.4**):

   ```
   ini_set ('display_errors', 1);
   ```

   Again, this line tells PHP you'd like to see any errors that occur. You should call it first thing in your PHP section so the rest of the PHP code will abide by this new setting.

Script 3.4 This addition to the PHP script turns on the display_errors directive so that any errors that occur are shown.

```
1   <!DOCTYPE html PUBLIC "-//W3C//DTD XHTML
    1.0 Transitional//EN"
2       "http://www.w3.org/TR/xhtml1/DTD/
        xhtml1-transitional.dtd">
3   <html xmlns="http://www.w3.org/1999/
    xhtml" xml:lang="en" lang="en">
4   <head>
5       <meta http-equiv="Content-Type"
        content="text/html; charset=utf-8"/>
6       <title>Your Feedback</title>
7   </head>
8   <body>
9   <?php // Script 3.4 - handle_form.php #2
10
11  ini_set ('display_errors', 1); // Let me
    learn from my mistakes!
12
13  // This page receives the data from
    feedback.html.
14  // It will receive: title, name, email,
    response, comments, and submit in $_POST.
15  $title = $_POST['title'];
16  $name = $_POST['name'];
17  $response = $_POST['response'];
18  $comments = $_POST['comments'];
19
20  // Print the received data:
21  print "<p>Thank you, $title $name, for
    your comments.</p>
22  <p>You stated that you found this
    example to be '$response' and added:
    <br />$comments</p>";
23
24  ?>
25  </body>
26  </html>
```

Figure 3.10 Trying the form again...

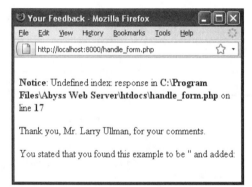

Figure 3.11 ...and now any error messages are displayed. The notices are generated by references to any form element for which there is no value.

3. Save the file as `handle_form.php`.

4. Upload the file to your Web server and test it in your Web browser (**Figures 3.10** and **3.11**).

If the resulting page has no errors in it, then the script will run as it did before. If you saw a blank page when you ran the form earlier, you should now see messages like those in Figure 3.11. Again, if you see such errors, you likely misspelled the name of a form element, misspelled the index in the $_POST array, or didn't fill out the form completely.

✔ Tips

■ Make sure `display_errors` is enabled any time you're having difficulties debugging a script. If you installed PHP on your computer, I *highly* recommend enabling it in your PHP configuration while you learn (again, see Appendix A).

■ If you see a blank page when running a PHP script, also check the HTML source code for errors or other problems.

■ The `ini_set()` function can only be used to alter certain settings. See the PHP manual for details.

■ Remember that the `display_errors` directive only controls whether error messages are sent to the Web browser. It doesn't create errors or prevent them from occurring in any way.

Error Reporting

Another PHP configuration issue you should be aware of, along with `display_errors`, is *error reporting*. There are eleven different types of errors in PHP—as of version 6, plus four user-defined types (which aren't covered in this book). **Table 3.1** lists the four most important general error types, along with a description and example.

You can set what errors PHP reports on using the `error_reporting()` function. The function takes either a number or some constants (nonquoted strings with predetermined meanings) to adjust the levels. The most important of these constants, which directly relate to the types of errors in Table 3.1, are listed in **Table 3.2**.

Table 3.1

PHP Error Types

Type	Description	Example
Notice	Nonfatal error that may or may not be indicative of a problem	Referring to a variable that has no value
Warning	Nonfatal error that is most likely problematic	Misusing a function
Parse error	Fatal error caused by a syntactical mistake	Omission of a semicolon or an imbalance of quotation marks, braces, or parentheses
Error	A general fatal error	Memory allocation problem

Table 3.2

Error Reporting Constants

Name
E_NOTICE
E_WARNING
E_PARSE
E_ERROR
E_ALL
E_STRICT

Script 3.5 Adjust a script's level of error reporting to give you more or less feedback on potential and existing problems.

```
1    <!DOCTYPE html PUBLIC "-//W3C//DTD XHTML
     1.0 Transitional//EN"
2        "http://www.w3.org/TR/xhtml1/DTD/
         xhtml1-transitional.dtd">
3    <html xmlns="http://www.w3.org/1999/
     xhtml" xml:lang="en" lang="en">
4    <head>
5        <meta http-equiv="Content-Type"
         content="text/html; charset=utf-8"/>
6        <title>Your Feedback</title>
7    </head>
8    <body>
9    <?php // Script 3.5 - handle_form.php #3
10
11   ini_set ('display_errors', 1); // Let me
     learn from my mistakes!
12   error_reporting (E_ALL | E_STRICT);
     // Show all possible problems!
13
14   // This page receives the data from
     feedback.html.
15   // It will receive: title, name, email,
     response, comments, and submit in $_POST.
16   $title = $_POST['title'];
17   $name = $_POST['name'];
18   $response = $_POST['response'];
19   $comments = $_POST['comments'];
20
21   // Print the received data:
22   print "<p>Thank you, $title $name, for
     your comments.</p>
23   <p>You stated that you found this
     example to be '$response' and added:
     <br />$comments</p>";
24
25   ?>
26   </body>
27   </html>
```

Using this information, you could add any of the following to a script:

```
error_reporting (0);
error_reporting (E_ALL);
error_reporting (E_ALL & ~E_NOTICE);
```

The first line says that no errors should be reported. The second requests that all errors be reported. The last example states that you want to see all error messages except notices (the & ~ means *and not*). Keep in mind that adjusting this setting doesn't prevent or create errors, it just affects whether or not errors are reported.

It's generally best to develop and test PHP scripts using the highest level of error reporting possible. To accomplish that, declare that you want to see all errors *plus strict* error reporting:

```
error_reporting (E_ALL | E_STRICT);
```

The E_ALL setting does not include E_STRICT, which is why that lines says that all errors should be shown *or* (the vertical bar, called the *pipe*) strict errors should be shown. This latter setting takes reporting a step further but also raises notices for things that could be a problem in future versions of PHP. Let's apply this setting to the handle_form.php page.

To adjust error reporting:

1. Open handle_form.php in your text editor (Script 3.4).

2. After the ini_set() line, add the following (**Script 3.5**):

   ```
   error_reporting (E_ALL | E_STRICT);
   ```

3. Save the file as handle_form.php.

   continues on next page

4. Place the file in the proper directory for your PHP-enabled server and test it in your Web browser by submitting the form (**Figures 3.12** and **3.13**).

At this point, if the form is filled out completely and the $_POST indexes exactly match the names of the form elements, you shouldn't see any errors (as in the figures). If any problems exist, including any potential problems (thanks to E_STRICT), they should be displayed and reported.

✔ Tips

- ■ The PHP manual lists all the error-reporting levels, but those listed here are the most important.

- ■ You can also adjust the level of PHP error reporting in the php.ini file, although such a change affects every script. If you are running your own PHP server, you'll probably want to tweak this while developing your scripts. See the section "Configuring PHP" of Appendix A.

Figure 3.12 Trying the form one more time...

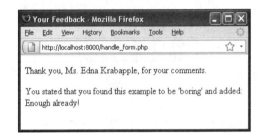

Figure 3.13 ...and the result (if filled out completely and without any programmer errors).

Manually Sending Data to a Page

The last example for this chapter is a slight tangent to the other topics but plays off the idea of handling form data with PHP. As discussed in the section "Using GET or POST," if a form uses the GET method, the resulting URL is something like

```
http://www.example.com/page.php?
→ some_var=some_value&age=20&...
```

The receiving page (here, page.php) is sent a series of *name=value* pairs, each of which is separated by an ampersand (&). The whole sequence is preceded by a question mark (immediately after the handling script's name).

To access the values passed to the page in this way, turn to the $_GET variable. Just as you would when using $_POST, refer to the specific name as an index in $_GET. In this example, page.php receives a $_GET['some_var'] variable with a value of *some_value*, a $_GET['age'] variable with a value of *20*, and so forth.

As I said, you can pass data in this way by creating an HTML form that uses the GET method. But you can also use this same idea to send data to a PHP page *without* the use of the form. Normally you'd do so by using links in another page:

```
<a href="page.php?id=22">Some Link</a>
```

That link, which could be dynamically generated by PHP after pulling some data from a database, will pass the value *22* to page.php, accessible in $_GET['id'].

To try this for yourself, this next pair of scripts will easily demonstrate this concept, using a hard-coded HTML page.

To create the HTML page:

1. Begin a new document in your text editor or IDE (**Script 3.6**):

```
<!DOCTYPE html PUBLIC "-//W3C//DTD
→ XHTML 1.0 Transitional//EN"
  "http://www.w3.org/TR/xhtml1/DTD/
  → xhtml1-transitional.dtd">
<html xmlns="http://www.w3.org/1999/
→ xhtml" xml:lang="en" lang="en">
<head>
  <meta http-equiv="Content-Type"
  → content="text/html;
  → charset=utf-8"/>
  <title>Greetings!</title>
</head>
<body>
<!-- Script 3.6 - hello.html -->
<div><p>Click a link to say
→ hello:</p>
```

2. Create links to a PHP script, passing values along in the URL:

```
<ul>
  <li><a href="hello.php?name=
  → Michael">Michael</a></li>
  <li><a href="hello.php?name=
  → Celia">Celia</a></li>
  <li><a href="hello.php?name=
  → Jude">Jude</a></li>
  <li><a href="hello.php?name=
  → Sophie">Sophie</a></li>
</ul>
```

Script 3.6 This HTML page uses links to pass values to a PHP script in the URL (thereby emulating a form that uses the GET method).

```
1   <!DOCTYPE html PUBLIC "-//W3C//DTD XHTML
    1.0 Transitional//EN"
2       "http://www.w3.org/TR/xhtml1/DTD/
        xhtml1-transitional.dtd">
3   <html xmlns="http://www.w3.org/1999/
    xhtml" xml:lang="en" lang="en">
4   <head>
5       <meta http-equiv="Content-Type"
        content="text/html; charset=utf-8"/>
6       <title>Greetings!</title>
7   </head>
8   <body>
9   <!-- Script 3.6 - hello.html -->
10  <div><p>Click a link to say hello:</p>
11
12  <ul>
13      <li><a href="hello.php?name=
        Michael">Michael</a></li>
14      <li><a href="hello.php?name=
        Celia">Celia</a></li>
15      <li><a href="hello.php?name=
        Jude">Jude</a></li>
16      <li><a href="hello.php?name=
        Sophie">Sophie</a></li>
17  </ul>
18
19  </div>
20  </body>
21  </html>
```

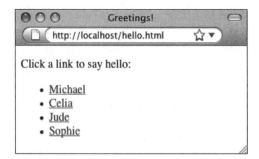

Figure 3.14 The simple HTML page, with four links to the PHP script.

The premise here is that the user sees a list of links, each associated with a specific name (**Figure 3.14**). When the user clicks a link, that name is passed to `hello.php` in the URL.

If you want to use different names, that's fine, but stick to one-word names without spaces or punctuation (or else they won't be passed to the PHP script properly, for reasons that will be explained in time).

3. Complete the HTML page:

```
</div>
</body>
</html>
```

4. Save the script as `hello.html` and place it within the proper directory on your PHP-enabled server.

5. Load the HTML page through a URL in your Web browser.

Although you can view HTML pages without going through a URL, you'll click links in this page to access the PHP script, so you'll need to start off using a URL here (see Figure 3.14). Don't click any of the links yet, though, as the PHP script doesn't exist.

To create the PHP script:

1. Begin a new document in your text editor or IDE (**Script 3.7**):

```
<!DOCTYPE html PUBLIC "-//W3C//DTD
→ XHTML 1.0 Transitional//EN"
   "http://www.w3.org/TR/xhtml1/DTD/
   → xhtml1-transitional.dtd">
<html xmlns="http://www.w3.org/1999/
→ xhtml" xml:lang="en" lang="en">
<head>
   <meta http-equiv="Content-Type"
   → content="text/html;
   → charset=utf-8"/>
   <title>Greetings!</title>
</head>
<body>
```

2. Begin the PHP code:

```
<?php // Script 3.7 - hello.php
```

3. Address the error management, if desired:

```
ini_set ('display_errors', 1);
error_reporting (E_ALL | E_STRICT);
```

These two lines, which configure how PHP responds to errors, are explained in the pages leading up to this section. They may or may not be necessary for your situation but can be helpful.

Script 3.7 This PHP page refers to the name value passed in the URL in order to print a greeting.

```
1   <!DOCTYPE html PUBLIC "-//W3C//DTD XHTML
    1.0 Transitional//EN"
2       "http://www.w3.org/TR/xhtml1/DTD/
        xhtml1-transitional.dtd">
3   <html xmlns="http://www.w3.org/1999/
    xhtml" xml:lang="en" lang="en">
4   <head>
5       <meta http-equiv="Content-Type"
        content="text/html; charset=utf-8"/>
6       <title>Greetings!</title>
7   </head>
8   <body>
9   <?php // Script 3.7 - hello.php
10
11  ini_set ('display_errors', 1); // Let me
    learn from my mistakes!
12  error_reporting (E_ALL | E_STRICT);
    // Show all possible problems!
13
14  // This page should receive a name value
    in the URL.
15
16  // Say "Hello":
17  $name = $_GET['name'];
18  print "<p>Hello, <span style=
    \"font-weight: bold;\">$name
    </span>!</p>";
19
20  ?>
21  </body>
22  </html>
```

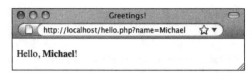

Hello, **Michael**!

Figure 3.15 By clicking the first link, *Michael* is passed along in the URL and is greeted by name.

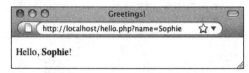

Hello, **Sophie**!

Figure 3.16 By clicking the last link, *Sophie* is sent along in the URL and is also greeted by name.

4. Use the name value passed in the URL to create a greeting:

```
$name = $_GET['name'];
print "<p>Hello, <span style=
→ \"font-weight: bold;\">$name
→ </span>!</p>";
```

The *name* variable is sent to the page through the URL (see Script 3.6). To access that value, refer to `$_GET['name']`. Again, you would use `$_GET` (as opposed to `$_POST`) because the value is coming from a GET method.

As with earlier PHP scripts, the value in the predefined variable (`$_GET`) is first assigned to another variable, to simplify the syntax in the `print()` statement.

5. Complete the PHP code and the HTML page:

```
?>
</body>
</html>
```

6. Save the script as `hello.php` and place it within the proper directory on your PHP-enabled server.

It should be saved in the same directory as `hello.html` (Script 3.6).

7. Click the links in `hello.html` to view the result (**Figures 3.15** and **3.16**).

✔ Tips

- If you run `hello.php` directly, you'll get an error notice because no name value would be passed along in the URL (**Figure 3.17**).

- Because `hello.php` reads a value from the URL, it works independently of `hello.html`. For example, you can directly edit the `hello.php` URL to greet anyone by name, even if `hello.html` does not have a link for that name (**Figure 3.18**).

- If you want to use a link to send multiple values to a script, separate the `variable=value` pairs (for example, `first_name=Larry`) with the ampersand (&). So, another link may be `hello.php?first_name=Larry&last_name=Ullman`.

- Although the example here—setting the value of a person's name—may not be very practical, this basic technique is useful on many occasions. For example, a PHP script might constitute a template, and the content of the resulting Web page would differ based on the values the page received in the URL.

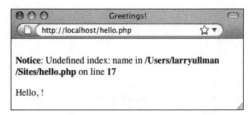

Figure 3.17 If the `$_GET['name']` variable isn't assigned a value, the browser prints out this awkward message, along with the error notice.

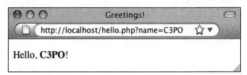

Figure 3.18 Any value assigned to name (lowercase) in the URL is greeted by the PHP script.

USING NUMBERS

Chapter 2, "Variables," loosely discussed the different types of variables, how to assign values to them, and how they're generally used. In this chapter, you'll work specifically with number variables—both integers (whole numbers) and floating-point numbers (aka floats or decimals).

The chapter begins by creating an HTML form that will be used to generate number variables. Then you'll learn how to perform basic arithmetic, how to format numbers, and how to cope with operator precedence. The last two sections of this chapter cover incrementing and decrementing numbers and generating random numbers. Throughout the chapter, you'll also find mentions of other useful number-related PHP functions.

Creating the Form

Most of the PHP examples in this chapter will perform various calculations based on an e-commerce premise. A form will take quantity, price, tax rate, shipping cost, and discount values, and the PHP script that handles the form will return a total cost. That cost will also be broken down by the number of payments the user wants to make in order to generate a monthly cost value.

To start, let's create an HTML page that allows the user to enter the different values (**Figure 4.1**).

To create the HTML form:

1. Begin a new HTML document in your text editor or IDE (**Script 4.1**):

   ```
   <!DOCTYPE html PUBLIC "-//W3C//DTD
   → XHTML 1.0 Transitional//EN"
     "http://www.w3.org/TR/xhtml1/DTD/
     → xhtml1-transitional.dtd">
   <html xmlns="http://www.w3.org/1999/
   → xhtml" xml:lang="en" lang="en">
   <head>
     <meta http-equiv="Content-Type"
     → content="text/html;
     → charset=utf-8"/>
     <title>Product Cost Calculator
     → </title>
   </head>
   <body><!-- Script 4.1 -
   → calculator.html -->
   <div><p>Fill out this form to
   → calculate the total cost:</p>
   ```

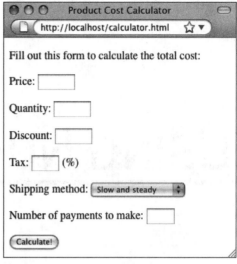

Figure 4.1 This form takes numbers from the user and sends them to the PHP page.

Script 4.1 This basic HTML form generates the numbers upon which mathematical calculations will be performed in a PHP script.

```
 1   <!DOCTYPE html PUBLIC "-//W3C//DTD XHTML
     1.0 Transitional//EN"
 2      "http://www.w3.org/TR/xhtml1/DTD/
        xhtml1-transitional.dtd">
 3   <html xmlns="http://www.w3.org/1999/
     xhtml" xml:lang="en" lang="en">
 4   <head>
 5      <meta http-equiv="Content-Type"
        content="text/html; charset=utf-8"/>
 6      <title>Product Cost Calculator</title>
 7   </head>
 8   <body><!-- Script 4.1 - calculator.html -->
 9   <div><p>Fill out this form to calculate
     the total cost:</p>
10
11   <form action="handle_calc.php"
     method="post">
12
13   <p>Price: <input type="text" name="price"
     size="5" /></p>
14
15   <p>Quantity: <input type="text"
     name="quantity" size="5" /></p>
16
17   <p>Discount: <input type="text"
     name="discount" size="5" /></p>
18
19   <p>Tax: <input type="text" name="tax"
     size="3" /> (%)</p>
20
21   <p>Shipping method: <select
     name="shipping">
22   <option value="5.00">Slow and steady
     </option>
23   <option value="8.95">Put a move on it.
     </option>
24   <option value="19.36">I need it
     yesterday!</option>
25   </select></p>
26
27   <p>Number of payments to make:
     <input type="text" name="payments"
     size="3" /></p>
28
29   <input type="submit" name="submit"
     value="Calculate!" />
30
31   </form>
32
33   </div>
34   </body>
35   </html>
```

2. Create the initial form tag:

```
<form action="handle_calc.php"
method="post">
```

This form tag begins the HTML form. Its action attribute indicates that the form data will be submitted to a page called handle_calc.php. The tag's method attribute tells the page to use POST to send the data. See Chapter 3, "HTML Forms and PHP," for more on any of this.

3. Create the inputs for the price, quantity, discount, and tax:

```
<p>Price: <input type="text"
→ name="price" size="5" /></p>

<p>Quantity: <input type="text"
→ name="quantity" size="5" /></p>

<p>Discount: <input type="text"
→ name="discount" size="5" /></p>

<p>Tax: <input type="text"
→ name="tax" size="3" /> (%)</p>
```

HTML has no input type for numbers, so you create text boxes for these values. A parenthetical indicates the formatting for the tax as a percent.

Also remember that the names used for the inputs have to correspond to valid PHP variable names (letters, numbers, and the underscore only; doesn't start with a number, and so forth).

continues on next page

CREATING THE FORM

4. Add a field in which the user can select a shipping method:

```
<p>Shipping method: <select
→ name="shipping">
<option value="5.00">Slow and
→ steady</option>
<option value="8.95">Put a move on
→ it.</option>
<option value="19.36">I need it
→ yesterday!</option>
</select></p>
```

The shipping selection is done using a drop-down menu. The value of the selected option is the cost for that option. Therefore, if the user selects, for example, the *Put a move on it.* option, the value of $_POST['shipping'] in handle_calc.php will be *8.95*.

5. Complete the HTML form:

```
<p>Number of payments to make:
→ <input type="text" name="payments"
→ size="3" /></p>
<input type="submit" name="submit"
→ value="Calculate!" />
</form>
```

The final two input types take a number for how many payments are required and then create a submit button (labeled *Calculate!*). The closing form tag marks the end of the form section of the page.

6. Complete the HTML page:

```
</div>
</body>
</html>
```

7. Save the script as calculator.html and view it in your Web browser.

Because this is an HTML page, you can view it directly in a Web browser.

Script 4.2 This PHP script performs all the standard mathematical calculations using the numbers submitted from the form.

```
      ● ● ●                   📄 Script
1     <!DOCTYPE html PUBLIC "-//W3C//DTD XHTML
      1.0 Transitional//EN"
2         "http://www.w3.org/TR/xhtml1/DTD/
          xhtml1-transitional.dtd">
3     <html xmlns="http://www.w3.org/1999/
      xhtml" xml:lang="en" lang="en">
4     <head>
5         <meta http-equiv="Content-Type"
          content="text/html; charset=utf-8"/>
6         <title>Product Cost Calculator</title>
7         <style type="text/css" media="screen">
8            .number { font-weight: bold;}
9         </style>
10    </head>
11    <body>
12    <?php // Script 4.2 - handle_calc.php
13    /* This script takes values from
      calculator.html and performs
14    total cost and monthly payment
      calculations. */
15
16    // Address error handling, if you want.
17
18    // Get the values from the $_POST array:
19    $price = $_POST['price'];
20    $quantity = $_POST['quantity'];
21    $discount = $_POST['discount'];
22    $tax = $_POST['tax'];
23    $shipping = $_POST['shipping'];
24    $payments = $_POST['payments'];
25
26    // Calculate the total:
27    $total = $price * $quantity;
28    $total = $total + $shipping;
29    $total = $total - $discount;
30
31    // Determine the tax rate:
32    $taxrate = $tax/100;
33    $taxrate = $taxrate + 1;
34
35    // Factor in the tax rate:
36    $total = $total * $taxrate;
37
38    // Calculate the monthly payments:
39    $monthly = $total / $payments;
40
```

(script continues on next page)

Performing Arithmetic

Just as you learned in grade school, basic mathematics involve the principles of addition, subtraction, multiplication, and division. These are accomplished in PHP using the most obvious operators:

◆ Addition (+)

◆ Subtraction (-)

◆ Multiplication (*)

◆ Division (/)

To demonstrate these principles, you'll create a PHP script that calculates the total cost for the sale of some widgets. This handling script could be the basis of a shopping-cart application—a very practical Web page feature (although in this case the relevant number values will come from calculator.html).

When you're writing this script, be sure to note the use of comments (**Script 4.2**) to illuminate the different lines of code and the reasoning behind them.

To create your sales-cost calculator:

1. Create a new document in your text editor or IDE (Script 4.2):

   ```
   <!DOCTYPE html PUBLIC "-//W3C//DTD
   → XHTML 1.0 Transitional//EN"
      "http://www.w3.org/TR/xhtml1/DTD/
      → xhtml1-transitional.dtd">
   <html xmlns="http://www.w3.org/1999/
   → xhtml" xml:lang="en" lang="en">
   <head>
      <meta http-equiv="Content-Type"
      → content="text/html;
      → charset=utf-8"/>
      <title>Product Cost Calculator
      → </title>
   ```

continues on next page

continues on next page

PERFORMING ARITHMETIC

```
<style type="text/css"
→ media="screen">
   .number { font-weight: bold;}
</style>
</head>
<body>
```

Note that I'm defining one CSS class here, called *number*. Any element within the page that has that class value will be given extra font weight. In other words, when the numbers from the form are reprinted in the script's output, I'd like them to be in bold.

2. Insert the PHP tags and address error handling, if desired:

```
<?php // Script 4.2 - handle_calc.php
```

Depending on your PHP configuration, you may or many not want to add a couple of lines that turn on `display_errors` and adjust the level of error reporting. See Chapter 3 for specifics.

3. Assign the $_POST elements to local variables:

```
$price = $_POST['price'];
$quantity = $_POST['quantity'];
$discount = $_POST['discount'];
$tax = $_POST['tax'];
$shipping = $_POST['shipping'];
$payments = $_POST['payments'];
```

The script will receive all of the form data in the predefined $_POST variable. To access individual form values, refer to $_POST['*index*'], replacing *index* with the corresponding form element's name value. These values are assigned to individual local variables here, to make it easier to use them throughout the rest of the script.

Note that each variable is given a descriptive name and is written entirely in lowercase letters.

Script 4.2 *continued*

```
41   // Print out the results:
42   print "<div>You have selected to
     purchase:<br />
43   <span class=\"number\">$quantity</span>
     widget(s) at <br />
44   $<span class=\"number\">$price</span>
     price each plus a <br />
45   $<span class=\"number\">$shipping</span>
     shipping cost and a <br />
46   <span class=\"number\">$tax</span>
     percent tax rate.<br />
47   After your $<span class=\"number\">
     $discount</span> discount, the total
     cost is
48   $<span class=\"number\">$total
     </span>.<br />
49   Divided over <span class=\"number\">
     $payments</span> monthly payments, that
     would be $<span class=\"number\">$monthly
     </span> each.</p></div>";
50
51   ?>
52   </body>
53   </html>
```

4. Begin calculating the total cost:

```
$total = $price * $quantity;
$total = $total + $shipping;
$total = $total - $discount;
```

The asterisk (*) indicates multiplication in PHP, so the total is first calculated as the number of items purchased ($quantity) multiplied by the price. Then the shipping cost is added to the total value (remember that the shipping cost correlates to the value attribute of the shipping drop-down menu), and the discount is subtracted.

Note that it's perfectly acceptable to determine a variable's value in part by using that variable's existing value (as you do in the last two lines).

5. Calculate the tax rate and the new total:

```
$taxrate = $tax/100;
$taxrate = $taxrate + 1;
$total = $total * $taxrate;
```

The tax rate should be entered as a percent—for example, 8 or 5.75. This number is then divided by 100 to get the decimal equivalent of the percent (.08 or .0575). Finally, you calculate how much something costs with tax by adding 1 to the percent and then multiplying that new rate by the total. This is the mathematical equivalent of multiplying the decimal tax rate times the total and then adding this result to the total (for example, a 5 percent tax on $100 is $5, making the total $105, which is the same as multiplying $100 times 1.05).

6. Calculate the monthly payment:

```
$monthly = $total / $payments;
```

As an example of division, assume that the widget(s) or whatever is being purchased can be paid for over the course of many months. Hence, you divide the total by the number of payments to find the monthly payment.

continues on next page

PERFORMING ARITHMETIC

7. Print the results:

```
print "<div>You have selected to
→ purchase:<br />
<span class=\"number\">$quantity
→ </span> widget(s) at <br />
$<span class=\"number\">$price
→ </span> price each plus a <br />
$<span class=\"number\">$shipping
→ </span> shipping cost and a <br />
<span class=\"number\">$tax</span>
→ percent tax rate.<br />
After your $<span class=\"number\">
→ $discount</span> discount, the
→ total cost is
$<span class=\"number\">$total
→ </span>.<br />
Divided over <span class=\"number\">
→ $payments</span> monthly payments,
→ that would be $<span class=
→ \"number\">$monthly</span>
→ each.</p></div>";
```

The `print()` statement sends every value to the Web browser along with some text. To make it easier to read, `<br />` tags are added to format the browser result; in addition, the `print()` function operates over multiple lines to make the PHP code cleaner. Each variable's value will be highlighted in the browser by wrapping it within span tags that have a class attribute of *number* (see Step 1).

8. Close the PHP section and complete the HTML page.

```
?>
</body>
</html>
```

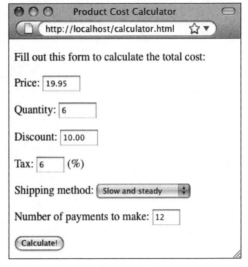

Figure 4.2 The HTML form...

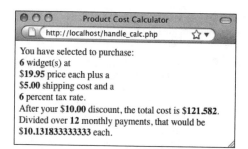

Figure 4.3 ...and the resulting calculations.

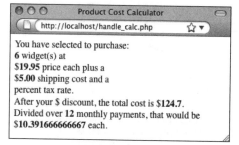

Figure 4.4 You can omit or change any value and rerun the calculator. Here I've omitted the tax and discount values.

9. Save your script as `handle_calc.php` and place it in the proper directory for your PHP-enabled server.

 Make sure that `calculator.html` is in this same directory.

10. Test the script in your Web browser (**Figures 4.2** and **4.3**).

 Not to belabor the point, but make sure you start by loading the HTML form through a URL (`http://something`) so that when it's submitted, the PHP script is also run through a URL.

 You can experiment with these values to see how effectively your calculator works. If you omit any values, the resulting message will just be a little odd but the calculations should still work (**Figure 4.4**).

✔ Tips

■ As you'll certainly notice, the calculator comes up with numbers that don't correspond well to real dollar values (see Figures 4.3 and 4.4). In the next section, "Formatting Numbers," you'll learn how to compensate for this result.

■ If you want to print the value of the total before tax or before the discount (or both), you can do so two ways. You can insert the appropriate `print()` statements immediately after the proper value has been determined but before the `$total` variable has been changed again. Or, you can use new variables to contain the values of the subsequent calculations (for example, `$total_with_tax` and `$total_less_discount`).

■ Because variables start with a dollar sign, using one to print out a figure such as `$2000.00` has to be handled carefully. You can't use `$$variable`, because the combination of two dollar signs creates a type of variable that's too complex to discuss in this book. One solution is to put something—a space or an HTML tag, as in this example—between the dollar sign and the variable name. Another option is to escape the first dollar sign:

```
print "The total is \$$total";
```

■ This script performs differently, depending on whether the various fields are submitted. The only truly problematic field is the number of monthly payments: If this is omitted, you'll see a division-by-zero warning. Chapter 6, "Control Structures," will cover validating form data before it's used.

Formatting Numbers

Although the calculator is on its way to being practical, it still has one legitimate problem: You can't ask someone to make a monthly payment of $10.13183333. To create more usable numbers, you need to format them.

There are two appropriate functions for this purpose. The first, round(), rounds a value to a specified number of decimal places. The function's first argument is the number to be rounded. This can be either a number or a variable with a number value. The second argument is optional; it represents the number of decimal places to round to. For example:

```
round (4.30); // 4
round (4.289, 2); // 4.29
$num = 236.26985;
round ($num); // 236
```

The other function you can use in this situation is number_format(). It works like round() in that it takes a number (or a variable with a numeric value) and an optional decimal specifier. This function has the added benefit of formatting the number with commas, the way it would commonly be written:

```
number_format (428.4959, 2); // 428.50
number_format (428, 2); // 428.00
number_format (123456789);
→ // 123,456,789
```

Let's rewrite the PHP script to format the numbers appropriately.

To format numbers:

1. Open handle_calc.php in your text editor or IDE (Script 4.2).

2. After all the calculations but before the print() statement, add the following (**Script 4.3**):

   ```
   $total = number_format ($total, 2);
   $monthly = number_format
   → ($monthly, 2);
   ```

Script 4.3 The number_format() function is applied to the values of the number variables, so they are more appropriate.

```
1   <!DOCTYPE html PUBLIC "-//W3C//DTD XHTML
    1.0 Transitional//EN"
2       "http://www.w3.org/TR/xhtml1/DTD/
        xhtml1-transitional.dtd">
3   <html xmlns="http://www.w3.org/1999/
    xhtml" xml:lang="en" lang="en">
4   <head>
5       <meta http-equiv="Content-Type"
        content="text/html; charset=utf-8"/>
6       <title>Product Cost Calculator</title>
7       <style type="text/css" media="screen">
8           .number { font-weight: bold;}
9       </style>
10  </head>
11  <body>
12  <?php // Script 4.3 - handle_calc.php #2
13  /* This script takes values from
    calculator.html and performs
14  total cost and monthly payment
    calculations. */
15
16  // Address error handling, if you want.
17
18  // Get the values from the $_POST array:
19  $price = $_POST['price'];
20  $quantity = $_POST['quantity'];
21  $discount = $_POST['discount'];
22  $tax = $_POST['tax'];
23  $shipping = $_POST['shipping'];
24  $payments = $_POST['payments'];
25
26  // Calculate the total:
27  $total = $price * $quantity;
28  $total = $total + $shipping;
29  $total = $total - $discount;
30
31  // Determine the tax rate:
32  $taxrate = $tax/100;
33  $taxrate = $taxrate + 1;
34
35  // Factor in the tax rate:
36  $total = $total * $taxrate;
37
38  // Calculate the monthly payments:
39  $monthly = $total / $payments;
40
```

(script continues on next page)

Script 4.3 *continued*

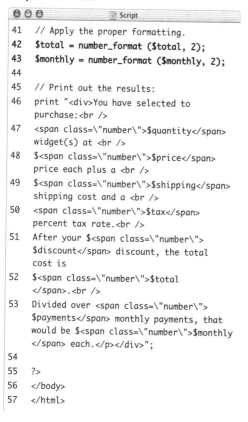

```
41    // Apply the proper formatting.
42    $total = number_format ($total, 2);
43    $monthly = number_format ($monthly, 2);
44
45    // Print out the results:
46    print "<div>You have selected to
      purchase:<br />
47    <span class=\"number\">$quantity</span>
      widget(s) at <br />
48    $<span class=\"number\">$price</span>
      price each plus a <br />
49    $<span class=\"number\">$shipping</span>
      shipping cost and a <br />
50    <span class=\"number\">$tax</span>
      percent tax rate.<br />
51    After your $<span class=\"number\">
      $discount</span> discount, the total
      cost is
52    $<span class=\"number\">$total
      </span>.<br />
53    Divided over <span class=\"number\">
      $payments</span> monthly payments, that
      would be $<span class=\"number\">$monthly
      </span> each.</p></div>";
54
55    ?>
56    </body>
57    </html>
```

To format the numbers, you apply this function after every calculation has been made but before they're sent to the Web browser. The second argument (the 2) indicates that the resulting number should have exactly two decimal places; this setting rounds the numbers and adds zeros at the end, as necessary.

3. Save the file, place it in the same directory as `calculator.html`, and test it in your browser (**Figures 4.5** and **4.6**).

✔ Tips

■ Another, much more complex, way to format numbers is to use the `printf()` and `sprintf()` functions. Due to their tricky syntax, they're not discussed in this book; see the PHP manual for more information.

■ Non-Windows versions of PHP also have a `money_format()` function, which can be used in lieu of `number_format()`.

■ For complicated reasons, the `round()` function rounds exact halves (`.5`, `.05`, `.005`, and so on) down half the time and up half the time.

■ The `number_format()` function takes two other optional arguments that let you specify what characters to use to indicate a decimal point and break up thousands. This is useful, for example, for cultures that write *1,000.89* as *1.000,89*. See the PHP manual for the proper syntax, if you want to use this option.

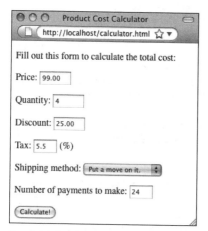

Figure 4.5 Another execution of the form.

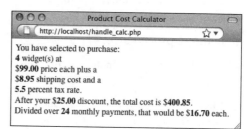

Figure 4.6 The updated version of the script returns more appropriate number values thanks to the `number_format()` function.

Understanding Precedence

Inevitably, after a discussion of the different sorts of mathematical operators comes the discussion of precedence. *Precedence* refers to the order in which a series of calculations are executed. For example, what is the value of the following variable?

```
$number = 10 - 4 / 2;
```

Is $number worth 3 (10 minus 4 equals 6, divided by 2 equals 3) or 8 (4 divided by 2 equals 2, subtracted from 10 equals 8)? The answer here is 8, because division takes precedence over subtraction.

Appendix B, "Resources and Next Steps," shows the complete list of operator precedence for PHP (including operators that haven't been covered yet). However, instead of attempting to memorize a large table of peculiar characters, you can bypass the whole concept by using parentheses. Parentheses always take precedence over any other operator. Thus:

```
$number = (10 - 4) / 2; // 3
$number = 10 - (4 / 2); // 8
```

Using parentheses in your calculations ensures that you never see peculiar results due to precedence issues. Parentheses can also be used to rewrite complex calculations in fewer lines of code. Let's rewrite the handle_calc.php script, combining multiple lines into one while maintaining accuracy by using parentheses.

To manage precedence:

1. Open handle_calc.php in your text editor or IDE (Script 4.3).

2. Change the way the total is first calculated (**Script 4.4**):

   ```
   $total = (($price * $quantity) +
   → $shipping) - $discount;
   ```

Script 4.4 By using parentheses, calculations made over multiple lines (see Script 4.3) can be compressed without affecting the script's mathematical accuracy.

```
1   <!DOCTYPE html PUBLIC "-//W3C//DTD XHTML
    1.0 Transitional//EN"
2       "http://www.w3.org/TR/xhtml1/DTD/
        xhtml1-transitional.dtd">
3   <html xmlns="http://www.w3.org/1999/
    xhtml" xml:lang="en" lang="en">
4   <head>
5       <meta http-equiv="Content-Type"
        content="text/html; charset=utf-8"/>
6       <title>Product Cost Calculator</title>
7       <style type="text/css" media="screen">
8           .number { font-weight: bold;}
9       </style>
10  </head>
11  <body>
12  <?php // Script 4.4 - handle_calc.php #3
13  /* This script takes values from
    calculator.html and performs
14  total cost and monthly payment
    calculations. */
15
16  // Address error handling, if you want.
17
18  // Get the values from the $_POST array:
19  $price = $_POST['price'];
20  $quantity = $_POST['quantity'];
21  $discount = $_POST['discount'];
22  $tax = $_POST['tax'];
23  $shipping = $_POST['shipping'];
24  $payments = $_POST['payments'];
25
26  // Calculate the total:
27  $total = (($price * $quantity) +
    $shipping) - $discount;
28
29  // Determine the tax rate:
30  $taxrate = ($tax/100) + 1;
31
32  // Factor in the tax rate:
33  $total = $total * $taxrate;
34
35  // Calculate the monthly payments:
36  $monthly = $total / $payments;
37
```

(script continues on next page)

Script 4.4 *continued*

```
                    Script
38   // Apply the proper formatting.
39   $total = number_format ($total, 2);
40   $monthly = number_format ($monthly, 2);
41
42   // Print out the results:
43   print "<div>You have selected to
     purchase:<br />
44   <span class=\"number\">$quantity</span>
     widget(s) at <br />
45   $<span class=\"number\">$price</span>
     price each plus a <br />
46   $<span class=\"number\">$shipping</span>
     shipping cost and a <br />
47   <span class=\"number\">$tax</span>
     percent tax rate.<br />
48   After your $<span class=\"number\">
     $discount</span> discount, the total
     cost is
49   $<span class=\"number\">$total
     </span>.<br />
50   Divided over <span class=\"number\">
     $payments</span> monthly payments, that
     would be $<span class=\"number\">$monthly
     </span> each.</p></div>";
51
52   ?>
53   </body>
54   </html>
```

There's no reason not to make all the calculations in one step, as long as you use parentheses to ensure that the math works properly. The other option is to memorize PHP's rules of precedence for multiple operators, but using parentheses is a lot easier.

3. Change how the tax is calculated:

`$taxrate = ($tax/100) + 1;`

Again, the tax calculations can be made in one line instead of two separate ones.

4. Save the script, place it in the same directory as `calculator.html`, and test it in your browser (**Figures 4.7** and **4.8**).

✔ Tips

- Be sure that you match your parentheses consistently as you create your formulas (every opening parenthesis requires a closing parenthesis). Failure to do so will cause parse errors.

- Granted, using the methods applied here, you could combine all the total calculations into just one line of code (instead of three)—but there is such a thing as oversimplifying.

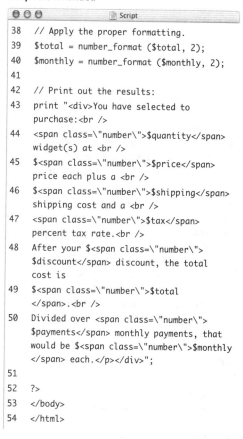

Figure 4.7 Testing the form one more time.

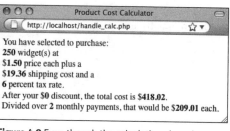

Figure 4.8 Even though the calculations have been condensed, the math works out the same. If you see different results or get an error message, double-check your parentheses for balance (an equal number of opening and closing parentheses).

Incrementing and Decrementing a Number

PHP, like Perl and most other programming languages, includes some shortcuts that let you avoid ugly constructs such as

`$tax = $tax + 1;`

When you need to increase the value of a variable by 1 (called an *incremental* adjustment) or decrease the value of a variable by 1 (a *decremental* adjustment), you can use ++ or --, respectively:

```
$var = 20; // 20
$var++; // 21
$var++; // 22
$var--; // 21
```

Solely for the sake of testing this concept, you'll rewrite the handle_calc.php script one last time.

To increment the value of a variable:

1. Open handle_calc.php in your text editor or IDE (Script 4.4).

2. Change the tax rate calculation from Script 4.3 to read as follows (**Script 4.5**):

   `$taxrate = $tax/100;`

   `$taxrate++;`

   The first line calculates the tax rate as the $tax value divided by 100. The second line increments this value by 1 so that it can be multiplied by the total to determine the total with tax.

Script 4.5 Incrementing or decrementing a number is a common operation using ++ or --, respectively.

```
1   <!DOCTYPE html PUBLIC "-//W3C//DTD XHTML
    1.0 Transitional//EN"
2       "http://www.w3.org/TR/xhtml1/DTD/
    xhtml1-transitional.dtd">
3   <html xmlns="http://www.w3.org/1999/
    xhtml" xml:lang="en" lang="en">
4   <head>
5       <meta http-equiv="Content-Type"
    content="text/html; charset=utf-8"/>
6       <title>Product Cost Calculator</title>
7       <style type="text/css" media="screen">
8           .number { font-weight: bold;}
9       </style>
10  </head>
11  <body>
12  <?php // Script 4.5 - handle_calc.php #4
13  /* This script takes values from
    calculator.html and performs
14  total cost and monthly payment
    calculations. */
15
16  // Address error handling, if you want.
17
18  // Get the values from the $_POST array:
19  $price = $_POST['price'];
20  $quantity = $_POST['quantity'];
21  $discount = $_POST['discount'];
22  $tax = $_POST['tax'];
23  $shipping = $_POST['shipping'];
24  $payments = $_POST['payments'];
25
26  // Calculate the total:
27  $total = (($price * $quantity) +
    $shipping) - $discount;
28
29  // Determine the tax rate:
30  $taxrate = $tax/100;
31  $taxrate++;
32
33  // Factor in the tax rate:
34  $total = $total * $taxrate;
35
36  // Calculate the monthly payments:
37  $monthly = $total / $payments;
38
```

(script continues on next page)

Script 4.5 *continued*

```
 39    // Apply the proper formatting.
 40    $total = number_format ($total, 2);
 41    $monthly = number_format ($monthly, 2);
 42
 43    // Print out the results:
 44    print "<div>You have selected to
       purchase:<br />
 45    <span class=\"number\">$quantity</span>
       widget(s) at <br />
 46    $<span class=\"number\">$price</span>
       price each plus a <br />
 47    $<span class=\"number\">$shipping</span>
       shipping cost and a <br />
 48    <span class=\"number\">$tax</span>
       percent tax rate.<br />
 49    After your $<span class=\"number\">
       $discount</span> discount, the total
       cost is
 50    $<span class=\"number\">$total
       </span>.<br />
 51    Divided over <span class=\"number\">
       $payments</span> monthly payments, that
       would be $<span class=\"number\">$monthly
       </span> each.</p></div>";
 52
 53    ?>
 54    </body>
 55    </html>
```

3. Save the script, place it in the same directory as `calculator.html`, and test it in your browser (**Figures 4.9** and **4.10**).

✔ Tips

■ Although functionally it doesn't matter whether you code $taxrate = $taxrate + 1; or the abbreviated $taxrate++, the latter method (using the increment operator) is more professional and common.

■ In Chapter 6, "Control Structures," you'll see how the increment operator is commonly used in conjunction with loops.

■ PHP also supports a combination of mathematical and assignment operators. These are + =, - =, * =, and /=. Each will assign a value to a variable by performing a calculation upon it. For example:

```
$tax = 5;
$tax /= 100; // Now $tax is .05
$tax += 1; // 1.05
```

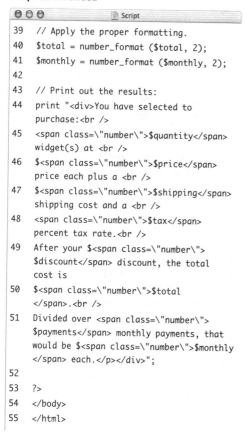

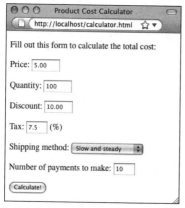

Figure 4.9 The last execution of the form.

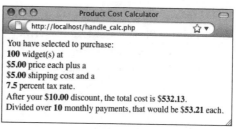

Figure 4.10 It won't affect your calculations if you use the long or short version of incrementing a variable (compare Scripts 4.4 and 4.5).

INCREMENTING AND DECREMENTING A NUMBER

Creating Random Numbers

The last function you'll learn about here is rand( ), a random-number generator:

```
$n = rand(); // 31
$n = rand(); // 87
```

The rand( ) function can also take minimum and maximum parameters, if you prefer to limit the generated number to a specific range:

```
$n = rand (0, 10);
```

These values are inclusive, so in this case 0 and 10 are feasible returned values.

As an example of generating random numbers, let's create a simple "Lucky Numbers" script.

To generate random numbers:

1. Begin a new document in your text editor or IDE (**Script 4.6**):

   ```
   <!DOCTYPE html PUBLIC "-//W3C//DTD
   → XHTML 1.0 Transitional//EN"
       "http://www.w3.org/TR/xhtml1/DTD/
       → xhtml1-transitional.dtd">
   <html xmlns="http://www.w3.org/1999/
   → xhtml" xml:lang="en" lang="en">
   <head>
       <meta http-equiv="Content-Type"
       → content="text/html;
       → charset=utf-8"/>
       <title>Lucky Numbers</title>
   </head>
   <body>
   ```

2. Include the PHP tags and address error management, if you need to:

   ```
   <?php // Script 4.6 - random.php
   ```

Script 4.6 The rand( ) function generates random numbers.

```
1   <!DOCTYPE html PUBLIC "-//W3C//DTD XHTML
    1.0 Transitional//EN"
2       "http://www.w3.org/TR/xhtml1/DTD/
        xhtml1-transitional.dtd">
3   <html xmlns="http://www.w3.org/1999/
    xhtml" xml:lang="en" lang="en">
4   <head>
5       <meta http-equiv="Content-Type"
        content="text/html; charset=utf-8"/>
6       <title>Lucky Numbers</title>
7   </head>
8   <body>
9   <?php // Script 4.6 - random.php
10  /* This script generates 3 random
    numbers. */
11
12  // Address error handling, if you want.
13
14  // Create three random numbers:
15  $n1 = rand (1, 99);
16  $n2 = rand (1, 99);
17  $n3 = rand (1, 99);
18
19  // Print out the numbers:
20  print "<p>Your lucky numbers are:<br />
21  $n1<br />
22  $n2<br />
23  $n3</p>";
24
25  ?>
26  </body>
27  </html>
```

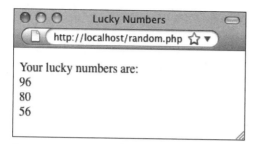

Figure 4.11 The three random numbers created by invoking the rand() function.

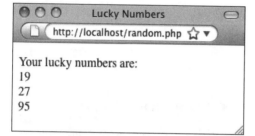

Figure 4.12 Running the script again produces different results.

3. Create three random numbers:

```
$n1 = rand (1, 99);
$n2 = rand (1, 99);
$n3 = rand (1, 99);
```

This script prints out a person's lucky numbers, like those found on the back of a fortune cookie's fortune. These numbers are generated by calling the rand() function three separate times and assigning each result to a variable.

4. Print out the numbers:

```
print "<p>Your lucky numbers
→ are:<br />
$n1<br />
$n2<br />
$n3</p>";
```

The print() statement is fairly simple. The numbers are printed, each on its own line, by preceding them with an HTML break tag.

5. Close the PHP code and the HTML page:

```
?>
</body>
</html>
```

6. Save the file as random.php, place it in the proper directory for your PHP-enabled server, and test it in your Web browser (**Figures 4.11** and **4.12**).

CREATING RANDOM NUMBERS

✔ Tips

■ The `getrandmax()` function returns the largest possible random number that can be created using `rand()`. This value differs by operating system.

■ PHP has another function that generates random numbers: `mt_rand()`. It works similarly to (but, arguably, better than) `rand()` and is the smarter choice for sensitive situations like cryptography. Also see the PHP manual's page for the `mt_rand()` function for more discussion of the topic as a whole.

Other Mathematical Functions

PHP has a number of built-in functions for manipulating mathematical data. This chapter introduced `round()`, `number_format()`, and `rand()`.

PHP has broken `round()` into two other functions. The first, `ceil()`, rounds every number to the next highest integer. The second, `floor()`, rounds every number to the next lowest integer.

Another function the calculator page could make good use of is `abs()`, which returns the absolute value of a number. In case you don't remember your absolute values, the function works like this:

```
$number = abs(-23); // 23
$number = abs(23); // 23
```

In layman's terms, the absolute value of a number is always a positive number.

Beyond these functions, PHP supports all the trigonometry, exponent, base conversion, and logarithm functions you'll ever need. See the PHP manual for more information.

USING STRINGS

As introduced in Chapter 2, "Variables," the second category of variables used by PHP is *strings*—a collection of characters enclosed within either single or double quotation marks. A string variable may consist of a single letter, a word, a sentence, a paragraph, HTML code, or even a jumble of nonsensical letters, numbers, and symbols (which might represent a password). Strings may be the most common variable type used in PHP.

Passwords, names, email addresses, comments, and similar input from HTML forms all become strings in your PHP script. You would have witnessed this behavior if you tried the `feedback.html` and `handle_form.php` pages in Chapter 3, "HTML Forms and PHP."

This chapter covers PHP's most basic built-in functions and operators for manipulating string data, regardless of whether the string originates from a form or is first declared within the script. Some common techniques will be introduced—trimming strings, joining strings together, and encoding strings. Other uses for strings will be illustrated in subsequent chapters.

Creating the HTML Form

As in Chapter 3, let's begin by creating an HTML form that sends different values—in the form of string variables—to a PHP script. The theoretical example being used is an online bulletin board or forum where users can post a message, their email address, and their first and last names (**Figure 5.1**).

To create an HTML form:

1. Begin a new HTML document in your text editor or IDE (**Script 5.1**):

```
<!DOCTYPE html PUBLIC "-//W3C//DTD
→ XHTML 1.0 Transitional//EN"
   "http://www.w3.org/TR/xhtml1/DTD/
   → xhtml1-transitional.dtd">
<html xmlns="http://www.w3.org/1999/
→ xhtml" xml:lang="en" lang="en">
<head>
   <meta http-equiv="Content-Type"
   → content="text/html;
   → charset=utf-8"/>
   <title>Forum Posting</title>
</head>
<body>
<!-- Script 5.1 - posting.html -->
<div><p>Please complete this form to
→ submit your posting:</p>
```

2. Create the initial form tag:

```
<form action="handle_post.php"
→ method="post">
```

This form will send its data to a `handle_post.php` script and will use the POST method.

Figure 5.1 This HTML form is the basis for most of the examples in this chapter.

Script 5.1 This form sends string data to a PHP script.

```
1    <!DOCTYPE html PUBLIC "-//W3C//DTD XHTML
     1.0 Transitional//EN"
2        "http://www.w3.org/TR/xhtml1/DTD/
         xhtml1-transitional.dtd">
3    <html xmlns="http://www.w3.org/1999/
     xhtml" xml:lang="en" lang="en">
4    <head>
5        <meta http-equiv="Content-Type"
         content="text/html; charset=utf-8"/>
6        <title>Forum Posting</title>
7    </head>
8    <body>
9    <!-- Script 5.1 - posting.html -->
10   <div><p>Please complete this form to
     submit your posting:</p>
11
12   <form action="handle_post.php"
     method="post">
13
14       <p>First Name: <input type="text"
         name="first_name" size="20" /></p>
15
16       <p>Last Name: <input type="text"
         name="last_name" size="20" /></p>
17
18       <p>Email Address: <input type="text"
         name="email" size="30" /></p>
19
20       <p>Posting: <textarea name="posting"
         rows="9" cols="30"></textarea></p>
21
22       <input type="submit" name="submit"
         value="Send My Posting" />
23
24   </form>
25   </div>
26   </body>
27   </html>
```

3. Add inputs for the first name, last name, and email address:

```
<p>First Name: <input type="text"
→ name="first_name" size="20" /></p>
<p>Last Name: <input type="text"
→ name="last_name" size="20" /></p>
<p>Email Address: <input type="text"
→ name="email" size="30" /></p>
```

These are all basic text input types, which were covered back in Chapter 3. Remember that the various inputs' name values should adhere to the rules of PHP variable names (no spaces; must not begin with a number; consists only of letters, numbers, and the underscore).

4. Add an input for the posting:

```
<p>Posting: <textarea name="posting"
→ rows="9" cols="30"></textarea></p>
```

The posting field is a textarea, which is a larger type of text input box.

5. Create a submit button and close the form:

```
<input type="submit" name="submit"
→ value="Send My Posting" />
</form>
```

Every form must have a submit button (or a submit image).

continues on next page

6. Complete the HTML page:

```
</div>
</body>
</html>
```

7. Save the file as `posting.html`, place it in the appropriate directory on your PHP-enabled server, and view it in your Web browser (Figure 5.1).

This is an HTML page, so it doesn't have to be on a PHP-enabled server in order for you to view it. But because it will eventually send data to a PHP script, it's best to go ahead and place the file on your server.

✔ Tips

■ Many forum systems written in PHP are freely available for your use. This book doesn't discuss how to fully develop one, but a multilingual forum is developed in my *PHP 6 and MySQL 5 for Dynamic Web Sites: Visual QuickPro Guide* (Peachpit Press, 2007).

■ This book's Web site has a forum where readers can post questions and other readers (and the author) answer questions. You can find it at

```
www.dmcinsights.com/phorum/
→ list.php?23
```

Connecting Strings (Concatenation)

Concatenation is an unwieldy term but a useful concept. It refers to the process of linking items together. Specifically, in programming, you concatenate *strings*. The period (.) is the operator for performing this action, and it's used like so:

```
$s1 = 'Hello, ';
$s2 = 'world!';
$greeting = $s1 . $s2;
```

The end result of this concatenation is that the $greeting variable has a value of *Hello, world!*.

Due to the way PHP deals with variables, the same effect could be accomplished using

```
$greeting = "$s1$s2";
```

This works because variables put within double quotation marks are replaced with their value when handled by PHP. However, the formal method of using the period to concatenate strings is more commonly used and is recommended (it will be more obvious what's occurring in your code).

Another way of performing concatenation involves the concatenation assignment operator:

```
$greeting = 'Hello, ';
$greeting .= 'world!';
```

This second line roughly means "assign to $greeting its current value plus the concatenation of *world!*" The end result is $greeting having the value *Hello, world!*

The posting.html script sends several string variables to the handle_post.php page. Of those variables, the first and last names could logically be concatenated. It's quite common and even recommended to take a user's first and last names as separate inputs, as this form does. On the other hand, it would be advantageous to be able to refer to the two together as one name. You'll write the PHP script with this in mind.

To use concatenation:

1. Begin a new document in your text editor or IDE (**Script 5.2**):

   ```
   <!DOCTYPE html PUBLIC "-//W3C//DTD
   → XHTML 1.0 Transitional//EN"
      "http://www.w3.org/TR/xhtml1/DTD/
   → xhtml1-transitional.dtd">
   <html xmlns="http://www.w3.org/1999/
   → xhtml" xml:lang="en" lang="en">
   <head>
      <meta http-equiv="Content-Type"
   → content="text/html;
   → charset=utf-8"/>
      <title>Forum Posting</title>
   </head>
   <body>
   ```

2. Create the initial PHP tag, and address error management, if necessary:

   ```
   <?php // Script 5.2 - handle_post.php
   ```

   If you don't have display_errors enabled, or if error_reporting is set to the wrong level, see Chapter 3 for the lines to include here to alter those settings.

Script 5.2 This PHP script demonstrates concatenation, one of the most common manipulations of a string variable. Think of it as addition for strings.

```
1    <!DOCTYPE html PUBLIC "-//W3C//DTD XHTML
     1.0 Transitional//EN"
2       "http://www.w3.org/TR/xhtml1/DTD/
        xhtml1-transitional.dtd">
3    <html xmlns="http://www.w3.org/1999/
     xhtml" xml:lang="en" lang="en">
4    <head>
5       <meta http-equiv="Content-Type"
        content="text/html; charset=utf-8"/>
6       <title>Forum Posting</title>
7    </head>
8    <body>
9    <?php // Script 5.2 - handle_post.php
10   /* This script receives five values from
     posting.html:
11   first_name, last_name, email, posting,
     submit */
12
13   // Address error management, if you want.
14
15   // Get the values from the $_POST array:
16   $first_name = $_POST['first_name'];
17   $last_name = $_POST['last_name'];
18   $posting = $_POST['posting'];
19
20   // Create a full name variable:
21   $name = $first_name . ' ' . $last_name;
22
23   // Print a message:
24   print "<div>Thank you, $name, for your
     posting:
25   <p>$posting</p></div>";
26
27   ?>
28   </body>
29   </html>
```

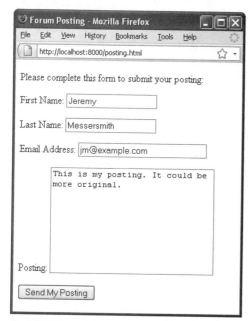

Figure 5.2 The HTML form in use...

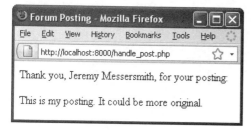

Figure 5.3 ...and the resulting PHP page.

3. Assign the form data to local variables:

```
$first_name = $_POST['first_name'];
$last_name = $_POST['last_name'];
$posting = $_POST['posting'];
```

The form uses the POST method, so all of the form data will be available in `$_POST`.

This example doesn't have a line for the email address because you won't be using it yet, but you can duplicate this code to reference that value as well.

4. Create a new `$name` variable using concatenation:

```
$name = $first_name . ' ' .
→ $last_name;
```

This act of concatenation takes two variables plus a space and joins them all together to create a new variable, called `$name`. Assuming you entered *Elliott* and *Smith* as the names, then `$name` would be equal to *Elliott Smith*.

5. Print out the message to the user:

```
print "<div>Thank you, $name, for
your posting:

<p>$posting</p></div>";
```

This message reports back to the user what was entered in the form.

6. Close the PHP section and complete the HTML page:

```
?>
</body>
</html>
```

7. Save your script as `handle_post.php`, place it in the same directory as `posting.html` (on your PHP-enabled server), and test both the form and the script in your Web browser (**Figures 5.2** and **5.3**).

As a reminder, you must load the form through a URL (`http://something`) so that, when the form is submitted, the handling PHP script is also run through a URL.

✔ Tips

- If you used quotation marks of any kind in your form and saw extraneous slashes in the printed result, see the sidebar "Magic Quotes" in Chapter 3 for an explanation of the cause and for the fix.

- As a reminder, it's very important to understand the difference between single and double quotation marks in PHP. Characters within single quotation marks are treated literally; characters within double quotation marks are *interpreted* (for example, a variable's name will be replaced by its value). See Chapter 3 for a refresher.

- You can link as many strings as you want using concatenation. You can even join numbers to strings:

  ```
  $new_string = $s1 . $s2 . $number;
  ```

  This works because PHP is *weakly typed*, meaning that its variables aren't locked in to one particular format. Here, the `$number` variable will be turned into a string and appended to the value of the `$new_string` variable.

- All form data, aside from uploaded files, is sent to the handling script as strings. This includes numeric data entered into text boxes, options selected from drop-down menus, checkbox or radio button values, and so forth.

- Concatenation can be used in many ways, even when you're feeding arguments to a function. An uncommon but functional example would be

  ```
  print 'Hello, ' . $first_name . '!';
  ```

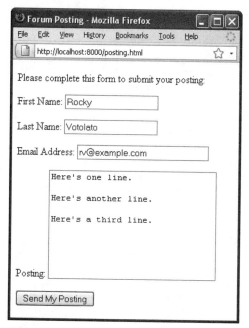

Figure 5.4 Newlines in form data like textareas...

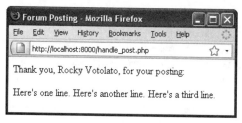

Figure 5.5 ...are not rendered by the Web browser.

Handling Newlines

A common question beginning PHP developers have involves newlines in strings. A user can enter text over multiple lines in a form element by pressing Return or Enter. Each use of Return or Enter equates to a newline in the resulting string. These newlines work within a textarea but have no effect on a rendered PHP page (**Figures 5.4** and **5.5**).

To create the equivalent of newlines in a rendered Web page, you would use the break tag: <br />. Fortunately, PHP has the nl2br() function that automatically converts newlines into break tags:

$var = nl2br($var);

Let's apply this to handle_post.php so that the user's posting retains its formatting.

To convert newlines:

1. Open handle_post.php (Script 5.2) in your text editor, if it is not already.

2. Apply the nl2br( ) function when assigning a value to the $posting variable (**Script 5.3**):

   $posting = nl2br($_POST['posting']);

   Now $posting will be assigned the value of $_POST['posting'], with any newlines converted to HTML break tags.

3. Save the file, place it in the same directory as posting.html (on your PHP-enabled server), and test again in your Web browser (**Figure 5.6**).

✔ Tips

■ Newlines can also be inserted into strings by placing the newline character—\n—between double quotation marks.

■ Other HTML tags, like paragraph tags, also affect spacing in the rendered Web page. You can turn newlines (or any character) into paragraph tags using a replace function, but the code for doing so is far more involved than just invoking nl2br( ).

Figure 5.6 Now the same submitted data as seen in Figure 5.4 is properly displayed.

Script 5.3 By using the nl2br( ) function, newlines entered into the posting textarea are honored when displayed in the Web browser.

```
1   <!DOCTYPE html PUBLIC "-//W3C//DTD XHTML
    1.0 Transitional//EN"
2      "http://www.w3.org/TR/xhtml1/DTD/
       xhtml1-transitional.dtd">
3   <html xmlns="http://www.w3.org/1999/
    xhtml" xml:lang="en" lang="en">
4   <head>
5      <meta http-equiv="Content-Type"
       content="text/html; charset=utf-8"/>
6      <title>Forum Posting</title>
7   </head>
8   <body>
9   <?php // Script 5.3 - handle_post.php #2
10  /* This script receives five values from
    posting.html:
11  first_name, last_name, email, posting,
    submit */
12
13  // Address error management, if you want.
14
15  // Get the values from the $_POST array:
16  $first_name = $_POST['first_name'];
17  $last_name = $_POST['last_name'];
18  $posting = nl2br($_POST['posting']);
19
20  // Create a full name variable:
21  $name = $first_name . ' ' . $last_name;
22
23  // Print a message:
24  print "<div>Thank you, $name, for your
    posting:
25  <p>$posting</p></div>";
26
27  ?>
28  </body>
29  </html>
```

HANDLING NEWLINES

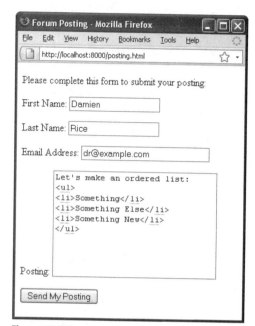

Figure 5.7 If the user enters HTML code in the posting...

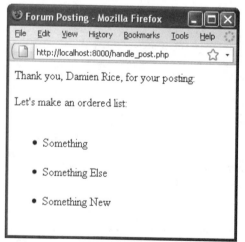

Figure 5.8 ...it's rendered by the Web browser when reprinted.

HTML and PHP

As I've said several times over by now, PHP is a server-side technology that's frequently used to send data to the Web browser. This data can be in the form of plain text, HTML code, or both.

In this chapter's primary example, data is entered in an HTML form and then printed back to the Web browser using PHP. A potential problem is that the user can enter HTML characters in the form, which can affect the resulting page's formatting (**Figures 5.7** and **5.8**)—or, worse, cause security problems.

Because of the relationship between HTML and PHP, you can use a couple of PHP functions to manipulate HTML tags within PHP string variables:

◆ `htmlspecialchars()` turns certain HTML tags into an entity version.

◆ `htmlentities()` turns all HTML tags into their entity versions.

◆ `strip_tags()` removes all HTML and PHP tags.

The first two functions turn an HTML tag (for example, `<span>`) into an entity version like `&lt;span&gt;`. The entity version appears in the output but isn't rendered. You might use either of these if you wanted to display code without enacting it. The third function, `strip_tags()`, removes HTML and PHP tags entirely.

HTML AND PHP

You ought to watch for special tags in user-provided data for two reasons. The first, as already mentioned, is that submitted HTML would likely affect the rendered page (e.g., mess up a table, tweak the CSS, or just add formatting where there shouldn't be any). The second concern is more important. Because JavaScript is placed within HTML tags, a malicious user could submit JavaScript that would be executed when it's redisplayed on the page. This is how *cross-site scripting* (XSS) attacks are performed.

To see the impact these functions have, this next rewrite of handle_post.php will use them each and display the respective results.

To work with HTML and PHP:

1. Open handle_post.php (Script 5.3) in your text editor or IDE, if it is not already.

2. Before the print() line, add the following lines (**Script 5.4**):

   $html_post = htmlentities($_POST
   → ['posting']);

   $strip_post = strip_tags($_POST
   → ['posting']);

   To clarify the difference between how these two functions work, apply them both to the posting, creating two new variables in the process. I refer to $_POST['posting'] here and not $posting because $posting already reflects the application of the nl2br() function, which means that break tags may be introduced that were not explicitly entered by the user.

Script 5.4 This version of the PHP script addresses HTML tags in two different ways.

```
1   <!DOCTYPE html PUBLIC "-//W3C//DTD XHTML
    1.0 Transitional//EN"
2       "http://www.w3.org/TR/xhtml1/DTD/
        xhtml1-transitional.dtd">
3   <html xmlns="http://www.w3.org/1999/
    xhtml" xml:lang="en" lang="en">
4   <head>
5       <meta http-equiv="Content-Type"
        content="text/html; charset=utf-8"/>
6       <title>Forum Posting</title>
7   </head>
8   <body>
9   <?php // Script 5.4 - handle_post.php #3
10  /* This script receives five values from
    posting.html:
11  first_name, last_name, email, posting,
    submit */
12
13  // Address error management, if you want.
14
15  // Get the values from the $_POST array:
16  $first_name = $_POST['first_name'];
17  $last_name = $_POST['last_name'];
18  $posting = nl2br($_POST['posting']);
19
20  // Create a full name variable:
21  $name = $first_name . ' ' . $last_name;
22
23  // Adjust for HTML tags:
24  $html_post = htmlentities($_POST
    ['posting']);
25  $strip_post = strip_tags($_POST
    ['posting']);
26
27  // Print a message:
28  print "<div>Thank you, $name, for your
    posting:
29  <p>$posting</p>
30  <p>$html_post</p>
31  <p>$strip_post</p></div>";
32
33  ?>
34  </body>
35  </html>
```

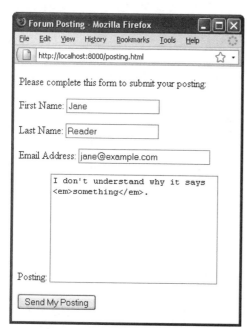

Figure 5.9 The HTML characters you enter as part of a posting will now be addressed by PHP.

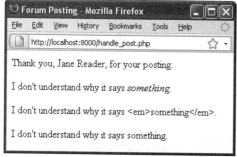

Figure 5.10 The resulting PHP page shows the original post as it would look if printed without modification, the effect of htmlentities( ), and the effect of strip_tags( ).

3. Alter the print statement to read as follows:

```
print "<div>Thank you, $name, for
→ your posting:
<p>$posting</p>
<p>$html_post</p>
<p>$strip_post</p></div>";
```

To highlight the different results, print out the three different versions of the postings. First is the original posting as it was entered, followed by the htmlentities( ) version of the posting. It will show the HTML tags without rendering them. Finally, the strip_tags( ) version will be printed; it doesn't include any HTML (or PHP) tags.

4. Save the file, place it in the same directory as posting.html (on your PHP-enabled server), and test it again in your Web browser (**Figures 5.9** and **5.10**).

continues on next page

If you view the HTML source code of the resulting PHP page (**Figure 5.11**), you'll also see the effect that applying these functions has.

✔ Tips

■ For security purposes, it's almost always a good idea to use htmlentities( ), html-specialchars( ), or strip_tags( ) to any user-provided data that's being printed to the Web browser. I don't do so through the course of this book only to minimize clutter.

■ The html_entity_decode( ) function does just the opposite of htmlentities( ), turning HTML entities into their respective HTML code.

■ Another useful function for outputting strings in the Web browser is wordwrap( ). This function wraps a string to a certain number of characters.

■ To turn newlines into breaks while still removing any HTML or PHP tags, apply nl2br( ) after strip_tags( ):

```
$posting = nl2br(strip_tags($_POST
↪['posting']));
```

In that line, the strip_tags( ) function will be called first, and its result will be sent to the nl2br( ) function.

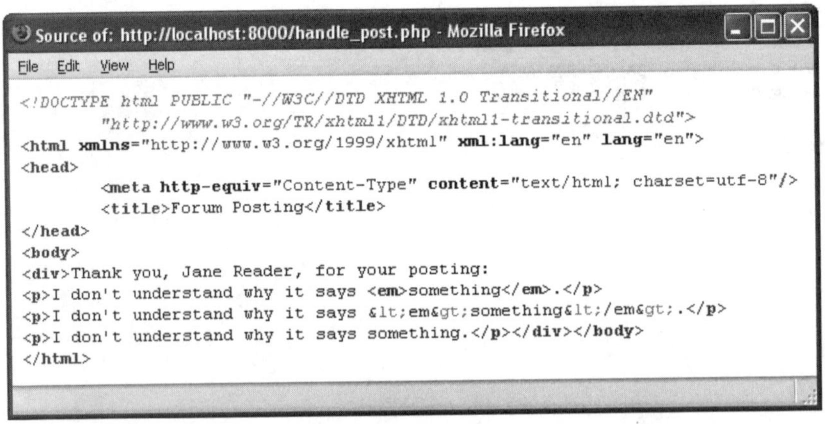

Figure 5.11 The HTML source for the content displayed in Figure 5.10.

Script 5.5 This script encodes two variables before adding them to a link. This way, the variables are successfully passed to the other page.

```
1   <!DOCTYPE html PUBLIC "-//W3C//DTD XHTML
    1.0 Transitional//EN"
2       "http://www.w3.org/TR/xhtml1/DTD/
    xhtml1-transitional.dtd">
3   <html xmlns="http://www.w3.org/1999/
    xhtml" xml:lang="en" lang="en">
4   <head>
5       <meta http-equiv="Content-Type"
        content="text/html; charset=utf-8"/>
6       <title>Forum Posting</title>
7   </head>
8   <body>
9   <?php // Script 5.5 - handle_post.php #4
10  /* This script receives five values from
    posting.html:
11  first_name, last_name, email, posting,
    submit */
12
13  // Address error management, if you want.
14
15  // Get the values from the $_POST array:
16  $first_name = $_POST['first_name'];
17  $last_name = $_POST['last_name'];
18  $posting = nl2br($_POST['posting']);
19
20  // Create a full name variable:
21  $name = $first_name . ' ' . $last_name;
22
23  // Print a message:
24  print "<div>Thank you, $name, for your
    posting:
25  <p>$posting</p></div>";
26
27  // Make a link to another page:
28  $name = urlencode($name);
29  $email = urlencode($_POST['email']);
30  print "<p>Click <a href=\"thanks.php?
    name=$name&email=$email\">here</a> to
    continue.</p>";
31
32  ?>
33  </body>
34  </html>
```

Encoding and Decoding Strings

At the end of Chapter 3, the section "Manually Sending Data to a Page" demonstrates how to use the thinking behind the GET method to send data to a page by appending it to the URL. At that time, you used this technique to send a variable with a single word value. But what if you want to pass several words as one variable value?

In these instances you can use the urlencode() function. As its name implies, this function takes a string and *encodes* it (changes its format) so that it can properly be passed as part of a URL. The function replaces spaces with plus signs (+) and translates special characters (for example, the apostrophe) into less problematic versions. To use this function, you might code:

```
$string = urlencode($string);
```

To demonstrate one application of urlencode(), let's rewrite the handle_post.php page, adding a link that passes the user's name and email address to a third page.

To use urlencode():

1. Open handle_post.php (Script 5.4) in your text editor or IDE, if it is not already.

2. Delete the htmlentities() and strip_tags() lines added in the previous set of steps (**Script 5.5**).

3. Revert to the older version of the print() invocation.

continues on next page

4. After the print statement, add the following:

```
$name = urlencode($name);
$email = urlencode($_POST['email']);
```

This script will pass these two variables to a second page. In order for it to do so, they must both be encoded.

Because you haven't previously referred to or used the `$email` variable, the second line both retrieves the email value from the `$_POST` array and encodes it in one step. This is the same as having these two separate lines:

```
$email = $_POST['email'];
$email = urlencode($email);
```

5. Add another print statement that creates the link:

```
print "<p>Click <a href=\"thanks.php
→ ?name=$name&email=$email\">here
→ </a> to continue.</p>";
```

The core purpose of this `print()` statement is to create an HTML link in the Web page, the source code of which would be something like

```
<a href="thanks.php?name=Larry+
→ Ullman&email=larry%40example.
→ com">here</a>
```

To accomplish this, you begin by hard-coding most of the HTML and then include the appropriate variable names. Because the HTML code requires that the URL for the link be in double quotation marks—and the `print()` statement already uses double quotation marks—you must escape them in order for them to be printed.

6. Save the file, place it in the proper directory of your PHP-enabled server, and test it again in your Web browser (**Figures 5.12** and **5.13**).

Figure 5.12 Another use of the form.

Figure 5.13 The handling script now displays a link to another page.

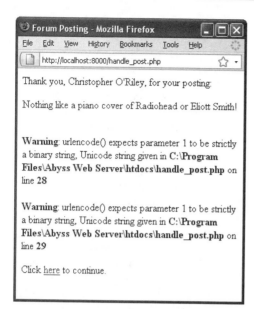

Figure 5.14 These error messages are due to a change in PHP 6, still being worked out at the time of this writing (see the sidebar).

---

urlencode() and PHP 6

At the time of this writing, PHP 6 is still in development, as it has been for some time. Some things, like the urlencode() function, are still being finalized. When I ran this example, I saw the warnings shown in Figure 5.14. To fix this, you'll need to change two lines in the script to:

```
$name = urlencode((binary) $name);
$email = urlencode((binary)
→ $_POST['email']);
```

In short, this code converts the strings to a binary format so that they can be used in the urlencode() function. The primary reason I didn't put this code into the printed script already is that it won't work if you're using a version of PHP before 5.2.1. Also, it's likely that the urlencode() function will change before PHP 6 is officially released.

If you see a PHP warning about the urlencode() function expecting the first parameter to be a binary string (**Figure 5.14**), see the sidebar for the cause and solution.

Also note that clicking the link will result in a server error, as that other PHP script hasn't yet been written.

7. View the HTML source code of the handling page to see the resulting link in the HTML code.

✔ Tips

- The urldecode() function does just the opposite of urlencode()—it takes an encoded URL and turns it back into a standard form. You'll use it less frequently, though, as PHP will automatically decode most values it receives.

- Since you can use concatenation with functions, the new print() statement could be written as follows:

```
print 'Click <a href="thanks.php?
→ name=' . $name . '&email=' .
→ $email . '">here</a> to continue.';
```

This method has two added benefits. First, it uses single quotation marks to start and stop the statement, meaning you don't need to escape the double quotation marks. Second, the variables used are more obvious—they aren't buried in a lot of other code.

- You do not need to encode numeric PHP values in order to use them in a URL, as they do not contain problematic characters. That being said, it won't hurt to encode them either.

Just in case it's not clear, let's quickly write the thanks.php page to which users are directed when they click the link in handle_post.php (see Figure 5.13).

To write thanks.php:

1. Begin a new document in your text editor or IDE (**Script 5.6**):

```
<!DOCTYPE html PUBLIC "-//W3C//DTD
→ XHTML 1.0 Transitional//EN"
    "http://www.w3.org/TR/xhtml1/DTD/
    → xhtml1-transitional.dtd">
<html xmlns="http://www.w3.org/1999/
→ xhtml" xml:lang="en" lang="en">
<head>
    <meta http-equiv="Content-Type"
    → content="text/html;
    → charset=utf-8"/>
    <title>Thanks!</title>
</head>
<body>
```

2. Create the initial PHP tag:

```
<?php // Script 5.6 - thanks.php
```

3. Assign the values to local variables:

```
$name = $_GET['name'];
$email = $_GET['email'];
```

Because the variable values will come from the URL and not from an HTML form using the POST method, you use $_GET instead of $_POST to access the values.

4. Print out a simple message:

```
print "<p>Thank you, $name. We will
→ contact you at $email.</p>";
```

Script 5.6 The thanks.php script prints a greeting based on two values it receives in the URL.

```
1   <!DOCTYPE html PUBLIC "-//W3C//DTD XHTML
    1.0 Transitional//EN"
2       "http://www.w3.org/TR/xhtml1/DTD/
        xhtml1-transitional.dtd">
3   <html xmlns="http://www.w3.org/1999/
    xhtml" xml:lang="en" lang="en">
4   <head>
5       <meta http-equiv="Content-Type"
        content="text/html; charset=utf-8"/>
6       <title>Thanks!</title>
7   </head>
8   <body>
9   <?php // Script 5.6 - thanks.php
10  /* This is the page the user sees after
    clicking on the link in handle_post.php
    (Script 5.5).
11  This page receives name and email
    variables in the URL. */
12
13  // Address error management, if you want.
14
15  // Get the values from the $_GET array:
16  $name = $_GET['name'];
17  $email = $_GET['email'];
18
19  // Print a message:
20  print "<p>Thank you, $name. We will
    contact you at $email.</p>";
21
22  ?>
23  </body>
24  </html>
```

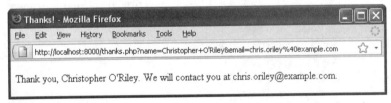

Figure 5.15 The third page in this process prints a message based on values it receives in the URL.

5. Complete the PHP code and the HTML page:

```
?>
</body>
</html>
```

6. Save the page as `thanks.php`, place it in the same directory as `posting.html` and `handle_post.php`, and test it in your Web browser by clicking the link in `handle_post.php` (**Figure 5.15**).

✔ Tip

■ Values sent directly from a form are automatically URL-encoded prior to being sent and decoded upon arrival at the receiving script. You only need the `urlencode()` function to manually encode data (as in the example).

Encrypting and Decrypting Strings

Frequently, in order to protect data, programmers *encrypt* it—alter its state by transforming it to a form that's more difficult, if not virtually impossible, to discern. Passwords are an example of a value you might want to encrypt. Depending on the level of security you want to establish, usernames, email addresses, and phone numbers are likely candidates for encryption, too.

You can use the `crypt()` function to encrypt data, but be aware that no decryption option is available (it's known as *one-way* encryption). So, a password may be encrypted using it and then stored, but the decrypted value of the password can never be determined. Using this function in a Web application, you might encrypt a user's password upon registration; then, when the user logged in, the password they entered at that time would also be encrypted, and the two protected versions of the password would be compared. The syntax for using `crypt()` is

```
$data = crypt($data);
```

A second encryption function is `mcrypt_encrypt()`, which can be decrypted using the appropriately named `mcrypt_decrypt()` function. Unfortunately, in order for you to be able to use these two functions, the Mcrypt extension must be installed with the PHP module. Its usage and syntax is also more complex (I discuss it in my *PHP 5 Advanced: Visual QuickPro Guide* [Peachpit Press, 2007]).

If the data is being stored in a database, you can also use functions built into the database application (for example, MySQL, PostgreSQL, Oracle, or SQL Server) to perform encryption and decryption. Depending on the technology you're using, it most likely provides both one-way and two-way encryption tools.

Finding Substrings

PHP has a few functions you can use to pull apart strings, search through them, and perform comparisons. Although these functions are normally used with conditionals, discussed in Chapter 6, "Control Structures," they are important enough that I want to introduce them here; later chapters will use them more formally.

Earlier in this chapter you learned how to join strings using concatenation. Besides making larger strings out of smaller pieces, you can also extract subsections of a string (which is to say, *tokenize* them). The trick to using any method to pull out a subsection of a string is that you must know something about the string itself in order to do so effectively.

The `strtok()` function creates a substring, referred to as a *token*, from a larger string by using a predetermined separator (such as a comma or a space). For example, if you have users enter their full name in one field (presumably with their first and last names separated by a space), you can ascertain their first name with this code:

```
$first = strtok($_POST['name'], ' ');
```

This line tells PHP to pull out everything from `$_POST['name']` until it finds a blank space.

If you have users enter their full name in the format *Surname, First*, you can find their surname by writing:

```
$last = strtok($_POST['name'], ', ');
```

A second way to pull out sections of a string is by referring to the *indexed position* of the characters within the string. The *index* of a string is the numerical location of a character, counting from the beginning. However, PHP—like most programming languages—begins all indexes with the number 0. For example, to index the string *Larry*, you begin with the *L* at position 0, followed by *a* at 1, *r* at 2, the second *r* at 3, and *y* at 4. Even though the string length of *Larry* is 5, its index goes from 0 to 4 (i.e., indexes always go from 0 to the string's length minus 1).

With this in mind, you can utilize the `substr()` function to create a substring based on the index position of the substring's characters, like this:

`$sub = substr($string, 0, 10);`

The first argument is the master string from which your substring will be derived. Second, indicate where the substring begins, as its indexed position (0 means that you want to start with the first character). Third, from that starting point, state how many characters the substring is composed of (10). In this case, if `$string` isn't 10 characters long, the resulting `$sub` will end with the end of `$string`.

You can also use negative numbers to count from the end of the string:

```
$string = 'ardvark';
$sub = substr($string, -3, 3); // ark
```

The second line says that three characters should be returned starting at the third character from the end.

To see how many characters are in a string, use `strlen()`:

`print strlen('Hello, world!'); // 13`

That count will include spaces and punctuation. To see how many words are in a string, use `str_word_count()`. This function, along with `substr()`, will be used in this next revision of the `handle_post.php` script.

Comparing Strings

To compare two strings, you can always use the equality operator, which you'll learn about in the next chapter. Otherwise, you can use these functions:

◆ `strcmp()` indicates how two strings compare by returning a whole number.

◆ `strnatcmp()` is similar but linguistically more precise.

These also have case-insensitive companions, `strcasecmp()` and `strnatcasecmp()`.

To see if a substring is contained within another string (i.e., to find a needle in a haystack), you'll use these functions:

◆ `strstr()` returns the haystack from the first occurrence of a needle to the end.

◆ `strpos()` searches through a haystack and returns the numeric location of a particular needle.

Both of these functions also have a case-insensitive alternative: `stristr()` and `stripos()`, respectively. Each of these functions is normally used in a conditional to test if the substring was found.

FINDING SUBSTRINGS

To create substrings:

1. Open handle_post.php (Script 5.5) in your text editor or IDE, if it is not already.

2. Before the print statement, add the following (**Script 5.7**):

   $words = str_word_count($posting);

   In this version of the script, I'd like to do two things with the user's posting. One will be to display the number of words it contains. That information is gathered here, and assigned to the $words variable.

3. On the next line (also before the print statement), add:

   $posting = substr($posting, 0, 50);

   The second thing I want this script to do is limit the displayed posting to its first fifty characters. You might use this, for example, if one page shows the beginning of a post, then a link takes the user to the full posting. To implement this limit, the substr( ) function is called.

Script 5.7 This version of handle_post.php counts the number of words in the posting and trims the displayed posting down to just the first 50 characters.

```
1   <!DOCTYPE html PUBLIC "-//W3C//DTD XHTML
    1.0 Transitional//EN"
2       "http://www.w3.org/TR/xhtml1/DTD/
        xhtml1-transitional.dtd">
3   <html xmlns="http://www.w3.org/1999/
    xhtml" xml:lang="en" lang="en">
4   <head>
5       <meta http-equiv="Content-Type"
        content="text/html; charset=utf-8"/>
6       <title>Forum Posting</title>
7   </head>
8   <body>
9   <?php // Script 5.7 - handle_post.php #5
10  /* This script receives five values from
    posting.html:
11  first_name, last_name, email, posting,
    submit */
12
13  // Address error management, if you want.
14
15  // Get the values from the $_POST array:
16  $first_name = $_POST['first_name'];
17  $last_name = $_POST['last_name'];
18  $posting = nl2br($_POST['posting']);
19
20  // Create a full name variable:
21  $name = $first_name . ' ' . $last_name;
22
23  // Get a word count:
24  $words = str_word_count($posting);
25
26  // Get a snippet of the posting:
27  $posting = substr($posting, 0, 50);
28
29  // Print a message:
30  print "<div>Thank you, $name, for your
    posting:
31  <p>$posting...</p>
32  <p>($words words)</p></div>";
33
34  ?>
35  </body>
36  </html>
```

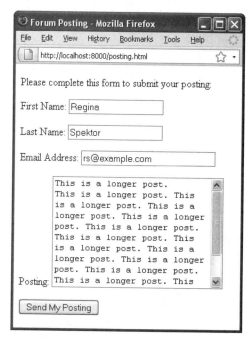

Figure 5.16 Postings longer than 50 characters...

Figure 5.17 ...will be cut short. The word count is also displayed.

4. Update the print statement to read:

```
print "<div>Thank you, $name, for
→ your posting:
<p>$posting...</p>
<p>($words words)</p></div>";
```

There are two changes here. First, ellipses are added after the posting to indicate that this is just part of the whole posting. Then, within another paragraph, the number of words is printed.

5. Delete the two urlencode( ) lines and the corresponding print( ) line.

6. Save the file, place it in the proper directory of your PHP-enabled server, and test it again in your Web browser (**Figures 5.16** and **5.17**).

✔ Tip

■ If you want to check whether a string matches a certain format—for example, to see if it's a valid email address—you need to use regular expressions. *Regular expressions* are an advanced concept in which you define patterns and then see if a value fits the mold. See Chapter 13, "Regular Expressions," for more information.

Replacing Parts of a String

Instead of just finding substrings within a string, as the preceding section of the chapter discusses, you might find that you need to *replace substrings* with new values. You can do so using the str_ireplace() function:

```
$string = str_ireplace($needle,
→ $replacement, $haystack);
```

This function replaces every occurrence of $needle found in $haystack with $replacement. For example:

```
$me = 'Larry E. Ullman';
$me = str_ireplace('E.', 'Edward', $me);
```

The $me variable now has a value of *Larry Edward Ullman.*

That function performs a *case-insensitive* search. To be more restrictive, you can perform a case-sensitive search using str_replace(). In this next example, str_ireplace() will be used to cross out "bad words" in submitted text.

There's one last string-related function I want to discuss: trim(). This function removes any white space—spaces, newlines, and tabs—from the beginning and end of a string. It's quite common for extra spaces to be added to a string variable, either because a user enters information carelessly or due to sloppy HTML code. For purposes of clarity, data integrity, and Web design, it's worth your while to delete those spaces from the strings before you use them. Extra spaces sent to the Web browser could make the page appear oddly, and those sent to a database or cookie could have unfortunate consequences at a later date (for example, if a password has a superfluous space, it might not match when it's entered without the space).

Adjusting String Case

A handful of PHP functions are used to change the case of a string's letters:

◆ ucfirst() capitalizes the first letter of the string.

◆ ucwords() capitalizes the first letter of words in a string.

◆ strtoupper() makes an entire string uppercase.

◆ strtolower() makes an entire string lowercase.

Do note that due to the variance in people's names around the globe, there's really no flawless way to automatically format names with PHP (or any programming language). In fact, I would be hesitant to alter the case of user-supplied data unless you have really good cause to do so.

Script 5.8 This final version of the handling script applies the trim( ) function and then replaces uses of badword with a bunch of Xs.

```
1   <!DOCTYPE html PUBLIC "-//W3C//DTD XHTML
    1.0 Transitional//EN"
2       "http://www.w3.org/TR/xhtml1/DTD/
    xhtml1-transitional.dtd">
3   <html xmlns="http://www.w3.org/1999/
    xhtml" xml:lang="en" lang="en">
4   <head>
5       <meta http-equiv="Content-Type"
    content="text/html; charset=utf-8"/>
6       <title>Forum Posting</title>
7   </head>
8   <body>
9   <?php // Script 5.8 - handle_post.php #6
10  /* This script receives five values from
    posting.html:
11  first_name, last_name, email, posting,
    submit */
12
13  // Address error management, if you want.
14
15  // Get the values from the $_POST array.
16  // Strip away extra spaces using trim():
17  $first_name = trim($_POST['first_name']);
18  $last_name = trim($_POST['last_name']);
19  $posting = trim($_POST['posting']);
20
21  // Create a full name variable:
22  $name = $first_name . ' ' . $last_name;
23
24  // Get a word count:
25  $words = str_word_count($posting);
26
27  // Take out the bad words:
28  $posting = str_ireplace('badword',
    'XXXXX', $posting);
29
30  // Print a message:
31  print "<div>Thank you, $name, for your
    posting:
32  <p>$posting</p>
33  <p>($words words)</p></div>";
34
35  ?>
36  </body>
37  </html>
```

The trim( ) function automatically strips away any extra spaces from both the beginning and the end of a string (but not the middle). The format for using trim( ) is as follows:

```
$string = ' extra space before and
→ after text ';
$string = trim($string);
// $string is now equal to 'extra
→ space before and after text'.
```

To use str_ireplace( ):

1. Open handle_post.php (Script 5.7) in your text editor or IDE, if it is not already.

2. Apply trim( ) to the form data (**Script 5.8**):

   ```
   $first_name = trim($_POST['first_
   → name']);
   $last_name = trim($_POST['last_
   → name']);
   $posting = trim($_POST['posting']);
   ```

   Just in case the incoming data has extraneous white space at its beginning or end, the trim( ) function is applied.

3. Remove the use of substr( ):

   I'll want to see the entire posting for this example, so I remove the invocation of substr( ).

4. Before the print statement, add:

   ```
   $posting = str_ireplace('badword',
   → 'XXXXX', $posting);
   ```

   This specific example flags the use of a bad word in a posting by crossing it out. Rather than an actual curse word, the code uses *badword*. (You can use whatever you want, of course.)

   continues on next page

REPLACING PARTS OF A STRING

If you'd like to catch many bad words, you can use multiple lines, like so:

```
$posting = str_ireplace('badword1',
→ 'XXXXX', $posting);

$posting = str_ireplace('badword2',
→ 'XXXXX', $posting);

$posting = str_ireplace('badword3',
→ 'XXXXX', $posting);
```

5. Update the print statement so that it no longer uses the ellipses:

```
print "<div>Thank you, $name, for
→ your posting:
<p>$posting</p>
<p>($words words)</p></div>";
```

6. Save the file, place it in the proper directory of your PHP-enabled server, and test again in your Web browser (**Figures 5.18** and **5.19**).

✔ Tips

- The str_ireplace() function will even catch bad words in context. For example, if you entered *I feel like using badwords*, the result would be *I feel like using XXXXXs*.

- The str_ireplace() function can also take an array of needle terms, an array of replacement terms, and even an array as the haystack. Because you may not know what an array is yet, this technique isn't demonstrated here.

- If you need to trim excess spaces from the beginning or the end of a string but not both, PHP breaks the trim() function into two more specific functions: rtrim() removes spaces found at the end of a string variable, and ltrim() handles those at the beginning. They're both used just like trim():

```
$string = rtrim($string);
$string = ltrim($string);
```

Figure 5.18 If a user enters a word you'd prefer they not use...

Figure 5.19 ...you can have PHP replace it.

REPLACING PARTS OF A STRING

CONTROL
STRUCTURES

Control structures—conditionals and loops—are a staple of programming languages. PHP includes two general conditionals—if and switch—both of which you'll master in this chapter. They allow you to establish a test and then perform actions based on the results. This functionality gives you the ability to make your Web sites even more dynamic. The discussion of if conditionals will introduce two last categories of operators: comparison and logical (you've already seen the arithmetic and assignment operators in the previous chapters). You'll commonly use these in your conditionals along with the Boolean concepts of *TRUE* and *FALSE*.

Finally, this chapter begins programming with loops, which allow you to repeat an action for a specified number of iterations. Loops can save you programming time and help you get the most functionality out of arrays, as you'll see in the next chapter.

Creating the HTML Form

As with the previous chapters, the examples in this chapter are based on an HTML form that sends data to a PHP page. In this case, the form is a simple registration page that requests the following information (**Figure 6.1**):

◆ Email Address

◆ Password

◆ Date of birth

◆ Favorite color

The following steps walk through this form before getting into the PHP code.

To create the HTML form:

1. Begin a new HTML document in your text editor or IDE (**Script 6.1**):

```
<!DOCTYPE html PUBLIC "-//W3C//DTD
→ XHTML 1.0 Transitional//EN"
  "http://www.w3.org/TR/xhtml1/DTD/
  → xhtml1-transitional.dtd">
<html xmlns="http://www.w3.org/1999/
→ xhtml" xml:lang="en" lang="en">
<head>
  <meta http-equiv="Content-Type"
  → content="text/html;
  → charset=utf-8"/>
  <title>Registration Form</title>
</head>
<body>
<!-- Script 6.1 - register.html -->
<div><p>Please complete this form to
register:</p>
```

2. Create the initial form tag:

```
<form action="handle_reg.php"
→ method="post">
```

As with many of the previous examples, this page uses the POST method. The handling script, identified by the action attribute, will be handle_reg.php.

Figure 6.1 The HTML form used in this chapter.

Script 6.1 This pseudo-registration form is the basis for the examples in this chapter.

```
1    <!DOCTYPE html PUBLIC "-//W3C//DTD XHTML
     1.0 Transitional//EN"
2        "http://www.w3.org/TR/xhtml1/DTD/
     xhtml1-transitional.dtd">
3    <html xmlns="http://www.w3.org/1999/
     xhtml" xml:lang="en" lang="en">
4    <head>
5        <meta http-equiv="Content-Type"
         content="text/html; charset=utf-8"/>
6        <title>Registration Form</title>
7    </head>
8    <body>
9    <!-- Script 6.1 - register.html -->
10   <div><p>Please complete this form to
     register:</p>
11
12   <form action="handle_reg.php"
     method="post">
13
14       <p>Email Address: <input type="text"
         name="email" size="30" /></p>
15
16       <p>Password: <input type="password"
         name="password" size="20" /></p>
17
18       <p>Confirm Password: <input type=
         "password" name="confirm" size="20" />
         </p>
19
```

(script continues on next page)

Figure 6.2 A password input type, as it's being filled out.

Script 6.1 *continued*

```
 ⊙ ⊙ ⊙                📄 Script
20        <p>Date Of Birth:
21        <select name="month">
22        <option value="">Month</option>
23        <option value="1">January</option>
24        <option value="2">February</option>
25        <option value="3">March</option>
26        <option value="4">April</option>
27        <option value="5">May</option>
28        <option value="6">June</option>
29        <option value="7">July</option>
30        <option value="8">August</option>
31        <option value="9">September</option>
32        <option value="10">October</option>
33        <option value="11">November</option>
34        <option value="12">December</option>
35        </select>
36        <select name="day">
37        <option value="">Day</option>
38        <option value="1">1</option>
39        <option value="2">2</option>
40        <option value="3">3</option>
41        <option value="4">4</option>
42        <option value="5">5</option>
43        <option value="6">6</option>
44        <option value="7">7</option>
45        <option value="8">8</option>
46        <option value="9">9</option>
47        <option value="10">10</option>
48        <option value="11">11</option>
49        <option value="12">12</option>
50        <option value="13">13</option>
51        <option value="14">14</option>
52        <option value="15">15</option>
53        <option value="16">16</option>
54        <option value="17">17</option>
55        <option value="18">18</option>
56        <option value="19">19</option>
57        <option value="20">20</option>
58        <option value="21">21</option>
59        <option value="22">22</option>
60        <option value="23">23</option>
```

(script continues on next page)

3. Create inputs for the email address and password:

```
<p>Email Address: <input type="text"
→ name="email" size="30" /></p>
<p>Password: <input type="password"
→ name="password" size="20" /></p>
<p>Confirm Password: <input
→ type="password" name="confirm"
→ size="20" /></p>
```

These lines should be self-evident. Each line is wrapped in HTML <p></p> tags to improve the spacing in the Web browser. Also, note that two password inputs are created—the second is used to confirm the text entered in the first. Password input types don't reveal what the user types (**Figure 6.2**), so it's a good insurance policy to make them type it again.

4. Begin making the inputs for the date of birth:

```
<p>Date Of Birth:
<select name="month">
<option value="">Month</option>
<option value="1">January</option>
<option value="2">February</option>
<option value="3">March</option>
<option value="4">April</option>
<option value="5">May</option>
<option value="6">June</option>
<option value="7">July</option>
<option value="8">August</option>
<option value="9">September</option>
<option value="10">October</option>
<option value="11">November</option>
<option value="12">December</option>
</select>
```

continues on next page

CREATING THE HTML FORM

The date of birth will be broken into three separate inputs—month, day, and year—rather than have the user enter it all at once (for example, *10/23/1970* or *January 26, 1974*). This approach gives you more control for validating and formatting the information submitted.

5. Create a drop-down menu for the birthday:

```
<select name="day">
<option value="">Day</option>
<option value="1">1</option>
<option value="2">2</option>
<option value="3">3</option>
<option value="4">4</option>
<option value="5">5</option>
<option value="6">6</option>
<option value="7">7</option>
<option value="8">8</option>
<option value="9">9</option>
<option value="10">10</option>
<option value="11">11</option>
<option value="12">12</option>
<option value="13">13</option>
<option value="14">14</option>
<option value="15">15</option>
<option value="16">16</option>
<option value="17">17</option>
<option value="18">18</option>
<option value="19">19</option>
<option value="20">20</option>
<option value="21">21</option>
<option value="22">22</option>
<option value="23">23</option>
<option value="24">24</option>
<option value="25">25</option>
<option value="26">26</option>
<option value="27">27</option>
<option value="28">28</option>
<option value="29">29</option>
<option value="30">30</option>
<option value="31">31</option>
</select>
```

Script 6.1 *continued*

```
61    <option value="24">24</option>
62    <option value="25">25</option>
63    <option value="26">26</option>
64    <option value="27">27</option>
65    <option value="28">28</option>
66    <option value="29">29</option>
67    <option value="30">30</option>
68    <option value="31">31</option>
69    </select>
70    <input type="text" name="year"
      value="YYYY" size="4" /></p>
71
72    <p>Favorite Color:
73    <select name="color">
74    <option value="">Pick One</option>
75    <option value="red">Red</option>
76    <option value="yellow">Yellow</option>
77    <option value="green">Green</option>
78    <option value="blue">Blue</option>
79    </select></p>
80
81    <input type="submit" name="submit"
      value="Register" />
82
83    </form>
84
85    </div>
86    </body>
87    </html>
```

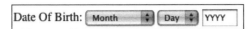

Date Of Birth: Month ▲▼ Day ▲▼ YYYY

Figure 6.3 The date of birth inputs; the year input has a preset value.

6. Create a text input for the birth year:

```
<input type="text" name="year"
→ value="YYYY" size="4" /></p>
```

Rather than use a drop-down menu that displays 50 or 100 years, you have the user enter their birth year in a text box. By presetting the value of the input, you make the text box indicate the proper format for the year (**Figure 6.3**). Also, just to clarify, the closing </p> tag completes the paragraph begun in Step 4.

7. Create a drop-down menu for the user's favorite color:

```
<p>Favorite Color:
<select name="color">
<option value="">Pick One</option>
<option value="red">Red</option>
<option value="yellow">Yellow
→ </option>
<option value="green">Green</option>
<option value="blue">Blue</option>
</select></p>
```

The truth is that I'm adding this input so that it can be used for a specific example later in the chapter, but it might be used to customize the look of the site after the user logs in. Naturally, you can add as many colors as you want here.

continues on next page

8. Add a submit button and close the form:

```
<input type="submit"
→ name="submit"
→ value="Register" />
</form>
```

9. Complete the HTML page:

```
</div>
</body>
</html>
```

10. Save the file as `register.html`, place it in the proper directory for your PHP-enabled server, and load the page in your Web browser.

✔ Tips

- Registration pages should always have users confirm their password and possibly their username or email address (whatever information will be used to log in).

- Most registration pages use either a nickname or an email address for the username. If you use the email address as a username, it's easier for your users to remember their registration information (a user may have only a few email addresses but a gazillion usernames for different sites around the Web). Furthermore, email addresses are, by their nature, unique.

The if Conditional

The basic programming conditional is the standard if (what used to be called an if-then conditional—the then is now implied). The syntax for this kind of conditional is very simple:

```
if (condition) {
    statement(s);
}
```

The condition must go within parentheses; then the statement(s) are placed within curly braces. These are commands to be executed (for example, printing a string or adding two numbers together). Each separate statement (or command) must have its own semicolon indicating the end of the line, but there is no limit on the number of statements that can be associated with a conditional.

Programmers commonly indent these statements from the initial if line to indicate that they're the result of a conditional, but that format isn't syntactically required. You'll also see people use this syntax:

```
if (condition)
{
    statement(s);
}
```

Failure to use a semicolon after each statement, forgetting an opening or closing parenthesis or curly brace, or using a semicolon after either of the braces will cause errors to occur. So, be mindful of your syntax as you code with conditionals.

PHP uses the Boolean concepts of TRUE and FALSE when determining whether to execute the statements. If the condition is TRUE, the statements are executed; if it's FALSE, they are not executed.

Over the course of this chapter (most of it, anyway), a PHP script will be developed until it fully validates the feedback.html form data. To start, this first version of the script will just create the basic shell of the validation process, defining and using a variable with a Boolean value that'll track the success of the validation process.

To create an if conditional:

1. Begin a new document in your text editor or IDE (**Script 6.2**):

```
<!DOCTYPE html PUBLIC "-//W3C//DTD
→ XHTML 1.0 Transitional//EN"
    "http://www.w3.org/TR/xhtml1/DTD/
    → xhtml1-transitional.dtd">
<html xmlns="http://www.w3.org/1999/
→ xhtml" xml:lang="en" lang="en">
<head>
    <meta http-equiv="Content-Type"
    → content="text/html;
    → charset=utf-8"/>
    <title>Registration</title>
</head>
<body>
<h2>Registration Results</h2>
```

2. Begin the PHP section and address error management, if necessary:

```
<?php // Script 6.2 - handle_reg.php
```

If you don't have display_errors enabled, or if error_reporting is set to the wrong level, see Chapter 3, "HTML Forms and PHP," for the lines to include here to alter those settings.

3. Create a flag variable:

```
$okay = TRUE;
```

This variable is initialized with a Boolean value of *TRUE* (Booleans are case-insensitive, so you could also write *True* or *true*). I call this a "flag" variable because its value in itself isn't important; it'll just be used to indicate the status of something.

Script 6.2 This shell of a PHP script will be built upon to validate the form data.

```
1   <!DOCTYPE html PUBLIC "-//W3C//DTD XHTML
    1.0 Transitional//EN"
2       "http://www.w3.org/TR/xhtml1/DTD/
        xhtml1-transitional.dtd">
3   <html xmlns="http://www.w3.org/1999/
    xhtml" xml:lang="en" lang="en">
4   <head>
5       <meta http-equiv="Content-Type"
        content="text/html; charset=utf-8"/>
6       <title>Registration</title>
7   </head>
8   <body>
9   <h2>Registration Results</h2>
10  <?php // Script 6.2 - handle_reg.php
11  /* This script receives eight values from
    register.html:
12  email, password, confirm, month, day,
    year, color, submit */
13
14  // Address error management, if you want.
15
16  // Flag variable to track success:
17  $okay = TRUE;
18
19  // If there were no errors, print a
    success message:
20  if ($okay) {
21      print '<p>You have been successfully
        registered (but not really).</p>';
22  }
23  ?>
24  </body>
25  </html>
```

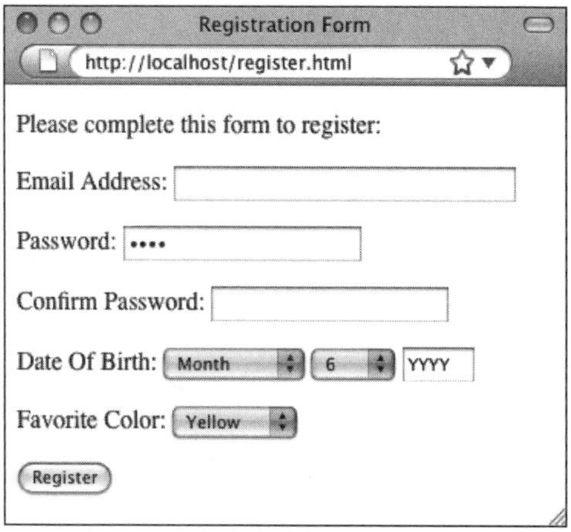

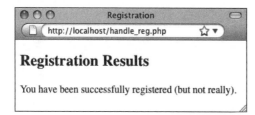

Figure 6.4 Filling out the HTML form to any degree...

Registration Results

You have been successfully registered (but not really).

Figure 6.5 ...results in just this.

4. Print a message if everything is all right:

```
if ($okay) {
    print '<p>You have been
    → successfully registered (but
    → not really).</p>';
}
```

Over the course of this chapter, validation routines will be added to this script, checking the submitted form data. If any data fails a routine, then $okay will be set to FALSE. In that case, this conditional will also be FALSE, so the message won't be printed. However, if the data passes every validation routine, then $okay will still be TRUE, in which case this message will be printed.

5. Complete the PHP section and the HTML page:

```
?>
</body>
</html>
```

6. Save the file as handle_reg.php, place it in the proper directory for your PHP-enabled server (in the same directory as register.html), and test both in your Web browser (**Figures 6.4** and **6.5**).

Of course, the fact is that this script will always print the success message, as nothing will set $okay to FALSE. You can even run the script directly and see the same result.

✔ Tip

■ If the statement area of your conditional is only one line long, you technically don't need the curly braces. In that case, you can place the whole conditional on one line, like so:

```
if (condition) statement;
```

You may run across code in this format. However, I think it's best to always use the multiline format (as demonstrated in the syntax introduction) to improve consistency and minimize errors.

Validation Functions

PHP has dozens of functions that are commonly used to validate form data. Of these functions, three are used in this chapter's examples.

First up is the `empty()` function, which checks to see if a given variable has a value other than 0 or an empty string. It returns TRUE if the variable doesn't have a value (or has a value of 0 or an empty string) and FALSE otherwise:

```
$v1 = 0;
$v2 = 'something';
empty($v); // TRUE
empty($v1); // TRUE
empty($v2); // FALSE
```

This function is perfect for making sure that text boxes in forms have been filled out. For example, if you have a text input named *email* and the user doesn't enter anything in it before submitting the form, then the `$_POST['email']` variable will exist but will have an empty value.

Next is the `isset()` function, which is almost the opposite of `empty()`, albeit with a slight difference. The `isset()` function returns TRUE if a variable has a value (including 0 or an empty string) or FALSE otherwise. For example:

```
$v1 = 0;
$v2 = 'something';
isset($v); // FALSE
isset($v1); // TRUE
isset($v2); // TRUE
```

The `isset()` function is commonly used to validate non-text form elements like checkboxes, radio buttons, and select menus.

Finally, the `is_numeric()` function returns TRUE if the submitted variable has a valid numerical value and FALSE otherwise.

Script 6.3 Using `if` conditionals and the `empty()` function, this PHP script checks if email address and password values were provided.

```
 1   <!DOCTYPE html PUBLIC "-//W3C//DTD XHTML
     1.0 Transitional//EN"
 2       "http://www.w3.org/TR/xhtml1/DTD/
         xhtml1-transitional.dtd">
 3   <html xmlns="http://www.w3.org/1999/
     xhtml" xml:lang="en" lang="en">
 4   <head>
 5       <meta http-equiv="Content-Type"
         content="text/html; charset=utf-8"/>
 6       <title>Registration</title>
 7       <style type="text/css" media="screen">
 8           .error { color: red; }
 9       </style>
10   </head>
11   <body>
12   <h2>Registration Results</h2>
13   <?php // Script 6.3 - handle_reg.php #2
14   /* This script receives eight values from
     register.html:
15   email, password, confirm, month, day,
     year, color, submit */
16
17   // Address error management, if you want.
18
19   // Flag variable to track success:
20   $okay = TRUE;
21
22   // Validate the email address:
23   if (empty($_POST['email'])) {
24       print '<p class="error">Please enter
         your email address.</p>';
25       $okay = FALSE;
26   }
27
28   // Validate the password:
29   if (empty($_POST['password'])) {
30       print '<p class="error">Please enter
         your password.</p>';
31       $okay = FALSE;
32   }
33
34   // If there were no errors, print a
     success message:
35   if ($okay) {
36       print '<p>You have been successfully
         registered (but not really).</p>';
37   }
38   ?>
39   </body>
40   </html>
```

Integers, decimals, and even strings (if they're a valid number) can all pass the `is_numeric()` test:

```
is_numeric(2309); // TRUE
is_numeric('80.23'); // TRUE
is_numeric('Bears'); // FALSE
```

Let's start applying these functions to the PHP script in order to perform some actual data validation.

To validate form data:

1. Open `handle_reg.php` (Script 6.2) in your text editor or IDE, if it is not already.

2. Within the document's head, define a CSS class (**Script 6.3**):

   ```
   <style type="text/css" media=
   → "screen">
       .error { color: red; }
   </style>
   ```

   This CSS class will be used to format any printed registration errors.

3. Validate the email address:

   ```
   if (empty($_POST['email'])) {
       print '<p class="error">Please
   → enter your email address.</p>';
       $okay = FALSE;
   }
   ```

   This `if` conditional uses the code `empty($_POST['email'])` as its condition. If that variable is empty, meaning it has no value, a value of 0, or a value of an empty string, the conditional is TRUE. In that case, the print statement will be executed and the $okay variable will be assigned a value of FALSE (indicating that everything is not okay).

   If the variable isn't empty, then the conditional is FALSE, the `print()` function is never called, and $okay will retain its original value.

continues on next page

4. Repeat the validation for the password:

```
if (empty($_POST['password'])) {
    print '<p class="error">Please
 → enter your password.</p>';
    $okay = FALSE;
}
```

This is a repeat of the email validation, but with the variable name and print statement changed accordingly. The other form inputs will be validated in time.

All of the printed error messages are placed within HTML paragraph tags that have a class value of *error*. By doing so, the CSS formatting will be applied (i.e., the errors will be printed in red).

5. Save the file as `handle_reg.php`, place it in the same directory as `register.html` (on your PHP-enabled server), and test both the form and the script in your Web browser (**Figures 6.6** and **6.7**).

6. Resubmit the form in different states of completeness to test the results some more.

If you do provide both email address and password values, the result will be exactly like that in Figure 6.5, because the $okay variable will still have a value of TRUE.

✔ Tips

- When you use functions within your conditionals, as you use empty() here, it's easy to forget a closing parenthesis and see a parse error. Be extra careful with your syntax when you're coding any control structure.

- One use of the isset() function is to avoid referring to a variable unless it exists. If PHP is set to report notices (see "Error Reporting" in Chapter 3), then, for example, using $var if it has not been defined will cause an error. You can avoid this by coding

```
if (isset ($var)) {
    // Do whatever with $var.
}
```

Figure 6.6 If you omit the email address or password form input...

Figure 6.7 ...you'll see messages like these.

- Even though all form data is sent to a PHP script as strings, the is_numeric() function can still be used for values coming from a form because it can handle strings that contain only numbers.

- The isset() function can take any number of variables as arguments:

```
if (isset($var1, $var2)) {
    print 'Both variables exist.';
}
```

If all of the named variables are set, the function returns TRUE; if any variable is not set, the function returns FALSE.

Script 6.4 By adding if-else conditionals, you can validate the date of birth and create a new variable in the process.

```
 1   <!DOCTYPE html PUBLIC "-//W3C//DTD XHTML
     1.0 Transitional//EN"
 2       "http://www.w3.org/TR/xhtml1/DTD/
     xhtml1-transitional.dtd">
 3   <html xmlns="http://www.w3.org/1999/
     xhtml" xml:lang="en" lang="en">
 4   <head>
 5       <meta http-equiv="Content-Type"
     content="text/html; charset=utf-8"/>
 6       <title>Registration</title>
 7       <style type="text/css" media="screen">
 8           .error { color: red; }
 9       </style>
10   </head>
11   <body>
12   <h2>Registration Results</h2>
13   <?php // Script 6.4 - handle_reg.php #3
14   /* This script receives eight values from
     register.html:
15   email, password, confirm, month, day,
     year, color, submit */
16
17   // Address error management, if you want.
18
19   // Flag variable to track success:
20   $okay = TRUE;
21
22   // Validate the email address:
23   if (empty($_POST['email'])) {
24       print '<p class="error">Please enter
     your email address.</p>';
25       $okay = FALSE;
26   }
27
28   // Validate the password:
29   if (empty($_POST['password'])) {
30       print '<p class="error">Please enter
     your password.</p>';
31       $okay = FALSE;
32   }
33
34   // Validate the birthday:
35   $birthday = '';
36
```

(script continues on next page)

Using else

The next logical formation after an if conditional is the if-else (sometimes called the if-then-else) conditional. It allows you to establish a condition that indicates when one statement would be executed and then execute other statement(s) if that condition isn't met:

```
if (condition) {
    statement(s);
} else {
    other_statement(s);
}
```

The important thing to remember when using this construct is that unless the condition is explicitly met, the else statement will be executed. In other words, the statements after the else constitute the default action, whereas the statements after the if condition are the exception to the rule.

Let's rewrite the handle_reg.php page, incorporating if-else conditionals, to validate the birthday data. In the process, a new variable will be created, a string representing the birthday in the format *MM-DD-YYYY*.

To use else:

1. Open handle_reg.php (Script 6.3) in your text editor or IDE, if it is not already.

2. Before the $okay conditional, create a new variable (**Script 6.4**):

   ```
   $birthday = '';
   ```

   This variable will be built up over the course of the script until it stores the registrant's birth month, day, and year. It's initialized as an empty string here, which isn't required by PHP but is an arguably more professional step to take.

continues on next page

3. Validate the month value:

```
if (is_numeric($_POST['month'])) {

    $birthday = $_POST['month'] . '-';
} else {
    print '<p class="error">Please
select the month you were born.</
p>';

    $okay = FALSE;

}
```

Because the month variable should be a number, you can use the `is_numeric()` function to check its value, rather than `empty()`.

If the variable has a numeric value (meaning that the conditional is TRUE), then the `$birthday` variable is assigned the month value, followed by a hyphen, using concatenation. This is the first step in the process of creating a birthday in the format *MM-DD-YYYY*.

If the month does not have a numeric value, an error message is printed and the `$okay` variable is set to FALSE (as is the case if any validation routine fails).

4. Repeat this structure to validate the day and year variables:

```
if (is_numeric($_POST['day'])) {
    $birthday .= $_POST['day'] . '-';
} else {
    print '<p class="error">Please
→ select the day you were born.</p>';
    $okay = FALSE;
}
if (is_numeric($_POST['year'])) {
    $birthday .= $_POST['year'];
} else {
    print '<p class="error">Please
→ enter the year you were born as
→ four digits.</p>';
    $okay = FALSE;
}
```

Script 6.4 *continued*

```
37   // Validate the month:
38   if (is_numeric($_POST['month'])) {
39       $birthday = $_POST['month'] . '-';
40   } else {
41       print '<p class="error">Please select
          the month you were born.</p>';
42       $okay = FALSE;
43   }
44
45   // Validate the day:
46   if (is_numeric($_POST['day'])) {
47       $birthday .= $_POST['day'] . '-';
48   } else {
49       print '<p class="error">Please select
          the day you were born.</p>';
50       $okay = FALSE;
51   }
52
53   // Validate the year:
54   if (is_numeric($_POST['year'])) {
55       $birthday .= $_POST['year'];
56   } else {
57       print '<p class="error">Please enter
          the year you were born as four
          digits.</p>';
58       $okay = FALSE;
59   }
60
61   // If there were no errors, print a
     success message:
62   if ($okay) {
63       print '<p>You have been successfully
          registered (but not really).</p>';
64       print "<p>You entered your birthday as
          $birthday.</p>";
65   }
66   ?>
67   </body>
68   </html>
```

Figure 6.8 Test the form again, omitting some of the date-of-birth information.

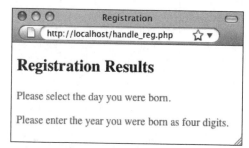

Figure 6.9 If you skip any of the date-of-birth fields, error messages are printed.

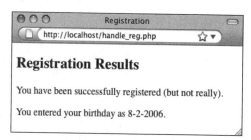

Figure 6.10 If the user completes the date-of-birth section properly, his or her birth date is printed in a new format.

The day validation is identical to the month validation. You also check whether the year has a numeric value using the is_numeric() function, even though its value comes from a text box and not a drop-down menu. If the user changed the default year value (*YYYY*, see Figure 6.3) to a number, this conditional is TRUE, and the year is added to the $birthday variable. Otherwise, an error message is printed and $okay is set to FALSE.

5. After the final print statement, also print out the value of the $birthday:

```
print "<p>You entered your birthday
→ as $birthday.</p>";
```

If the $okay variable still has a value of TRUE, then the submitted data passed every validation routine. This means that the birthday routines also passed, so the accumulated $birthday variable can be printed within context.

6. Save your script, place it in the same directory as register.html (on your PHP-enabled server), and test it in your Web browser again (**Figures 6.8**, **6.9**, and **6.10**).

✔ Tip

■ Another good validation function is checkdate(), which you can use to confirm that a date exists (or existed in the past). You would use it like so:

```
if (checkdate($month, $day,
→ $year)) {…
```

More Operators

Previous chapters discussed most of PHP's operators along with the variable types that use them. These operators include arithmetic for numbers: addition (+), subtraction (-), multiplication (*), and division (/), along with the incremental (++) and decremental (--) shortcuts for increasing or decreasing the value of a number by 1. Then there is the assignment operator (=), which is used to set the value of a variable, regardless of type. You've also learned about concatenation (.), which appends one string to another.

These operators are all handy for establishing the value of a variable, but they're of less use when it comes to conditionals. Now you'll explore comparison and logical operators that widen your conditional possibilities. **Table 6.1** lists a fuller assortment of PHP's operators.

Comparison

When the assignment operator (the equals sign) was first introduced in Chapter 2, "Variables," you learned that its meaning isn't exactly what you'd conventionally think it to be. The line $variable = 5; doesn't state that $variable *is equal to* 5 but that it *is assigned the value of* 5. This is an important distinction.

When you're writing conditionals, you'll often want to see if a variable is equal to a specific value (to match usernames or passwords, perhaps), which you can't do with the equals sign alone (because it's used for assigning a value, not equating values). For this purpose, you have the equality operator (==), which is created by using two equals signs together:

```
$variable = 5;
if ($variable == 5) { ...
```

Table 6.1

OPERATOR	USAGE	TYPE
+	Addition	Arithmetic
-	Subtraction	Arithmetic
*	Multiplication	Arithmetic
/	Division	Arithmetic
%	Modulus (remainder of a division)	Arithmetic
++	Incrementation	Arithmetic
--	Decrementation	Arithmetic
=	Assigns a value to a variable	Assignment
==	Equality	Comparison
!=	Inequality	Comparison
<	Less than	Comparison
>	Greater than	Comparison
<=	Less than or equal to	Comparison
>=	Greater than or equal to	Comparison
!	Negation	Logical
AND	And	Logical
&&	And	Logical
OR	Or	Logical
||	Or	Logical
XOR	Or not	Logical
.	Concatenation	String

PHP's Operators

Script 6.5 This version of the form-handling script uses comparison operators to validate the password and year values.

```
     ⊙ ⊙ ⊙                    Script
1    <!DOCTYPE html PUBLIC "-//W3C//DTD XHTML
     1.0 Transitional//EN"
2        "http://www.w3.org/TR/xhtml1/DTD/
     xhtml1-transitional.dtd">
3    <html xmlns="http://www.w3.org/1999/
     xhtml" xml:lang="en" lang="en">
4    <head>
5        <meta http-equiv="Content-Type"
         content="text/html; charset=utf-8"/>
6        <title>Registration</title>
7        <style type="text/css" media="screen">
8            .error { color: red; }
9        </style>
10   </head>
11   <body>
12   <h2>Registration Results</h2>
13   <?php // Script 6.5 - handle_reg.php #4
14   /* This script receives eight values from
     register.html:
15   email, password, confirm, month, day,
     year, color, submit */
16
17   // Address error management, if you want.
18
19   // Flag variable to track success:
20   $okay = TRUE;
21
22   // Validate the email address:
23   if (empty($_POST['email'])) {
24       print '<p class="error">Please enter
         your email address.</p>';
25       $okay = FALSE;
26   }
27
28   // Validate the password:
29   if (empty($_POST['password'])) {
30       print '<p class="error">Please enter
         your password.</p>';
31       $okay = FALSE;
32   }
33
34   // Check the two passwords for equality:
35   if ($_POST['password'] != $_POST
     ['confirm']) {
36       print '<p class="error">Your
         confirmed password does not match
         the original password.</p>';
37       $okay = FALSE;
38   }
39
```

(script continues on next page)

Using these two lines of code together first establishes the value of $variable as 5 and then makes a TRUE conditional when you see whether $variable is equal to 5. This example demonstrates the significant difference one more equals sign makes in your PHP code and why you must distinguish carefully between the assignment and comparison operators.

The next comparison operator—not equal to—is represented by an exclamation mark coupled with an equals sign (!=). The remaining comparison operators are identical to their mathematical counterparts: less than (<), greater than (>), less than or equal to (<=), and greater than or equal to (>=).

As a demonstration of comparison operators, you'll make sure that the user's birth year is before 2009 and that the confirmed password matches the original password.

To use comparison operators:

1. Open handle_reg.php (Script 6.4) in your text editor or IDE, if it is not already.

2. After the password validation, check that the two passwords match (**Script 6.5**):

   ```
   if ($_POST['password'] !=
   → $_POST['confirm']) {
       print '<p class="error">Your
   → confirmed password does not
   → match the original password.
   → </p>';
       $okay = FALSE;
   }
   ```

   To compare these two string values, you use the not-equal-to operator. You could use one of the string comparison functions (see Chapter 5, "Using Strings"), but this will suffice.

continues on next page

3. After the year validation, check that the year is before 2009:

```
if ($_POST['year'] >= 2009) {
    print '<p class="error">Either
    → you entered your birth year
    → wrong or you come from the
    → future!</p>';
    $okay = FALSE;
}
```

If the user entered their year of birth as 2009 or later, it's presumably a mistake.

Script 6.5 *continued*

```
40   // Validate the birthday:
41   $birthday = '';
42
43   // Validate the month:
44   if (is_numeric($_POST['month'])) {
45       $birthday = $_POST['month'] . '-';
46   } else {
47       print '<p class="error">Please select
         the month you were born.</p>';
48       $okay = FALSE;
49   }
50
51   // Validate the day:
52   if (is_numeric($_POST['day'])) {
53       $birthday .= $_POST['day'] . '-';
54   } else {
55       print '<p class="error">Please select
         the day you were born.</p>';
56       $okay = FALSE;
57   }
58
59   // Validate the year:
60   if (is_numeric($_POST['year'])) {
61       $birthday .= $_POST['year'];
62   } else {
63       print '<p class="error">Please enter
         the year you were born as four
         digits.</p>';
64       $okay = FALSE;
65   }
66
67   // Check that they were born before 2009:
68   if ($_POST['year'] >= 2009) {
69       print '<p class="error">Either you
         entered your birth year wrong or you
         come from the future!</p>';
70       $okay = FALSE;
71   }
72
73   // If there were no errors, print a
     success message:
74   if ($okay) {
75       print '<p>You have been successfully
         registered (but not really).</p>';
76       print "<p>You entered your birthday
         as $birthday.</p>";
77   }
78   ?>
79   </body>
80   </html>
```

Figure 6.11 Run the form once again...

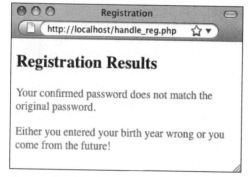

Figure 6.12 ...with two new validation checks in place.

4. Save your script, place it in the same directory as `register.html` (on your PHP-enabled server), and test it in your Web browser again (**Figures 6.11** and **6.12**).

✔ Tips

- Before you compare two string values that come from a form (like the password and confirmed password), it's a good idea to apply the `trim()` function to both, to get rid of any errant spaces. I didn't do so here, so as not to overcomplicate matters, but this habit is recommended.

- Another method of checking that a text input type has been filled out (as opposed to using the `empty()` function) is this:

```
if (strlen ($var) > 0 ) {
    // $var is okay.
}
```

- In an `if` conditional, if you make the mistake of writing `$variable = 5` in place of `$variable == 5`, you'll see that the corresponding conditional statements are always executed. This happens because although the condition `$variable == 5` may or may not be TRUE, the condition `$variable = 5` is always TRUE.

- Some programmers advocate reverse conditionals—for example, writing `5 == $variable`. Although it looks awkward, if you inadvertently code `5 = $variable`, an error results (allowing you to catch the mistake more easily) because the number 5 can't be assigned another value.

MORE OPERATORS

Logical

Writing conditions in PHP comes down to identifying TRUE or FALSE situations. This can be accomplished using functions and comparative operators, as you've already seen. Logical operators—the final operator type discussed in this chapter—help you create more elaborate or obvious constructs.

In PHP, one example of a TRUE condition is simply a variable name that has a value that isn't zero or an empty string, such as

```
$variable = 5;
if ($variable) { ...
```

You've already seen this with the $okay variable being used in the handling PHP script.

A condition is also TRUE if it makes logical sense:

```
if (5 >= 3) { ...
```

A condition will be FALSE if it refers to a variable and that variable has no value (or a value of 0 or an empty string), or if you've created an illogical construct. The following condition is always false:

```
if (5 <= 3) { ...
```

In PHP, the exclamation mark (!) is the NOT operator. You can use it to invert the TRUE/FALSE status of a statement. For example:

```
$var = 'value';
if ($var) {... // TRUE
if (!$var) {... // FALSE
isset($var); // TRUE
!isset($var); // FALSE
!empty($var); // TRUE
```

To go beyond simple one-part conditions, PHP supports five more types of logical operators: two versions of *and* (AND and &&), two versions of *or* (OR and ||—a character called the *pipe*, put together twice), and *or not* (XOR). When you have two options for one

Nesting Conditionals

Besides using logical operators to create more complex conditionals, you can use *nesting* for this purpose (the process of placing one control structure inside of another). The key to doing so is to place the interior conditional as the statement(s) section of the exterior conditional. For example:

```
if (condition1) {
    if (condition2) {
        2statement(s);
    } else { // condition2 else
        2other_statement(s);
    } // End of 2
} else { // condition1 else
    1other_statement(s);
} // End of 1
```

As you can see from this example, you can cut down on the complexity of these structures by using extensive indentations and comments. As long as every conditional is syntactically correct, there are no rules as to how many levels of nesting you can have, whether you use an else clause, or even whether a subconditional is part of the if or the else section of the main conditional.

MORE OPERATORS

Script 6.6 Here the handling PHP script is changed so that the year validation routine uses both multiple and nested conditions. The color conditional also uses a logical operator.

```
1    <!DOCTYPE html PUBLIC "-//W3C//DTD XHTML
     1.0 Transitional//EN"
2        "http://www.w3.org/TR/xhtml1/DTD/
         xhtml1-transitional.dtd">
3    <html xmlns="http://www.w3.org/1999/
     xhtml" xml:lang="en" lang="en">
4    <head>
5        <meta http-equiv="Content-Type"
         content="text/html; charset=utf-8"/>
6        <title>Registration</title>
7        <style type="text/css" media="screen">
8            .error { color: red; }
9        </style>
10   </head>
11   <body>
12   <h2>Registration Results</h2>
13   <?php // Script 6.6 - handle_reg.php #5
14   /* This script receives eight values from
     register.html:
15   email, password, confirm, month, day,
     year, color, submit */
16
17   // Address error management, if you want.
18
19   // Flag variable to track success:
20   $okay = TRUE;
21
22   // Validate the email address:
23   if (empty($_POST['email'])) {
24       print '<p class="error">Please enter
         your email address.</p>';
25       $okay = FALSE;
26   }
27
28   // Validate the password:
29   if (empty($_POST['password'])) {
30       print '<p class="error">Please enter
         your password.</p>';
31       $okay = FALSE;
32   }
33
34   // Check the two passwords for equality:
35   if ($_POST['password'] != $_POST
     ['confirm']) {
36       print '<p class="error">Your
         confirmed password does not match the
         original password.</p>';
37       $okay = FALSE;
38   }
39
```

(script continues on next page)

operator (as with *and* and *or*), they differ only in precedence. For almost every situation, you can use either version of *and* or either version of *or* interchangeably.

Using parentheses and logical operators, you can create even more complex if conditionals. For an AND conditional, every conjoined part must be TRUE in order for the whole conditional to be TRUE. With OR, at least one subsection must be TRUE to render the whole condition TRUE. These conditionals are TRUE:

```
if ( (5 <= 3) OR (5 >= 3) ) { ...
if ( (5 > 3) AND (5 < 10) ) { ...
```

These conditionals are FALSE:

```
if ( (5 != 5) AND (5 > 3) ) { ...
if ( (5 != 5) OR (5 < 3) ) { ...
```

As you construct your conditionals, remember two important things: first, in order for the statements that are the result of a conditional to be executed, the conditional must have a TRUE value; second, by using parentheses, you can ignore rules of precedence and ensure that your operators are addressed in the order of your choosing.

To demonstrate logical operators, you'll add two more conditionals to the handle_reg. php page. You'll also nest one of the year conditionals inside another conditional (see the sidebar "Nesting Conditionals" for more).

To use logical operators:

1. Open handle_reg.php (Script 6.5) in your text editor or IDE, if it is not already.

2. Delete the existing year validations (**Script 6.6**).

   You'll entirely rewrite these conditionals as one nested conditional, so it's best to get rid of the old versions entirely.

continues on next page

MORE OPERATORS

3. Check that the year variable is a four-digit number:

```
if ( is_numeric($_POST['year']) AND
→ (strlen($_POST['year']) == 4) ) {
```

This conditional has two parts. The first you've already seen—it tests for a valid numeric value. The second part gets the length of the year variable (using the strlen() function) and checks if this value is equal to 4. Because of the AND, this conditional is TRUE only if both conditions are met.

4. Create a subconditional to verify the year value isn't after 2009:

```
if ($_POST['year'] >= 2009) {
    print '<p class="error">Either you
    → entered your birth year wrong or
    → you come from the future!</p>';
    $okay = FALSE;
} else {
    $birthday .= $_POST['year'];
}
```

This if-else conditional acts as the statements part of the main conditional, being executed only if that condition is TRUE. This if-else checks whether the year variable is greater than or equal to 2009. If it is, an error message is printed and the $okay variable is set to FALSE (indicating a problem occurred). Otherwise, the year value is appended to the $birthday variable as before.

5. Complete the main year conditional:

```
} else { // Else for 1st conditional.
    print '<p class="error">Please
    → enter the year you were born
    → as four digits.</p>';
    $okay = FALSE;
} // End of 1st conditional.
```

Script 6.6 *continued*

```
40   // Validate the birthday:
41   $birthday = '';
42
43   // Validate the month:
44   if (is_numeric($_POST['month'])) {
45       $birthday = $_POST['month'] . '-';
46   } else {
47       print '<p class="error">Please select
         the month you were born.</p>';
48       $okay = FALSE;
49   }
50
51   // Validate the day:
52   if (is_numeric($_POST['day'])) {
53       $birthday .= $_POST['day'] . '-';
54   } else {
55       print '<p class="error">Please select
         the day you were born.</p>';
56       $okay = FALSE;
57   }
58
59   // Validate the year:
60   if ( is_numeric($_POST['year']) AND
     (strlen($_POST['year']) == 4) ) {
61
62       // Check that they were born before
         2009.
63       if ($_POST['year'] >= 2009) {
64           print '<p class="error">Either you
             entered your birth year wrong or
             you come from the future!</p>';
65           $okay = FALSE;
66       } else {
67           $birthday .= $_POST['year'];
68       } // End of 2nd conditional.
69
70   } else { // Else for 1st conditional.
71
72       print '<p class="error">Please enter
         the year you were born as four
         digits.</p>';
73       $okay = FALSE;
74
75   } // End of 1st conditional.
76
77   // If there were no errors, print a
     success message:
78   if ($okay) {
79       print '<p>You have been successfully
         registered (but not really).</p>';
80       print "<p>You entered your birthday as
         $birthday.</p>";
81   }
82   ?>
83   </body>
84   </html>
```

Figure 6.13 The PHP script now catches if the year isn't a four-digit number, as will be the case with this form submission.

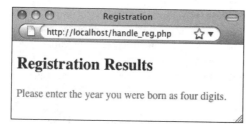

Figure 6.14 Error messages are printed if fields are incorrectly filled out.

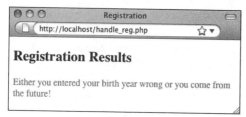

Figure 6.15 The year validation still checks that the date is before 2009.

This `else` section completes the conditional begun in Step 3. If at least one of the conditions set forth there is FALSE, this message is printed and `$okay` is set to FALSE.

6. Those are the only changes to the script, so you can now save it again, place it in the same directory as `register.html` (on your PHP-enabled server), and test it in your Web browser again (**Figures 6.13** and **6.14**).

7. If desired, change your year value to be in the future and submit the form again (**Figure 6.15**).

✔ Tips

- It's another common programming convention—which is maintained in this book—to write the terms TRUE and FALSE in all capitals. This isn't a requirement of PHP, though. For example, the following conditional is TRUE:

  `if (true) {...`

- It's very easy in long, complicated conditionals to forget an opening or closing parenthesis or curly brace, which will produce either error messages or unexpected results. Find a system (like spacing out your conditionals and using comments) to help clarify your code. Another good technique is to create the entire conditional's structure first, and then go back to add the details.

- If you have problems getting your `if-else` statements to execute, print out the values of your variables to help debug the problem. A conditional may not be TRUE because a variable doesn't have the value you think it does.

Using elseif

Similar to the if-else conditional is if-elseif (or if-elseif-else). It acts like a running if statement and can be expanded to whatever length you require:

```
if (condition1) {
    statement(s);
} elseif (condition2) {
    other_statement(s);
}
```

Here's another example:

```
if (condition1) {
    statement(s);
} elseif (condition2) {
    other_statement(s);
} else {
    other_other_statement(s);
}
```

You must always make the else the last part of a conditional because it's executed unless one of the conditions to that point has been met (again, it represents the default behavior). You can, however, continue to use elseifs as many times as you want as part of one if conditional.

As an example of this, let's create a conditional that prints a message based upon the selected color value.

Using elseif

Script 6.7 This multiline if-elseif-else conditional prints a color-specific message and validates that a submitted color has an allowed value.

```
1    <!DOCTYPE html PUBLIC "-//W3C//DTD XHTML
     1.0 Transitional//EN"
2       "http://www.w3.org/TR/xhtml1/DTD/
        xhtml1-transitional.dtd">
3    <html xmlns="http://www.w3.org/1999/
     xhtml" xml:lang="en" lang="en">
4    <head>
5       <meta http-equiv="Content-Type"
        content="text/html; charset=utf-8"/>
6       <title>Registration</title>
7       <style type="text/css" media="screen">
8          .error { color: red; }
9       </style>
10   </head>
11   <body>
12   <h2>Registration Results</h2>
13   <?php // Script 6.7 - handle_reg.php #6
14   /* This script receives eight values from
     register.html:
15   email, password, confirm, month, day,
     year, color, submit */
16
17   // Address error management, if you
     want.
18
19   // Flag variable to track success:
20   $okay = TRUE;
21
22   // Validate the email address:
23   if (empty($_POST['email'])) {
24      print '<p class="error">Please enter
        your email address.</p>';
25      $okay = FALSE;
26   }
27
28   // Validate the password:
29   if (empty($_POST['password'])) {
30      print '<p class="error">Please enter
        your password.</p>';
31      $okay = FALSE;
32   }
33
```

(script continues on next page)

Script 6.7 *continued*

```
34   // Check the two passwords for equality:
35   if ($_POST['password'] !=
     $_POST['confirm']) {
36       print '<p class="error">Your
         confirmed password does not match the
         original password.</p>';
37       $okay = FALSE;
38   }
39
40   // Validate the birthday:
41   $birthday = '';
42
43   // Validate the month:
44   if (is_numeric($_POST['month'])) {
45       $birthday = $_POST['month'] . '-';
46   } else {
47       print '<p class="error">Please select
         the month you were born.</p>';
48       $okay = FALSE;
49   }
50
51   // Validate the day:
52   if (is_numeric($_POST['day'])) {
53       $birthday .= $_POST['day'] . '-';
54   } else {
55       print '<p class="error">Please select
         the day you were born.</p>';
56       $okay = FALSE;
57   }
58
59   // Validate the year:
60   if ( is_numeric($_POST['year']) AND
     (strlen($_POST['year']) == 4) ) {
61
62       // Check that they were born before
         2009.
63       if ($_POST['year'] >= 2009) {
64           print '<p class="error">Either you
             entered your birth year wrong or
             you come from the future!</p>';
65           $okay = FALSE;
66       } else {
67           $birthday .= $_POST['year'];
68       } // End of 2nd conditional.
69
```

(script continues on next page)

To use elseif:

1. Open `handle_reg.php` (Script 6.6) in your text editor or IDE, if it is not already.

2. Before the $okay conditional, begin a new conditional (**Script 6.7**):

   ```
   if ($_POST['color'] == 'red') {
       print '<p style="color:red;">Red
       → is your favorite color.</p>';
   ```

   The color value comes from a select menu with four possible options: red, yellow, green, and blue. This conditional will print a message, repeating back their color choice, also formatted in that color. The first condition checks if the value of `$_POST['color']` is equal to the string *red*.

3. Add an `elseif` clause for the second color:

   ```
   } elseif ($_POST['color'] ==
   → 'yellow') {
       print '<p style="color:yellow;">
       → Yellow is your favorite
       → color.</p>';
   ```

   The `elseif` continues the main conditional begun in Step 2. The condition itself is a replication of the condition in Step 2, using a new color comparison.

continues on next page

USING ELSEIF

4. Add `elseif` clauses for the other two colors:

```
} elseif ($_POST['color'] ==
→ 'green') {
  print '<p
style="color:green;">Green is your
→ favorite color.</p>';
} elseif ($_POST['color'] ==
→ 'blue') {
  print '<p style="color:blue;">
  → Blue is your favorite color.
  → </p>';
```

Once you understand the main concept, it's just a matter of repeating the `elseif`s for every possible color value.

5. Add an `else` clause:

```
} else { // Problem!
  print '<p class="error">Please
  → select your favorite color.</p>';
  $okay = FALSE;
}
```

If the user didn't select a color, or if they manipulated the form to submit a different color value (other than *red, yellow, green,* or *blue*), none of the conditions will be TRUE, meaning this `else` clause will take effect. It prints an error and assigns a value of FALSE to $okay, indicating a problem.

Script 6.7 *continued*

```
70  } else { // Else for 1st conditional.
71
72      print '<p class="error">Please enter
        the year you were born as four
        digits.</p>';
73      $okay = FALSE;
74
75  } // End of 1st conditional.
76
77  // Validate the color:
78  if ($_POST['color'] == 'red') {
79      print '<p style="color:red;">Red is
        your favorite color.</p>';
80  } elseif ($_POST['color'] == 'yellow') {
81      print '<p style="color:yellow;">Yellow
        is your favorite color.</p>';
82  } elseif ($_POST['color'] == 'green') {
83      print '<p style="color:green;">Green
        is your favorite color.</p>';
84  } elseif ($_POST['color'] == 'blue') {
85      print '<p style="color:blue;">Blue is
        your favorite color.</p>';
86  } else { // Problem!
87      print '<p class="error">Please select
        your favorite color.</p>';
88      $okay = FALSE;
89  }
90
91  // If there were no errors, print a
    success message:
92  if ($okay) {
93      print '<p>You have been successfully
        registered (but not really).</p>';
94      print "<p>You entered your birthday as
        $birthday.</p>";
95  }
96  ?>
97  </body>
98  </html>
```

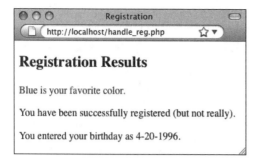

Figure 6.16 The script now prints a message acknowledging the user's color choice (although you can't really tell in this black and white book).

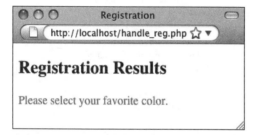

Figure 6.17 Failure to select a color results in this error message.

6. Save the script, place it in the same directory as `register.html` (on your PHP-enabled server), and test it in your Web browser again, using different color options (**Figures 6.16** and **6.17**).

✔ Tip

■ PHP also allows you to write `elseif` as two words, if you prefer:

```
if (condition1) {
    statement(s);
} else if (condition2) {
    2statement(s);
}
```

The Switch Conditional

Once you get to the point where you have longer if-elseif-else conditionals, you may find that you can save time and clarify your programming by using a switch conditional instead. The switch conditional takes only one possible condition, normally just a variable:

```
switch ($variable) {
    case 'value1':
        1statement(s);
        break;
    case 'value2':
        2statement(s);
        break;
    default:
        3statement(s);
        break;
}
```

It's critical that you comprehend how a switch conditional works in order to use it properly. Starting at the beginning, once PHP finds the case that matches the value of the conditional variable, it continues to execute those statements until it either comes to the end of the switch conditional (the closing curly brace) or hits a break statement, at which point it exits the switch construct. Thus, it's imperative that you close every case —even the default case, for consistency's sake—with a break (the sidebar "Break, Exit, Die, and Continue" discusses this keyword in more detail).

This previous switch conditional is like a rewrite of this:

```
if ($variable == 'value1') {
    1statement(s);
} elseif ($variable == 'value2') {
    2statement(s);
} else {
    3statement(s);
}
```

Script 6.8 Switch conditionals can simplify complicated if-elseif conditionals.

```
1    <!DOCTYPE html PUBLIC "-//W3C//DTD XHTML
     1.0 Transitional//EN"
2        "http://www.w3.org/TR/xhtml1/DTD/
     xhtml1-transitional.dtd">
3    <html xmlns="http://www.w3.org/1999/
     xhtml" xml:lang="en" lang="en">
4    <head>
5        <meta http-equiv="Content-Type"
     content="text/html; charset=utf-8"/>
6        <title>Registration</title>
7        <style type="text/css" media="screen">
8            .error { color: red; }
9        </style>
10   </head>
11   <body>
12   <h2>Registration Results</h2>
13   <?php // Script 6.8 - handle_reg.php #7
14   /* This script receives eight values from
     register.html:
15   email, password, confirm, month, day,
     year, color, submit */
16
17   // Address error management, if you want.
18
19   // Flag variable to track success:
20   $okay = TRUE;
21
22   // Validate the email address:
23   if (empty($_POST['email'])) {
24       print '<p class="error">Please enter
     your email address.</p>';
25       $okay = FALSE;
26   }
27
28   // Validate the password:
29   if (empty($_POST['password'])) {
30       print '<p class="error">Please enter
     your password.</p>';
31       $okay = FALSE;
32   }
33
34   // Check the two passwords for equality:
35   if ($_POST['password'] !=
     $_POST['confirm']) {
36       print '<p class="error">Your
     confirmed password does not match the
     original password.</p>';
37       $okay = FALSE;
38   }
39
```

(script continues on next page)

Script 6.8 *continued*

```
40   // Validate the birthday:
41   $birthday = '';
42
43   // Validate the month:
44   if (is_numeric($_POST['month'])) {
45       $birthday = $_POST['month'] . '-';
46   } else {
47       print '<p class="error">Please select
         the month you were born.</p>';
48       $okay = FALSE;
49   }
50
51   // Validate the day:
52   if (is_numeric($_POST['day'])) {
53       $birthday .= $_POST['day'] . '-';
54   } else {
55       print '<p class="error">Please select
         the day you were born.</p>';
56       $okay = FALSE;
57   }
58
59   // Validate the year:
60   if ( is_numeric($_POST['year']) AND
     (strlen($_POST['year']) == 4) ) {
61
62       // Check that they were born before
         2009.
63       if ($_POST['year'] >= 2009) {
64           print '<p class="error">Either you
             entered your birth year wrong or
             you come from the future!</p>';
65           $okay = FALSE;
66       } else {
67           $birthday .= $_POST['year'];
68       } // End of 2nd conditional.
69
70   } else { // Else for 1st conditional.
71
72       print '<p class="error">Please enter
         the year you were born as four
         digits.</p>';
73       $okay = FALSE;
74
75   } // End of 1st conditional.
76
77   // Validate the color:
78   switch ($_POST['color']) {
79       case 'red':
80           print '<p style="color:red;">Red is
             your favorite color.</p>';
81           break;
```

(script continues on next page)

Because the `switch` conditional uses the value of `$variable` as its condition, it first checks to see if `$variable` is equal to *value1* and, if so, executes *1statement(s)*. If not, it checks to see if `$variable` is equal to *value2* and, if so, executes *2statement(s)*. If neither condition is met, the default action of the `switch` condition is to execute *3statement(s)*.

With this in mind, let's rewrite the colors conditional as a `switch`.

To use a switch conditional:

1. Open `handle_reg.php` (Script 6.7) in your text editor or IDE, if it is not already.

2. Delete the extended colors conditional (**Script 6.8**).

3. Begin the `switch`:

   ```
   switch ($_POST['color']) {
   ```

   As mentioned earlier, a `switch` conditional takes only one condition: a variable's name. In this case, it's `$_POST['color']`.

4. Create the first case:

   ```
   case 'red':
       print '<p style="color:red;">Red
       → is your favorite color.</p>';
       break;
   ```

   The first `case` checks to see if `$_POST['color']` has a value of *red*. If so, then the same print statement is executed as before. Then you include a `break` statement to exit the `switch`.

continues on next page

5. Add a case for the second color:

```
case 'yellow':
    print '<p style="color:yellow;">
    →Yellow is your favorite color.
    →</p>';
    break;
```

6. Add cases for the remaining colors:

```
case 'green':
    print '<p style="color:green;">
    →Green is your favorite color.
    →</p>';
    break;
case 'blue':
    print '<p style="color:blue;">
    →Blue is your favorite color.
    →</p>';
    break;
```

7. Add a default case and complete the switch:

```
default:
    print '<p class="error">Please
    →select your favorite color.
    →</p>';
    $okay = FALSE;
    break;
} // End of switch.
```

This default case is the equivalent of the else clause used in the original conditional.

Script 6.8 *continued*

```
82    case 'yellow':
83        print '<p style="color:yellow;">
          Yellow is your favorite color.
          </p>';
84        break;
85    case 'green':
86        print '<p style="color:green;">
          Green is your favorite color.</p>';
87        break;
88    case 'blue':
89        print '<p style="color:blue;">Blue
          is your favorite color.</p>';
90        break;
91    default:
92        print '<p class="error">Please
          select your favorite color.</p>';
93        $okay = FALSE;
94        break;
95    } // End of switch.
96
97    // If there were no errors, print a
      success message:
98    if ($okay) {
99        print '<p>You have been successfully
          registered (but not really).</p>';
100       print "<p>You entered your birthday as
          $birthday.</p>";
101   }
102   ?>
103   </body>
104   </html>
```

Figure 6.18 The handling script still works the same, whether the user selects a color...

Figure 6.19 ...or fails to.

8. Save your script, place it in the same directory as `register.html` (on your PHP-enabled server), and test it in your Web browser again (**Figures 6.18** and **6.19**).

✔ Tips

- A default case isn't required in your `switch` conditional (you could set it up so that if the value isn't explicitly met by one of the cases, nothing happens), but if it's used, it must be listed as the last case.

- If you're using a string in your `switch` conditional as the case value, keep in mind that it's case sensitive, meaning that *Value* won't match *value*.

THE SWITCH CONDITIONAL

Break, Exit, Die, and Continue

PHP includes many language constructs: tools that aren't functions but still do something in your scripts. The first of these is `break`, which is demonstrated in the `switch`. `Break` exits the current structure, be it a switch, an `if-else` conditional, or a loop.

Similar to this is `continue`, which terminates the current iteration of the loop. Any remaining statements within the loop aren't executed, but the loop's condition is checked again to see if the loop should be entered.

`Exit` and `die` are more potent versions of `break` (and they're synonymous). Instead of exiting the current structure, these two language constructs terminate the execution of the PHP script. Therefore, all PHP code after a use of `exit` or `die` is never executed. For that matter, any HTML after these constructs is never sent to the Web browser. You'll see `die` used most frequently in code that accesses files and databases. `Exit` is often used in conjunction with the `header()` function.

The for Loop

Loops are the final type of control structure discussed in this chapter. As suggested earlier, you use loops to execute a section of code repeatedly. You may want print something a certain number of times, or you may want to print out each value of an array. For either of these cases, and many more, you can use a loop. (The latter example is demonstrated in the next chapter.)

PHP supports three kinds of loops: for, while, and foreach. The while loop is similar to for, but it's used most frequently when retrieving values from a database or reading from a text file (it's introduced in the sidebar). Foreach is related to using arrays and is introduced in the next chapter.

The for loop is designed to perform specific statements for a determined number of iterations (unlike while, which runs until the condition is FALSE—similar, but significantly different, concepts). You normally use a dummy variable in the loop for this purpose:

```
for (initial expression; condition;
→ closing expression) {
    statement(s);
}
```

The initial expression is executed once: the first time the loop is called. Then the condition is used to determine whether to execute the statements. The closing expression is executed each time the condition is found to be TRUE, but only after the statements are executed (**Figure 6.20**).

Here's a simple loop that prints out the numbers 1 through 10:

```
for ($v = 1; $v <= 10; $v++) {
    print $v;
}
```

To practice with the for loop, you'll use it to create the day drop-down menu in the HTML form.

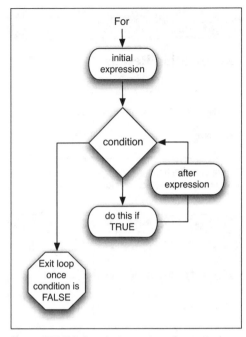

Figure 6.20 This flowchart represents how a for loop is executed in PHP.

Script 6.9 This script uses a PHP for loop to dynamically generate the day of the month drop-down menu.

```
1   <!DOCTYPE html PUBLIC "-//W3C//DTD XHTML
    1.0 Transitional//EN"
2       "http://www.w3.org/TR/xhtml1/DTD/
        xhtml1-transitional.dtd">
3   <html xmlns="http://www.w3.org/1999/
    xhtml" xml:lang="en" lang="en">
4   <head>
5       <meta http-equiv="Content-Type"
        content="text/html; charset=utf-8"/>
6       <title>Registration Form</title>
7   </head>
8   <body>
9   <!-- Script 6.9 - register.php -->
10  <div><p>Please complete this form to
    register:</p>
11
12  <form action="handle_reg.php"
    method="post">
13
14      <p>Email Address: <input type="text"
        name="email" size="30" /></p>
15
16      <p>Password: <input type="password"
        name="password" size="20" /></p>
17
18      <p>Confirm Password: <input
        type="password" name="confirm"
        size="20" /></p>
19
20      <p>Date Of Birth:
21      <select name="month">
22      <option value="">Month</option>
23      <option value="1">January</option>
24      <option value="2">February</option>
25      <option value="3">March</option>
26      <option value="4">April</option>
27      <option value="5">May</option>
28      <option value="6">June</option>
29      <option value="7">July</option>
30      <option value="8">August</option>
31      <option value="9">September</option>
32      <option value="10">October</option>
33      <option value="11">November</option>
34      <option value="12">December</option>
35      </select>
```

(script continues on next page)

To write a for loop:

1. Open `register.html` (Script 6.1) in your text editor or IDE, if it is not already.

2. Delete all the lines between <option value="">Day</option> and </select> (lines 38–68 of the original script), which create the different drop-down options (**Script 6.9**).

3. Create a new PHP section:

   `<?php`

   Because PHP can be embedded within HTML, you'll use it to populate the drop-down menu. You begin with the standard PHP tag.

4. Create a for loop to print out 31 days as menu options:

   ```
   for ($d = 1; $d <= 31; $d++) {
       print "<option value=\"$d\">$d
    → </option>\n";
   }
   ```

   The loop begins with creating a dummy variable called $d. On the first use of the loop, this variable is set to 1. Then, as long as $d is less than or equal to 31, the contents of the loop are executed. These contents are the print() line, which creates code like <option value="1">1 </option>, followed by a return (created with \n). After this statement is executed, the $d variable is incremented by one. Then the condition ($d <= 31) is checked again, and the process is repeated.

   continues on next page

5. Close the PHP section:

```
?>
```

6. Save the file as `register.php`.

You must save the file with the `.php` extension now, in order for the PHP code to be executed.

7. Place the file in the proper directory for your PHP-enabled server and test it in your Web browser (**Figure 6.21**).

As long as this script is in the same directory as `handle_reg.php`, you can even fill out and submit the form as you would with the plain HTML version.

Script 6.9 *continued*

```
36      <select name="day">
37      <option value="">Day</option>
38      <?php // Print out 31 days:
39      for ($d = 1; $d <= 31; $d++) {
40          print "<option value=\"$d\">$d
            </option>\n";
41      }
42      ?>
43      </select>
44      <input type="text" name="year"
        value="YYYY" size="4" /></p>
45
46      <p>Favorite Color:
47      <select name="color">
48      <option value="">Pick One</option>
49      <option value="red">Red</option>
50      <option value="yellow">Yellow</option>
51      <option value="green">Green</option>
52      <option value="blue">Blue</option>
53      </select></p>
54
55      <input type="submit" name="submit"
        value="Register" />
56
57  </form>
58
59  </div>
60  </body>
61  </html>
```

Figure 6.21 The form looks exactly as it did before, even though PHP created some of the HTML.

THE FOR LOOP

8. If desired, view the HTML source code
(**Figure 6.22**).

✔ Tips

■ Just as you can write the `if` conditional
on one line if you have only one statement, you can do the same with the `while`
and `for` loops. Again, though, this isn't
recommended.

■ Loops can be nested inside each other.
You can also place conditionals within
loops, loops within conditionals, and so
forth.

■ Pay close attention to your loop's condition so that the loop ends at some point.
Otherwise, you'll create an infinite loop,
and the script will run and run and run.

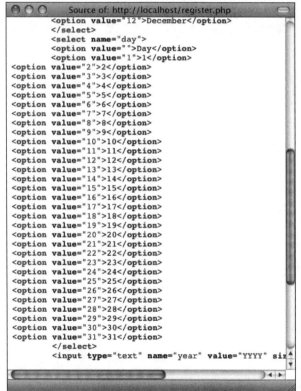

Figure 6.22 If you view the
HTML source code for the
form, you'll see the data
generated by the `for` loop.

The while Loop

The second of the three types of loops that exist in PHP—the `while` loop—is designed to continue working as long as the condition you establish is TRUE. Like the `for` loop, it checks the value of the condition before each iteration. Once the condition becomes FALSE, the `while` loop is exited:

```
while (condition) {
    statement(s);
}
```

The main difference between the `for` and the `while` is that `while` doesn't include a system for setting initial conditions or for executing closing expressions

You also have the option of using the `do...while` loop, which guarantees that the statements are executed at least once (this isn't necessarily true of the `while` loop):

```
do {
    statement(s);
} while (condition);
```

Although there is a fair amount of overlap regarding when you can use the two major loop constructs (`while` and `for`), you'll discover as you program that sometimes one is more logical than the other. The `while` loop is frequently used in the retrieval of data from a database (see Chapter 12, "Introduction to Databases").

USING ARRAYS

The next—and last—variable type you'll learn about in this book is the array. Arrays are significantly different than either numbers or strings, and you can't make the most of programming in PHP without comprehending them.

Because of their unique nature, this chapter will cover arrays more deliberately and slowly than the other variable types. The chapter begins with a thorough introduction to the concept, along with the basics of creating and using arrays. Then it covers multidimensional arrays and some of the array-related functions. The chapter concludes with array-string conversions and a demonstration on how to create an array from an HTML form.

What Is an Array?

Arrays constitute a complicated but very useful notion. Whereas numbers and strings are *scalar* variables (meaning they only ever have a single value), an array is a collection of multiple values assembled into one overriding variable. An array can consist of numbers and/or strings (and/or other arrays), which allows this one variable to hold exponentially more information than a simple string or number can. For example, if you wanted to create a grocery list using strings, your code would look something like this:

```
$item1 = 'apples';
$item2 = 'bananas';
$item3 = 'oranges';
```

For each added item, you'd need to create a new string. This approach is cumbersome, and it makes it difficult to refer back to the entire list or any specific value later in your code. You can greatly simplify matters by placing your entire list into one array (say, `$items`), which contains everything you need (**Table 7.1**).

As an array, your list can be added to, sorted, searched, and so forth. With this context in mind, let's look into the syntax of arrays.

Table 7.1

Grocery List Array

Item Number	Item
1	apples
2	bananas
3	oranges

Syntactical rules for arrays

The other variable types you've dealt with—numbers and strings—have a variable name and a corresponding value (for example, $first_name could be equal to *Larry*). Arrays also have a name, derived using the same conventions—they:

◆ Begin with a dollar sign.

◆ Continue with a letter or underscore.

◆ Finish with any combination of letters, numbers, or the underscore.

But arrays differ in that they contain multiple *elements* (think of each row in Table 7.1 as an element). An element consists of an *index* or *key* (the two words can be used interchangeably) and a value. In Table 7.1, the Item Number is the key, and the Item is the value.

An array's index is used as a reference point to the values. An array can use either numbers or strings as its keys (or both), depending on how you set it up.

Generally, when you use an array it looks the same as any other variable, except that you include a key in square brackets ([ ]) when referring to particular values. So, $items refers to the array as a whole, but $items[1] points to a specific element in the array (in this example, *apples*).

Superglobals and You

Throughout this book, you've already dealt with some arrays: $_SERVER, $_GET, and $_POST. These are all called *superglobals*, along with $_COOKIE, $_SESSION, and $_ENV.

The $_POST array receives all the data sent from a form using the POST method. Its indexes are the names of the form inputs, and its values are the values for those form elements. Therefore, $_POST['name'] refers to the value typed in a form input created by the code

```
<input type="text" name="name" />
```

Similarly, $_GET refers to data sent from a form using the GET method or from data otherwise passed in the URL. $_COOKIE refers to data stored in a cookie, and $_SESSION refers to data stored in a session (you'll encounter these two in Chapter 9, "Cookies and Sessions"). $_ENV is like $_SERVER, containing values pertaining to the computer on which PHP is running.

WHAT IS AN ARRAY?

Creating an Array

The formal method of creating an array is to use the `array()` function. Its syntax follows the form shown here:

```
$list = array ('apples', 'bananas',
'oranges');
```

Arrays automatically begin their indexing at 0, unless otherwise indicated. In this example—which doesn't specify an index for the elements—the first item, apples, is automatically indexed at 0, the second item at 1, and the third at 2.

You can assign the index when using `array()`:

```
$list = array (1 => 'apples', 2 =>
→ 'bananas', 3 => 'oranges');
```

Because PHP is very liberal when it comes to blank space in your scripts, you can make this structure easier to read by writing it over multiple lines:

```
$list = array (
1 => 'apples',
2 => 'bananas',
3 => 'oranges'
);
```

Finally, the index value you specify doesn't have to be a number—you can use words as well. This indexing technique is practical for making more meaningful lists. As an example, you could create an array that records the soup of the day for each day of the week, as in the following script. This example will also demonstrate how you can, and cannot, print out an array.

Script 7.1 The $soups array contains three elements and uses strings for its keys.

```
1    <!DOCTYPE html PUBLIC "-//W3C//DTD XHTML
     1.0 Transitional//EN"
2        "http://www.w3.org/TR/xhtml1/DTD/
     xhtml1-transitional.dtd">
3    <html xmlns="http://www.w3.org/1999/
     xhtml" xml:lang="en" lang="en">
4    <head>
5        <meta http-equiv="Content-Type"
     content="text/html; charset=utf-8"/>
6        <title>No Soup for You!</title>
7    </head>
8    <body>
9    <h1>Mmm...soups</h1>
10   <?php // Script 7.1 - soups1.php
11   /* This script creates and prints out an
     array. */
12   // Address error management, if you want.
13
14   // Create the array:
15   $soups = array (
16   'Monday' => 'Clam Chowder',
17   'Tuesday' => 'White Chicken Chili',
18   'Wednesday' => 'Vegetarian'
19   );
20
21   // Try to print the array:
22   print "<p>$soups</p>";
23
24   // Print the contents of the array:
25   print_r ($soups);
26
27   ?>
28   </body>
29   </html>
```

To create an array:

1. Begin a new document in your text editor or IDE (**Script 7.1**):

   ```
   <!DOCTYPE html PUBLIC "-//W3C//DTD
   → XHTML 1.0 Transitional//EN"
      "http://www.w3.org/TR/xhtml1/DTD/
   → xhtml1-transitional.dtd">
   <html xmlns="http://www.w3.org/1999/
   → xhtml" xml:lang="en" lang="en">
   <head>
      <meta http-equiv="Content-Type"
   → content="text/html;
   → charset=utf-8"/>
      <title>No Soup for You!</title>
   </head>
   <body>
   <h1>Mmm...soups</h1>
   ```

2. Begin the PHP section of the script and address error handling, if necessary:

   ```
   <?php // Script 7.1 - soups1.php
   ```

   If you don't have display_errors enabled, or if error_reporting is set to the wrong level, see Chapter 3, "HTML Forms and PHP," for the lines to include here to alter those settings.

3. Use the array() function to create an array:

   ```
   $soups = array (
   'Monday' => 'Clam Chowder',
   'Tuesday' => 'White Chicken Chili',
   'Wednesday' => 'Vegetarian'
   );
   ```

   This is the proper format for initializing (creating and assigning a value to) an array in PHP, using strings as the indices. Because both the keys and values are strings, you surround them with single quotation marks.

   Do not inadvertently add a comma after the final array element (indexed at *Wednesday*) as this will cause a parse error.

continues on next page

4. Attempt to print the array:

`print "<p>$soups</p>";`

As you'll soon see, arrays are also different in that they can't be printed the way you'd print other (scalar) variables.

5. Use the `print_r()` function to print out the array differently:

`print_r ($soups);`

In Chapter 2, "Variables," you learned how to use the `print_r()` function to show the contents and structure of any variable. You use it here so that you can see the difference between the way this function and `print()` work with arrays.

6. Close the PHP and the HTML sections:

`?>`

`</body>`

`</html>`

7. Save your document as `soups1.php`, place it in the proper directory for your PHP-enabled server, and test it in your Web browser (**Figure 7.1**).

Do remember to run the PHP script through a URL.

Figure 7.1 Because an array is structured differently than other variable types, a request to print an array results in the word Array (and an error, depending upon the version of PHP and its settings). On the other hand, the `print_r()` function prints the array's contents and structure.

✔ Tips

■ The practice of beginning any index at 0 is standard in PHP and most other programming languages. As unnatural as this counting system may seem, it's here to stay, so you have two possible coping techniques. First, manually start all of your arrays indexed at position 1. Second, unlearn a lifetime of counting from 1. You can decide which is easier, but most programmers just get used to this odd construct.

Figure 7.2 The var_dump() function (used with Script 7.1 instead of the print_r() function) shows how many elements are in an array and how long each string value is.

- You must refer to an array's elements using the same index used to create the array. In the $soups example, $soups[0] has no value even though the array obviously has a first element (the first element being indexed at 0 numerically).

- If you use the array() function to define an index, you can associate the first index, and the others will follow sequentially. For example:

```
$list = array (1 => 'apples',
'bananas', 'oranges');
```

Now *bananas* is indexed at 2 and *oranges* at 3.

- The range() function can also be used to create an array of items based on a range of values. Here are two examples:

```
$ten = range (1, 10);
$alphabet = range ('a', 'z');
```

- As of PHP version 5, the range() function includes a step parameter that lets you specify increments:

```
$evens = range (0, 100, 2);
```

- If you use the var_dump() function in your script in lieu of print_r(), it shows not only the contents of the array but also its structure in a more detailed format (**Figure 7.2**). As of PHP 6, this function also indicates if a string uses Unicode encoding.

- An array whose keys are numbers is called an *indexed* array. If the keys are strings, it's referred to as an *associative* array. Other languages refer to associative arrays as *hashes*.

CREATING AN ARRAY

157

Adding Items to an Array

In PHP, once an array exists, you can add extra elements to the array with the assignment operator (the equals sign), in a way similar to how you assign a value to a string or a number. When doing so, you can either specify the key of the added element or not, but in either case, you must refer to the array with the square brackets. To add two items to the $list array, you'd write

```
$list[] = 'pears';
$list[] = 'tomatoes';
```

If you don't specify the key, each element is appended to the existing array, indexed with the next sequential number. Assuming this is the same array from the preceding section, which was indexed at 1, 2, and 3, *pears* is now located at 4 and *tomatoes* at 5.

If you do specify the index, the value is assigned at that location. Any existing value already indexed at that point is overwritten, like so:

```
$list[3] = 'pears';
$list[4] = 'tomatoes';
```

Now, the value of the element in the fourth position of the array is *tomatoes*, and no element of $list is equal to *oranges* (that value was overwritten by *pears*). With this in mind, unless you intend to overwrite any existing data, you'll be better off not naming a specific key when adding values to your arrays. However, if the array uses strings for indices, you'll probably want to specify keys so that you don't end up with an odd combination of string and number keys.

To test this process, in the following task you'll rewrite soups1.php to add more elements to the array. In order to see the difference adding more elements makes, you'll print out the number of elements in the array before and after the new additions.

Deleting Arrays and Array Elements

You won't frequently need to delete an individual item from an array, but it's possible to do so using the unset() function. This function eliminates a variable and frees up the memory it used. When applied to an array element, that element is deleted:

```
unset($array[4]);
unset($array['name']);
```

If you apply unset() to an entire array or any other variable type, the whole variable is deleted:

```
unset($array);
unset($string);
```

You can also *reset* an array (empty it without deleting the variable altogether) using the array() function:

```
$array = array();
```

This has the effect of initializing the variable: making it exist and defining its type without assigning a value.

Script 7.2 You can directly add elements to an array one at a time by assigning each element a value with the assignment operator. The count() function will help you keep track of how many elements the array contains.

```
1    <!DOCTYPE html PUBLIC "-//W3C//DTD XHTML
     1.0 Transitional//EN"
2        "http://www.w3.org/TR/xhtml1/DTD/
     xhtml1-transitional.dtd">
3    <html xmlns="http://www.w3.org/1999/
     xhtml" xml:lang="en" lang="en">
4    <head>
5        <meta http-equiv="Content-Type"
         content="text/html; charset=utf-8"/>
6        <title>No Soup for You!</title>
7    </head>
8    <body>
9    <h1>Mmm...soups</h1>
10   <?php // Script 7.2 - soups2.php
11   /* This script creates and prints out an
     array. */
12   // Address error management, if you want.
13
14   // Create the array:
15   $soups = array (
16   'Monday' => 'Clam Chowder',
17   'Tuesday' => 'White Chicken Chili',
18   'Wednesday' => 'Vegetarian'
19   );
20
21   // Count and print the current number of
     elements:
22   $count1 = count ($soups);
23   print "<p>The soups array originally had
     $count1 elements.</p>";
24
25   // Add three items to the array:
26   $soups['Thursday'] = 'Chicken Noodle';
27   $soups['Friday'] = 'Tomato';
28   $soups['Saturday'] = 'Cream of Broccoli';
29
30   // Count and print the number of elements
     again:
31   $count2 = count ($soups);
32   print "<p>After adding 3 more soups, the
     array now has $count2 elements.</p>";
33
34   // Print the contents of the array:
35   print_r ($soups);
36
37   ?>
38   </body>
39   </html>
```

Just as you can find the length of a string—how many characters it contains—using strlen(), you can determine the number of elements in an array, using count():

```
$how_many = count($array);
```

To add elements to an array:

1. Open soups1.php in your text editor or IDE, if it is not already.

2. After the array is initialized using array(), add the following (**Script 7.2**):

   ```
   $count1 = count ($soups);
   print "<p>The soups array originally
   → had $count1 elements.</p>";
   ```

   The count() function determines how many elements are in $soups. By assigning that value to a variable, you can easily print it out.

3. Add three more elements to the array:

   ```
   $soups['Thursday'] = 'Chicken
   → Noodle';
   $soups['Friday'] = 'Tomato';
   $soups['Saturday'] = 'Cream of
   → Broccoli';
   ```

   This code adds three more soups—indexed at *Thursday*, *Friday*, and *Saturday*—to the existing array.

4. Recount how many elements are in the array, and print this value.

   ```
   $count2 = count ($soups);
   print "<p>After adding 3 more
   → soups, the array now has $count2
   → elements.</p>";
   ```

   This second print() call is a repetition of the first, letting you know how many elements the array now contains.

continues on next page

ADDING ITEMS TO AN ARRAY

159

5. If you want to, delete the print
"<p>$soups</p>"; line.

This line isn't needed anymore, so you can get rid of it (you now know that you can't print an array that easily).

6. Save your script as soups2.php, place it in the proper directory for your PHP-enabled server, and test it in your Web browser (**Figure 7.3**).

✔ Tips

- Be very careful when you directly add elements to an array. There's a correct way to do it ($array[] = 'Add This'; or $array[1] = 'Add This';) and an incorrect way ($array = 'Add This';). If you forget to use the brackets, the added value will replace the entire existing array, leaving you with a simple string or number.

- The code
$array[] = 'Value';
creates the $array variable if it doesn't yet exist.

- While working with these arrays, I'm using single quotation marks to enclose both the keys and the values. Nothing needs to be interpolated (like a variable), so double quotation marks aren't required. It's perfectly acceptable to use double quotation marks, though, if you want to.

- You don't (and, in fact, shouldn't) quote your keys if they're numbers, variables, or constants (you'll learn about constants in Chapter 8, "Creating Web Applications"). For example:
$day = 'Sunday';
$soups[$day] = 'Mushroom';

- The sizeof() function is an alias to count(). It also returns the number of elements in an array.

Figure 7.3 A direct way to ensure that the new elements were successfully added to the array is to count the number of elements before and after you make the additions.

Merging Arrays

PHP has a function that allows you to append one array onto another. Think of it as concatenation for arrays. The function, array_merge(), works like so:

```
$new_array = array_merge($array1,
→ $array2);
```

You could also write the soups2.php page using this function:

```
$soups2 = array (
'Thursday' => 'Chicken Noodle',
'Friday' => 'Tomato',
'Saturday' => 'Cream of Broccoli',
);
$soups = array_merge($soups,
$soups2);
```

You could even accomplish this result with the plus sign (thus adding two arrays together):

```
$soups = $soups + $soups2;
```

or

```
$soups += $soups2;
```

Accessing Array Elements

Regardless of how you establish an array, there's only one way to retrieve a specific element (or value) from it, and that is to refer to its index:

```
print "The first item is $array[0]";
```

If the array uses strings for indexes, which should be quoted, you must adjust for the quotation marks you'd use around the index, because they conflict with the print( ) syntax. This line will cause problems:

```
print "The total of your order comes to
→ $array['total']";
```

To combat this issue, you can wrap the whole array construct within curly braces:

```
print "The total of your order comes to
→ {$array['total']}";
```

Ironically, the feature that makes arrays so useful—being able to store multiple values in one variable—also gives it a limitation the other variable types don't have: You must know the keys of the array in order to access its elements. If the array was set using strings, like the $soups array, then referring to $soups[1] points to nothing. For that matter, because variables are case sensitive, $soups['monday'] is meaningless because *Clam Chowder* was indexed at $soups['Monday'].

The fastest and easiest way to access all the values of an array is to use a foreach loop. This construct loops through every element of an array:

```
foreach ($array as $key => $value) {
    print "Key is $key. Value is
    → $value";
}
```

You can now write a new soups script to use this knowledge. Instead of merely being able to print out how many elements are in an array (as you've done to this point), you can access the actual values.

To print the values of any array:

1. Begin a new document in your text editor
   or IDE (**Script 7.3**):

   ```
   <!DOCTYPE html PUBLIC "-//W3C//DTD
   → XHTML 1.0 Transitional//EN"
       "http://www.w3.org/TR/xhtml1/DTD/
   → xhtml1-transitional.dtd">
   <html xmlns="http://www.w3.org/1999/
   → xhtml" xml:lang="en" lang="en">
   <head>
       <meta http-equiv="Content-Type"
   → content="text/html;
   → charset=utf-8"/>
       <title>No Soup for You!</title>
   </head>
   <body>
   <h1>Mmm...soups</h1>
   ```

2. Start the PHP section of the page and
   address error management, if you want:

   ```
   <?php // Script 7.3 - soups3.php
   ```

3. Create the $soups array:

   ```
   $soups = array (
   'Monday' => 'Clam Chowder',
   'Tuesday' => 'White Chicken Chili',
   'Wednesday' => 'Vegetarian',
   'Thursday' => 'Chicken Noodle',
   'Friday' => 'Tomato',
   'Saturday' => 'Cream of Broccoli'
   );
   ```

   Here you create the entire array at once,
   although you could use the same method
   (creating the array in steps) as in the
   preceding script.

Script 7.3 A foreach loop is the easiest way to access every element in an array.

```
1   <!DOCTYPE html PUBLIC "-//W3C//DTD XHTML
    1.0 Transitional//EN"
2       "http://www.w3.org/TR/xhtml1/DTD/
    xhtml1-transitional.dtd">
3   <html xmlns="http://www.w3.org/1999/
    xhtml" xml:lang="en" lang="en">
4   <head>
5       <meta http-equiv="Content-Type"
    content="text/html; charset=utf-8"/>
6       <title>No Soup for You!</title>
7   </head>
8   <body>
9   <h1>Mmm...soups</h1>
10  <?php // Script 7.3 - soups3.php
11  /* This script creates and prints out an
    array. */
12
13  // Address error management, if you want.
14
15  // Create the array:
16  $soups = array (
17  'Monday' => 'Clam Chowder',
18  'Tuesday' => 'White Chicken Chili',
19  'Wednesday' => 'Vegetarian',
20  'Thursday' => 'Chicken Noodle',
21  'Friday' => 'Tomato',
22  'Saturday' => 'Cream of Broccoli'
23  );
24
25  // Print each key and value:
26  foreach ($soups as $day => $soup) {
27      print "<p>$day: $soup</p>\n";
28  }
29
30  ?>
31  </body>
32  </html>
```

Figure 7.4 The execution of the loop for every element in the array generates this page. The foreach construct allows the script to access each key and value without prior knowledge of what they were.

4. Create a foreach loop to print out each day's soup:

```
foreach ($soups as $day => $soup) {
    print "<p>$day: $soup</p>\n";
}
```

The foreach loop iterates through every element of the $soups array, assigning each index to $day and each value to $soup. These values are then printed out within HTML paragraph tags. The print statement concludes with a newline character (created by \n), which will affect the HTML source code of the page.

5. Close the PHP section and the HTML page:

```
?>
</body>
</html>
```

6. Save the page as soups3.php, place it in the proper directory for your PHP-enabled server, and test it in your Web browser (**Figure 7.4**).

✔ Tips

- One option for working with arrays is to assign a specific element's value to a separate variable using the assignment operator:

```
$total = $array[1];
```

By doing this, you can preserve the original value in the array and still manipulate it separately as a variable.

- If you only need to access an array's values (and not its keys), you can use this `foreach` structure:

```
foreach ($array as $value) {
    // Do whatever.
}
```

- Remember that the curly braces are used to avoid errors when printing array values that have strings for keys. Here's an example where using quotation marks is not problematic, so the curly braces aren't required:

```
$name = trim ($array['Name']);
```

- Another way to access all of an array's elements is to use a `for` loop:

```
for ($n = 0; $n < count($array);
→ $n++) {
    print "The value is $array[$n]";
}
```

Creating Multidimensional Arrays

Multidimensional arrays are both simple and complicated at the same time. The structure and concept may be somewhat difficult to grasp, but creating and accessing multidimensional arrays in PHP is surprisingly easy.

A multidimensional array is used so that you can create an array containing more information than a standard array. This is accomplished by using other arrays for values instead of just strings and numbers. For example:

```
$fruits = array ('apples', 'bananas',
→ 'oranges');
$meats = array ('steaks', 'hamburgers',
→ 'pork chops');
$groceries = array (
'fruits' => $fruits,
'meats' => $meats,
'other' => 'peanuts',
'cash' => 30.00
);
```

This array, $groceries, now consists of one string (*peanuts*), one floating-point number (*30.00*), and two arrays ($fruits and $meats).

Pointing to an element in an array within an array is tricky. The key (pardon the pun) is to continue adding indices in square brackets as necessary. So in this example, *bananas* is at $groceries['fruits'][1].

First, you point to the element (in this case, an array) in the $groceries array, by using ['fruits']. Then, you point to the element in that array based on its position—it's the second item, so you use the index [1].

In this next task, you'll write a script that creates another multidimensional array example.

To use multidimensional arrays:

1. Begin a new document in your text editor or IDE (**Script 7.4**):

```
<!DOCTYPE html PUBLIC "-//W3C//DTD
→ XHTML 1.0 Transitional//EN"
  "http://www.w3.org/TR/xhtml1/DTD/
  → xhtml1-transitional.dtd">
<html xmlns="http://www.w3.org/1999/
→ xhtml" xml:lang="en" lang="en">
<head>
  <meta http-equiv="Content-Type"
  → content="text/html;
  → charset=utf-8"/>
  <title>My Books and Chapters
  → </title>
</head>
<body>
```

2. Create the initial PHP tags, and address error management, if necessary:

```
<?php // Script 7.4 - books.php
```

3. Create the first array:

```
$phpvqs = array (1 => 'Getting
→ Started', 'Variables', 'HTML Forms
→ and PHP', 'Using Numbers');
```

To build up the multidimensional array, you'll create three standard arrays and then use them as the values for the larger array. This array (called **$phpvqs**, which is short for *PHP for the World Wide Web: Visual QuickStart Guide*) uses numbers for the keys and strings for the values. The numbers begin with 1 and correspond to the chapter numbers. The values are the chapter titles.

Script 7.4 The multidimensional $books array stores a lot of information in one big variable.

```
1    <!DOCTYPE html PUBLIC "-//W3C//DTD XHTML
     1.0 Transitional//EN"
2      "http://www.w3.org/TR/xhtml1/DTD/
       xhtml1-transitional.dtd">
3    <html xmlns="http://www.w3.org/1999/
     xhtml" xml:lang="en" lang="en">
4    <head>
5      <meta http-equiv="Content-Type"
       content="text/html; charset=utf-8"/>
6      <title>My Books and Chapters</title>
7    </head>
8    <body>
9    <?php // Script 7.4 - books.php
10   /* This script creates and prints out a
     multidimensional array. */
11   // Address error management, if you want.
12
13   // Create the first array:
14   $phpvqs = array (1 => 'Getting Started',
     'Variables', 'HTML Forms and PHP', 'Using
     Numbers');
15
16   // Create the second array:
17   $phpadv = array (1 => 'Advanced PHP
     Techniques', 'Developing Web
     Applications', 'Advanced Database
     Concepts', 'Security Techniques');
18
19   // Create the third array:
20   $phpmysql = array (1 => 'Introduction
     to PHP', 'Programming with PHP',
     'Creating Dynamic Web Sites',
     'Introduction to MySQL');
21
22   // Create the multidimensional array:
23   $books = array (
24   'PHP VQS' => $phpvqs,
25   'PHP 5 Advanced VQP' => $phpadv,
26   'PHP 6 and MySQL 5 VQP' => $phpmysql
27   );
28
```

(script continues on next page)

Script 7.4 *continued*

```
000                    Script
29   // Print out some values:
30   print "<p>The third chapter of my first
     book is <i>{$books['PHP VQS'][3]}</i>.
     </p>";
31   print "<p>The first chapter of my second
     book is <i>{$books['PHP 5 Advanced VQP']
     [1]}</i>.</p>";
32   print "<p>The fourth chapter of my fourth
     book is <i>{$books['PHP 6 and MySQL 5
     VQP'][4]}</i>.</p>";
33
34   // See what happens with foreach:
35   foreach ($books as $key => $value) {
36      print "<p>$key: $value</p>\n";
37   }
38
39   ?>
40   </body>
41   </html>
```

4. Create the next two arrays:

```
$phpadv = array (1 => 'Advanced
→ PHP Techniques', 'Developing Web
→ Applications', 'Advanced Database
→ Concepts', 'Security Techniques');
$phpmysql = array (1 => 'Introduction
→ to PHP', 'Programming with PHP',
→ 'Creating Dynamic Web Sites',
→ 'Introduction to MySQL');
```

For each array, add only the books' first four chapters for simplicity's sake.

5. Create the main, multidimensional array:

```
$books = array (
'PHP VQS' => $phpvqs,
'PHP 5 Advanced VQP' => $phpadv,
'PHP 6 and MySQL 5 VQP' => $phpmysql
);
```

The $books array is the master array for this script. It uses strings for keys (which are shortened versions of the book titles) and arrays for values. You use the array() function to create it, as you would any other array.

6. Print out the name of the third chapter of the *PHP Visual QuickStart Guide* book:

```
print "<p>The third chapter of my
→ first book is <i>{$books['PHP
→ VQS'][3]}</i>.</p>";
```

Following the rules stated earlier, all you need to do to access any individual chapter name is to begin with $books, follow that with the first index (['PHP VQS']), and follow that with the next index ([3]). Because you're placing this in a print() call, you enclose the whole construct in curly braces to avoid parse errors.

continues on next page

CREATING MULTIDIMENSIONAL ARRAYS

7. Print out two more examples:

```
print "<p>The first chapter of my
→ second book is <i>{$books['PHP 5
→ Advanced VQP'][1]}</i>.</p>";

print "<p>The fourth chapter of my
→ fourth book is <i>{$books['PHP 6
→ and MySQL 5 VQP'][4]}</i>.</p>";
```

8. Run the $books array through a foreach loop to see the results:

```
foreach ($books as $key => $value) {
    print "<p>$key: $value</p>\n";
}
```

The $key variable stores each abbreviated book title, and the $value variable ends up containing each chapter array.

9. Close the PHP section and complete the HTML page:

```
?>
</body>
</html>
```

10. Save the file as books.php, place it in the proper directory for your PHP-enabled server, and test it in your browser (**Figure 7.5**).

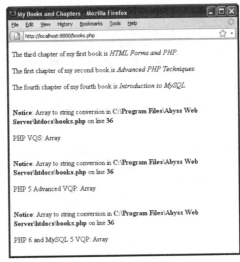

Figure 7.5 The first three lines are generated by print() statements. The last three show the results of the foreach loop (and the notices come from attempting to print an array).

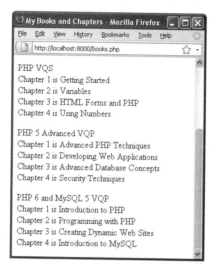

Figure 7.6 One foreach loop within another can access every element of a two-dimensional array.

```
array(3) {
  [u"PHP VQS"]=>
  array(4) {
    [1]=>
    unicode(15) "Getting Started"
    [2]=>
    unicode(9) "Variables"
    [3]=>
    unicode(18) "HTML Forms and PHP"
    [4]=>
    unicode(13) "Using Numbers"
  }
  [u"PHP 5 Advanced VQP"]=>
  array(4) {
    [1]=>
    unicode(23) "Advanced PHP Techniques"
    [2]=>
    unicode(27) "Developing Web Applications"
    [3]=>
    unicode(26) "Advanced Database Concepts"
    [4]=>
    unicode(19) "Security Techniques"
  }
  [u"PHP 6 and MySQL 5 VQP"]=>
  array(4) {
    [1]=>
    unicode(19) "Introduction to PHP"
    [2]=>
    unicode(20) "Programming with PHP"
    [3]=>
    unicode(26) "Creating Dynamic Web Sites"
    [4]=>
    unicode(21) "Introduction to MySQL"
  }
}
```

Figure 7.7 The var_dump() function shows the structure and contents of the $books array.

✔ Tips

- To access every element of every array, you can nest two foreach loops like this (**Figure 7.6**):

```
foreach ($books as $title =>
→ $chapters) {
    print "<p>$title";
    foreach ($chapters as $number =>
    → $chapter) {
    print "<br />Chapter $number is
    → $chapter";
    }
    print '</p>';
}
```

- Using the print_r() or var_dump() function (preferably enclosed in HTML <pre> tags for better formatting), you can view an entire multidimensional array (**Figure 7.7**).

- You can create a multidimensional array in one statement by using a series of nested array() calls (instead of using several steps as in this example). However, doing so isn't recommended, because it's all too easy to make syntactical errors as a statement becomes more and more nested.

- Although all the sub-arrays in this example have the same structure (numbers for indexes and four elements), that isn't required with multidimensional arrays.

- To learn about the greater "Larry Ullman Collection," including the three books referenced here, go to this book's Web site: www.DMCInsights.com/phpvqs3/.

Sorting Arrays

PHP supports a variety of ways to sort an array (*sort* refers to an alphabetical sort if the values being sorted are strings, or a numerical sort if the values being sorted are numbers). When you're sorting an array, you must keep in mind that an array consists of pairs of *keys and values*. Thus, an array can be sorted based on the keys or the values. This is further complicated by the fact that you can sort the values and keep the corresponding keys aligned, or you can sort the values and have them be assigned new keys.

To sort the values without regard to the keys, you use sort(). To sort these values (again, without regard to the keys) in reverse order, you use rsort(). The syntax for every sorting function is:

```
function($array);
```

So, sort() and rsort() are used as follows:

```
sort($array);
rsort($array);
```

To sort the values while maintaining the correlation between each value and its key, you use asort(). To sort the values in reverse while maintaining the key correlation, you use arsort().

To sort by the keys while maintaining the correlation between the key and its value, you use ksort(). Conversely, krsort() sorts the keys in reverse. **Table 7.2** lists all these functions.

Last, shuffle() randomly reorganizes the order of an array.

As an example of sorting arrays, you'll create a list of students and the grades they received on a test, and then sort this list first by grade and then by name.

Table 7.2

Array Sorting Functions

FUNCTION	SORTS BY	MAINTAINS KEY-VALUES?
sort()	Values	No
rsort()	Values (inverse)	No
asort()	Values	Yes
arsort()	Values (inverse)	Yes
ksort()	Keys	Yes
krsort()	Keys (inverse)	Yes

SORTING ARRAYS

Script 7.5 PHP provides a number of different functions for sorting arrays, including `arsort()` and `ksort()` (used here).

```
1    <!DOCTYPE html PUBLIC "-//W3C//DTD XHTML
     1.0 Transitional//EN"
2        "http://www.w3.org/TR/xhtml1/DTD/
         xhtml1-transitional.dtd">
3    <html xmlns="http://www.w3.org/1999/
     xhtml" xml:lang="en" lang="en">
4    <head>
5        <meta http-equiv="Content-Type"
         content="text/html; charset=utf-8"/>
6        <title>My Little Gradebook</title>
7    </head>
8    <body>
9    <?php // Script 7.5 - sort.php
10   /* This script creates, sorts, and prints
     out an array. */
11
12   // Address error management, if you want.
13
14   // Create the array:
15   $grades = array(
16   'Richard' => 95,
17   'Sherwood' => 82,
18   'Toni' => 98,
19   'Franz' => 87,
20   'Melissa' => 75,
21   'Roddy' => 85
22   );
23
24   // Print the original array:
25   print '<p>Originally the array looks like
     this: <br />';
26   foreach ($grades as $student => $grade) {
27       print "$student: $grade<br />\n";
28   }
29   print '</p>';
30
31   // Sort by value in reverse order, then
     print again.
32   arsort ($grades);
33   print '<p>After sorting the array by
     value using arsort(), the array looks
     like this: <br />';
```

(script continues on next page)

To sort an array:

1. Begin a new document in your text editor or IDE (**Script 7.5**):

```
<!DOCTYPE html PUBLIC "-//W3C//DTD
→ XHTML 1.0 Transitional//EN"
    "http://www.w3.org/TR/xhtml1/DTD/
    → xhtml1-transitional.dtd">
<html xmlns="http://www.w3.org/1999/
→ xhtml" xml:lang="en" lang="en">
<head>
    <meta http-equiv="Content-Type"
    → content="text/html;
    → charset=utf-8"/>
    <title>My Little Gradebook</title>
</head>
<body>
```

2. Begin the PHP section, and address error handling, if desired:

```
<?php // Script 7.5 - sort.php
```

3. Create the array:

```
$grades = array(
'Richard' => 95,
'Sherwood' => 82,
'Toni' => 98,
'Franz' => 87,
'Melissa' => 75,
'Roddy' => 85
);
```

The `$grades` array consists of six students' names along with their corresponding grades. Because the grades are number values, they don't need to be quoted when assigning them.

continues on next page

4. Print a caption, and then print each element of the array using a `foreach` loop:

```
print '<p>Originally the array looks
→ like this: <br />';
foreach ($grades as $student =>
→ $grade) {
    print "$student: $grade<br />\n";
}
print '</p>';
```

The caption tells you what point in the script you're at. At first, it prints the array in the original order. To do that, you use a `foreach` loop, where each index (the student's name) is assigned to `$student`, and each value (the student's grade) is assigned to `$grade`. The final `print()` call closes the HTML paragraph.

5. Sort the array in reverse order by value to determine who has the highest grade:

```
arsort ($grades);
```

Because you're determining who has the highest grade, you need to use `arsort()` instead of `asort()`. The latter, which sorts the array in numeric order, would order the grades 75, 82, 85, and so on, rather than the desired 98, 95, 87.

You also must use `arsort()` and not `rsort()` in order to maintain the key-value relationship (`rsort()` would eliminate the student's name associated with each grade).

6. Print the array again (with a caption), using another loop:

```
print '<p>After sorting the array
→ by value using arsort(), the array
→ looks like this: <br />';
foreach ($grades as $student =>
→ $grade) {
    print "$student: $grade<br />\n";
}
print '</p>';
```

Script 7.5 *continued*

```
34  foreach ($grades as $student => $grade) {
35      print "$student: $grade<br />\n";
36  }
37  print '</p>';
38
39  // Sort by key, then print again.
40  ksort ($grades);
41  print '<p>After sorting the array by
        key using ksort(), the array looks like
        this: <br />';
42  foreach ($grades as $student => $grade) {
43      print "$student: $grade<br />\n";
44  }
45  print '</p>';
46
47  ?>
48  </body>
49  </html>
```

Figure 7.8 You can sort an array in a number of ways with varied results. Pay close attention to whether you want to maintain your key-value association when choosing a sort function.

7. Sort the array by key to put the array in alphabetical order by student name:

```
ksort ($grades);
```

The `ksort()` function organizes the array by key (in this case, alphabetically) while maintaining the key-value correlation.

8. Print a caption and the array one last time:

```
print '<p>After sorting the array
→ by key using ksort(), the array
→ looks like this: <br />';
foreach ($grades as $student =>
→ $grade) {
    print "$student: $grade<br />\n";
}
print '</p>';
```

9. Complete the script with the standard PHP and HTML tags:

```
?>
</body>
</html>
```

10. Save your script as `sort.php`, place it in the proper directory for your PHP-enabled server, and test it in your Web browser (**Figure 7.8**).

✔ Tips

- The `$grades` array could have been created using the grades as the keys and the names of the students as values. It works either way.

- The `natsort()` and `natcasesort()` functions sort a string (while maintaining key-value associations) using *natural order*. The most obvious example of natural order sorting is that it places *name2* before *name12*, whereas `sort()` orders them *name12* and then *name2*.

- The `usort()`, `uasort()`, and `ursort()` functions let you sort an array using a user-defined comparison function. These functions are most often used with multidimensional arrays.

Transforming Between Strings and Arrays

Now that you understand both strings and arrays, this section introduces two functions for switching between the two formats. The first, implode( ), turns an array into a string. The second, explode( ), does just the opposite. Here are some reasons to use these functions:

◆ To turn an array into a string in order to pass that value appended to a URL (which you can't do as easily with an array)

◆ To turn an array into a string in order to store that information in a database

◆ To turn a string into an array to convert a comma-delimited text field (say a keyword search area of a form) into its separate parts

The syntax for using explode( ) is as follows:

```
$array = explode($separator, $string);
```

The *separator* refers to whatever character(s) define where one value ends and another begins. Commonly this is a comma, a tab, or a blank space. Thus your code might be

```
$array = explode(',', $string);
```

or

```
$array = explode(' ', $string);
```

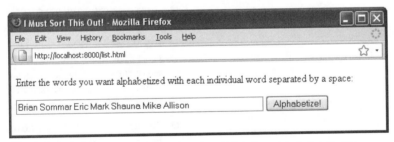

Figure 7.9 This HTML form takes a list of words, which is then alphabetized by the handle_list.php script (Figure 7.10).

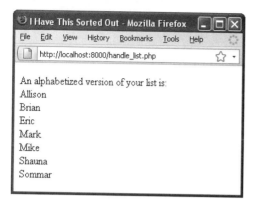

Figure 7.10 Here's the same list, alphabetized for the user. This process is quick and easy to code, but doing so would be impossible without arrays.

Script 7.6 This is a simple HTML form where a user can submit a list of words. Including detailed instructions for how the form should be used is a prudent Web design policy.

```
1    <!DOCTYPE html PUBLIC "-//W3C//DTD XHTML
     1.0 Transitional//EN"
2        "http://www.w3.org/TR/xhtml1/DTD/
         xhtml1-transitional.dtd">
3    <html xmlns="http://www.w3.org/1999/
     xhtml" xml:lang="en" lang="en">
4    <head>
5        <meta http-equiv="Content-Type"
         content="text/html; charset=utf-8"/>
6        <title>I Must Sort This Out!</title>
7    </head>
8    <body>
9    <!-- Script 7.6 - list.html -->
10   <div><p>Enter the words you want
     alphabetized with each individual word
     separated by a space:</p>
11
12   <form action="handle_list.php"
     method="post">
13
14       <input type="text" name="words"
         size="60" />
15       <input type="submit" name="submit"
         value="Alphabetize!" />
16
17   </form>
18   </div>
19   </body>
20   </html>
```

To go from an array to a string, you need to define what the separator (aka the *glue*) should be, and PHP does the rest:

```
$string = implode($glue, $array);
$string = implode(',', $array);
```

or

```
$string = implode(' ', $array);
```

To demonstrate how to use explode() and implode(), you'll create an HTML form that takes a space-delimited string of names from the user (**Figure 7.9**). The PHP script will then turn the string into an array so that it can sort the list. Finally, the code will create and return the alphabetized string (**Figure 7.10**).

To create the HTML form:

1. Begin a new document in your text editor or IDE (**Script 7.6**):

```
<!DOCTYPE html PUBLIC "-//W3C//DTD
→ XHTML 1.0 Transitional//EN"
    "http://www.w3.org/TR/xhtml1/DTD/
    → xhtml1-transitional.dtd">
<html xmlns="http://www.w3.org/1999/
→ xhtml" xml:lang="en" lang="en">
<head>
    <meta http-equiv="Content-Type"
    → content="text/html;
    → charset=utf-8"/>
    <title>I Must Sort This Out!
    → </title>
</head>
<body>
<!-- Script 7.6 - list.html -->
```

continues on next page

2. Create an HTML form with a text input:

```
<div><p>Enter the words you want
→ alphabetized with each individual
→ word separated by a space:</p>
<form action="handle_list.php"
→ method="post">
    <input type="text" name="words"
    → size="60" />
```

It's important in cases like this to instruct the user. For example, if they enter a comma-delimited list, you won't be able to handle the string properly (after completing both scripts, try using commas in lieu of spaces and see what happens).

3. Create a submit button, and then close the form and the HTML page:

```
    <input type="submit" name="submit"
    → value="Alphabetize!" />
</form>
</div>
</body>
</html>
```

4. Save your script as list.html and place it in the proper directory for your PHP-enabled server.

Now you'll write the handle_list.php page to process the data generated by list.html.

Script 7.7 Because the explode() and implode() functions are so simple and powerful, you can quickly and easily sort a submitted list of words (of practically any length) in just a couple of lines.

```
000                    Script
1   <!DOCTYPE html PUBLIC "-//W3C//DTD XHTML
    1.0 Transitional//EN"
2       "http://www.w3.org/TR/xhtml1/DTD/
        xhtml1-transitional.dtd">
3   <html xmlns="http://www.w3.org/1999/
    xhtml" xml:lang="en" lang="en">
4   <head>
5       <meta http-equiv="Content-Type"
        content="text/html; charset=utf-8"/>
6       <title>I Have This Sorted Out</title>
7   </head>
8   <body>
9   <?php // Script 7.7 - handle_list.php
10  /* This script receives a string in
    $_POST['words']. It then turns it into
    an array,
11  sorts the array alphabetically, and
    reprints it. */
12
13  // Address error management, if you want.
14
15  // Turn the incoming string into an array:
16  $words_array = explode(' ' , $_POST
    ['words']);
17
18  // Sort the array:
19  sort($words_array);
20
21  // Turn the array back into a string:
22  $string_words = implode('<br />',
    $words_array);
23
24  // Print the results:
25  print "<p>An alphabetized version of your
    list is: <br />$string_words</p>";
26
27  ?>
28  </body>
29  </html>
```

To convert between strings and arrays:

1. Begin a new document in your text editor or IDE (**Script 7.7**):

```
<!DOCTYPE html PUBLIC "-//W3C//DTD
→ XHTML 1.0 Transitional//EN"
   "http://www.w3.org/TR/xhtml1/DTD/
   → xhtml1-transitional.dtd">
<html xmlns="http://www.w3.org/1999/
→ xhtml" xml:lang="en" lang="en">
<head>
   <meta http-equiv="Content-Type"
   → content="text/html;
   → charset=utf-8"/>
   <title>I Have This Sorted Out
   → </title>
</head>
<body>
<?php // Script 7.7 - handle_list.php
```

2. Turn the incoming string, $_POST ['words'], into an array:

```
$words_array = explode(' ' ,
→ $_POST['words']);
```

This line of code creates a new array, $words_array, out of the string $_POST['words']. Each space between the words in $_POST['words'] indicates that the next word should be a new array element. Hence the first word becomes $words_array[0], then there is a space in $_POST['words'], then the second word becomes $words_array[1], and so forth, until the end of $_POST['words'].

3. Sort the array alphabetically:

```
sort($words_array);
```

Because you don't need to maintain key-value associations in the $words_array, you can use sort() instead of asort() (which you used before).

continues on next page

4. Create a new string out of the sorted array:

```
$string_words = implode('<br />',
→ $words_array);
```

Arrays don't print as easily as strings, so you turn $words_array into a string called $string_words. The resulting string starts with the value of $words_array[0], followed by the HTML <br /> tag, the value of $words_array[1], and so on. Using <br /> instead of a space or comma gives the list a more readable format when it's printed to the browser.

5. Print the new string to the browser:

```
print "<p>An alphabetized version
→ of your list is: <br />
→ $string_words</p>";
```

6. Close the PHP section and the HTML page:

```
?>
</body>
</html>
```

7. Save your page as handle_list.php, place it in the same directory as list.html, and test both scripts in your Web browser (Figures 7.9 and 7.10).

✔ Tips

■ The conversion from $words_array back to $string_words was more of an example than a requirement. You could also print out $words_array using a foreach loop.

■ You'll also run across code written using the join() function, which is synonymous with implode().

Figure 7.11 Checkboxes in an HTML form (using Firefox on Mac OS X).

Creating an Array from a Form

Throughout this chapter, you've established arrays entirely from within a PHP page. You can, however, send an array of data to a PHP script via an HTML form. In fact, every time you use $_POST, this is the case. But you can take this one step further by creating arrays with an HTML form, which are then a part of the greater $_POST array (thereby making $_POST a multidimensional array).

The most logical use of this capability is in dealing with checkboxes, where users might need to select multiple related options (**Figure 7.11**). The HTML source code for a checkbox is as follows:

```
<input type="checkbox" name="some_input"
→ value="some_value" />
```

The problem is that in order to send multiple values to a PHP script, each form element must have a unique name. If you created several checkboxes, each with a name of *some_input*, only the value of the last checked box would be received in the PHP script. The workaround is to use an array.

To create an array with an HTML form:

1. Begin a new document in your text editor or IDE (**Script 7.8**):

   ```
   <!DOCTYPE html PUBLIC "-//W3C//DTD
   → XHTML 1.0 Transitional//EN"
     "http://www.w3.org/TR/xhtml1/DTD/
     → xhtml1-transitional.dtd">
   <html xmlns="http://www.w3.org/1999/
   → xhtml" xml:lang="en" lang="en">
   <head>
     <meta http-equiv="Content-Type"
   → content="text/html;
   → charset=utf-8"/>
     <title>Add an Event</title>
   </head>
   <body>
   <!-- Script 7.8 - event.html -->
   <div><p>Use this form to add an
   → event:</p>
   ```

2. Begin the HTML form:

   ```
   <form action="handle_event.php"
   → method="post">
   ```

3. Create a text input for an event name:

   ```
   <p>Event Name: <input type="text"
   → name="name" size="30" /></p>
   ```

   This example allows the user to enter an event name and the days of the week when it takes place.

Script 7.8 This HTML form has an array for the checkbox input names.

```
1    <!DOCTYPE html PUBLIC "-//W3C//DTD XHTML
     1.0 Transitional//EN"
2        "http://www.w3.org/TR/xhtml1/DTD/
         xhtml1-transitional.dtd">
3    <html xmlns="http://www.w3.org/1999/
     xhtml" xml:lang="en" lang="en">
4    <head>
5        <meta http-equiv="Content-Type"
         content="text/html; charset=utf-8"/>
6        <title>Add an Event</title>
7    </head>
8    <body>
9    <!-- Script 7.8 - event.html -->
10   <div><p>Use this form to add an event:</p>
11
12   <form action="handle_event.php"
     method="post">
13
14       <p>Event Name: <input type="text"
         name="name" size="30" /></p>
15       <p>Event Days:
16       <input type="checkbox" name=
         "weekdays[]" value="Sunday" /> Sun
17       <input type="checkbox" name=
         "weekdays[]" value="Monday" /> Mon
18       <input type="checkbox" name=
         "weekdays[]" value="Tuesday" /> Tue
19       <input type="checkbox" name=
         "weekdays[]" value="Wednesday" /> Wed
20       <input type="checkbox" name=
         "weekdays[]" value="Thursday" /> Thu
21       <input type="checkbox" name=
         "weekdays[]" value="Friday" /> Fri
22       <input type="checkbox" name=
         "weekdays[]" value="Saturday" /> Sat
23       </p>
24       <input type="submit" name="submit"
         value="Add the Event!" />
25
26   </form>
27   </div>
28   </body>
29   </html>
```

4. Create the weekday checkboxes:

```
<p>Event Days:
<input type="checkbox" name=
→ "weekdays[]" value="Sunday" /> Sun
<input type="checkbox" name=
→ "weekdays[]" value="Monday" /> Mon
<input type="checkbox" name=
→ "weekdays[]" value="Tuesday" /> Tue
<input type="checkbox" name=
→ "weekdays[]" value="Wednesday"
→ /> Wed
<input type="checkbox" name=
→ "weekdays[]" value="Thursday"
/> Thu
<input type="checkbox" name=
→ "weekdays[]" value="Friday" /> Fri
<input type="checkbox" name=
→ "weekdays[]" value="Saturday"
/> Sat
</p>
```

All of these checkboxes use *weekdays[ ]* as the name value, which creates a `$_POST['weekdays']` array in the PHP script. The value attributes differ for each checkbox, corresponding to the day of the week.

5. Complete the HTML form:

```
<input type="submit" name="submit"
→ value="Add the Event!" />
</form>
```

6. Complete the HTML page:

```
</div>
</body>
</html>
```

7. Save your page as `event.html` and place it in the proper directory for your PHP-enabled server.

You also need to write a `handle_event.php` page to handle this HTML form.

To handle the HTML form:

1. Begin a new document in your text editor or IDE (**Script 7.9**):

```
<!DOCTYPE html PUBLIC "-//W3C//DTD
→ XHTML 1.0 Transitional//EN"
   "http://www.w3.org/TR/xhtml1/DTD/
   → xhtml1-transitional.dtd">
<html xmlns="http://www.w3.org/1999/
→ xhtml" xml:lang="en" lang="en">
<head>
   <meta http-equiv="Content-Type"
   → content="text/html;
   → charset=utf-8"/>
   <title>Add an Event</title>
</head>
<body>
```

2. Create the initial PHP tag, address error management (if need be), and print an introductory message:

```
<?php // Script 7.9 - handle_
→ event.php

print "<p>You want to add an event
→ called <b>{$_POST['name']}</b>
→ which takes place on: <br />";
```

The print( ) line prints out the value of the event's name. In a real-world version of this script, you would add a conditional to check that a value was entered (see Chapter 6, "Control Structures").

Script 7.9 This PHP script receives an array of values in $_POST['weekdays'].

```
1    <!DOCTYPE html PUBLIC "-//W3C//DTD XHTML
     1.0 Transitional//EN"
2        "http://www.w3.org/TR/xhtml1/DTD/
         xhtml1-transitional.dtd">
3    <html xmlns="http://www.w3.org/1999/
     xhtml" xml:lang="en" lang="en">
4    <head>
5        <meta http-equiv="Content-Type"
         content="text/html; charset=utf-8"/>
6        <title>Add an Event</title>
7    </head>
8    <body>
9    <?php // Script 7.9 - handle_event.php
10   /* This script creates, sorts, and prints
     out an array. */
11
12   // Address error management, if you want.
13
14   // Print an introductory text:
15   print "<p>You want to add an event called
     <b>{$_POST['name']}</b> which takes place
     on: <br />";
16
17   // Print each weekday:
18   if (isset($_POST['weekdays']) AND
     is_array($_POST['weekdays'])) {
19
20       foreach ($_POST['weekdays'] as $day) {
21           print "$day<br />\n";
22       }
23
24   } else {
25       print 'Please select at least once
         weekday for this event!';
26   }
27
28   // Complete the paragraph:
29   print '</p>';
30   ?>
31   </body>
32   </html>
```

3. Begin a conditional to check that at least one weekday was selected:

```
if (isset($_POST['weekdays']) AND
→ is_array($_POST['weekdays'])) {
```

If no checkbox was clicked, then `$_POST['weekdays']` won't be an existing variable. To avoid an error caused by referring to a variable that does not exist, the first part of the conditional checks that `$_POST['weekdays']` is set.

The second part of the condition—and both must be TRUE for the entire condition to be TRUE—confirms that `$_POST['weekdays']` is an array. This is a good step to take because a `foreach` loop will create an error if it receives a variable that isn't an array.

4. Print each selected weekday:

```
foreach ($_POST['weekdays'] as
→ $day) {
    print "$day<br />\n";
}
```

To print out each checked weekday, you run the `$_POST['weekdays']` array through a `foreach` loop. The array contains the values (from the HTML form inputs, for example, *Monday*, *Tuesday*, and so on) for every box that was selected.

5. Complete the `is_array()` conditional:

```
} else {
    print 'Please select at least once
    → weekday for this event!';
}
```

If no weekday was selected, then the `isset()` AND `is_array()` condition is FALSE, and this message is printed.

continues on next page

6. Complete the main paragraph, the PHP section, and the HTML page:

```
print '</p>';
?>
</body>
</html>
```

7. Save the page as handle_event.php, place it in the same directory as event.html, and test both pages in your Web browser (**Figures 7.12** and **7.13**).

✔ Tip

■ The same technique demonstrated here can be used to allow a user to select multiple options in a drop-down menu. Just give the menu a name with a syntax like *something*[ ], then the PHP script will receive every selection in $_POST['*something*'].

Figure 7.12 The HTML form with its checkboxes (using Firefox on Windows XP).

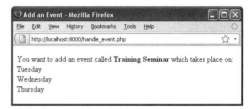

Figure 7.13 The results of the HTML form.

The List Function

The list() function is used to assign array element values to individual variables. To start with an example:

```
$date = array('Thursday', 23, 'October');
list($weekday, $day, $month) = $date;
```

Now there is a $weekday variable with a value of *Thursday*, a $day variable with a value of *23*, and a $month variable with a value of *October*.

There are two caveats for using list(). First, list() only works on arrays numerically indexed starting at 0. Second, when you're using the list() function, you must acknowledge each array element. But you can use empty values to ignore elements:

```
list ($weekday, , $month) = $date;
```

or

```
list (, , $month) = $date;
```

But you cannot do this:

```
list ($month) = $date;
```

The list() function is often used when retrieving values from a database.

CREATING WEB APPLICATIONS

8

The chapters to this point cover the fundamentals of programming with PHP; now it's time to begin tying it all together into actual Web applications. In this chapter, you'll learn about a number of functions and techniques that you can utilize to make your Web sites more professional, more feature-rich, and easier to maintain.

First, you'll begin learning how to use external files to break your Web pages into individual pieces (allowing you to separate the logic from the formatting, to a degree). Then you'll tinker with constants, a special data type in PHP. After that, you'll be introduced to some of the date- and time-related functions built into PHP.

Two of the chapter's topics discuss useful techniques: having the same page both display and handle an HTML form, and having a form remember user-submitted values. After that, you'll see how easy it can be to send email from PHP. The chapter concludes with the slightly more advanced topics of output buffering and using HTTP headers.

Creating Templates

Every example thus far has been a one-page script that handles an HTML form, sorts arrays, or performs calculations. However, as you begin to develop multiple-page Web sites (which is to say *Web applications*), it quickly becomes impractical to repeat common elements over the course of several pages.

Certain features, such as the HTML design, will be used by every page within the site. You can put these elements into each individual page, but when you need to make a change, you'll be required to make that change over and over again. You can save time by creating templates that separate out the repeating content from the page-specific materials. For example, a Web site may have navigation, copyright, and other features that repeat across multiple pages (**Figures 8.1** and **8.2**).

The key to using templates is to create a prototype and then divide it into parts. Using the PHP functions introduced in the next section of this chapter, the repeating parts can be easily included in each page while the new content is generated on a page-by-page basis. You'll first learn how to develop the template files.

To create the layout model:

1. Begin a new HTML document in your text editor or IDE (**Script 8.1**):

```
<!DOCTYPE html PUBLIC "-//W3C//DTD
→ XHTML 1.0 Transitional//EN"
  "http://www.w3.org/TR/xhtml1/DTD/
  → xhtml1-transitional.dtd">
<html xmlns="http://www.w3.org/1999/
→ xhtml" xml:lang="en" lang="en">
<head>
  <meta http-equiv="Content-Type"
  → content="text/html;
  → charset=utf-8"/>
  <title>Elliott Smith Fan Club
  → </title>
```

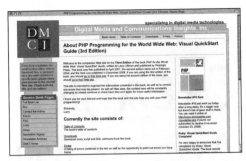

Figure 8.1 The book's home page has its page-specific content in the middle column.

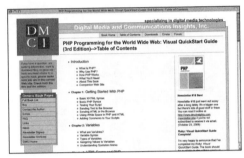

Figure 8.2 The book's table of contents page uses the same left and right columns as the home page (Figure 8.1), thanks to the templates.

Script 8.1 This script represents the desired end result with the template system.

```
1   <!DOCTYPE html PUBLIC "-//W3C//DTD XHTML
    1.0 Transitional//EN"
2       "http://www.w3.org/TR/xhtml1/DTD/
        xhtml1-transitional.dtd">
3   <html xmlns="http://www.w3.org/1999/
    xhtml" xml:lang="en" lang="en">
4   <head>
5       <meta http-equiv="Content-Type"
        content="text/html; charset=utf-8"/>
6       <title>Elliott Smith Fan Club</title>
7
8       <style type="text/css">
9       body {
10          margin:0px 0px 0px 0px;
11          background: #9F9;
12          }
13      #leftcontent {
14          float:left;
15          width:67%;
16          background:#fff;
17          border-right:2px solid #000;
18          border-bottom:2px solid #000;
19          margin-right:15px;
20          padding-bottom:20px;
21          }
22      p,h1,pre {
23          margin:0px 30px 10px 30px;
24          }
25      h1 {
26          font-size:14px;
27          padding-top:10px;
28          }
29      #rightcontent p {
30          font-size:14px;
31          margin-left:0px;
32          }
33      </style>
34
35  </head>
36  <body>
37  <div id="leftcontent">
38  <!-- BEGIN CHANGEABLE CONTENT. -->
39
```

(script continues on next page)

The first step in developing any template system is to create a model document—an example of what a basic page should look like. Once you've created this, you can break it down into its parts.

2. Add the CSS code:

```
<style type="text/css">
    body {
        margin:0px 0px 0px 0px;
        background: #9F9;
        }
    #leftcontent {
        float:left;
        width:67%;
        background:#fff;
        border-right:2px solid #000;
        border-bottom:2px solid #000;
        margin-right:15px;
        padding-bottom:20px;
        }
    p,h1,pre {
        margin:0px 30px 10px 30px;
        }
    h1 {
        font-size:14px;
        padding-top:10px;
        }
    #rightcontent p {
        font-size:14px;
        margin-left:0px;
        }
</style>
```

This example uses CSS for most of the formatting and layout controls. The sidebar talks a little bit about this example: how it works and where it came from.

continues on next page

187

3. Close the HTML head, begin the body, and mark the start of the changeable content:

```
</head>
<body>
<div id="leftcontent">
<!-- BEGIN CHANGEABLE CONTENT. -->
```

Everything up until this point will remain the same for every page in the Web application. To indicate this (for your own benefit), include an HTML comment.

Just before that, the *leftcontent* area is begun. This area is defined in the CSS code and properly formats the main content part of the page. In other words, on every page, that page's content will go within the one div that has an id of *leftcontent*.

4. Create the page's content:

```
<h1>Welcome to the Elliott Smith Fan
→ Club!</h1>
<p>Here's a whole lotta text.</p>
<p>Here's a whole lotta text.</p>
```

For the example, the content is just a header and a whole lot of text (there's more in the actual script than I've included in this step).

5. Mark the end of the changeable content:

```
<!-- END CHANGEABLE CONTENT. -->
```

The code in Step 4 is the only text that will change on a page-by-page basis. Just as an HTML comment indicates where that section starts, one here indicates where it ends.

Script 8.1 *continued*

```
40      <h1>Welcome to the Elliott Smith Fan
        Club!</h1>
41      <p>Here's a whole lotta text. Here's
        a whole lotta text. Here's a whole
        lotta text. Here's a whole lotta text.
        Here's a whole lotta text. Here's
        a whole lotta text. Here's a whole
        lotta text. Here's a whole lotta text.
        Here's a whole lotta text. Here's a
        whole lotta text. </p>
42      <p>Here's a whole lotta text. Here's
        a whole lotta text. Here's a whole
        lotta text. Here's a whole lotta text.
        Here's a whole lotta text. Here's
        a whole lotta text. Here's a whole
        lotta text. Here's a whole lotta text.
        Here's a whole lotta text. Here's a
        whole lotta text. </p>
43
44      <!-- END CHANGEABLE CONTENT. -->
45      </div>
46
47      <div id="rightcontent">
48          <h1>Navigation</h1>
49          <p><a href="index.php">Home</a><br />
50          <a href="albums.php">Discography
            </a><br />
51          <a href="login.php">Login</a><br />
52          <a href="register.php">Register
            </a></p>
53      </div>
54
55      </body>
56      </html>
```

6. Create the navigation area:

```
</div>
<div id="rightcontent">
  <h1>Navigation</h1>
  <p><a href="index.php">Home</a>
  → <br />
  <a href="albums.php">Discography
  → </a><br />
  <a href="login.php">Login</a>
  → <br />
  <a href="register.php">Register
  → </a></p>
</div>
```

The *rightcontent* area (also defined in the CSS code) contains links to the other pages in the Web application. This is preceded by the closing </div> tag, which completes the leftcontent section.

7. Finish the HTML page:

```
</body>
</html>
```

8. Save the file as layout.html and test it in your Web browser (**Figure 8.3**).

Once you've completed a model that you like, you can break it into its various parts to generate the template system.

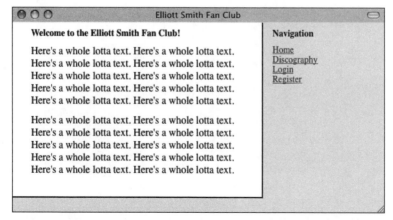

Figure 8.3 Although this design isn't very fancy, it provides a model to work toward with the PHP templates.

To create the header file:

1. Open layout.html (Script 8.1) in your text editor or IDE, if it isn't already open.

2. Select everything from the initial HTML code to the `<!-- BEGIN CHANGEABLE CONTENT -->` HTML comment (**Figure 8.4**).

   Part of the benefit of identifying the start of the page-specific content with an HTML comment is that it simplifies breaking the model into its parts.

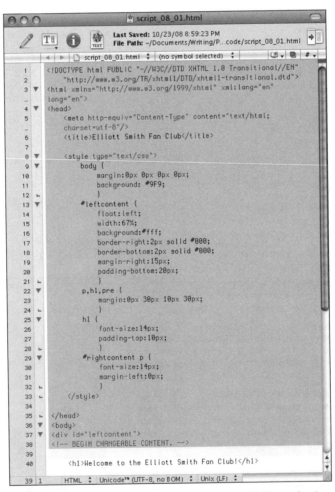

Figure 8.4 Using the example file, select and copy the initial lines of code to create the header.

Script 8.2 This is a basic header file that creates the HTML head information (including the CSS) and begins the body.

```
1    <!DOCTYPE html PUBLIC "-//W3C//DTD XHTML
     1.0 Transitional//EN"
2        "http://www.w3.org/TR/xhtml1/DTD/
         xhtml1-transitional.dtd">
3    <html xmlns="http://www.w3.org/1999/
     xhtml" xml:lang="en" lang="en">
4    <head>
5        <meta http-equiv="Content-Type"
         content="text/html; charset=utf-8"/>
6        <title>Elliott Smith Fan Club</title>
7
8        <style type="text/css">
9        body {
10            margin:0px 0px 0px 0px;
11            background: #9F9;
12            }
13        #leftcontent {
14            float:left;
15            width:67%;
16            background:#fff;
17            border-right:2px solid #000;
18            border-bottom:2px solid #000;
19            margin-right:15px;
20            padding-bottom:20px;
21            }
22        p,h1,pre {
23            margin:0px 30px 10px 30px;
24            }
25        h1 {
26            font-size:14px;
27            padding-top:10px;
28            }
29        #rightcontent p {
30            font-size:14px;
31            margin-left:0px;
32            }
33        </style>
34
35    </head>
36    <body>
37    <div id="leftcontent">
38    <!-- Script 8.2 - header.html -->
39    <!-- BEGIN CHANGEABLE CONTENT. -->
```

3. Copy this code.

Using your Edit menu or keyboard shortcut (Ctrl+C on Windows, Command+C on the Macintosh), copy all of the highlighted code to your computer's temporary memory (which is to say, the clipboard).

4. Create a new, blank document in your text editor or IDE.

5. Paste the copied text into the document (**Script 8.2**).

Using your Edit menu or keyboard shortcut (Ctrl+V on Windows, Command+V on the Macintosh), paste all of the highlighted code into this new document.

6. Save the file as header.html.

Now that the header file has been created, you'll make the footer file using the same process.

CREATING TEMPLATES

To create the footer file:

1. Open layout.html (Script 8.1) in your text editor or IDE, if it isn't already open.

2. Select everything from the <!-- END CHANGEABLE CONTENT --> HTML comment to the end of the script (**Figure 8.5**).

3. Copy this code.

4. Create a new, blank document in your text editor.

5. Paste the copied text into the document (**Script 8.3**).

6. Save the file as footer.html.

Script 8.3 This is a basic footer file that creates the navigation column and concludes the HTML page.

```
1    <!-- END CHANGEABLE CONTENT. -->
2    <!-- Script 8.3 - footer.html -->
3    </div>
4
5    <div id="rightcontent">
6        <h1>Navigation</h1>
7        <p><a href="index.php">Home</a><br />
8        <a href="albums.php">Discography
         </a><br />
9        <a href="login.php">Login</a><br />
10       <a href="register.php">Register</a>
         </p>
11   </div>
12
13   </body>
14   </html>
```

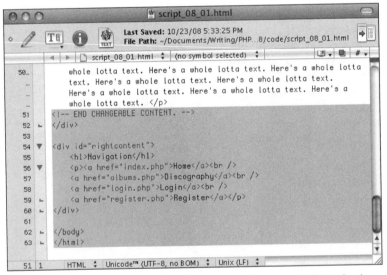

Figure 8.5 Again using the example file, select and copy the concluding lines of code for the footer.

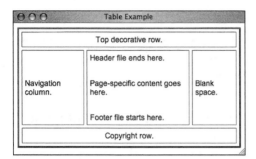

Figure 8.6 This mundane example shows how a table is used with template files to create a design.

✔ Tips

■ There are many far more complex template systems you can use in PHP to separate the design from the logic. The best known of these is probably Smarty (www.smarty.net).

■ Although this example used CSS for its layout, you can certainly use tables instead (**Figure 8.6**). Your header file might begin the HTML page and the table. Each content page would then create its own specific content, and the footer file would complete the table and the HTML page. To turn this into a template, copy all of the code up to *Page-specific content goes here.* into a header file and everything after that into a footer file.

This CSS Template

Cascading Style Sheets (CSS) have been an increasingly important part of the World Wide Web for some time. Their initial usage was focused on cosmetics (font sizes, colors, and so on), but now CSS are frequently used in lieu of tables to control the layout of pages. The Web application in this chapter uses this approach.

This example defines two areas of the page—*leftcontent* and *rightcontent*. The leftcontent area changes for each page. The rightcontent contains standard items, such as navigation links, that appear on each page of the application. The example used in this chapter is based on one of the many CSS examples displayed at glish.com (http://glish.com/css). This specific example, in turn, comes from the excellent site A List Apart (www.alistapart.com).

Just to be clear: There is no relationship between PHP and CSS other than the fact that you *can* use PHP to generate CSS, just as you can use PHP to generate HTML. In this example, though, the CSS is hard-coded into the head section of the HTML document.

Using External Files

As the preceding section said, you can save development time by creating separate pages for particular elements and then incorporating them into the main PHP pages using specific functions. These functions are include() and require():

```
include ('file.php');
require ('file.html');
```

Both functions work the same way, with one relatively insignificant difference: If the include() function fails, the PHP script generates a warning (**Figure 8.7**) but continues to run. Conversely, if require() fails, it terminates the execution of the script (**Figure 8.8**).

But what do these two functions do? Both include() and require() incorporate the file referenced into the main file (for clarity's sake, this chapter refers to the file that has the include() or require() line as the *including* or *parent* file). Any code within the included file is treated as HTML unless it's within the PHP tags in the included file itself. This way, included files behave exactly as if you were running them in the Web browser.

There are many reasons to use included files. You could put your own defined functions into a common file (see Chapter 10, "Creating Functions," for information on writing your own functions). You might also want to place your database access information into a configuration file (see Chapter 12, "Introduction to Databases"). First, however, let's include the template files created in the preceding section of the chapter in order to make pages abide by a consistent design.

Figure 8.7 When an include() fails, warnings are issued, but the script continues to execute.

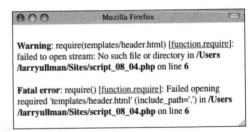

Figure 8.8 When a require() function call fails, warnings and errors are issued, and the script stops running.

To use external files:

1. Create a new document in your text editor or IDE.

2. Start with the initial PHP tags and add any comments (**Script 8.4**):

   ```
   <?php // Script 8.4 - index.php
   /* This is the home page for this
   → site.
   It uses templates to create the
   → layout. */
   ```

   Notice that, with the template system, the very first line of the script is the PHP tag. There's no need to begin with the initial HTML stuff, because it's now stored in the header.html file.

3. Address error management, if necessary.

   This topic is discussed in Chapter 3, "HTML Forms and PHP," and may or may not need to be addressed in your scripts. See that chapter for more; this will be the last time I specifically mention it in this chapter.

continues on next page

Script 8.4 Once the two included files have been created, the require() function incorporates them into the parent file to create the entire page on the fly.

```
1    <?php // Script 8.4 - index.php
2    /* This is the home page for this site.
3    It uses templates to create the layout. */
4
5    // Include the header:
6    require('templates/header.html');
7    // Leave the PHP section to display lots of HTML:
8    ?>
9
10   <h1>Welcome to the Elliott Smith Fan Club!</h1>
11   <p>Here's a whole lotta text. Here's a whole lotta text. Here's a whole lotta text. Here's a
     whole lotta text. Here's a whole lotta text. Here's a whole lotta text. Here's a whole lotta
     text. Here's a whole lotta text. Here's a whole lotta text. Here's a whole lotta text. </p>
12   <p>Here's a whole lotta text. Here's a whole lotta text. Here's a whole lotta text. Here's a
     whole lotta text. Here's a whole lotta text. Here's a whole lotta text. Here's a whole lotta
     text. Here's a whole lotta text. Here's a whole lotta text. Here's a whole lotta text. </p>
13
14   <?php // Return to PHP.
15   require('templates/footer.html'); // Include the footer.
16   ?>
```

4. Include the header file:

```
require('templates/header.html');
```

To use the template system, you include the header file here by invoking the `require()` function. Because the header file contains only HTML, all of its contents will be immediately sent to the Web browser as if they were part of this file. This line uses a relative path to refer to the included file (see the sidebar) and assumes that the file is stored in the `templates` directory.

5. Close the PHP section and create the page-specific content:

```
?>
<h1>Welcome to the Elliott Smith Fan
→ Club!</h1>
<p>Here's a whole lotta text.</p>
<p>Here's a whole lotta text.</p>
```

Because the bulk of this page is standard HTML, you exit out of the PHP section and then type the HTML (rather than using `print()` to send it to the Web browser). Again, there's more blather in the actual script than I've included here.

6. Create another PHP section and require the footer file:

```
<?php
require('templates/footer.html');
?>
```

To finish the page, you need to include the footer file (which displays the navigation and closes the HTML code). To do this, you create a new section of PHP—you can have multiple sections of PHP code within a script—and call the `require()` function again.

7. Save the file as `index.php`.

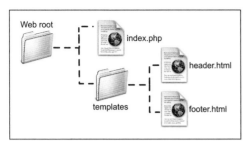

Figure 8.9 How the three files should be organized on your PHP-enabled server.

8. Create a folder called `templates` within the main Web document directory on your PHP-enabled computer or Web server.

   To further separate the design elements from the main content, the header and footer files go within their own directory.

9. Place `header.html` and `footer.html` in the `templates` directory you just created.

10. Place `index.php` in the same directory as the `templates` folder (**Figure 8.9**).

    The relative locations on the computer between the index page and the two HTML pages must be correct in order for the code to work.

11. Run `index.php` in your Web browser (**Figure 8.10**).

    The resulting page should look exactly like the original layout (Figure 8.3).

12. View the page's source code in your Web browser.

    The source code should be exactly like the source code of the `layout.html` script (Script 8.1), aside from the added comments for the script names and numbers.

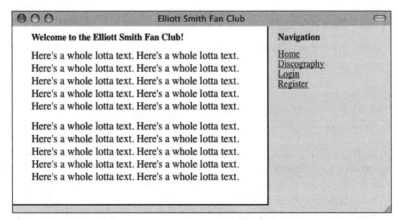

Figure 8.10 This page has been dynamically generated using included files.

USING EXTERNAL FILES

✔ Tips

■ All three files in this template system—
header.html, footer.html, and index.
php—must use the same encoding in order
to avoid problems (see Chapter 1, "Getting
Started with PHP," for more on encoding).
Each file's encoding must also match the
encoding established in the HTML code.

■ The require() and include() functions
can be used with or without parentheses:

```
require 'filename.html';
```

You might also use a variable that stores
the name of the file to be included:

```
require $filename;
```

File Navigation and Site Structure

To be able to use external files, you need to understand file navigation on your computer
or server. Just as you'd refer to other pages in HTML links or images in Web sites, you must
properly point your parent file to the included scripts. You can do this using *absolute* or *relative*
paths. An absolute path is a specific address, like the following:

```
require('C:\inetpub\wwwfiles\file.php');
require('/Users/larry/Sites/file.php');
```

As long as the included file isn't moved, an absolute path will always work.

A relative path indicates where the included file is in relation to the parent file. These examples
assume both are within the same directory:

```
require('file.php');
require('./file.php');
```

The included file can also be in a directory below the parent one, as in this chapter's example
(also see Figure 8.9):

```
require('templates/header.html');
```

Or, the included file could be in the directory above the parent:

```
require('../file.php');
```

Finally, a note on site structure: Once you divvy your Web application into multiple pieces, you
should begin thinking about arranging the files in appropriate folders. Complex sites might
have the main folder, another for images, one for administration files, and a special directory
for templates and included files. As long as you properly reference the files in your include()
or require() statements, structuring your applications will work fine and give the added benefit of making them easier to maintain.

- Both `include()` and `require()` have variations: `include_once()` and `require_once()`. Each is identical to its counterpart except that it allows the same file to be included only one time (in a parent script).

- If you see error messages like those in Figures 8.7 and 8.8, the parent script can't locate an included file. This problem is most likely caused by a misspelled included filename or an error in the path (for example, using `header.html` instead of `templates/header.html`).

- A file's extension is less important for included files because they aren't intended to be run directly. As a general rule of thumb, you'll be safe using `.html` for an included file containing only or mostly HTML (in which case the extension indicates it's an HTML-related file) and `.php` for included files containing only or mostly PHP. Some programmers use an `.inc` extension (for *include*), but security risks can be associated with this practice. For that reason, use the `.php` extension for any file containing sensitive information (like database access parameters). And, of course, always use the `.php` extension for any PHP script that will be executed directly.

- Another good use of an external file is to place your error settings code there so that the settings changes are applied to every page in the Web site.

Using Constants

Many of PHP's data types have already been discussed in this book: primarily numbers, strings, and arrays. Constants are another data type, but unlike variables, they retain their initial value throughout the course of a script. You can't change the value of a constant once it has been set!

You can only create a constant by assigning it a value. Unlike variables, which are assigned values via the assignment operator (=), constants are assigned values using the define() function:

```
define('CONSTANT_NAME', value);
```

Notice that—as a rule of thumb—constants are named using all capital letters, although this isn't required. Most important, constants don't use the initial dollar sign as variables do (because constants are not variables). Here are two constants:

```
define ('PI', 3.14);
define ('CURRENCY', 'euros');
```

Referring to constants is generally straightforward:

```
print CURRENCY;
number_format(PI, 1);
```

But using constants within quotation marks is more complicated. You can't print constants within single or double quotation marks, like this:

```
print "468 CURRENCY";
print '468 CURRENCY';
```

In both cases, the literal text *468 CURRENCY* will be sent to the Web browser. Instead, concatenation or multiple print() statements are used:

```
print '468 ' . CURRENCY;
```

or

```
print '468 ';
print CURRENCY;
```

Script 8.5 This script uses the same template system as index.php (Script 8.4) but also uses a constant to identify the page's title.

```
      ⬤ ⬤ ⬤              📄 Script
1     <?php // Script 8.5 - albums.php
2     /* This page lists Elliott Smith's
      discography. */
3
4     // Set the page title and include the
      header file:
5     define ('TITLE', 'Records by Elliott
      Smith');
6     require('templates/header.html');
7
8     // Leave the PHP section to display lots
      of HTML:
9     ?>
10
11    <h1>Elliott Smith's Albums</h1>
12    <p><ul>
13       <li>Roman Candle</li>
14       <li>Elliott Smith</li>
15       <li>Either/Or</li>
16       <li>XO</li>
17       <li>Figure 8</li>
18       <li>From a Basement On the Hill</li>
19       <li>New Moon</li>
20    </ul></p>
21
22    <?php // Return to PHP and include the
      footer:
23    require('templates/footer.html');
24    ?>
```

Not to confuse you, but along with the define() function for making constants is the defined() function, which returns TRUE if the submitted constant has been defined:

```
defined('CONSTANT_NAME'); // TRUE
defined('OOPS'); //FALSE
```

As an example of working with constants, you'll give the example application the ability to display a different title (which appears at the top of the browser window) for each page. To accomplish this, you'll define a constant in the parent script that will then be printed by the header file. This technique works because any variables or constants that exist in the parent document before the include() or require() call are available to the included file (it's as if the included file were part of the parent file).

To use constants:

1. Create a new PHP document in your text editor or IDE, beginning with the initial PHP tag (**Script 8.5**):

   ```
   <?php // Script 8.5 - albums.php
   ```

2. Define the page title as a constant:

   ```
   define ('TITLE', 'Records by Elliott
   → Smith');
   ```

   Here one constant is defined, named TITLE, and given the value *Records by Elliott Smith*.

   continues on next page

3. Include the header file:

```
require('templates/header.html');
```

This script uses the same header file as all the others, although you'll modify that file shortly to take the constant into account.

4. Close the PHP section and create the HTML:

```
?>
<h1>Elliott Smith's Albums</h1>
<p><ul>
   <li>Roman Candle</li>
   <li>Elliott Smith</li>
   <li>Either/Or</li>
   <li>XO</li>
   <li>Figure 8</li>
   <li>From a Basement On the Hill
   → </li>
   <li>New Moon</li>
</ul></p>
```

The content here is simple but serves the page's purpose nicely.

5. Create a new PHP section that includes the footer file:

```
<?php
require('templates/footer.html');
?>
```

6. Save the file as albums.php.

To take advantage of the constant, you now need to modify the header.html file.

Script 8.6 The header.html file is modified so that it can set the page title value based on the existence and value of a constant.

```
1    <!DOCTYPE html PUBLIC "-//W3C//DTD XHTML
     1.0 Transitional//EN"
2        "http://www.w3.org/TR/xhtml1/DTD/
     xhtml1-transitional.dtd">
3    <html xmlns="http://www.w3.org/1999/
     xhtml" xml:lang="en" lang="en">
4    <head>
5        <meta http-equiv="Content-Type"
         content="text/html; charset=utf-8"/>
6        <title><?php // Print the page title.
7        if (defined('TITLE')) { // Is the
         title defined?
8            print TITLE;
9        } else { // The title is not defined.
10           print 'Elliott Smith Fan Club';
11       }
12       ?></title>
13
14       <style type="text/css">
15           body {
16               margin:0px 0px 0px 0px;
17               background: #9F9;
18               }
19           #leftcontent {
20               float:left;
21               width:67%;
22               background:#fff;
23               border-right:2px solid #000;
24               border-bottom:2px solid #000;
25               margin-right:15px;
26               padding-bottom:20px;
27               }
28           p,h1,pre {
29               margin:0px 30px 10px 30px;
30               }
31           h1 {
32               font-size:14px;
33               padding-top:10px;
34               }
35           #rightcontent p {
36               font-size:14px;
37               margin-left:0px;
38               }
39       </style>
40
41   </head>
42   <body>
43   <div id="leftcontent">
44   <!-- Script 8.6 - header.html -->
45   <!-- BEGIN CHANGEABLE CONTENT. -->
```

To print out a constant:

1. Open header.html (Script 8.2) in your text editor or IDE.

2. Delete the *Elliott Smith Fan Club* text that appears between the title tags (line 6).

   Now that the page title will be determined on a page-by-page basis, you don't need it to be hard-coded into the page.

3. In the place of the deleted text (between the title tags), add the following **(Script 8.6)**:

```php
<?php
if (defined('TITLE')) {
    print TITLE;
} else {
    print 'Elliott Smith Fan Club';
}
?>
```

   To have PHP create the page title, you need to begin by starting a section of PHP code between the title tags. Then you use a conditional to see if the TITLE constant has been defined. If it has, you print its value as the page title. If TITLE hasn't been defined, you print a default title.

4. Save the file as header.html.

5. Upload albums.php and header.html to your PHP-enabled server. The new PHP script, albums.php, should go in the same directory as index.php; header.html should replace the previous version, in the same directory—templates—as footer.html.

continues on next page

6. Run `albums.php` in your Web browser (**Figure 8.11**).

7. View `index.php` (the home page) in your Web browser (**Figure 8.12**).

8. If you want, add the constant definition line to `index.php` to change its title.

✔ Tips

■ The formal rules for naming constants are exactly like those for variables except for the omission of a dollar sign. Constant names must begin with a letter; can contain any combination of letters, numbers, and the underscore; and are case-sensitive.

■ PHP runs with several predefined constants. These include `PHP_VERSION` (the version of PHP running) and `PHP_OS` (the operating system of the server).

■ In Chapter 9, "Cookies and Sessions," you'll learn about another constant, `SID` (which stands for *session ID*).

■ An added benefit of using constants is that they're global in scope. This concept will mean more to you after you read the section "Understanding Variable Scope" of Chapter 10.

■ Not only can the value of a constant never be changed, a constant can't be deleted. Also, unlike arrays, a constant can only ever contain a single value, like a string or a number.

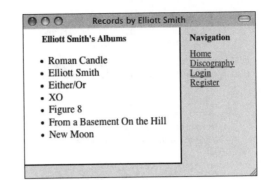

Figure 8.11 The albums page uses a PHP constant to create its title.

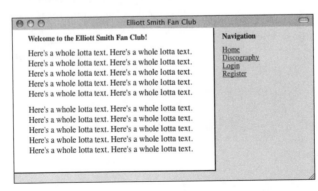

Figure 8.12 Because the index page didn't have a TITLE constant defined in it, the default page title is used (thanks to the conditional in Script 8.6).

Table 8.1

Date( ) Function Formatting

CHARACTER	MEANING	EXAMPLE
Y	Year as 4 digits	2004
y	Year as 2 digits	04
L	Is it a leap year?	1 (for yes)
n	Month as 1 or 2 digits	2
m	Month as 2 digits	02
F	Month	February
M	Month as 3 letters	Feb
j	Day of the month as 1 or 2 digits	8
d	Day of the month as 2 digits	08
l (lowercase L)	Day of the week	Monday
D	Day of the week as 3 letters	Mon
w	Day of the week as a single digit	0 (Sunday)
z	Day of the year: 0 to 365	189
t	Number of days in the month	31
S	English ordinal suffix for a day, as 2 characters	rd
g	Hour; 12-hour format as 1 or 2 digits	6
G	Hour; 24-hour format as 1 or 2 digits	18
h	Hour; 12-hour format as 2 digits	06
H	Hour; 24-hour format as 2 digits	18
i	Minutes	45
s	Seconds	18
u	Microseconds	1234
a	am or pm	am
A	AM or PM	PM
U	Seconds since the epoch	1048623008
e	Timezone	UTC
I (capital i)	Is it daylight savings?	1 (for yes)
O	Difference from GMT	+0600

Working with the Date and Time

PHP has a few functions for working with the date and time, the most important of which is date(). The only thing the date() function does is return date and time information in a format based on the arguments it's fed, but you'd be surprised how useful that can be! The basic usage of the date() function is just

```
date('formatting');
```

A long list of possible options is available for formatting, as indicated in **Table 8.1**. These parameters can also be combined—for example, date('l F j, Y') returns *Friday January 26, 2004*.

The date() function can take another argument called a *timestamp*. A timestamp is a number representing how many seconds have passed since midnight on January 1, 1970—a moment referred to as the *epoch*. The time() function returns the timestamp for the current moment. The mktime() function can return a timestamp for a particular time and date:

```
mktime(hour, minute, second, month, day,
→ year);
```

So the code

```
$ts = mktime(12, 30, 0, 11, 5, 2009);
```

assigns to $timestamp the number of seconds from the epoch to 12:30 on November 5, 2009. That number can then be fed into the date() function like so:

```
date('D', $ts);
```

This returns *Thu*, which is the three-letter format for that day of the week.

As of PHP 5.1, you should establish the server's time zone prior to calling any date- or time-related function. To do so, use:

```
date_default_timezone_set(timezone);
```

The *timezone* value is a string like *America/New_York* or *Pacific/Auckland*. There are too many to list here (Africa alone has over 50), but see the PHP manual for them all. If you don't take this step, you might see errors (**Figure 8.13**).

To demonstrate the date() function, let's update the footer file so that it shows the current date and time.

To use date():

1. Open footer.html (Script 8.3) in your text editor or IDE.

2. Before the closing </div> tag, add the following (**Script 8.7**):

   `<p><em><?php`

   The initial HTML tags format the date and time slightly, putting them in italics (thanks to the emphasis tag). Then you open a PHP section so that you can call the date() function.

3. Establish the time zone:

   `date_default_timezone_set('America/`
   `↪ New_York');`

   Before calling date(), the time zone has to be set. To find yours, see www.php.net/timezones.

Script 8.7 The modified footer.html file uses the date() function to print the current date and time.

```
1    <!-- END CHANGEABLE CONTENT. -->
2    <!-- Script 8.7 - footer.html -->
3    </div>
4
5    <div id="rightcontent">
6        <h1>Navigation</h1>
7        <p><a href="index.php">Home</a><br />
8        <a href="albums.php">Discography
         </a><br />
9        <a href="login.php">Login</a><br />
10       <a href="register.php">Register</a></p>
11
12       <p><em><?php // Print the current date
         and time:
13       // Set the timezone:
14       date_default_timezone_set('America/
         New_York');
15
16       // Now print the date and time:
17       print date('g:i a l F j');
18       ?><em></p>
19
20   </div>
21
22   </body>
23   </html>
```

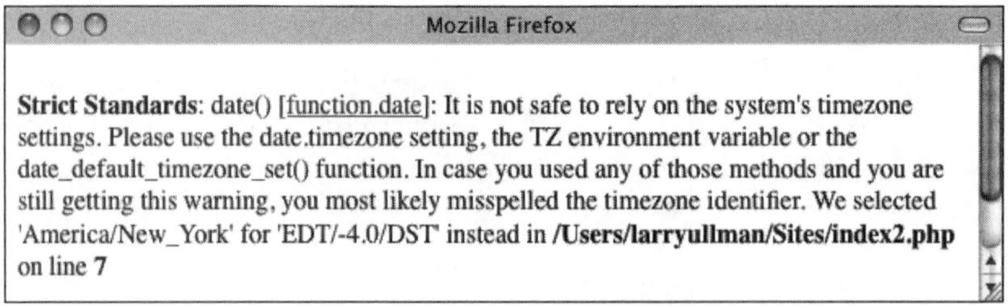

Figure 8.13 As of PHP 5.1, notices will be generated when a date or time function is used without the time zone being set.

> **Strict Standards**: date() [function.date]: It is not safe to rely on the system's timezone settings. Please use the date.timezone setting, the TZ environment variable or the date_default_timezone_set() function. In case you used any of those methods and you are still getting this warning, you most likely misspelled the timezone identifier. We selected 'America/New_York' for 'EDT/-4.0/DST' instead in **/Users/larryullman/Sites/index2.php** on line **7**

4. Use the date() function to print out today's date and time:

```
print date('g:i a l F j');
```

Using the formatting parameters from Table 8.1, the date() function will return a value like *4:15 pm Sunday February 22*. This value will immediately be printed.

5. Close the PHP section and finish the HTML code:

```
?><em></p>
```

6. Save the file as footer.html, place it in the templates directory of your PHP-enabled server, and test it in your Web browser (**Figure 8.14**).

✔ Tips

■ Because PHP is a server-side technology, these functions reflect the date and time on the server. To get the time on the client (in other words, on the computer where the Web browser viewing the page is located), you must use JavaScript.

■ The server's time zone can also be set in the PHP configuration file (see Appendix A, "Installation and Configuration"). Establishing the time zone there is generally a better idea than doing so on a script-by-script basis.

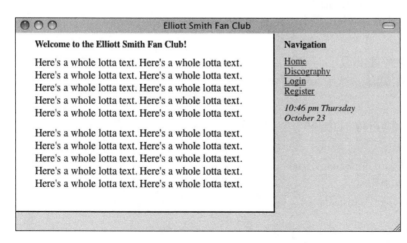

Figure 8.14 The Web site now displays the date and time in the sidebar, thanks to the date() function.

WORKING WITH THE DATE AND TIME

Handling HTML Forms with PHP, Revisited

All the examples in this book so far have used two separate scripts for handling HTML forms: one that displayed the form and another that received and processed the form's data. There's certainly nothing wrong with this method, but there are advantages to having the entire process in one script. To make a page both display and handle a form, use a conditional:

```
if (/* form has been submitted */) {
    // Handle the form.
} else {
    // Display the form.
}
```

To determine if the form has been submitted, you can check whether any variable is set:

```
if (isset($_POST['something'])) { …
```

However, if the user submitted the form without completing it, that variable may not be set. For this and other reasons, I like to include a hidden input in my forms that I can check for:

```
<input type="hidden" name="submitted"
→ value="true" />
```

Again, the only purpose of this hidden input is to reliably indicate that the form has been submitted. To check for that, the handling PHP code would use this conditional:

```
if (isset($_POST['submitted'])) { …
```

As an example of this, you'll create the basics of a login form.

To use one page to display and handle a form:

1. Begin a new PHP document in your text editor or IDE (**Script 8.8**):

   ```
   <?php // Script 8.8 - login.php
   ```

continues on page 210

Script 8.8 The login page serves two purposes. It displays the login form (Figure 8.15) and handles its submission (Figures 8.16, 8.17, and 8.18).

```php
1    <?php // Script 8.8 - login.php
2    /* This page lets people log into the site (in theory). */
3
4    // Set the page title and include the header file:
5    define('TITLE', 'Login');
6    require('templates/header.html');
7
8    // Print some introductory text:
9    print '<h1>Login Form</h1>
10       <p>Users who are logged in can take advantage of certain features like this, that, and the
         other thing.</p>';
11
12   // Check if the form has been submitted:
13   if ( isset($_POST['submitted']) ) {
14
15       // Handle the form:
16       if ( (!empty($_POST['email'])) && (!empty($_POST['password'])) ) {
17
18           if ( (strtolower($_POST['email']) == 'me@example.com') && ($_POST['password'] ==
             'testpass') ) { // Correct!
19
20               print '<p>You are logged in!<br />Now you can blah, blah, blah...</p>';
21
22           } else { // Incorrect!
23
24               print '<p>The submitted email address and password do not match those on file!<br
                 />Go back and try again.</p>';
25
26           }
27
28       } else { // Forgot a field.
29
30           print '<p>Please make sure you enter both an email address and a password!<br />Go back
             and try again.</p>';
31
32       }
33
34   } else { // Display the form.
35
36       print '<form action="login.php" method="post">
37       <p>Email Address: <input type="text" name="email" size="20" /></p>
38       <p>Password: <input type="password" name="password" size="20" /></p>
39       <p><input type="submit" name="submit" value="Log In!" /></p>
40       <input type="hidden" name="submitted" value="true" />
41       </form>';
42
43   }
44
45   require('templates/footer.html'); // Need the footer.
46   ?>
```

2. Define the page title as a constant and include the header file:

```
define('TITLE', 'Login');
require('templates/header.html');
```

Using the constant system developed earlier in the chapter, give this page its own unique page title.

3. Add some introductory text:

```
print '<h1>Login Form</h1>
    <p>Users who are logged in can
    → take advantage of certain
    → features like this, that, and
    → the other thing.</p>';
```

This text, which appears outside of the main conditional, will always show in the Web browser, whether the form is being displayed or has been submitted. Because the core of this script revolves around a PHP conditional, you print out the HTML from PHP rather than exit out of the PHP code as you did in the previous two examples (`index.php` and `albums.php`).

4. Begin the conditional to check whether the form has been submitted:

```
if ( isset($_POST['submitted']) ) {
```

To test whether the form has been submitted, check whether the `$_POST['submitted']` variable has a value (is set). This will be a hidden variable with a preset value, so it will always be set if the form has been submitted.

5. Create a nested pair of conditionals to process the form data:

```
if ( (!empty($_POST['email'])) &&
→ (!empty($_POST['password'])) ) {
  if ( (strtolower($_POST['email'])
→ == 'me@example.com') &&
→ ($_POST['password'] ==
→ 'testpass') ) {
    print '<p>You are logged in!
→ <br />Now you can blah, blah,
→ blah...</p>';
  } else {
    print '<p>The submitted email
→ address and password do not
→ match those on file!<br />Go
→ back and try again.</p>';
  }
} else {
  print '<p>Please make sure you
→ enter both an email address and
→ a password!<br />Go back and try
→ again.</p>';
}
```

These conditionals handle the form data. The first conditional checks that both the email address and password variables have values. If they don't, a message is displayed (*Please make sure...*). Within that first conditional, another conditional checks whether the email address is equal to *me@example.com* and the password is equal to *testpass*. If so, let's say the user is logged in (it would be too advanced at this juncture to store and retrieve user information). Otherwise, a message indicates that the wrong values were entered.

Be certain to use the equals operator (==) here and not the assignment operator (=) in this conditional, which is a common mistake. Also, in case the user enters their address as *Me@example.com*, or any other capitalized permutation, the `strtolower()` function is first applied to the email address, prior to checking for equality.

continues on next page

6. Complete the main conditional:

```
} else { // Display the form.
   print '<form action="login.php"
   → method="post">
   <p>Email Address: <input
   → type="text" name="email"
   → size="20" /></p>
   <p>Password: <input type=
   → "password" name="password"
   → size="20" /></p>
   <p><input type="submit" name=
   → "submit" value="Log In!" /></p>
   <input type="hidden" name=
   → "submitted" value="true" />
   </form>';
}
```

This concludes the main conditional, which checks whether the form has been submitted. If it hasn't been, then the form is displayed. The form itself is very simple (**Figure 8.15**).

In order for this process to work—where the same page both handles and displays the form—the name attribute of your hidden input must exactly match the name of the variable used as the conditional (and it's case-sensitive, remember).

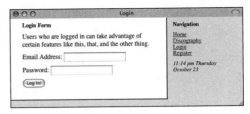

Figure 8.15 This simple login page takes an email address and a password.

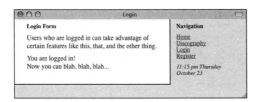

Figure 8.16 Upon successfully logging in, the user sees this message.

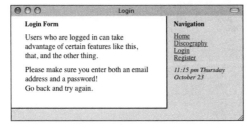

Figure 8.17 Failure to submit either an email address or a password results in this message.

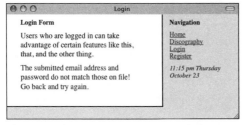

Figure 8.18 If either the email address or the password doesn't match that in the script, the user sees this error message.

7. Require the footer file and complete the PHP page:

```
require('templates/footer.html');
?>
```

8. Save the file as login.php, place it in the same directory as index.php, and test it in your Web browser (**Figures 8.16**, **8.17**, and **8.18**).

✔ Tips

■ In the real world, I'd probably add some CSS formatting to the error messages so that they stand out. The next section of the chapter will include this feature.

■ This little trick of checking for the presence of a hidden input can be confusing. This works because the same script— login.php—will be accessed twice by the user. The first time the form will not have been submitted, so the main conditional will be FALSE and the form will be displayed. Then the page will be accessed again after the user clicks submit, at which point the conditional becomes TRUE.

■ If you want a page to handle a form and then immediately display the form again, do this:

```
if (isset($_POST['submitted'])) { …
    // Handle the form.
}
// Display the form.
```

Making Forms Sticky

A *sticky* form remembers values entered into it. A common example is a search engine, which always displays your terms in the search box, even when showing the results of the search. You might also want to use sticky forms on occasions where the user failed to complete a form accurately and therefore must resubmit it.

From a technological standpoint, sticky forms work by having your form element values be predetermined. You can do this by setting the value input when you create the form:

```
<input type="text" name="first_name"
→ value="Stephanie" />
```

To have PHP preset that value, print the appropriate variable between the quotation marks:

```
<input type="text" name="first_name"
→ value="<?php print $first_name; ?>" />
```

The first time the form is run, the PHP code prints nothing (because the variable has no value). If the form is displayed again after submission, values that the user originally entered in the form input will be displayed there automatically. That's the basic idea, but a more professional implementation would address two things...

First, it's best not to refer to variables that don't exist, so to avoid that, check that the variable is set before printing it. Second, certain characters that could be in a submitted value will cause problems if printed as a form element's value. To prevent such problems, apply the htmlspecialchars() function (discussed in Chapter 5, "Using Strings"). With this in mind, a longer but better version of this code is:

```
<input type="text" name="first_name"
→ value="<?php if (isset($first_name)
→ { print htmlspecialchars($first_name);
→ } ?>" />
```

To demonstrate, you'll create the shell of a registration form (**Figure 8.19**).

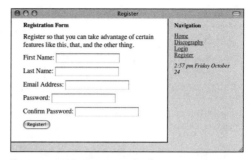

Figure 8.19 The registration form as the user first sees it.

Script 8.9 The registration form uses a so-called *sticky* feature so that it recalls the values entered into it.

```
         ● ● ●                   📄 Script
1    <?php // Script 8.9 - register.php
2    /* This page lets people register for the
     site (in theory). */
3
4    // Set the page title and include the
     header file:
5    define('TITLE', 'Register');
6    require('templates/header.html');
7
8    // Print some introductory text:
9    print '<h1>Registration Form</h1>
10      <p>Register so that you can take
        advantage of certain features like
        this, that, and the other thing.</p>';
11
12   // Add the CSS:
13   print '<style type="text/css" media=
     "screen">
14      .error { color: red; }
15   </style>';
16
17   // Check if the form has been submitted:
18   if ( isset($_POST['submitted']) ) {
19
20      $problem = FALSE; // No problems so far.
21
22      // Check for each value...
23      if (empty($_POST['first_name'])) {
24          $problem = TRUE;
25          print '<p class="error">Please
            enter your first name!</p>';
26      }
27
28      if (empty($_POST['last_name'])) {
29          $problem = TRUE;
30          print '<p class="error">Please
            enter your last name!</p>';
31      }
32
33      if (empty($_POST['email'])) {
34          $problem = TRUE;
35          print '<p class="error">Please
            enter your email address!</p>';
36      }
37
```

(script continues on next page)

To make a sticky form:

1. Create a new PHP script in your text editor or IDE (**Script 8.9**):

   ```
   <?php // Script 8.9 - register.php
   ```

2. Set the page title and include the HTML header:

   ```
   define('TITLE', 'Register');
   require('templates/header.html');
   ```

3. Add some introductory text and define a CSS class:

   ```
   print '<h1>Registration Form</h1>
       <p>Register so that you can take
   → advantage of certain features
   → like this, that, and the other
   → thing.</p>';
   print '<style type="text/css"
   → media="screen">
       .error { color: red; }
   </style>';
   ```

   So that the error messages, generated by improperly completing the registration form, stand out, a CSS class is defined that colors the applicable text in red. Although CSS is normally defined in the page's head, you can put it anywhere.

4. Check whether the form has been submitted:

   ```
   if ( isset($_POST['submitted']) ) {
   ```

   Like the login page, this script both displays and handles the registration form. After the form is submitted, there will be a $_POST['submitted'] variable that is set, making this conditional TRUE, indicating that the form data should be validated.

   You don't have to use this technique to make a sticky form, but it makes the process significantly easier.

continues on page 217

Script 8.9 *continued*

```
38     if (empty($_POST['password1'])) {
39         $problem = TRUE;
40         print '<p class="error">Please enter a password!</p>';
41     }
42
43     if ($_POST['password1'] != $_POST['password2']) {
44         $problem = TRUE;
45         print '<p class="error">Your password did not match your confirmed password!</p>';
46     }
47
48     if (!$problem) { // If there weren't any problems...
49
50         // Print a message:
51         print '<p>You are now registered!<br />Okay, you are not really registered but...</p>';
52
53         // Clear the posted values:
54         $_POST = array();
55
56     } else { // Forgot a field.
57
58         print '<p class="error">Please try again!</p>';
59
60     }
61
62 } // End of handle form IF.
63
64 // Create the form:
65 ?>
66 <form action="register.php" method="post">
67
68 <p>First Name: <input type="text" name="first_name" size="20" value="<?php if (isset($_POST
   ['first_name'])) { print htmlspecialchars($_POST['first_name']); } ?>" /></p>
69
70 <p>Last Name: <input type="text" name="last_name" size="20" value="<?php if (isset($_POST
   ['last_name'])) { print htmlspecialchars($_POST['last_name']); } ?>" /></p>
71
72 <p>Email Address: <input type="text" name="email" size="20" value="<?php if (isset($_POST
   ['email'])) { print htmlspecialchars($_POST['email']); } ?>" /></p>
73
74 <p>Password: <input type="password" name="password1" size="20" /></p>
75 <p>Confirm Password: <input type="password" name="password2" size="20" /></p>
76 <p><input type="submit" name="submit" value="Register!" /></p>
77 <input type="hidden" name="submitted" value="true" />
78 </form>
79
80 <?php require('templates/footer.html'); // Need the footer. ?>
```

5. Create a flag variable:

```
$problem = FALSE;
```

The $problem variable will be used to indicate whether a problem occurred. Specifically, you want to make sure that every form input has been filled out before you formally register the user. Initially, this variable is set to FALSE, because no problems have occurred.

6. Check that a first name was entered:

```
if (empty($_POST['first_name'])) {
    $problem = TRUE;
    print '<p class="error">Please
→ enter your first name!</p>';
}
```

As a simple test to determine whether the user has entered a first name value, you check that the variable isn't empty. (This technique was first discussed in Chapter 6, "Control Structures.") If the variable is empty, then you indicate a problem by setting that variable to TRUE and print an error message. The error message has a class type of *error*, so that the CSS formatting is applied.

7. Repeat the validation for the last name and email address:

```
if (empty($_POST['last_name'])) {
    $problem = TRUE;
    print '<p class="error">Please
→ enter your last name!</p>';
}
if (empty($_POST['email'])) {
    $problem = TRUE;
    print '<p class="error">Please
→ enter your email address!</p>';
}
```

Both of these checks are variations on the username validation routine.

continues on next page

MAKING FORMS STICKY

8. Validate the passwords:

```
if (empty($_POST['password1'])) {
    $problem = TRUE;
    print '<p class="error">Please
    → enter a password!</p>';
}
if ($_POST['password1'] != $_POST
→ ['password2']) {
    $problem = TRUE;
    print '<p class="error">Your
    → password did not match your
    → confirmed password!</p>';
}
```

The password validation requires two conditionals. The first checks whether the $_POST['password1'] variable is empty. The second checks whether the $_POST['password1'] variable isn't equal to the $_POST['password2'] variable. You don't need to see if $_POST['password2'] is empty because if it is and $_POST['password1'] isn't, the second conditional will catch that problem. If $_POST['password2'] and $_POST['password1'] are both empty, the first conditional will catch the situation.

9. Check whether a problem occurred:

```
if (!$problem) {
    print '<p>You are now registered!
    → <br />Okay, you are not really
    → registered but...</p>';
    $_POST = array();
```

If there were no problems, the $problem variable is still FALSE, and the initial condition here is TRUE (the condition being that $problem has a value of FALSE). In that case, the registration process would take place. The formal registration process, where the data is stored in a file or database, has not yet been developed, so a simple message appears in its stead here.

Next, the $_POST variable is assigned the value of array(). This line has the effect of wiping out the contents of the $_POST variable (i.e., resetting it as an empty array). I take this step only upon a successful (theoretical) registration so that the values are not redisplayed in the registration form (e.g., see Step 12).

10. Complete the conditionals:

```
} else { // Forgot a field.
    print '<p class="error">Please
    → try again!</p>';
}
} // End of handle form IF.
```

The else clause applies if a problem occurred, in which case the user is asked to complete the form again.

11. Begin the HTML form:

```
?>
<form action="register.php"
→ method="post">
```

Unlike the login example, this page always displays the form. Therefore, the form isn't part of any conditional. Also, because there's a lot of HTML to be generated, I think it'll be easier to leave the PHP section of the page and just output the HTML directly.

12. Create the sticky first name input:

```
<p>First Name: <input type="text"
→ name="first_name" size="20"
→ value="<?php if (isset($_POST
→ ['first_name'])) { print
→ htmlspecialchars($_POST
→ ['first_name']); } ?>" /></p>
```

continues on next page

MAKING FORMS STICKY

To make the first name input sticky, you preset its value attribute by printing out the $_POST['first_name'] variable, but only if it's set. The conditional is therefore put within PHP tags within the HTML's value section of the form element. As already mentioned, the htmlspecialchars() function is used to handle any potentially problematic characters.

13. Repeat the process for the last name and email address:

```
<p>Last Name: <input type="text"
→ name="last_name" size="20"
→ value="<?php if (isset($_POST
→ ['last_name'])) { print
→ htmlspecialchars($_POST['last_
→ name']); } ?>" /></p>
<p>Email Address: <input type=
→ "text" name="email" size="20"
→ value="<?php if (isset($_POST
→ ['email'])) { print
→ htmlspecialchars($_POST
→ ['email']); } ?>" /></p>
```

These are variations on Step 12, switching the variable names as appropriate.

14. Add the rest of the form:

```
<p>Password: <input type="password"
→ name="password1" size="20" /></p>
<p>Confirm Password: <input
→ type="password" name="password2"
→ size="20" /></p>
<p><input type="submit" name=
→ "submit" value="Register!" /></p>
<input type="hidden" name=
→ "submitted" value="true" />
</form>
```

You can't preset a value for a password input, so there's no point in trying. Then you have the submit button and the hidden form input (to trigger the form validation in the PHP code).

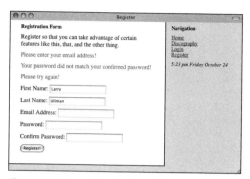

Figure 8.20 The registration form indicates any problems and retains the form values, except for the passwords.

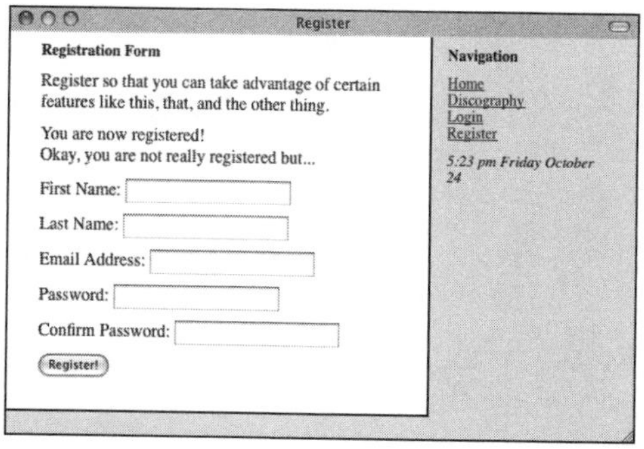

Figure 8.21 The registration form after the user successfully fills it out.

15. Complete the PHP page:

```
<?php require('templates/footer.
→ html'); ?>
```

The last step is to include the HTML footer.

16. Save the file as `register.php`, place it in the proper directory on your PHP-enabled server, and test it in your Web browser (**Figures 8.20** and **8.21**).

✔ Tips

- According to (X)HTML rules, you must quote all attributes in form inputs. Specifically, you should use double quotation marks. If you don't quote your values, any spaces in them mark the end of the value (for example, *Larry Ullman* will display as just *Larry* in the form input).

- To preset the status of radio buttons or check boxes as checked, add the code `checked="checked"` to their input tag:

```
<input type="checkbox" name=
→ "interests[]" value="Skiing"
→ checked="checked" />
```

Of course, you'd need to use a PHP conditional to see if that text should be added to the element's definition.

- To preselect a pull-down menu, use `selected="selected"`:

```
<select name="year">
<option value="2009">2009</option>
<option value="2010" selected=
→ "selected">2010</option>
</select>
```

Again, you'd need to use a PHP conditional to see if that text should be added to the element's definition.

- To preset the value of a textarea, place the value between the `textarea` tags:

```
<textarea name="comments" rows="10"
cols="50">preset value</textarea>
```

Sending Email

Sending email using PHP is theoretically simple, merely requiring the `mail()` function. The `mail()` function uses the server's email application (such as sendmail on Unix or Mac OS X) or an SMTP (Simple Mail Transfer Protocol) server to send out the messages. The basic usage of this function is:

```
mail(to, subject, body);
```

The first argument is the email address (or addresses, separated by commas) to which the email should be sent. The second argument establishes the message's subject line, and the third argument creates the message's content.

This function can take another argument through which you can add more details (*additional headers*) to the email, including a *From* address, email priority, and carbon-copy addresses:

```
mail('someone@example.com', 'Test
→ Email', 'This is a test email', 'From:
→ 'email@address.com');
```

Although this is theoretically easy, actual usage of this function in real-world code can be far more complex. For starters, setting up your own computer to send out email can be hard (again, see the sidebar). Second, you should take some steps to prevent malicious people from trying to use your forms to send out spam. Unfortunately the necessary steps are well beyond the scope of this beginner's book, but I discuss it in my *PHP 6 and MySQL 5 for Dynamic Web Sites: Visual QuickPro Guide* (Peachpit Press, 2007) and online in my forums (`www.DMCInsights.com/phorum/`).

All that being said, let's add a `mail()` function call to the registration page so that you get a sense of how the function might be used.

Script 8.10 In PHP, you can send email by calling the `mail()` function.

```
        ⊖ ○ ⊖                    📄 Script
1    <?php // Script 8.10 - register.php #2
2    /* This page lets people register for the
     site (in theory). */
3
4    // Set the page title and include the
     header file:
5    define('TITLE', 'Register');
6    require('templates/header.html');
7
8    // Print some introductory text:
9    print '<h1>Registration Form</h1>
10       <p>Register so that you can take
         advantage of certain features like
         this, that, and the other thing.</p>';
11
12   // Add the CSS:
13   print '<style type="text/css" media=
     "screen">
14       .error { color: red; }
15   </style>';
16
17   // Check if the form has been submitted:
18   if ( isset($_POST['submitted']) ) {
19
20       $problem = FALSE; // No problems so
         far.
21
22       // Check for each value...
23       if (empty($_POST['first_name'])) {
24           $problem = TRUE;
25           print '<p class="error">Please
             enter your first name!</p>';
26       }
27
28       if (empty($_POST['last_name'])) {
29           $problem = TRUE;
30           print '<p class="error">Please
             enter your last name!</p>';
31       }
32
33       if (empty($_POST['email'])) {
34           $problem = TRUE;
35           print '<p class="error">Please
             enter your email address!</p>';
36       }
37
```

(script continues on next page)

To send email with PHP:

1. Open `register.php` (Script 8.9) in your text editor or IDE.

2. After the registration message (line 51), add the following (**Script 8.10**):

   ```
   $body = "Thank you for registering
   → with the Elliott Smith fan club!
   → Your password is '{$_POST
   → ['password1']}'.";

   mail($_POST['email'], 'Registration
   → Confirmation', $body, 'From:
   → admin@example.com');
   ```

   Sometimes the easiest way to use this function is to establish the body as a variable and then feed it into the `mail()` function. The message itself is sent to the address with which the user registered, with the subject *Registration Confirmation*, from the address *admin@example.com*. If you'll be running this on a live server, you should use an actual email address for that site as the *from* value.

continues on page 225

Script 8.10 *continued*

```
███ ⬤                          Script
38    if (empty($_POST['password1'])) {
39        $problem = TRUE;
40        print '<p class="error">Please enter a password!</p>';
41    }
42
43    if ($_POST['password1'] != $_POST['password2']) {
44        $problem = TRUE;
45        print '<p class="error">Your password did not match your confirmed password!</p>';
46    }
47
48    if (!$problem) { // If there weren't any problems...
49
50        // Print a message:
51        print '<p>You are now registered!<br />Okay, you are not really registered but...</p>';
52
53        // Send the email:
54        $body = "Thank you for registering with the Elliott Smith fan club! Your password is
          '{$_POST['password1']}'.";
55        mail($_POST['email'], 'Registration Confirmation', $body, 'From: admin@example.com');
56
57        // Clear the posted values:
58        $_POST = array();
59
60    } else { // Forgot a field.
61
62        print '<p class="error">Please try again!</p>';
63
64    }
65
66  } // End of handle form IF.
67
68  // Create the form:
69  ?>
70  <form action="register.php" method="post">
71
72  <p>First Name: <input type="text" name="first_name" size="20" value="<?php if (isset($_POST
    ['first_name'])) { print htmlspecialchars($_POST['first_name']); } ?>" /></p>
73
74  <p>Last Name: <input type="text" name="last_name" size="20" value="<?php if (isset($_POST
    ['last_name'])) { print htmlspecialchars($_POST['last_name']); } ?>" /></p>
75
76  <p>Email Address: <input type="text" name="email" size="20" value="<?php if (isset($_POST
    ['email'])) { print htmlspecialchars($_POST['email']); } ?>" /></p>
77
78  <p>Password: <input type="password" name="password1" size="20" /></p>
79  <p>Confirm Password: <input type="password" name="password2" size="20" /></p>
80  <p><input type="submit" name="submit" value="Register!" /></p>
81  <input type="hidden" name="submitted" value="true" />
82  </form>
83
84  <?php require('templates/footer.html'); // Need the footer. ?>
```

Figure 8.22 Testing the registration form again.

Figure 8.23 This email was sent by the PHP script upon successful pseudo-registration.

3. Save the file, place it in the proper directory of your PHP- and email-enabled server, and test it in your Web browser (**Figure 8.22**).

4. Check your email for the message (**Figure 8.23**).

✔ Tips

- If you have problems receiving the PHP-sent email, start by confirming that the mail server works on its own without involving PHP. Then make sure you're using a valid *from* address. Finally, try using different recipient addresses and keep an eye on your junk folder to see that the message isn't getting put there (if applicable).

- It's possible to send email with attachments or HTML email, although doing so requires far more sophisticated coding (normally involving classes and objects). Fortunately, a number of programmers have already developed workable solutions that are available for use. See Appendix B, "Resources and Next Steps," for Web sites that may be of assistance.

- The `mail()` function returns a value (*1* or *0*) indicating its successful use. This value only indicates whether PHP was able to *attempt* to send the email (by using whatever email system is in place). There's no easy way to use PHP to tell whether an email address is valid or whether the end user received the message.

continues on next page

- To send an email to multiple addresses, either use the *CC* parameter or separate each *TO* address with a comma.

- To create new lines within the email body, either create the message over multiple lines or use the newline character (\n) within double quotation marks.

- If you want to send multiple headers in addition to the *From* address, separate them with a combination of \r\n:

```
mail ('email@example.com',
→ 'Testing', $body, "From:email@
→ example.org\r\nBcc:hidden@example.
→ net,third@example.com");
```

Configuring Your Server to Send Email

Sending email with PHP is easy, as long as your Web server (or computer) is set up to send email. If you're using a Web hosting service or your own Unix computer (like Linux), this shouldn't be a problem. However, if you're running your own Windows or Mac OS X machine—as you may well be—this could be a sticking point.

To start, go ahead and try this example using a valid email address. If you don't receive the email, see Appendix A for information about getting mail() to work. I'll also add that I almost never worry about getting PHP on my own computer to send out emails because I'll never be running actual, live Web sites from my computer. In other words, why waste time getting something to work that you'll never end up using (whereas getting PHP to send out email on a live server does matter).

Output Buffering

There are a handful of functions that you'll use in this chapter and the next that can only be called if nothing has been sent to the Web browser. These functions include header( ), setcookie( ), and session_start( ). If you use them after the Web browser has already received some text, HTML, or even a blank space, you'll get a dreaded *headers already sent* error message (**Figure 8.24**).

One solution that I recommend for beginning PHP developers is to make use of *output buffering* (also called output control). In a normal PHP script, any HTML outside of the PHP tags is immediately sent to the Web browser, as is all printed content, as soon as the print( ) statement is executed. With output buffering, the HTML and printed data—the output—will instead be put into a buffer (i.e., memory). At the end of the script, the buffer will then be sent to the Web browser, or if appropriate, the buffer can be cleared without being sent to the Web browser. There are many reasons to use output buffering, but for beginners, one benefit is that you can use certain functions without worrying about headers already sent errors. Although you haven't dealt with any of these functions yet, this chapter introduces output buffering

continues on next page

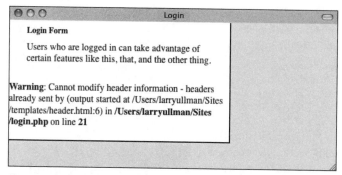

Figure 8.24 If the browser receives any HTML prior to a header( ) call, you'll see this error message.

now because it will greatly reduce errors as you begin using headers (in the next section of this chapter), cookies (in the next chapter), and sessions (also in the next chapter).

To begin output buffering, use the ob_start() function at the very top of your page. Once you call it, every print() and similar function will send data to a memory buffer rather than to the Web browser. Conversely, HTTP calls (like header() and setcookie()) won't be buffered and will operate as usual.

At the conclusion of the script, call the ob_end_flush() function to send the accumulated buffer to the Web browser. Or, use the ob_end_clean() function to delete the buffered data without passing it along. Both functions also turn off output buffering for that script.

From a programmer's perspective, output buffering allows you to structure a script in a more linear form, without concern for HTTP headers. Let's remake header.html and footer.html so that every page uses output buffering. You won't appreciate the benefits yet, but the number of errors you *won't see* over the rest of this book will go a long way toward preserving your programming sanity.

To use output buffering:

1. Open header.html (Script 8.6) in your text editor or IDE.

2. At the very top of the page, before any HTML code, add the following (**Script 8.11**):

```php
<?php
ob_start();
?>
```

The key to using output buffering is to call the ob_start() function as early as possible in a script. In this example, you create a special section of PHP prior to any

Script 8.11 Add output buffering to the Web application by placing the ob_start() function at the top of the header.html script.

```php
1   <?php // Script 8.11 - header.html #3
2
3   // Turn on output buffering:
4   ob_start();
5
6   ?><!DOCTYPE html PUBLIC "-//W3C//DTD
    XHTML 1.0 Transitional//EN"
7       "http://www.w3.org/TR/xhtml1/DTD/
        xhtml1-transitional.dtd">
8   <html xmlns="http://www.w3.org/1999/
    xhtml" xml:lang="en" lang="en">
9   <head>
10      <meta http-equiv="Content-Type"
        content="text/html; charset=utf-8"/>
11      <title><?php // Print the page title.
12      if (defined('TITLE')) { // Is the
        title defined?
13          print TITLE;
14      } else { // The title is not defined.
15          print 'Elliott Smith Fan Club';
16      }
17      ?></title>
18
19      <style type="text/css">
20          body {
21              margin:0px 0px 0px 0px;
22              background: #9F9;
23          }
24          #leftcontent {
25              float:left;
26              width:67%;
27              background:#fff;
28              border-right:2px solid #000;
29              border-bottom:2px solid #000;
30              margin-right:15px;
31              padding-bottom:20px;
32          }
33          p,h1,pre {
34              margin:0px 30px 10px 30px;
35          }
36          h1 {
37              font-size:14px;
38              padding-top:10px;
39          }
```

(script continues on next page)

OUTPUT BUFFERING

Script 8.11 *continued*

```
000                    Script
40          #rightcontent p {
41              font-size:14px;
42              margin-left:0px;
43              }
44      </style>
45
46  </head>
47  <body>
48  <div id="leftcontent">
49  <!-- BEGIN CHANGEABLE CONTENT. -->
```

HTML and call `ob_start()` there. By turning on output buffering in your header file and turning it off in your footer file, you buffer every page in the Web application.

3. Open `footer.html` (Script 8.7) in your text editor or IDE.

4. At the end of the script, after all of the HTML, add (**Script 8.12**):

```
<?php
ob_end_flush();
?>
```

This code turns off output buffering and sends the accumulated buffer to the Web browser. In other words, all the HTML is sent at this point.

continues on next page

Script 8.12 Output buffering is completed at the end of the footer file using `ob_end_flush()`, which sends the accumulated buffer to the Web browser.

```
000                                Script
1   <!-- END CHANGEABLE CONTENT. -->
2   </div>
3
4   <div id="rightcontent">
5       <h1>Navigation</h1>
6       <p><a href="index.php">Home</a><br />
7       <a href="albums.php">Discography</a><br />
8       <a href="login.php">Login</a><br />
9       <a href="register.php">Register</a></p>
10
11      <p><em><?php // Print the current date and time:
12      // Set the timezone:
13      date_default_timezone_set('America/New_York');
14
15      // Now print the date and time:
16      print date('g:i a l F j');
17      ?><em></p>
18
19  </div>
20
21  </body>
22  </html><?php // Script 8.12 - footer.html #3
23
24  // Send the buffer to the browser and turn off buffering:
25  ob_end_flush();
26  ?>
```

5. Save both files and place them in the `templates` directory of your PHP-enabled server.

6. Test any page in your Web browser (**Figure 8.25**).

✔ Tips

■ Just to clarify, PHP code can be placed in a file with a `.html` extension—as in these two examples here—if that file is being included by a PHP script (like `index.php`).

■ For some time now, output buffering is automatically enabled in PHP's default configuration.

■ You can set the maximum buffer size in the `php.ini` file. The default is 4,096 bytes.

■ The `ob_get_length()` function returns the length (in number of characters) of the current buffer contents.

■ The `ob_get_contents()` function returns the current buffer so that it can be assigned to a variable, should the need arise.

■ The `ob_flush()` function sends the current contents of the buffer to the Web browser and then discards them, allowing a new buffer to be started. This function lets your scripts maintain more moderate buffer sizes.

■ The `ob_clean()` function deletes the current contents of the buffer without stopping the buffer process.

■ PHP automatically runs `ob_end_flush()` at the conclusion of a script if it isn't otherwise done. But it's still a good idea to call it yourself.

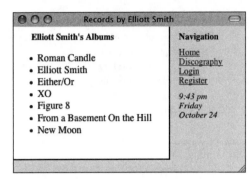

Figure 8.25 The site works the same as it did previously, but it will be easier to work with when you use HTTP headers later in this chapter.

Manipulating HTTP Headers

An HTTP (Hypertext Transfer Protocol) header is used to send information back and forth between the server and the client (the Web browser). Normally this information is in the form of HTML, which is why the addresses for Web pages begin with http://.

But the subject of HTTP headers is complicated enough to warrant a little more attention. There are dozens of uses for HTTP headers, all of which you can take advantage of using PHP's header() function.

This section demonstrates a common use: redirecting the user from one page to another. To redirect the user's browser with PHP, you send a location header:

```
header('Location: page.php');
```

Normally, the header() function is followed by exit(), to cancel the execution of the script (because the browser has been redirected to another page):

```
header('Location: page.php');
exit();
```

The most important thing to understand about using header() is that the function must be called before anything else is sent to the Web browser—otherwise, you'll see the all-too-common *headers already sent* error message (Figure 8.24). If your Web page receives *any* HTML or even blank space, the header() function won't work.

Fortunately for you, the preceding section introduced output buffering. Because output buffering is turned on in the Web application, nothing is sent to the Web browser until the very last line of the footer script (when ob_end_flush() is called). By using this method, you can avoid errors like those in Figure 8.24.

continues on next page

MANIPULATING HTTP HEADERS

To demonstrate redirection, you'll rewrite the login page to take the user to a welcome page upon successful login.

To use the header() function:

1. Open login.php in your text editor or IDE (Script 8.8):

2. Delete the *You are logged in...* print() statement (**Script 8.13**).

   Because the user is redirected to another page, there's no need to include this message.

Script 8.13 The new version of the login page redirects the user to another page using the header() function.

```
1    <?php // Script 8.13 - login.php #2
2    /* This page lets people log into the site
     (in theory). */
3
4    // Set the page title and include the
     header file:
5    define('TITLE', 'Login');
6    require('templates/header.html');
7
8    // Print some introductory text:
9    print '<h1>Login Form</h1>
10       <p>Users who are logged in can take
         advantage of certain features like
         this, that, and the other thing.</p>';
11
12   // Check if the form has been submitted:
13   if ( isset($_POST['submitted']) ) {
14
15       // Handle the form:
16       if ( (!empty($_POST['email'])) &&
         (!empty($_POST['password'])) ) {
17
18           if ( (strtolower($_POST['email'])
             == 'me@example.com') && ($_POST
             ['password'] == 'testpass') )
             { // Correct!
19
20               // Redirect the user to the
                 welcome page!
21               ob_end_clean(); // Destroy the
                 buffer!
22               header ('Location: welcome.php');
23               exit();
24
25           } else { // Incorrect!
26
27               print '<p>The submitted email
                 address and password do not
                 match those on file!<br />Go
                 back and try again.</p>';
28
29           }
30
```

(script continues on next page)

3. Where the print() statement was, add:

ob_end_clean();

header ('Location: welcome.php');

exit();

The first line destroys the page buffer (because the accumulated buffer won't be used). This isn't strictly required but is a good idea. The next line redirects the user to welcome.php. The third line terminates the execution of the rest of the script.

4. Save the file and place it in the proper directory for your PHP-enabled server (along with the other scripts from this chapter).

Now you need to create the welcome.php page to which the user will be redirected.

Script 8.13 *continued*

```
31      } else { // Forgot a field.
32
33          print '<p>Please make sure you enter both an email address and a password!<br />Go back
            and try again.</p>';
34
35      }
36
37  } else { // Display the form.
38
39      print '<form action="login.php" method="post">
40      <p>Email Address: <input type="text" name="email" size="20" /></p>
41      <p>Password: <input type="password" name="password" size="20" /></p>
42      <p><input type="submit" name="submit" value="Log In!" /></p>
43      <input type="hidden" name="submitted" value="true" />
44      </form>';
45
46  }
47
48  require('templates/footer.html'); // Need the footer.
49  ?>
```

To write welcome.php:

1. Begin a new PHP document in your text editor or IDE (**Script 8.14**):

   ```php
   <?php // Script 8.14 - welcome.php
   ```

2. Define the page title and include the header:

   ```php
   define('TITLE', 'Welcome to the
   → Elliott Smith Fan Club!');
   require('templates/header.html');
   ```

Script 8.14 The welcome page greets the user after they've logged in.

```php
1   <?php // Script 8.14 - welcome.php
2   /* This is the welcome page. The user is redirected here
3   after they successfully log in. */
4
5   // Set the page title and include the header file:
6   define('TITLE', 'Welcome to the Elliott Smith Fan Club!');
7   require('templates/header.html');
8
9   // Leave the PHP section to display lots of HTML:
10  ?>
11
12  <h1>Welcome to the Elliott Smith Fan Club!</h1>
13  <p>You've successfully logged in and can now take advantage of everything the site has to
    offer.</p>
14  <p>Here's a whole lotta text. Here's a whole lotta text. Here's a whole lotta text. Here's a
    whole lotta text. Here's a whole lotta text. Here's a whole lotta text. Here's a whole lotta
    text. Here's a whole lotta text. Here's a whole lotta text. Here's a whole lotta text. </p>
15
16  <?php require('templates/footer.html'); // Need the footer. ?>
```

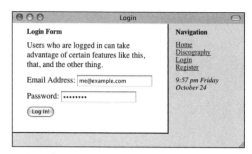

Figure 8.26 The login form...

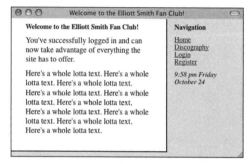

Figure 8.27 ...and the redirection if the user properly logged in.

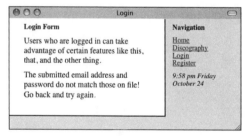

Figure 8.28 If the user didn't properly log in, they remain on the login page.

3. Create the page content:

```
?>
<h1>Welcome to the Elliott Smith Fan
→ Club!</h1>
<p>You've successfully logged in
→ and can now take advantage of
→ everything the site has to offer.
→ </p>
<p>Here's a whole lotta text. Here's
→ a whole lotta text. Here's a whole
→ lotta text. Here's a whole lotta
→ text. Here's a whole lotta text.
→ Here's a whole lotta text. Here's
→ a whole lotta text. Here's a whole
→ lotta text. Here's a whole lotta
→ text. Here's a whole lotta text.
→ </p>
```

4. Return to PHP and include the footer:

```
<?php require('templates/footer.
→ html'); ?>
```

5. Save the script as welcome.php, place it in the same directory as the new version of login.php, and test it in your Web browser (**Figures 8.26**, **8.27**, and **8.28**).

MANIPULATING HTTP HEADERS

235

✔ Tips

■ The `headers_sent()` function returns TRUE if the page has already received HTTP headers and the `header()` function can't be used.

■ Using the GET method trick, you can pass values from one page to another using `header()`:

```
$var = urlencode('Pass this text');
header ("Location: page.php?
→ message=$var");
```

■ The `header()` function should technically use a full path to the target page when redirecting. For example, it should be

```
header ('Location: http://www.
→ example.com/welcome.php');
```

or

```
header ('Location: http://localhost/
→ welcome.php');
```

In my book *PHP 6 and MySQL 5 for Dynamic Web Sites: Visual QuickPro Guide* I show some code for dynamically generating an absolute URL based upon the location of the current script.

COOKIES AND SESSIONS

Chapter 8, "Creating Web Applications," covers a number of techniques for developing more complete Web applications. One of the problems you'll encounter as you begin to assemble a multipage Web site is that the Hypertext Transfer Protocol (HTTP) is a stateless technology. This means that you as a Web developer have no built-in method for tracking a user or remembering data from one page of an application to the next. This is a serious problem, because e-commerce applications, user registration and login systems, and other common online services rely on this functionality. Fortunately, maintaining state from one page to another is fairly simple using PHP.

This chapter discusses the two main methods for tracking data: cookies and sessions. You'll start by learning how to create, read, modify, and delete cookies. Then you'll see how easy it is to master sessions, a more potent option for maintaining state.

What Are Cookies?

Prior to the existence of cookies, traversing a Web site was a trip without a history. Although your browser tracks the pages you visit, allowing you to use the Back button to return to previously visited pages and indicating visited links in a different color, the server keeps no record of who has seen what. This is still true for sites that don't use cookies, as well as for users who have disabled cookies in their Web browsers (**Figure 9.1**).

Why is that a problem? If the server can't track a user, there can be no shopping carts for you to use to make purchases online. If cookies didn't exist (or if they're disabled in your Web browser), people wouldn't be able to use popular sites that require user registration.

Cookies are a way for a server to store information about the user—on the user's machine—so that the server can remember the user over the course of the visit or through several visits. Think of a cookie like a name tag: You tell the server your name, and it gives you a name tag. Then it can know who you are by referring back to the name tag.

This brings up another point about the security issues involved with cookies. Cookies have gotten a bad rap because users believe cookies allow a server to know too much about them. However, a cookie can only be used to store information that you give it, so it's as secure as you want it to be.

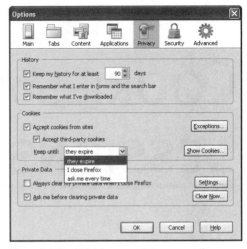

Figure 9.1 Most Web browsers let users set the cookie-handling preferences. This is Firefox 3's Privacy tab.

PHP has very good support for cookies. In this chapter, you'll learn how to set a cookie, retrieve information from a cookie, and then delete the cookie. You'll also see some of the optional parameters you can use to apply limits to a cookie's existence.

Before moving on, there are two more things you ought to know about cookies. The first is how to debug cookie-related problems. This is discussed in the sidebar. The second is how a cookie is transmitted and received (**Figure 9.2**). Cookies are stored in the Web browser, but only the site that originally sent a cookie can read it. Also, the cookies are read by the site when the page on that site is requested by the Web browser. In other words, when the user enters a URL in the address bar and clicks Go (or whatever), the site reads any cookies it has access to and then serves up the requested page. This order is important because it dictates when and how cookies can be accessed.

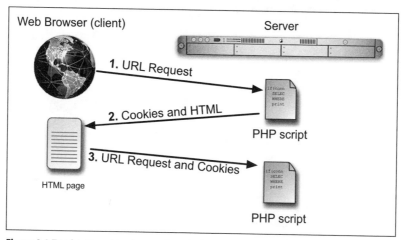

Figure 9.2 Two basic cookies transactions in the client/server relationship.

Debugging Cookies

When you begin working with cookies in PHP, you'll need to know how to debug your scripts when problems occur. Three areas might cause you concern:

◆ Sending the cookie with PHP

◆ Receiving the cookie in your Web browser

◆ Accessing a cookie in a PHP script

The first and last issues can be debugged by printing out the variable values in your PHP scripts (as you'll soon learn). The second issue requires that you know how to work with cookies in your Web browser. For debugging purposes, you'll want your Web browser to notify you when a cookie is being sent.

With Internet Explorer 7 on Windows, you can do this by choosing Internet Options under the Tools menu. Then click the Privacy tab, followed by the Advanced button under Settings. Click "Override automatic cookie handling," and then choose Prompt for both First-party and Third-party Cookies. Other versions of Internet Explorer use different variations on this process.

Firefox users on any platform can control cookies through the Cookies subsection of the Privacy tab in the Preferences (on Mac OS X) or Options (on Windows) window. Safari on Mac OS X doesn't give you as many cookie options, but they can be found on the Security tab of the Preferences window.

Some browsers also let you browse through the existing cookies to see their names and values. Doing so is a great asset in the debugging war.

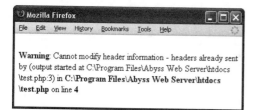

Figure 9.3 A message like this is what you'll see if the setcookie() function is called after anything, even a blank line, has already been sent to the Web browser.

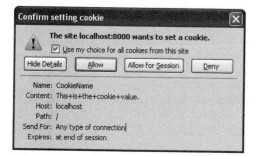

Figure 9.4 If the browser is set to prompt the user for cookies, a message like this will appear for each cookie sent.

Creating Cookies

An important thing to understand about cookies is that they must be sent from the server to the client prior to any other information. Should the server attempt to send a cookie after the Web browser has already received HTML—even an extraneous white space—an error message will result and the cookie won't be sent (**Figure 9.3**). This is by far the most common cookie-related error.

Cookies are sent using the setcookie() function:

```
setcookie(name, value);
setcookie('CookieName', 'This is the
→ cookie value.');
```

That line of code sends to the browser a cookie with the name *CookieName* and the value *This is the cookie value*. (**Figure 9.4**).

You can continue to send more cookies to the browser with subsequent uses of the setcookie() function, although you're limited by the Web browser as to how many cookies can be sent from the same site:

```
setcookie('name2', 'some value');
setcookie('name3', 'another value');
```

Finally, when creating cookies, you can—as you'll see in this example—use a variable for the name or value attribute of your cookies:

```
setcookie($cookie_name, $cookie_value);
```

For an example of setting cookies, you'll create a script that allows the user to specify the text size and color for a page. The page displays a form for choosing these values and then handles the form submission. A separate page, created in the next section of this chapter, will use these settings.

To send cookies:

1. Create a new PHP document in your text editor or IDE (**Script 9.1**):

```
<?php // Script 9.1 - customize.php
```

The most critical issue with cookies is that they're created before anything is sent to the Web browser. To accomplish this, the script begins with a PHP section that handles the sending of cookies.

Script 9.1 Two cookies will be used to store the user's choices for the text size and color. This page both displays and handles the form.

```
1    <?php // Script 9.1 - customize.php
2
3    // Handle the form if it has been submitted:
4    if (isset($_POST['submitted'])) {
5
6       // Send the cookies:
7       setcookie('font_size', $_POST['font_size']);
8       setcookie('font_color', $_POST['font_color']);
9
10      // Message to be printed later:
11      $msg = '<p>Your settings have been entered! Click <a href="view_settings.php">here</a> to
         see them in action.</p>';
12
13   } // End of submitted IF.
14   ?><!DOCTYPE html PUBLIC "-//W3C//DTD XHTML 1.0 Transitional//EN"
15      "http://www.w3.org/TR/xhtml1/DTD/xhtml1-transitional.dtd">
16   <html xmlns="http://www.w3.org/1999/xhtml" xml:lang="en" lang="en">
17   <head>
18      <meta http-equiv="Content-Type" content="text/html; charset=utf-8"/>
19      <title>Customize Your Settings</title>
20   </head>
21   <body>
22   <?php // If the cookies were sent, print a message.
23   if (isset($msg)) {
24      print $msg;
25   }
26   ?>
27
```

(script continues on next page)

Script 9.1 *continued*

```
●●●                        Script
28   <p>Use this form to set your
     preferences:</p>
29
30   <form action="customize.php"
     method="post">
31   <select name="font_size">
32   <option value="">Font Size</option>
33   <option value="xx-small">xx-small</option>
34   <option value="x-small">x-small</option>
35   <option value="small">small</option>
36   <option value="medium">medium</option>
37   <option value="large">large</option>
38   <option value="x-large">x-large</option>
39   <option value="xx-large">xx-large</option>
40   </select>
41   <select name="font_color">
42   <option value="">Font Color</option>
43   <option value="999">Gray</option>
44   <option value="0c0">Green</option>
45   <option value="00f">Blue</option>
46   <option value="c00">Red</option>
47   <option value="000">Black</option>
48   </select>
49   <input type="submit" name="submit"
     value="Set My Preferences" />
50   <input type="hidden" name="submitted"
     value="true" />
51   </form>
52
53   </body>
54   </html>
```

2. Check whether the form has been submitted:

```
if (isset($_POST['submitted'])) {
```

Using the technique described in the preceding chapter, this page both displays and handles the form. If the form has been submitted, the `$_POST['submitted']` variable is set and this condition will be TRUE.

3. Create the cookies:

```
setcookie('font_size', $_POST['font_
→ size']);
setcookie('font_color', $_POST
→ ['font_color']);
```

These two lines create two separate cookies. One is named *font_size* and the other *font_color*. Their values will be based on the selected values from the HTML form, which are stored in the `$_POST['font_size']` and `$_POST['font_color']` variables.

In a more fully developed application, I'd validate that the user selected a value for both form elements prior to using them for cookies.

4. Create a message and complete the conditional and the PHP section:

```
$msg = '<p>Your settings have
→ been entered! Click <a href=
→ "view_settings.php">here</a>
→ to see them in action.</p>';
} // End of submitted IF.
?>
```

When the form has been submitted, the cookies will be sent and the `$msg` variable will be assigned a string value. This variable will be used later in the script to print a message.

continues on next page

CREATING COOKIES

5. Create the HTML head and opening body tag:

```
<!DOCTYPE html PUBLIC "-//W3C//DTD
→ XHTML 1.0 Transitional//EN"
  "http://www.w3.org/TR/xhtml1/DTD/
  → xhtml1-transitional.dtd">
<html xmlns="http://www.w3.org/1999/
→ xhtml" xml:lang="en" lang="en">
<head>
  <meta http-equiv="Content-Type"
  → content="text/html;
  → charset=utf-8"/>
  <title>Customize Your Settings
  → </title>
</head>
<body>
```

All of this code must come after the setcookie() lines. Not to overstate the fact, but no text, HTML, or blank spaces can be sent to the Web browser prior to the setcookie() calls.

6. Create another PHP section to report on the cookies' being sent:

```
<?php
if (isset($msg)) {
   print $msg;
}
?>
```

This code prints out a message if the cookies have been sent. The first time the user comes to the page, the cookies haven't been sent, so $msg is not set, making this conditional FALSE, and this print() invocation never runs. Once the form has been submitted, $msg has been set by this point, so this conditional is TRUE.

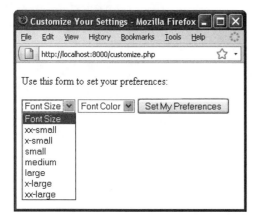

Figure 9.5 This form is used to select the font size and color used by another PHP page.

7. Begin the HTML form:

```
<p>Use this form to set your
→ preferences:</p>
<form action="customize.php"
→ method="post">
<select name="font_size">
<option value="">Font Size</option>
<option value="xx-small">xx-small
→ </option>
<option value="x-small">x-small
→ </option>
<option value="small">small</option>
<option value="medium">medium
→ </option>
<option value="large">large</option>
<option value="x-large">x-large
→ </option>
<option value="xx-large">xx-large
→ </option>
</select>
```

The HTML form itself is very simple (**Figure 9.5**). The user is given one drop-down menu to select the font size. The value for each corresponds to the CSS code used to set the document's font size: from *xx-small* to *xx-large*.

Because this script both displays and handles the form, the form's action attribute points to this same file.

continues on next page

CREATING COOKIES

8. Complete the HTML form:

```
<select name="font_color">
<option value="">Font Color</option>
<option value="999">Gray</option>
<option value="0c0">Green</option>
<option value="00f">Blue</option>
<option value="c00">Red</option>
<option value="000">Black</option>
</select>
<input type="submit" name="submit"
→ value="Set My Preferences" />
<input type="hidden" name=
→ "submitted" value="true" />
</form>
```

The second drop-down menu is used to select the font color. The menu displays the colors in text form, but the values are HTML color values. Normally such values are written using six characters plus a pound sign (e.g., *#00cc00*), but CSS allows you to use just a three-character version and the pound sign will be added on the page that uses these values.

Finally, a hidden input is added that will trigger the handling of the form data (see Step 2). Be certain that the name of the hidden input (here, *submitted*) exactly matches the key used in the conditional at the top of the script ($_POST['submitted']). Otherwise, the form will never be processed.

9. Complete the HTML page:

```
</body>
</html>
```

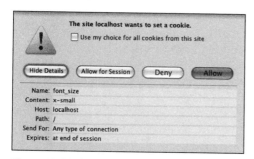

Figure 9.6 The user sees this message when the first setcookie() call is made, if they've opted to be prompted before accepting a cookie. This cookie is storing the value of *x-small* in a cookie named *font_size*.

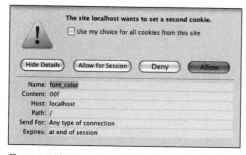

Figure 9.7 The second cookie that's sent is called *font_color* and has a value of *oof*, representing the color blue.

Figure 9.8 After submitting the form, the page shows a message and a link to another page (where the user's preferences will be used). That page will be created next.

10. Save the file as customize.php and place it in the proper directory for your PHP-enabled server.

11. Make sure you've set your Web browser to prompt for each cookie.

To guarantee that the script is working, you want the browser to prompt you for each cookie. See the "Debugging Cookies" sidebar.

12. Run the script in your Web browser (**Figures 9.6, 9.7,** and **9.8**).

✔ Tips

■ Cookies are one of the few PHP tools that can behave differently from browser to browser or operating system to operating system. You should test your cookie-based applications on as many browsers and operating systems as you can.

■ If you use the output buffering technique taught in Chapter 8, then you can place your setcookie() calls anywhere within the script (because the Web browser won't receive the data until the ob_end_flush() function is called).

■ Cookies are limited to approximately 4 KB of total data. This is more than sufficient for most applications.

■ To test whether it's safe to send a cookie, use the headers_sent() function. It reports on whether HTTP headers have already been sent to the Web browser.

Reading from Cookies

Just as form data is stored in the $_POST array (assuming it used the POST method) and values passed to a script in the URL are stored in the $_GET array, the setcookie() function places cookie data in the $_COOKIE array. To retrieve a value from a cookie, you only need to refer to the cookie name as the index of this array. For example, to retrieve the value of the cookie established with the line

```
setcookie('user', 'trout');
```

you would use the variable $_COOKIE['user'].

Unless you change the cookie's parameters (as you'll see later in this chapter), the cookie will automatically be accessible to every other page in your Web application. You should understand, however, that a cookie is never accessible to a script immediately after it's been sent. You can't do this:

```
setcookie('user', 'trout');
print $_COOKIE['user']; // No value.
```

The reason for this is the order in which cookies are read and sent (see Figure 9.2).

To see how simple it is to access cookie values, let's write a script that uses the preferences set in customize.php to specify the page's text size and color. The script relies on CSS to achieve this effect.

To retrieve cookie data with PHP:

1. Begin a new PHP document in your text editor or IDE (**Script 9.2**):

```
<!DOCTYPE html PUBLIC "-//W3C//DTD
→ XHTML 1.0 Transitional//EN"
    "http://www.w3.org/TR/xhtml1/DTD/
    → xhtml1-transitional.dtd">
<html xmlns="http://www.w3.org/1999/
→ xhtml" xml:lang="en" lang="en">
<head>
    <meta http-equiv="content-type"
    → content="text/html;
    → charset=utf-8" />
    <title>View Your Settings</title>
```

continues on next page

Script 9.2 This script sets the font size and color using the values stored in the cookies.

```
1    <!DOCTYPE html PUBLIC "-//W3C//DTD XHTML 1.0 Transitional//EN"
2        "http://www.w3.org/TR/xhtml1/DTD/xhtml1-transitional.dtd">
3    <html xmlns="http://www.w3.org/1999/xhtml" xml:lang="en" lang="en">
4    <head>
5        <meta http-equiv="content-type" content="text/html; charset=utf-8" />
6        <title>View Your Settings</title>
7        <style type="text/css">
8            body {
9    <?php // Script 9.2 - view_settings.php
10
11   // Check for a font_size value:
12   if (isset($_COOKIE['font_size'])) {
13       print "\t\tfont-size: " . htmlentities($_COOKIE['font_size']) . ";\n";
14   } else {
15       print "\t\tfont-size: medium;\n";
16   }
17
18   // Check for a font_color value:
19   if (isset($_COOKIE['font_color'])) {
20       print "\t\tcolor: #" . htmlentities($_COOKIE['font_color']) . ";\n";
21   } else {
22       print "\t\tcolor: #000; \n";
23   }
24
```

(script continues on next page)

2. Start the CSS section:

```
<style type="text/css">
    body {
```

The page will use CSS to enact the user's preferences. The aim is to create code like

```
body {
    font-size: x-large;
    color: #000;
}
```

The two values will differ based on what the user selected in the customize.php page. In this step, you create the initial CSS code.

3. Open a section of PHP code:

```
<?php // Script 9.2 - view_settings.
→ php
```

The script will now use PHP to print out the remaining CSS, based on the cookies.

4. Use the font size cookie value, if it exists:

```
if (isset($_COOKIE['font_size'])) {
    print "\t\tfont-size: " .
    → htmlentities($_COOKIE['font_
    → size']) . ";\n";
} else {
    print "\t\tfont-size: medium;\n";
}
```

If the script can access a cookie with a name of *font_size*, it will print out that cookie's value as the CSS font-size value. The isset() function is sufficient to see if the cookie exists. If no such cookie exists, PHP will print out a default size, *medium*.

For security purposes, the cookie's value is not directly printed. Instead, it's run through the htmlentities() function, discussed in Chapter 5, "Using Strings." This function will prevent bad things from happening should the user manipulate the value of the cookie (which is easy to do).

Script 9.2 *continued*

```
25    ?>
26        }
27    </style>
28    </head>
29    <body>
30    <p><a href="customize.php">Customize Your
      Settings</a></p>
31    <p><a href="reset.php">Reset Your
      Settings</a></p>
32
33    <p>
34    yadda yadda yadda yadda yadda
35    yadda yadda yadda yadda yadda
36    yadda yadda yadda yadda yadda
37    yadda yadda yadda yadda yadda
38    yadda yadda yadda yadda yadda
39    </p>
40
41    </body>
42    </html>
```

Finally, just to clarify, each `print()` statement also creates two tabs (using \t) and one newline character (\n). The purpose of these is to give the CSS code some formatting, which will appear in the HTML source.

5. Repeat this process for the font color cookie:

```
if (isset($_COOKIE['font_color'])) {
    print "\t\tcolor: #" .
    → htmlentities($_COOKIE['font_
    → color']) . ";\n";
} else {
    print "\t\tcolor: #000; \n";
}
```

Here the CSS' color attribute is being assigned a value. The cookie itself is used the same as in Step 4.

6. Close the PHP section, complete the CSS code, and finish the HTML head:

```
?>
    }
  </style>
</head>
```

7. Start the HTML body and create links to two other pages:

```
<body>
<p><a href="customize.php">Customize
→ Your Settings</a></p>
<p><a href="reset.php">Reset Your
→ Settings</a></p>
```

These two links take the user to two other PHP pages. The first, `customize.php`, has already been written and lets the user define their settings. The second, `reset.php`, will be written later in the chapter and lets the user delete their customized settings.

continues on next page

READING FROM COOKIES

8. Add some text:

```
<p>
yadda yadda yadda yadda yadda
yadda yadda yadda yadda yadda
yadda yadda yadda yadda yadda
yadda yadda yadda yadda yadda
yadda yadda yadda yadda yadda
</p>
```

This text exists simply to show the effects of the cookie changes.

9. Complete the HTML page:

```
</body>
</html>
```

10. Save the file as view_settings.php, place it in the same directory as customize.php, and test it in your Web browser (**Figure 9.9**).

11. View the source of the page to see the resulting CSS code (**Figure 9.10**).

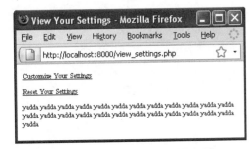

Figure 9.9 This page reflects the customized font choices made using the other PHP script.

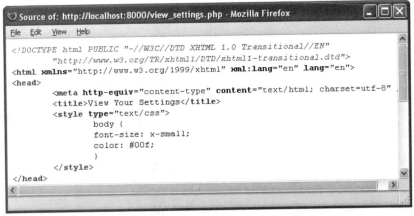

Figure 9.10 By viewing the source code of the page, you can also track how the CSS values change.

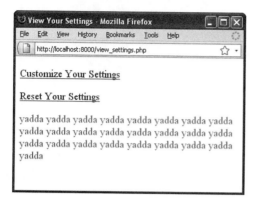

Figure 9.11 Change your settings to create new versions of the page.

12. Use the customize page to change your settings and return to this script (**Figure 9.11**).

Each submission of the form will create two new cookies storing the form values, thereby replacing the existing cookies.

✔ Tips

■ The value of a cookie is automatically encoded when it's sent and decoded on being received by the PHP page. The same is true of values sent by HTML forms.

■ If you want the customize.php page to also display the user's settings, you need to take into account the fact that the cookies aren't available immediately after they've been set. Instead, you would write the CSS code using the $_POST values after the form has been submitted, the $_COOKIE values upon first arriving at the page (if the cookies exist), and the default values otherwise.

Adding Parameters to a Cookie

Although passing just the name and value arguments to the setcookie() function will suffice for most of your cookie uses, you ought to be aware of the other arguments available. The function can take up to five more parameters, each of which limits the operation of the cookie:

```
setcookie(name, value, expiration,
→ path, domain, secure, httponly);
```

The expiration argument is used to set a specific length of time for a cookie to exist. If it isn't specified, the cookie will continue to be functional until the user closes their browser. Normally, you set the expiration time by adding a particular number of minutes or hours to the current time. This line of code sets the expiration time of the cookie to be one hour (60 seconds times 60 minutes) from the current moment:

```
setcookie(name, value, time()+3600);
```

Because the expiration time will be calculated as the value of time() plus 3600, this particular argument isn't put in quotes (you don't want to literally pass *time( ) + 3600* as the expiration but rather the result of that calculation).

The path and domain arguments are used to limit a cookie to a specific folder in a Web site (the path) or to a specific domain. Cookies are already specific to a domain, so this might be used to limit a cookie to a subdomain, such as forum.example.com.

Using the path option, you could limit a cookie to exist only while a user is in the user folder of the domain:

```
setcookie(name, value, time()+3600,
→'/user/');
```

The secure value dictates that a cookie should only be sent over a secure HTTPS connection. A value of 1 indicates that a secure connection must be used, whereas 0 indicates that a secure connection isn't necessary. You could ensure a secure cookie transmission for e-commerce sites:

```
setcookie(name, value, time()+3600,
→'', '', 1);
```

As with all functions that take arguments, you must pass all the values in order. In the preceding example, if you don't want to specify (or limit) the path and domain, you use empty quotes. By doing so, you maintain the proper number of arguments and can still indicate that a HTTPS connection is necessary.

The final argument—*httponly*—was added in PHP 5.2. It can be used to restrict access to the cookie (for example, preventing a cookie from being read using JavaScript) but isn't supported by all browsers.

Let's add an expiration date to the existing `customize.php` page so that the user's preferences will remain even after they've closed their browser and then returned to the site later.

ADDING PARAMETERS TO A COOKIE

To set a cookie's expiration date:

1. Open customize.php (Script 9.1) in your text editor or IDE.

2. Change the two setcookie() lines to read as follows (**Script 9.3**):

   ```
   setcookie('font_size', $_POST
   → ['font_size'], time()+10000000,
   → '/', '', 0);

   setcookie('font_color', $_POST
   → ['font_color'], time()+10000000,
   → '/', '', 0);
   ```

   To make these cookies persist for a long time (specifically, for a couple of months), you set the expiration time to be 10,000,000 seconds from now. While you're at it, set the path, domain, and secure arguments; doing so may improve the consistency of sending these cookies across the various browsers.

   Because the expiration date of the cookies is set months into the future, the user's preferences, which are stored in the cookies, will be valid even after the user has closed and reopened the browser. Without this expiration date, the user would see the default font size and color and have to reassign their preferences with every new browser session.

3. Save the file, place it in the proper directory for your PHP-enabled server, and test it again in your Web browser (**Figures 9.12** and **9.13**).

   Note that browsers may not adhere to a cookie's adjusted expiration time when the cookie is being sent from your own computer (i.e., from *localhost*).

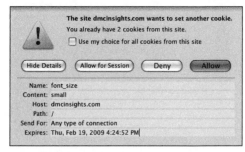

Figure 9.12 If you have your browser set to prompt you when receiving cookies, you'll see how the expiration time has been added (compare with Figure 9.6).

Figure 9.13 The new cookie parameters don't adversely affect the functionality of the application.

Script 9.3 By adding the expiration arguments to the two cookies, you make the cookies persist even after the user has closed out of and later returned to their browser.

```
1    <?php // Script 9.3 - customize.php #2
2
3    // Handle the form if it has been submitted:
4    if (isset($_POST['submitted'])) {
5
6       // Send the cookies:
7       setcookie('font_size', $_POST['font_size'], time()+10000000, '/', '', 0);
8       setcookie('font_color', $_POST['font_color'], time()+10000000, '/', '', 0);
9
10      // Message to be printed later:
11      $msg = '<p>Your settings have been entered! Click <a href="view_settings.php">here</a> to
        see them in action.</p>';
12
13   } // End of submitted IF.
14   ?><!DOCTYPE html PUBLIC "-//W3C//DTD XHTML 1.0 Transitional//EN"
15      "http://www.w3.org/TR/xhtml1/DTD/xhtml1-transitional.dtd">
16   <html xmlns="http://www.w3.org/1999/xhtml" xml:lang="en" lang="en">
17   <head>
18      <meta http-equiv="Content-Type" content="text/html; charset=utf-8"/>
19      <title>Customize Your Settings</title>
20   </head>
21   <body>
22   <?php // If the cookies were sent, print a message.
23   if (isset($msg)) {
24      print $msg;
25   }
26   ?>
27
28   <p>Use this form to set your preferences:</p>
29
30   <form action="customize.php" method=
     "post">
31   <select name="font_size">
32   <option value="">Font Size</option>
33   <option value="xx-small">xx-small</option>
34   <option value="x-small">x-small</option>
35   <option value="small">small</option>
36   <option value="medium">medium</option>
37   <option value="large">large</option>
38   <option value="x-large">x-large</option>
39   <option value="xx-large">xx-large</option>
40   </select>
```

(script continues on next page)

ADDING PARAMETERS TO A COOKIE

✔ Tips

- There's really no rule of thumb for what kind of expiration date to use with your cookies. Here are some general guidelines, though. If the cookie should last as long as the user browses through the site, don't set an expiration time. If the cookie should continue to exist after the user has closed and reopened their browser, set an expiration time that's months in the future. And if the cookie can constitute a security risk, set an expiration time of an hour or a fraction thereof so that the cookie doesn't continue to exist too long after a user has left their browser.

- There can be a big problem with cookie expirations if the server and the clients are in different time zones. The expiration time is set based on the server's time zone, but the browser may delete the cookie based on the client's time zone. Fortunately, some browsers do automatically correct for this.

- For security purposes, you can set a five- or ten-minute expiration time on a cookie and have the cookie re-sent with every new page the user visits. This way, the cookie will continue to persist as long as the user is active but will automatically die five or ten minutes after the user's last action.

- Setting the cookie's path to '/' makes the cookie accessible within an entire Web site.

Script 9.3 *continued*

```
41    <select name="font_color">
42    <option value="">Font Color</option>
43    <option value="999">Gray</option>
44    <option value="0c0">Green</option>
45    <option value="00f">Blue</option>
46    <option value="c00">Red</option>
47    <option value="000">Black</option>
48    </select>
49    <input type="submit" name="submit"
      value="Set My Preferences" />
50    <input type="hidden" name="submitted"
      value="true" />
51    </form>
52
53    </body>
54    </html>
```

Deleting a Cookie

The final thing to understand about using cookies is how to delete one. Although a cookie automatically expires when the user's browser is closed or when the expiration date/time is met, sometimes you'll want to manually delete the cookie as well. For example, Web sites that have registered users and login capabilities generally delete any cookies when the user logs out.

The setcookie() function can take up to seven arguments, but only one is required—the name. If you send a cookie that consists of a name without a value, it will have the same effect as deleting the existing cookie of the same name. For example, to create the cookie *username*, you use this line:

```
setcookie('username', 'Larry');
```

To delete the username cookie, you code

```
setcookie('username', '');
```

or

```
setcookie('username', FALSE);
```

As an added precaution, you can also set an expiration date that's in the past:

```
setcookie('username', '', time() - 600);
```

The only caveat when it comes to deleting a cookie is that you must use the same argument values that were used to set the cookie in the first place (aside from the value and expiration). For example, if you set a cookie while providing a domain value, you must also provide that value when deleting the cookie:

```
setcookie('user', 'larry', time() +
→ 3600, '', 'forums.example.com');
setcookie('user', '', time() - 600, '',
→ 'forums.example.com');
```

To demonstrate this feature, let's add a reset page to the Web application that will destroy the sent cookies so that the user's preferences are forgotten.

To delete a cookie:

1. Begin a new PHP script in your text editor or IDE (**Script 9.4**):

```
<?php // Script 9.4 - reset.php
```

2. Delete the existing cookies by sending blank cookies and complete the PHP code:

```
setcookie('font_size', '', time() -
→ 600, '/', '', 0);
setcookie('font_color', '', time() -
→ 600, '/', '', 0);
?>
```

These two lines send cookies named *font_size* and *font_color*, each with no value and an expiration time of ten minutes ago. As you did when creating cookies, you must call the `setcookie()` function before anything else is sent to the Web browser.

Script 9.4 To reset all the cookie values, send blank cookies with the same names as the existing cookies.

```
1    <?php // Script 9.4 - reset.php
2
3    // Delete the cookies:
4    setcookie('font_size', '', time() - 600, '/', '', 0);
5    setcookie('font_color', '', time() - 600, '/', '', 0);
6
7    ?><!DOCTYPE html PUBLIC "-//W3C//DTD XHTML 1.0 Transitional//EN"
8        "http://www.w3.org/TR/xhtml1/DTD/xhtml1-transitional.dtd">
9    <html xmlns="http://www.w3.org/1999/xhtml" xml:lang="en" lang="en">
10   <head>
11      <meta http-equiv="Content-Type" content="text/html; charset=utf-8"/>
12      <title>Reset Your Settings</title>
13   </head>
14   <body>
15
16   <p>Your settings have been reset! Click <a href="view_settings.php">here</a> to go back to the
     main page.</p>
17
18   </body>
19   </html>
```

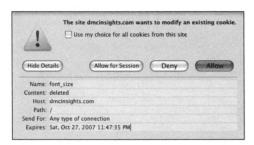

Figure 9.14 When the setcookie() function is used with a name but no value, the existing cookie of that name is deleted. The expiration date in the past also guarantees proper destruction of the existing cookie.

Figure 9.15 The reset page sends two blank cookies and then displays this message.

Figure 9.16 If the user has used the reset page, PHP destroys the cookies (Figure 9.14), which resets the main page to its default formatting.

■ Just as creating cookies has mixed results using different browsers, the same applies to deleting them. Test your scripts on many browsers and play with the setcookie() settings to ensure the best all-around compatibility.

3. Create the HTML head:

```
<!DOCTYPE html PUBLIC "-//W3C//DTD
→ XHTML 1.0 Transitional//EN"
   "http://www.w3.org/TR/xhtml1/DTD/
   → xhtml1-transitional.dtd">
<html xmlns="http://www.w3.org/1999/
→ xhtml" xml:lang="en" lang="en">
<head>
   <meta http-equiv="Content-Type"
   → content="text/html;
   → charset=utf-8"/>
   <title>Reset Your Settings</title>
</head>
```

4. Add the page's body:

```
<body>
<p>Your settings have been reset!
→ Click <a href="view_settings.
→ php">here</a> to go back to the
→ main page.</p>
</body>
```

The body of this script merely tells the user that their settings have been reset. A link is then provided to return to the main page.

5. Complete the HTML:

```
</html>
```

6. Save the page as reset.php, place it in the proper directory for your PHP-enabled server, and test it in your Web browser (**Figures 9.14**, **9.15**, and **9.16**).

To test this page, either click the appropriate link in view_settings.php (Script 9.2) or just go to this page directly.

✔ Tips

■ Just as creating a cookie doesn't take effect until another page is loaded, deleting a cookie doesn't take effect until another page. This is to say that you can delete a cookie on a page but still access that cookie on it (because the cookie was received by the page before the delete cookie was sent).

DELETING A COOKIE

What Are Sessions?

A session, like a cookie, provides a way for you to track data for a user over a series of pages. The difference between the two—and this is significant—is that a cookie stores the data on the client side (in the Web browser), whereas the session data is stored on the server. Because of this difference, sessions have numerous benefits over cookies:

◆ Sessions are generally more secure, because the data isn't transmitted back and forth between the client and server repeatedly.

◆ Sessions let you store more information than you can in a cookie.

◆ Sessions can be made to work even if the user doesn't accept cookies in their browser.

When you start a session, PHP generates a random session ID, a reference to that particular session and its stored data. By default, this session ID is sent to the Web browser as a cookie (**Figure 9.17**). Subsequent PHP pages will use this cookie to retrieve the session ID and access the session information.

Over the next few pages, you'll see just how easy sessions are to work with in PHP.

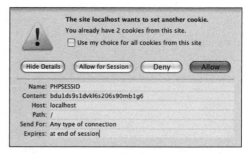

Figure 9.17 A session cookie being sent to the Web browser.

Choosing Between Sessions and Cookies

Sessions have many benefits over cookies, but there are still reasons why you would use the latter. Cookies have these advantages over sessions:

◆ Marginally easier to create and retrieve

◆ Require slightly less work from the server

◆ Normally persist over a longer period of time

As a rule of thumb, you should use cookies in situations where security is less of an issue and only a minimum of data is being stored. If security's a concern and there will be oodles of information to remember, you're best off with sessions. Understand, though, that using sessions may require a little more effort in writing your scripts.

Creating a Session

Creating, accessing, or deleting a session begins with the session_start( ) function. This function will attempt to send a cookie the first time a session is started (see Figure 9.17), so it absolutely must be called prior to any HTML or white space being sent to the Web browser. Therefore, on pages that use sessions, you should call the session_start( ) function as one of the very first lines in your script.

The first time a session is started, a random session ID is generated and a cookie is sent to the Web browser with a name of *PHPSESSID* (the session name) and a value like *4bcc48dc87cb4b54d63f99da23fb41e1*.

Once the session has been started, you can record data to it by assigning values to the $_SESSION array:

```
$_SESSION['first_name'] = 'Marc';
$_SESSION['age'] = 35;
```

Each time you do this, PHP writes that data to a temporary file stored on the server. To demonstrate, you'll rewrite the login script from Chapter 8, this time storing the email address in a session.

To create a session:

1. Open login.php (Script 8.13) in your text editor or IDE.

2. Before the ob_end_clean( ) line, add the following (**Script 9.5**):

   ```
   session_start( );
   $_SESSION['email'] = $_POST
   → ['email'];
   $_SESSION['loggedin'] = time( );
   ```

Script 9.5 This script stores two values in the session and then redirects the user to another page, where the session values are accessed.

```
    ●●●                                                    Script
1    <?php // Script 9.5 - login.php #3
2    /* This page lets people log into the site (almost!). */
3
4    // Set the page title and include the header file:
5    define('TITLE', 'Login');
6    require('templates/header.html');
7
8    // Print some introductory text:
9    print '<h1>Login Form</h1>
10      <p>Users who are logged in can take advantage of certain features like this, that, and the
        other thing.</p>';
11
12   // Check if the form has been submitted:
13   if ( isset($_POST['submitted']) ) {
14
15     // Handle the form:
16     if ( (!empty($_POST['email'])) && (!empty($_POST['password'])) ) {
17
18        if ( (strtolower($_POST['email']) == 'me@example.com') && ($_POST['password'] ==
           'testpass') ) { // Correct!
19
20           // Do session stuff:
21           session_start();
22           $_SESSION['email'] = $_POST['email'];
23           $_SESSION['loggedin'] = time();
24
25           // Redirect the user to the welcome page!
26           ob_end_clean(); // Destroy the buffer!
27           header ('Location: welcome.php');
28           exit();
29
```

(script continues on next page)

To store values in a session, begin by calling the session_start() function. Although you normally have to call this function first thing in your script (because it may attempt to send a cookie), that's not required here because the header file for this script begins output buffering (see Chapter 8).

The session first stores the user's submitted email address in $_SESSION['email']. Then the time the user logged in is assigned to $_SESSION['loggedin']. This is determined by calling the time() function, which returns the number of seconds that have elapsed since the epoch (midnight on January 1, 1970).

continues on next page

Script 9.5 *continued*

```
30        } else { // Incorrect!
31
32            print '<p>The submitted email address and password do not match those on file!<br
              />Go back and try again.</p>';
33
34        }
35
36    } else { // Forgot a field.
37
38        print '<p>Please make sure you enter both an email address and a password!<br />Go back
          and try again.</p>';
39
40    }
41
42 } else { // Display the form.
43
44    print '<form action="login.php" method="post">
45    <p>Email Address: <input type="text" name="email" size="20" /></p>
46    <p>Password: <input type="password" name="password" size="20" /></p>
47    <p><input type="submit" name="submit" value="Log In!" /></p>
48    <input type="hidden" name="submitted" value="true" />
49    </form>';
50
51 }
52
53 require('templates/footer.html'); // Need the footer.
54 ?>
```

3. Save the file as login.php and place it in the appropriate directory on your PHP-enabled computer.

This script should be placed in the same directory used in Chapter 8, as it requires some of those other files.

4. Load the form in your Web browser to ensure that it has no errors (**Figure 9.18**).

The welcome page needs to be updated prior to actually logging in.

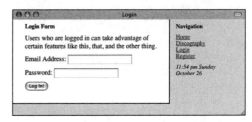

Figure 9.18 The login form.

✔ Tips

■ The php.ini configuration file includes many session-related settings that you can tinker with if you have administrative-level control over your server. Open the php.ini file in a text editor and see the manual for more information.

■ You can also alter some of the session settings using the ini_set() function.

■ The session_name() function lets you change the name of the session (instead of using the default *PHPSESSID*). It must be used before every session_start() call, like so:

```
session_name('YourVisit');
session_start();
```

■ The session_set_cookie_params() function alters the session cookie settings, like the expiration time, the path, and the domain.

■ The constant SID stores a string in the format *name=ID*. For example:

```
PHPSESSID=4bcc48dc87cb4b54d63f99da2
→ 3fb41e1
```

■ You can store any type of value—number, string, array, or object—or any combination thereof in your sessions.

Script 9.6 You can access stored session values using the $_SESSION array, as long as your script uses session_start() first.

```
1   <?php // Script 9.6 - welcome.php #2
2   /* This is the welcome page. The user is
    redirected here
3   after they successfully log in. */
4
5   // Need the session:
6   session_start();
7
8   // Set the page title and include the
    header file:
9   define('TITLE', 'Welcome to the Elliott
    Smith Fan Club!');
10  require('templates/header.html');
11
12  // Print a greeting:
13  print '<h1>Welcome to the Elliott
    Smith Fan Club, ' . $_SESSION['email'] .
    '!</h1>';
14
15  // Print how long they've been logged in:
16  date_default_timezone_set('America/New_
    York');
17  print '<p>You have been logged in since:
    ' . date('g:i a', $_SESSION['loggedin'])
    . '</p>';
18
19  // Make a logout link:
20  print '<p><a href="logout.php">Click here
    to logout.</a></p>';
21
22  require('templates/footer.html');
    // Need the footer.
23  ?>
```

Accessing Session Variables

Now that you've stored values in a session, you need to learn how to access them. You must begin with the session_start() function, whether you're creating a new session or accessing an existing one. This function indicates to PHP that this particular script will use sessions.

From there it's simply a matter of referencing the $_SESSION variable as you would any other array. With this in mind, you'll write another welcome page—similar to the one from Chapter 8—that accesses the stored *email* and *loggedin* values.

To access session variables:

1. Create a new PHP document in your text editor or IDE (**Script 9.6**):

   ```
   <?php // Script 9.6 - welcome.php
   ```

2. Begin the session:

   ```
   session_start();
   ```

   Even when you're accessing session values, you should call the session_start() function before any data is sent to the Web browser.

3. Define a page title, and include the HTML header:

   ```
   define('TITLE', 'Welcome to the
   → Elliott Smith Fan Club!');
   require('templates/header.html');
   ```

   Because this page uses the same template system developed in Chapter 8, it also uses the same header system.

4. Greet the user by email address:

   ```
   print '<h1>Welcome to the
   → Elliott Smith Fan Club, ' .
   → $_SESSION['email'] . '!</h1>';
   ```

continues on next page

To access the stored user's address, refer to $_SESSION['email']. Here, that value is concatenated to the rest of the string that's being printed out. You could also write:

```
print "<h1>Welcome to the
→ Elliott Smith Fan Club,
→ {$_SESSION['email']}!</h1>";
```

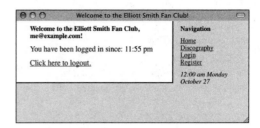

Figure 9.19 After successfully logging in (using *me@example.com* and *testpass* in the form), the user is redirected to this page, which greets them using the session values.

5. Show how long the user has been logged in:

```
date_default_timezone_set('America/
→ New_York');

print '<p>You have been logged
→ in since: ' . date('g:i a',
→ $_SESSION['loggedin']) . '</p>';
```

To show how long the user has been logged in, refer to the $_SESSION['loggedin'] variable. By using this as the second argument sent to the date() function, along with the appropriate formatting parameters, you make the PHP script create text like *11:22 pm*.

Before using the date() function, however, you need to set the default time zone (this is also discussed in Chapter 8). If you want, after setting the time zone here, you can remove the use of the same function from the footer file.

6. Complete the content:

```
print '<p><a href="logout.php">Click
→ here to logout.</a></p>';
```

The next script will provide logout functionality, so a link to it is added here.

7. Include the HTML footer, and complete the HTML page:

```
require('templates/footer.html');
?>
```

8. Save the file as welcome.php, place it in the proper directory for your PHP-enabled server, and test it (starting with login.php, Script 9.5) in your Web browser (**Figure 9.19**).

✔ Tip

■ To see whether a particular session variable exists, use isset($_SESSION['var']) as you would to check if any other variable is set.

Script 9.7 Deleting a session is a three-step process: start the session, delete the variable, and destroy the session data.

```
⬤ ⬤ ⬤                    📄 Script
1    <?php // Script 9.7 - logout.php
2    /* This is the logout page. It destroys
     the session information. */
3
4    // Need the session:
5    session_start();
6
7    // Delete the session variable:
8    unset($_SESSION);
9
10   // Destroy the session data:
11   session_destroy();
12
13   // Define a page title and include the
     header:
14   define('TITLE', 'Logout');
15   require('templates/header.html');
16
17   ?>
18
19   <h1>Welcome to the Elliott Smith Fan
     Club!</h1>
20   <p>You are now logged out.</p>
21   <p>Thank you for using this site. We hope
     that you liked it.<br />
22   Blah, blah, blah...
23   Blah, blah, blah...</p>
24
25   <?php require ('templates/footer.html'); ?>
```

Deleting a Session

It's important to know how to delete a session, just as it's important to know how to delete a cookie: Sometimes you'll want to get rid of the data you've stored. Session data exists in two areas, so you'll need to delete both. But first you must begin with the `session_start()` function, as always:

```
session_start();
```

Then, you delete the session variables by unsetting the `$_SESSION` array:

```
unset($_SESSION);
```

Finally, you remove the session data from the server (where it's stored in temporary files). To do this, use

```
session_destroy();
```

With that in mind, let's write `logout.php`, which will delete the session, effectively logging out the user.

To delete a session:

1. Start a new PHP script in your text editor or IDE (**Script 9.7**).

   ```
   <?php // Script 9.7 - logout.php
   ```

2. Begin the session:

   ```
   session_start();
   ```

   Remember that you can't delete a session until you activate the session using this function.

3. Delete the session variable:

   ```
   unset($_SESSION);
   ```

   You can use the `unset()` function to delete any variable, including `$_SESSION`. Doing so trashes any stored values.

4. Destroy the session data on the server:

   ```
   session_destroy();
   ```

   This step tells PHP to remove the actual session files on the server.

continues on next page

5. Include the HTML header, and complete this PHP section:

```
define('TITLE', 'Logout');
require('templates/header.html');
?>
```

6. Make the page content:

```
<h1>Welcome to the Elliott Smith Fan
→ Club!</h1>
<p>You are now logged out.</p>
<p>Thank you for using this site. We
→ hope that you liked it.<br />
Blah, blah, blah...
Blah, blah, blah...</p>
```

7. Include the HTML footer:

```
<?php require ('templates/footer.
→ html'); ?>
```

8. Save the file as logout.php, place it in the proper directory for your PHP-enabled server, and test it in your Web browser by clicking the link in welcome.php (**Figure 9.20**).

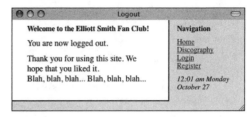

Figure 9.20 The logout page destroys the session data.

✔ Tips

- To delete an individual session value, use unset($_SESSION['*var*']);

- The PHP module on the server will automatically perform *garbage collection* based on settings in its configuration. PHP uses garbage collection to manually delete session files from the server, with the assumption that they're no longer needed.

- You can have PHP use sessions without cookies, in which case the session ID must be appended to every link in your site (so that each page receives the session ID). If you enable the enable_trans_side setting (in the php.ini file), PHP will handle this for you.

CREATING FUNCTIONS

Throughout this book, you've used dozens of functions that provide much-needed functionality, such as date( ), setcookie( ), and number_format( ). Whereas those functions have already been defined by PHP, here you'll be creating your own. However, once created, functions you've written and built-in PHP functions are used in the same manner.

Creating functions can save you oodles of time over the course of your programming life. In fact, they constitute a strong step in the process of creating Web applications and building a solid library of PHP code to use in future projects.

In this chapter, you'll see how to write your own functions that perform specific tasks. After that, you'll learn how to pass information to the function, use default values in a function, and have your function return a value. You'll also learn how functions and variables work together.

Creating and Using Simple Functions

As you program, you'll discover that you use certain sections of code frequently, either within a single script or over the course of several scripts. Placing these routines into a self-defined function can save you time and make your programming easier, especially as your Web sites become more complex. Once you create a function, the actions of that function take place each time the function is called, just as print() sends text to the browser with each use.

The syntax to create a user-defined function is

```
function function_name () {
    statement(s);
}
```

For example:

```
function whatever() {
    print 'whatever';
}
```

You can use roughly the same naming conventions for functions as you do for variables, just without the initial dollar sign. Second to that is the suggestion that you create meaningful function names, just as you ought to write representative variable names (create_header would be a better function name than function1). Remember not to use spaces, though—doing so constitutes two separate words for the function name, which will result in error messages (the underscore is a logical replacement for the space). Unlike variables, function names in PHP are *not case-sensitive*, but you should still stick with a consistent naming scheme.

Any valid PHP code can go within the statement(s) area of the function, including calls to other functions. There is also no limit on the number of statements a function contains; but make sure each statement ends with a semicolon, just as you would within the rest of the PHP script.

The formatting of a function isn't important as long as the requisite elements are there. These elements include the word *function*, the function's name, the opening and closing parentheses, the opening and closing braces, and the statement(s). It's conventional to indent a function's statement(s) from the previous line, for clarity's sake, as you would with a loop or conditional. In any case, select a format style that you like (which is both syntactically correct and logically sound) and stick to it.

You call (or invoke) the function by referring to it just as you do any built-in function. The line of code

```
whatever();
```

will cause the statement part of the previously defined function—the print() statement—to be executed.

Let's begin by creating a function that generates month, day, and year pull-down menus for a form.

To create and call a basic function:

1. Start a new PHP document in your text editor or IDE (**Script 10.1**):

```
<!DOCTYPE html PUBLIC "-//W3C//DTD
→ XHTML 1.0 Transitional//EN"
   "http://www.w3.org/TR/xhtml1/DTD/
   → xhtml1-transitional.dtd">
<html xmlns="http://www.w3.org/1999/
→ xhtml" xml:lang="en" lang="en">
<head>
  <meta http-equiv="content-type"
  → content="text/html;
  → charset=utf-8" />
  <title>Date Menus</title>
</head>
<body>
```

Script 10.1 The function defined in this script creates three pull-down menus for a form.

```
1    <!DOCTYPE html PUBLIC "-//W3C//DTD XHTML 1.0 Transitional//EN"
2        "http://www.w3.org/TR/xhtml1/DTD/xhtml1-transitional.dtd">
3    <html xmlns="http://www.w3.org/1999/xhtml" xml:lang="en" lang="en">
4    <head>
5        <meta http-equiv="content-type" content="text/html; charset=utf-8" />
6        <title>Date Menus</title>
7    </head>
8    <body>
9    <?php // Script 10.1 - menus1.php
10   /* This script defines and calls a function. */
11
12   // This function makes three pull-down menus for the months, days, and years.
13   function make_date_menus() {
14
15       // Array to store the months:
16       $months = array (1 => 'January', 'February', 'March', 'April', 'May', 'June', 'July',
         'August', 'September', 'October', 'November', 'December');
17
18       // Make the month pull-down menu:
19       print '<select name="month">';
20       foreach ($months as $key => $value) {
21           print "\n<option value=\"$key\">$value</option>";
22       }
23       print '</select>';
24
```

(script continues on next page)

Script 10.1 *continued*

```
25   // Make the day pull-down menu:
26   print '<select name="day">';
27   for ($day = 1; $day <= 31; $day++) {
28       print "\n<option value=\"$day\">
         $day</option>";
29   }
30   print '</select>';
31
32   // Make the year pull-down menu:
33   print '<select name="year">';
34   $start_year = date('Y');
35   for ($y = $start_year; $y <= ($start_
     year + 10); $y++) {
36       print "\n<option value=\"$y\">$y
         </option>";
37   }
38   print '</select>';
39
40   } // End of make_date_menus() function.
41
42   // Make the form:
43   print '<form action="" method="post">';
44   make_date_menus();
45   print '</form>';
46
47   ?>
48   </body>
49   </html>
```

2. Begin the PHP section:

```
<?php // Script 10.1 - menus1.php
```

3. Start defining a function:

```
function make_date_menus() {
```

The name of this function is *make_date_menus*, which is both descriptive of what the function does and easy to remember.

4. Create the month pull-down menu:

```
$months = array (1 => 'January',
→ 'February', 'March', 'April',
→ 'May', 'June', 'July', 'August',
→ 'September', 'October',
→ 'November', 'December');
print '<select name="month">';
foreach ($months as $key => $value) {
    print "\n<option value=\"$key\">
    → $value</option>";
}
print '</select>';
```

To generate a list of months, first create an array of the month names, indexed numerically beginning at 1 for *January*. When you specify the index for the first array element, the others will follow sequentially without the need to be explicit in naming them.

After the array has been created, the initial select tag is printed out. Then, a foreach loop runs through the $months array. For each element in the array, the HTML option tag is printed, using the array key (the numbers 1 through 12) as the option value and the array value (*January* through *December*) as the displayed text. Each line is also preceded by a newline character (\n) so that each option ends up on its own line within the HTML source.

continues on next page

5. Create the day pull-down menu:

```
print '<select name="day">';
for ($day = 1; $day <= 31; $day++) {
  print "\n<option value=\"$day\">
  → $day</option>";
}
print '</select>';
```

The day menu is a lot easier to create. To do so, you use a simple for loop, running through the numbers 1 through 31.

6. Create the year pull-down menu:

```
print '<select name="year">';
$start_year = date ('Y');
for ($y = $start_year; $y <=
→ ($start_year + 10); $y++) {
  print "\n<option value=\"$y\">$y
  → </option>";
}
print '</select>';
```

To create the year pull-down menu, you start by using the date() function to get the current year. Then you create options for this year plus the next 10, using a for loop.

7. Close the function:

```
} // End of make_date_menus()
→ function.
```

When you're creating functions, it's easy to create parse errors by forgetting the closing curly brace. You may want to add comments to help you remember this final step.

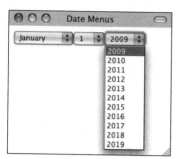

Figure 10.1 These pull-down menus were created by a user-defined function. This technique makes your code more portable without having an effect on the end result.

8. Make the form tags, and call the function:

```
print '<form action="" method=
→ "post">';
```

```
make_date_menus();
```

```
print '</form>';
```

The `print()` statements are used to create the HTML form tags. Without those, the date pull-down menus won't appear properly in your script.

Once you've created your function, you simply have to call it by name (being careful to use the exact spelling) to make the function work. Be sure to include the parentheses as well.

9. Complete the PHP and HTML:

```
?>
```

```
</body>
```

```
</html>
```

10. Save the file as `menus1.php`, place it in the proper directory for your PHP-enabled server, and run it in your Web browser (**Figure 10.1**).

✔ Tips

■ If you see a *Call to undefined function: some_ function...* error message, it means you're trying to call a function that doesn't exist. Recheck your spelling in both the definition of the function and its usage to see if you made a mistake.

■ The `function_exists()` function returns TRUE or FALSE based on whether a function exists in PHP. This applies to both user-defined functions and those that can be built into PHP:

```
if (function_exists('some_
→ function')) { …
```

■ Although you aren't required in PHP to define your functions before you call them, it's recommended that you habitually define your functions at the beginning of a script. The benefit of doing so is that it helps to separate the function definition code from the main workings of the script.

■ Some people prefer this syntax for laying out their functions:

```
function function_name()
{
    statement(s);
}
```

■ User-defined functions add extra memory requirements to your PHP scripts, so you should be judicious in using them. If you find that your function merely calls another PHP function or has but one line of code, it's probably not the best use of this capability.

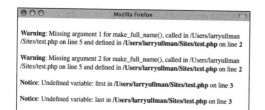

Figure 10.2 As with any function (user-defined or built into PHP), passing an incorrect number of arguments when calling it yields error messages.

Creating and Calling Functions That Take Arguments

Although being able to create a simple function is useful, writing one that takes input and does something with that input is even better. The input a function takes is called an *argument* (or a *parameter*). This is a concept you've seen before: the sort() function takes an array as an argument, which the function then sorts.

The syntax for writing functions that take arguments is as follows:

```
function function_name($arg1,
→ $arg2, …){
    statement(s);
}
```

The function's arguments are in the form of variables that are assigned the values sent to the function when you call it. The variables are defined using the same naming rules as any other variable in PHP:

```
function make_full_name($first, $last) {
    print $first . ' ' . $last;
}
```

Functions that take input are called much like those that don't—you just need to remember to pass along the necessary values (**Figure 10.2**). You can do this either by passing variables,

```
make_full_name($fn, $ln);
```

or by sending literal values, as in

```
make_full_name('Larry', 'Ullman');
```

or some combination thereof:

```
make_full_name('Larry', $ln);
```

continues on next page

The important thing to note is that arguments are passed quite literally: The first variable in the function definition is assigned the first value in the call line, the second function variable is assigned the second call value, and so forth. Functions aren't smart enough to intuitively understand how you meant the values to be associated. This is also true if you fail to pass a value, in which case the function will assume that value is null (*null* isn't the mathematical 0, which is actually a value, but closer to the idea of the word *nothing*). The same thing applies if a function takes four arguments and you pass three—the fourth will be null, which may create an error.

To demonstrate functions that take arguments, you'll rewrite the `make_date_menus()` function so that it takes a start year value and a number for how many years should be displayed. Then the function can easily create different year pull-down menus for different situations.

To create and call a function that takes an argument:

1. Open `menus1.php` (Script 10.1) in your text editor or IDE, if it is not already.

2. Change the function definition line (line 13 in Script 10.1) so that it takes two arguments (**Script 10.2**):

   ```
   function make_date_menus($start_year,
   → $num_years) {
   ```

   This function now takes two arguments, which will be assigned to the `$start_year` and `$num_years` variables.

3. Delete the `$start_year = date('Y');` code (line 34 of the original script).

   Because the start year is being passed to the function, the function no longer needs to calculate this value for itself.

continues on page 282

CREATING AND CALLING FUNCTIONS

Script 10.2 This version of the `make_date_menus()` function takes two arguments, dictating when the dates in the year pull-down menu begin and end.

```
1    <!DOCTYPE html PUBLIC "-//W3C//DTD XHTML 1.0 Transitional//EN"
2        "http://www.w3.org/TR/xhtml1/DTD/xhtml1-transitional.dtd">
3    <html xmlns="http://www.w3.org/1999/xhtml" xml:lang="en" lang="en">
4    <head>
5        <meta http-equiv="content-type" content="text/html; charset=utf-8" />
6        <title>Date Menus</title>
7    </head>
8    <body>
9    <?php // Script 10.2 - menus2.php
10   /* This script defines and calls a function that takes arguments. */
11
12   // This function makes three pull-down menus for the months, days, and years.
13   // This function requires two arguments be passed to it.
14   function make_date_menus($start_year, $num_years) {
15
16       // Array to store the months:
17       $months = array (1 => 'January', 'February', 'March', 'April', 'May', 'June', 'July',
         'August', 'September', 'October', 'November', 'December');
18
19       // Make the month pull-down menu:
20       print '<select name="month">';
21       foreach ($months as $key => $value) {
22           print "\n<option value=\"$key\">$value</option>";
23       }
24       print '</select>';
25
26       // Make the day pull-down menu:
27       print '<select name="day">';
28       for ($day = 1; $day <= 31; $day++) {
29           print "\n<option value=\"$day\">
             $day</option>";
30       }
31       print '</select>';
32
33       // Make the year pull-down menu:
34       print '<select name="year">';
35       for ($y = $start_year; $y <= ($start_year + $num_years); $y++) {
36           print "\n<option value=\"$y\">$y
             </option>";
37       }
38       print '</select>';
39
40   } // End of make_date_menus() function.
41
42   // Make the form:
43   print '<form action="" method="post">';
44   make_date_menus(2009, 15);
45   print '</form>';
46
47   ?>
48   </body>
49   </html>
```

4. Rewrite the year for loop to use the passed arguments:

```
for ($y = $start_year; $y <=
→ ($start_year + $num_years); $y++) {
```

To use the received values, you just need to change the second part of the for loop (the condition the for loop checks against). Instead of having the loop execute 10 times, it executes for $num_years times.

5. Change the function call so that it passes two arguments:

```
make_date_menus(2009, 15);
```

The function now needs to be passed two values. The first value is the first year to display in the pull-down menu. The second value is how many years to display. Because these are both number values, they don't need to be placed within quotation marks.

6. Save your script as menus2.php, place it in the proper directory for your PHP-enabled server, and test it in your Web browser (**Figure 10.3**).

7. If you want, change the arguments in your function call to create a different year pull-down menu (**Figure 10.4**).

✔ Tips

■ You could also use the date('Y') call outside of the function to have the pull-down menu automatically begin with the current year. This is what you could do:

```
make_date_menus(date('Y'), 20);
```

■ You can define as many functions as you want, not just one per script as the examples in this chapter portray.

■ There are no limits on how many arguments a function can take.

■ Once you've defined your own functions like this, you can place them in an external file and then require that file when you need access to the functions.

Figure 10.3 A slightly different variation on the original function (see Script 10.1 and Figure 10.1) lets you create different pull-down menus with ease.

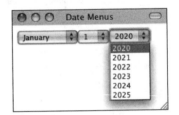

Figure 10.4 Minor changes to one line of code generate different results (compare with Figure 10.3).

Figure 10.5 Calling the function without any arguments uses the default value (the first greeting); calling it with an argument provided means that value will be used instead (the second).

Setting Default Argument Values

PHP allows functions to have default argument values. To do so, just assign a value to the argument in the function definition:

```
function greeting($who = 'world') {
    print "Hello, $who!";
}
```

Such a function will use the preset values unless it receives a value that then overwrites the default. In other words, by setting a default value for an argument, you render that particular argument optional when calling the function. You'd set an argument's default value if you wanted to assume a certain value but still allow for other possibilities (**Figure 10.5**):

```
greeting();
greeting('Sarah');
```

The default arguments should always be written after the other standard arguments (those without defaults). This is because PHP directly assigns values to arguments in the order they're received from the call line. Thus, it isn't possible to omit a value for the first argument but include one for the second (this would mean you sent one value, and it would automatically be equated to the first argument, not the second). For example, suppose you have:

```
function calculate_total($qty, $price =
→ 20.00, $tax = 0.06) {...
```

If you call the function with the line

```
calculate_total(3, 0.07);
```

with the intention of setting $qty to 3, leaving $price at 20.00, and changing the $tax to 0.07, there will be problems. The end result will be that $qty is set to 3, $price is set to 0.07, and $tax remains at 0.06, which isn't

continues on next page

the desired outcome. The proper way to achieve that affect would be to code

```
calculate_total(3, 20.00, 0.07);
```

Let's rework the make_date_menus() function to incorporate the notion of setting default argument values.

To write a function that uses default values:

1. Open menus2.php (Script 10.2) in your text editor or IDE, if it isn't open already.

2. Add a default value to the $num_years variable in the make_date_menus() function (**Script 10.3**):

   ```
   function make_date_menus($start_
   → year, $num_years = 10) {
   ```

   You've now set the value of $num_years to be 10 as a default. If two arguments are sent to the function, then $num_years will be set to the second value instead of the default, working as it did previously.

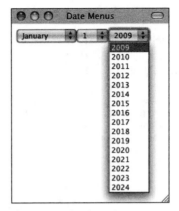

Figure 10.6 Now the script uses a default value for one function argument. This doesn't affect the end result but does make the function easier to use.

Script 10.3 The function still takes two arguments, but only one of them is required. If no $num_years value is passed to the function, its value will be 10.

```
1    <!DOCTYPE html PUBLIC "-//W3C//DTD XHTML 1.0 Transitional//EN"
2        "http://www.w3.org/TR/xhtml1/DTD/xhtml1-transitional.dtd">
3    <html xmlns="http://www.w3.org/1999/xhtml" xml:lang="en" lang="en">
4    <head>
5        <meta http-equiv="content-type" content="text/html; charset=utf-8" />
6        <title>Date Menus</title>
7    </head>
8    <body>
9    <?php // Script 10.3 - menus3.php
10   /* This script defines and calls a function that takes arguments. */
11
12   // This function makes three pull-down menus for the months, days, and years.
13   // This function requires two arguments be passed to it.
14   // The second argument has a default value of 10.
15   function make_date_menus($start_year, $num_years = 10) {
16
17       // Array to store the months:
18       $months = array (1 => 'January', 'February', 'March', 'April', 'May', 'June', 'July',
                 'August', 'September', 'October', 'November', 'December');
19
```

(script continues on next page)

Script 10.3 *continued*

```
000                    Script
20      // Make the month pull-down menu:
21      print '<select name="month">';
22      foreach ($months as $key => $value) {
23          print "\n<option value=\"$key\">
            $value</option>";
24      }
25      print '</select>';
26
27      // Make the day pull-down menu:
28      print '<select name="day">';
29      for ($day = 1; $day <= 31; $day++) {
30          print "\n<option value=\"$day\">
            $day</option>";
31      }
32      print '</select>';
33
34      // Make the year pull-down menu:
35      print '<select name="year">';
36      for ($y = $start_year; $y <= ($start_
        year + $num_years); $y++) {
37          print "\n<option value=\"$y\">$y
            </option>";
38      }
39      print '</select>';
40
41  } // End of make_date_menus() function.
42
43  // Make the form:
44  print '<form action="" method="post">';
45  make_date_menus(2009, 15);
46  print '</form>';
47
48  ?>
49  </body>
50  </html>
```

3. Save your script as `menus3.php`, place it in the proper directory of your PHP-enabled server, and test it in your Web browser (**Figure 10.6**).

4. If you want, change your function call to read

`make_date_menus(2009);`

Calling the function with this code works without a problem, only this time 10 more years are displayed in the pull-down menu instead of 15.

5. Save the script and run it again (**Figure 10.7**).

✔ Tips

■ To pass no value to a function for a particular argument, use an empty string (`''`) or the word `NULL` (without quotes). Either of these values will override the default value, if one is established.

■ As mentioned way back in Chapter 1, "Getting Started with PHP," the PHP manual marks optional function arguments using square brackets. For example, when you use the `number_format()` function, the number of decimals to round to is optional:

`string number_format(float number`
`→ [, int decimals])`

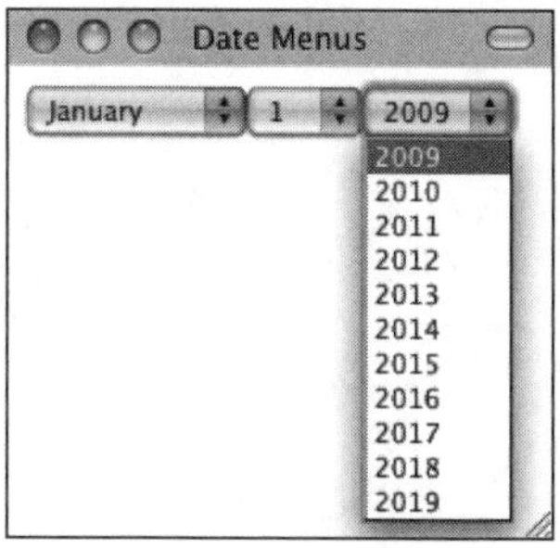

Figure 10.7
Passing only one parameter to the function causes it to use the default number of years to print (the start year plus ten more).

Creating and Using Functions That Return a Value

Functions do more than take arguments; they can also return values. To do so requires just two more steps. First, you use the `return` statement within the function. Second, you use the output somehow when you call the function. Commonly, you'll assign the returned value to a variable, but you can also, for example, directly print the output. Here is the basic format for a function that takes two arguments and returns a value:

```
function make_full_name($first, $last) {
    $name = $first . ' ' . $last;
    return $name;
}
```

This function could be used like so:

```
$full_name = make_full_name($fn, $ln);
```

There the returned value of the function is assigned to a variable. Here it's printed immediately:

```
print make_full_name($fn, $ln)
```

To best demonstrate this concept, let's create a function that performs a simple calculation and formats the result. This script will display an HTML form where a user enters a quantity and price (**Figure 10.8**). When the form is submitted (back to this same page), a total value will be determined and printed (**Figure 10.9**).

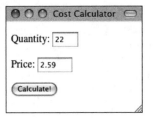

Figure 10.8 This simple form takes two values on which calculations will be made (see Figure 10.9).

Figure 10.9 The result of the calculation, which takes place within a user-defined function.

To create and use a function that returns a value:

1. Create a new PHP document in your text editor or IDE (**Script 10.4**):

```
<!DOCTYPE html PUBLIC "-//W3C//DTD
→ XHTML 1.0 Transitional//EN"
  "http://www.w3.org/TR/xhtml1/DTD/
  → xhtml1-transitional.dtd">
<html xmlns="http://www.w3.org/1999/
→ xhtml" xml:lang="en" lang="en">
<head>
  <meta http-equiv="Content-Type"
  → content="text/html;
  → charset=utf-8"/>
  <title>Cost Calculator</title>
</head>
<body>
```

continues on next page

Script 10.4 This script both displays and handles an HTML form in order to perform some basic calculations. The script uses a function that takes two arguments and returns a single value.

```
1   <!DOCTYPE html PUBLIC "-//W3C//DTD XHTML 1.0 Transitional//EN"
2       "http://www.w3.org/TR/xhtml1/DTD/xhtml1-transitional.dtd">
3   <html xmlns="http://www.w3.org/1999/xhtml" xml:lang="en" lang="en">
4   <head>
5       <meta http-equiv="Content-Type" content="text/html; charset=utf-8"/>
6       <title>Cost Calculator</title>
7   </head>
8   <body>
9   <?php // Script 10.4 - calculator.php
10  /* This script displays and handles an HTML form.
11  It uses a function to calculate a total from a quantity and price. */
12
13  // This function performs the calculations.
14  function calculate_total ($quantity, $price) {
15
16      $total = $quantity * $price; // Calculation
17      $total = number_format ($total, 2); // Formatting
18
19      return $total; // Return the value.
20
21  } // End of function.
22
```

(script continues on next page)

2. Begin the PHP code:

```
<?php // Script 10.4 - calculator.php
```

3. Define the function:

```
function calculate_total ($quantity,
→ $price) {
  $total = $quantity * $price;
  $total = number_format ($total, 2);
  return $total;
}
```

This function takes two arguments—a quantity and a price—and multiplies them to create a total. The total value is then formatted before it's returned by the function.

Script 10.4 *continued*

```
23   // Check for a form submission:
24   if (isset($_POST['submitted'])) {
25
26       // Check for values:
27       if ( is_numeric($_POST['quantity']) AND is_numeric($_POST['price']) ) {
28
29           // Call the function and print the results:
30           $total = calculate_total($_POST['quantity'], $_POST['price']);
31           print "<p>Your total comes to $<span style=\"font-weight: bold;\">$total</span>.</p>";
32
33       } else { // Inappropriate values entered.
34           print '<p style="color: red;">Please enter a valid quantity and price!</p>';
35       }
36
37   }
38   ?>
39   <form action="calculator.php" method="post">
40       <p>Quantity: <input type="text" name="quantity" size="3" /></p>
41       <p>Price: <input type="text" name="price" size="5" /></p>
42       <input type="submit" name="submit" value="Calculate!" />
43       <input type="hidden" name="submitted" value="true" />
44   </form>
45   </body>
46   </html>
```

Although this may seem like a silly use of a function, the benefits of putting even a one-step calculation into a function are twofold: First, the calculation will be easier to find and modify at a later date with your function located at the beginning of your script instead of hidden in the rest of the code; and second, should you want to repeat the action again in a script, you can do so without duplicating code.

4. Begin the conditional to see if the form was submitted:

```
if (isset($_POST['submitted'])) {
```

Because this page both displays and handles the HTML form, it has a conditional that checks for the presence of a $_POST['submitted'] variable. If this variable is set, the script should handle the form.

5. Validate the form data and use the function:

```
if ( is_numeric($_POST['quantity'])
→ AND is_numeric($_POST['price']) ) {
  $total = calculate_total($_POST
  → ['quantity'], $_POST['price']);
  print "<p>Your total comes
  → to $<span style=\"font-weight:
  → bold;\">$total</span>.</p>";
```

This part of the PHP code—which handles the form if it has been submitted—first checks that a numeric quantity and price were entered. If so, the total is determined by calling the calculate_total() function and assigning the result to the $total variable. This result is then printed out.

continues on next page

Returning Multiple Values

User-defined functions frequently return just a single value but can return multiple values by using arrays. Here's how you go about this:

```
function some_function($a1, $a2) {
    // Do whatever.
    return array($v1, $v2);
}
```

Then, to call this function, use the list() function to assign the array elements to individual variables:

```
list($var1, $var2) = some_function($p1,
→ $p2);
```

The end result is that $v1 from the function is assigned to $var1 in the PHP script, and $v2 from the function is assigned to $var2.

6. Complete the conditionals:

```
    } else {
        print '<p style="color: red;">
        → Please enter a valid quantity
        → and price!</p>';
    }
}
```

If either of the form variables was not properly submitted, a message is printed indicating such. The final curly brace closes the form submission conditional.

A little CSS is applied to both printed messages (here and in Step 5).

7. Display the HTML form:

```
?>
<form action="calculator.php"
→ method="post">
    <p>Quantity: <input type="text"
    → name="quantity" size="3" /></p>
    <p>Price: <input type="text"
    → name="price" size="5" /></p>
    <input type="submit" name="submit"
    → value="Calculate!" />
    <input type="hidden" name=
    → "submitted" value="true" />
</form>
```

The form itself is quite simple, requesting two different values from the user (Figure 10.8). The hidden form input is used as a trigger for the handling code, indicating that the form was submitted. Because this form is created outside of the main submission conditional, the form will always be displayed by the page.

8. Complete the HTML page:

```
</body>
</html>
```

9. Save the page as calculator.php, place it in the proper directory for your PHP-enabled server, and test it in your Web browser (Figure 10.9).

✔ Tip

■ You can have only one return statement *executed* in a function, but the same function can have multiple return statements. As an example, you may want to write a function that checks for a condition and returns a value indicating whether the condition was satisfied. In such a case, you'd code as follows in your function:

```
if (condition) {
    return TRUE;
} else {
    return FALSE;
}
```

The result returned by the function is either TRUE or FALSE, indicating whether the stated condition was met.

CREATING AND USING FUNCTIONS

Understanding Variable Scope

The concept of variable scope wasn't introduced earlier because without an understanding of functions, scope makes little sense. Now that you are acquainted with functions, this section will revisit the topic of variables and discuss in some detail just how variables and functions work together.

As you saw in the second section of this chapter, "Creating and Calling Functions That Take Arguments," you can send variables to a function by passing them as arguments. However, you can also reference an external variable from within a function using the `global` statement. This is possible because of variable scope. The *scope* of a variable is the realm in which it exists. By default, the variables you write in a script exist for the life of that script. Conversely, environment variables, such as `$_SERVER['PHP_SELF']`, exist throughout the server.

Functions, though, create a new level of scope. Function variables—the arguments of a function as well as any variables defined within the function—exist only within that function and aren't accessible outside of it (that is, they're *local variables* with *local scope*). Likewise, a variable from outside a function can only be referenced by passing it to the function as an argument or by using the `global` statement. The `global` statement roughly means, "I want this variable within the function to refer to the same named variable outside of the function." In other words, the `global` statement turns a local variable with local scope into a global variable with global scope. Any changes made to the variable within the function are also passed on to the variable when it's outside of the function (assuming the function is called, that is), without using the `return` command.

continues on next page

The syntax of the global statement is as follows:

```
function function_name($args) {
    global $variable;
    statement(s);
}
```

This leads to another issue regarding functions and variables: Because of variable scope, a local variable within a function is a different entity (perhaps with a different value) than a variable outside of the function, *even if the two variables use the exact same name*. Let's go over this more explicitly...

Say you have:

```
function test($arg) {
    // Do whatever.
}
$var = 1;
test($var);
```

When the function is called, the value of $var will be assigned $arg, so their values are the same but their names are different and they are different variables. However, if the name of the argument in the function is also $var—

```
function test($var) {
    // Do whatever.
}
$var = 1;
test($var);
```

—then the $var variable within the function is assigned the same value as the original $var outside of the function—but they're still two separate variables. The one has a scope within the function, and the other has a scope outside of it. This means that you can use the exact same name for variables in the function as exist outside of the function without conflict. Just remember they aren't the same variable. What happens to a variable's value within a function only affects that variable within the function.

Understanding Variable Scope

This is all true unless you use the global statement, of course, which does make the two variables the same:

```
function test() {
    global $var; // Same!
    print $var; // Prints 1
}
$var = 1;
test();
```

To demonstrate variable scope, let's rework the calculator.php script using the global statement.

To use the global statement:

1. Open calculator.php (Script 10.4) in your text editor or IDE, if it is not already.

2. Before the function definition, add the following (**Script 10.5**):

   ```
   $tax = 8.75;
   ```

   Create a $tax variable with a set value to be used in the cost calculations. It's assigned a value outside of the function because it will be used later in the main body of the script.

continues on page 295

Script 10.5 The function in this script can use the $tax variable—even though it hasn't been passed to the function—thanks to the global statement.

```
1   <!DOCTYPE html PUBLIC "-//W3C//DTD XHTML 1.0 Transitional//EN"
2       "http://www.w3.org/TR/xhtml1/DTD/xhtml1-transitional.dtd">
3   <html xmlns="http://www.w3.org/1999/xhtml" xml:lang="en" lang="en">
4   <head>
5       <meta http-equiv="Content-Type" content="text/html; charset=utf-8"/>
6       <title>Cost Calculator</title>
7   </head>
8   <body>
9   <?php // Script 10.5 - calculator.php #2
10  /* This script displays and handles an HTML form.
11  It uses a function to calculate a total from a quantity, price, and tax rate. */
12
13  // Define a tax rate:
14  $tax = 8.75;
15
```

(script continues on next page)

Script 10.5 *continued*

```
16   // This function performs the calculations.
17   function calculate_total ($quantity, $price) {
18
19       global $tax;
20
21       $total = $quantity * $price; // Calculation
22       $taxrate = ($tax / 100) + 1;
23       $total = $total * $taxrate; // Add the tax.
24       $total = number_format ($total, 2); // Formatting
25
26       return $total; // Return the value.
27
28   } // End of function.
29
30   // Check for a form submission:
31   if (isset($_POST['submitted'])) {
32
33       // Check for values:
34       if ( is_numeric($_POST['quantity']) AND is_numeric($_POST['price']) ) {
35
36           // Call the function and print the results:
37           $total = calculate_total($_POST['quantity'], $_POST['price']);
38           print "<p>Your total comes to $<span style=\"font-weight: bold;\">$total</span>,
             including the $tax percent tax rate.</p>";
39
40       } else { // Inappropriate values entered.
41           print '<p style="color: red;">Please enter a valid quantity and price!</p>';
42       }
43
44   }
45   ?>
46   <form action="calculator.php" method="post">
47       <p>Quantity: <input type="text" name="quantity" size="3" /></p>
48       <p>Price: <input type="text" name="price" size="5" /></p>
49       <input type="submit" name="submit" value="Calculate!" />
50       <input type="hidden" name="submitted" value="true" />
51   </form>
52   </body>
53   </html>
```

3. Within the function definition, add a `global` statement:

```
global $tax;
```

This statement tells the function to incorporate the same `$tax` variable as the one that exists outside of the function.

4. Before the `$total` in the function is formatted, recalculate the value using the tax rate:

```
$taxrate = ($tax / 100) + 1;
$total = $total * $taxrate;
```

To add the tax to the total value, you start by dividing the tax by `100`, to create a percentage. Then you add 1 to this value to get a multiplier. This result is then multiplied by the total to come up with the new, final total.

Notice that you use a `$taxrate` variable (based on `$tax`) to perform these calculations. This is because you'll print out the value of `$tax` later, and any changes made to it here will be reflected (because it's a global variable).

5. Alter the main `print()` line (after the function call) so that it prints the tax rate as well:

```
print "<p>Your total comes to
→ $<span style=\"font-weight:
→ bold;\">$total</span>, including
→ the $tax percent tax rate.</p>";
```

The `$tax` variable defined at the beginning of the script is printed out at the end. If you hadn't used the `$taxrate` variable within the function and made the alterations to the global `$tax` instead, those calculations would be reflected in the value printed here.

continues on next page

6. Save the script, place it in the proper directory for your PHP-enabled server, and test it in your Web browser (**Figures 10.10** and **10.11**).

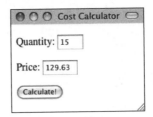

Figure 10.10 Run the form again...

✔ Tips

■ Constants and the superglobal arrays ($_GET, $_POST, $_COOKIE, and $_SESSION) have the added benefit that they're always available inside functions without requiring the global statement (which is why they are called *superglobal*).

■ Proper function design suggests that you should be cautious when using global variables. Arguably, a function should be passed all the information it needs, so that global variables are not required. By doing so, you make the function more independent and portable.

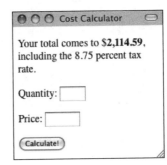

Figure 10.11 ...and the calculation now makes use of a global $tax variable.

FILES AND DIRECTORIES

To truly take your Web applications to the next level, you'll need a method of storing and retrieving data. There are two primary ways of storing data with PHP: using files (and directories) or databases. This chapter will discuss the former, and the next chapter will introduce the latter. It's worth your time to comprehend both methods (in fact, a database is just a really fancy system for writing to and reading from data stored in files on the server). Although a database can be more powerful and secure than a file-based system, you may be surprised at how much you can do by sending and retrieving information from simple text documents on the server!

In this chapter, you'll learn about file permissions and then learn to write to, read from, and lock files. After that, you'll see how to handle file uploads with PHP, how to create directories, and an alternate method for reading data from a file. These last two examples will also demonstrate a simple file-based registration and login system that you can use in your Web applications.

File Permissions

Before attempting to write to and read from a file, you must have an understanding of file permissions. The topic is large enough that you may want to pursue it further, but this discussion will get you started. Up front I will say that most of the information herein will be an issue only for non-Windows users. In my experience, the preparatory steps to be taken aren't necessary when running PHP on a Windows computer. Still, having an understanding of permissions as a whole is a good idea, especially if you might later be running your PHP scripts on a non-Windows server.

Permissions identify who can do what with a file or directory. The options are *read*, *write*, and *execute* (actually, files can be designated *executable*, whereas directories are made *searchable*). On top of that, these options can be set differently for three unique types of users: the *owner* of the file (the person who created it or put it on the server); members of a particular *group*, which a server administrator sets; and *others* (those who don't fall into the previous two categories). There is also the implied *everyone* level, which includes all of the previously mentioned users.

Normally, a file's *owner* is given read and write permissions by default, whereas *groups* and *others* are able to only read a file or directory. For the examples in this chapter, PHP needs to be able to write to some files and directories, so you must be able to expand the permissions. Being able to write to a file or directory can be a security issue and should only be designated an option when absolutely necessary. Keep this in mind, and pay attention to some of the security tips mentioned throughout this chapter.

A More Secure File Structure

Having writable files and directories on the server is a bit of a security risk. If the Web server (and everyone else) can write to the file or directory, then what's to stop malicious users from trying to hack your system using this same gateway?

In general, the security issue is more important for directories than for files. This is because anyone can write anything to an open directory, including viruses, evil scripts, and Trojan horses.

The best security measure you can take in such instances is to place your writable files and directories outside of the Web directory. In other words, if your Web pages go in C:\inetpub\wwwroot or /Users/~username/Sites, then if you place items in C:\inetpub or /Users/~username, they are accessible to the locally running PHP but not to others over the Internet. The examples in this chapter follow this structure, and you should do so as well.

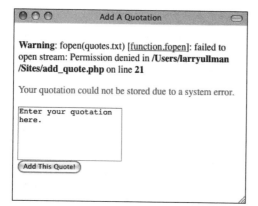

Figure 11.1 The ...failed to open stream: Permission denied... message is the result of attempting to do something to a file that isn't allowed by the server. Here the server is denying the fopen() function that is attempting to open quotes.txt for the purpose of writing to it.

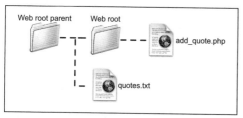

Figure 11.2 The quotes.txt file should ideally be placed in the same directory as your Web documents directory (i.e., not in the directory with the Web documents).

Creating the text file

In the first example, you'll work with a text file on the server named quotes.txt. If the file doesn't have the correct permissions to do what your PHP script is asking it to, you'll see an error message similar to that shown in **Figure 11.1**. Before proceeding through this chapter, you should create quotes.txt on the server and establish its permissions.

To create quotes.txt:

1. Open your text editor or IDE and create a new, blank document.

2. Without typing anything into the file, save it as quotes.txt.

3. Move the file just outside of the Web root directory of your PHP-enabled server (**Figure 11.2**)

   The sidebar "A More Secure File Structure" explains where you should put the file with respect to your Web directory and why.

✔ Tips

- The file_exists() function returns TRUE if a submitted filename is found on the server. This can be used to test for the existence of a file before doing anything with it.

  ```
  if (file_exists('somefile')) { …
  ```

- Assuming that PHP has write permissions on a directory, you can create a blank document within that directory using PHP. This is accomplished using the touch() function:

  ```
  touch('somefile');
  ```

Setting a file's permissions

The preceding sequence may seem like an odd series of steps, but in order to set the permissions on a file, the file must exist first. You do want the file to be blank, though, because you'll use PHP to write data to it later.

The desired end result for this example is to give either *others* or *everyone* permission to *read* and *write* (but not *execute*) quotes.txt. How you accomplish this depends on:

◆ Whether you're running PHP on your own computer or on a remote server

◆ The operating system of the PHP-enabled computer

Unfortunately, it would be impossible to offer steps for how every user should set the permissions under any circumstances, but here are some rough guidelines and steps to get you going.

To set a file's permissions on a remote server:

◆ Most ISPs offer their users a Web-based control panel where they can set file permissions (**Figure 11.3**) as well as set other hosting parameters.

◆ You may be able to change a file's permissions using your FTP client (**Figure 11.4**).

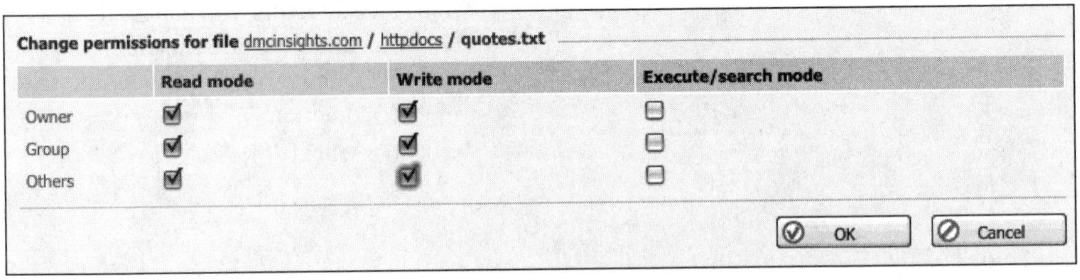

Figure 11.3 This control panel, provided by a hosting company, lets you adjust a file's permissions.

FILE PERMISSIONS

Figure 11.4 The FileZilla FTP application uses this pop-up window to allow you to set a file's permissions.

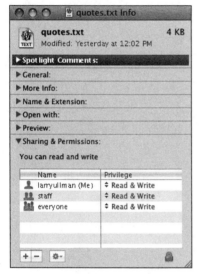

Figure 11.5 The Mac OS X Get Info panel lets you adjust a file's ownership and permissions, among other things.

To set a file's permissions on your computer:

◆ If you're working on your own Windows computer, you may not need to change the permissions. To test this theory, try each example first. If you see the *Permission denied* error message (Figure 11.1), use the next suggestion to rework the permissions.

◆ Windows users who need to change the permissions can do so by viewing the file or directory's properties. The resulting panel will differ for each version of Windows, but basically you just need to tweak who can access the file and how.

◆ Mac OS X users must select the file in the Finder and choose Get Info from the File menu. From there, use the Ownership & Permissions subpanel to adjust the file's permissions (**Figure 11.5**).

◆ On Unix (including users of Linux and Mac OS X) you can also use the chmod 0666 quotes.txt line in a terminal window, assuming that you have authority to do so.

✔ Tips

- Most operating systems have no *PHP* user. Instead, the *PHP* user is essentially the user the Web server application (for example, Apache or IIS) is running as. On the Unix family, Apache often runs as *nobody*. On Windows, the Web server frequently runs as the same user who is logged in (and who probably created the file), meaning there will be no need to alter a file's permissions.

- If you're already familiar with Telnet and chmod, you probably also understand what the 0666 number means; but here's an explanation for those of you who aren't familiar with it. The 0 is just a prefix indicating the number is written in an octal format. Each 6 corresponds to *read* (4) plus *write* (2) permission—first assigning 6 to the *owner*, then to the *group*, and then to *others*. Comparatively, 0777 allows *read* (4) plus *write* (2) plus *execute* (1) permission to all three types of users. This numbering is applicable for Unix variant operating systems (Linux, Solaris, and Mac OS X).

- PHP has several functions for changing a file or directory's permissions, including chgrp( ), chown( ), and chmod( ). However, they will only work if PHP already has permission to modify the file or directory in question.

Table 11.1

fopen( ) Modes	
MODE	MEANING
r	Reading only; begin reading at the start of the file.
r+	Reading or writing; begin at the start of the file.
w	Writing only; create the file if it doesn't exist, and overwrite any existing contents.
w+	Reading or writing; create the file if it doesn't exist, and overwrite any existing contents (when writing).
a	Writing only; create the file if it doesn't exist, and append the new data to the end of the file (retain any existing data and add to it).
a+	Reading or writing; create the file if it doesn't exist, and append the new data to the end of the file (when writing).
x	Writing only; create the file if it doesn't exist, but do nothing (and issue a warning) if the file does exist.
x+	Reading or writing; create the file if it doesn't exist, but do nothing (and issue a warning) if the file already exists (when writing).

Writing to Files

Because you need to write something to a file in order to read something from it, this chapter explores writing first. Writing to a file on the server is a three-step process: first, open the file; second, write your data to it; and third, close the file. Fortunately, PHP's built-in functions for doing these steps are quite obvious:

```
$fp = fopen(filename, mode);

fwrite($fp, data to be written);

fclose($fp);
```

To write to a file, you must create a file pointer when opening it. The first argument to the fopen( ) function is the name of the file. This can be an absolute or relative path (see the sidebar "File Paths"). The file pointer returned by the fopen( ) function will be used by PHP to refer to the open file.

The most important consideration when opening the file is what *mode* you use. Depending on what you intend to do with the file, the mode dictates how to open it. The most forgiving mode is a+, which allows you to read or write to a file. It creates the file if it doesn't exist, and it appends—hence *a*—new data to the end of the file automatically. Conversely, r only allows you to read from a file. **Table 11.1** lists all the possible modes. Each mode can also be appended with a b flag, which forces files to be opened in binary mode. This is a safer option for files that might be read on multiple operating systems.

The fwrite( ) function writes the new data (sent as the second argument in the function call) to the file in accordance with the selected mode. You normally want each piece of data to be written on its own line, so each submission should conclude with the appropriate

continues on next page

WRITING TO FILES

line break for the operating system of the computer running PHP. This would be

◆ \n on Unix and Mac OS X

◆ \r\n on Windows

For most users and many situations, just calling fwrite() may be all you need to do. But if the HTML page is using a different encoding than the default for the server, you'll need to add a line of code. For example, say the default encoding for the computer on which PHP is running *ISO Latin 9* (Chapter 1, "Getting Started with PHP," introduces the subject of encoding). If the HTML page uses the UTF-8 encoding—as all of the examples in this book do—then the form data will automatically be received as UTF-8 encoded. This means that PHP will attempt to write UTF-8 data but the computer is expecting ISO Latin 9 in its files (**Figure 11.6**). The solution is to indicate the encoding being used:

```
stream_encoding(file_pointer, encoding);
```

This line should be done once, before writing to or reading from a file.

As the last step of the writing process, you close the file by once again referring to the file pointer while calling the fclose() function:

```
fclose(file_pointer);
```

Let's create a form that stores user-submitted quotations in a plain text file (**Figure 11.7**). Later in this chapter, another PHP script will retrieve and randomly display these quotations.

Writing to Files

> **Notice**: fwrite() [function.fwrite]: 30 character unicode buffer downcoded for binary stream runtime_encoding in C:**Program Files\Abyss Web Server\htdocs\add_quote.php** on line **21**

Figure 11.6 This convoluted error message results from mixing encodings.

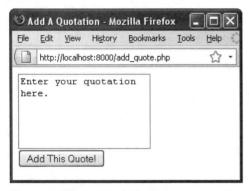

Figure 11.7 This very simple form lets a user submit a quotation that will be written to a text file.

To write to an external file:

1. Create a new PHP document in your text editor or IDE (**Script 11.1**):

   ```
   <!DOCTYPE html PUBLIC "-//W3C//DTD
   → XHTML 1.0 Transitional//EN"
      "http://www.w3.org/TR/xhtml1/DTD/
      → xhtml1-transitional.dtd">
   <html xmlns="http://www.w3.org/1999/
   → xhtml" xml:lang="en" lang="en">
   <head>
      <meta http-equiv="content-type"
      → content="text/html;
      → charset=utf-8" />
      <title>Add A Quotation</title>
   </head>
   <body>
   ```

continues on next page

WRITING TO FILES

Script 11.1 This script takes a user-submitted quotation and stores it in a text file.

```
1    <!DOCTYPE html PUBLIC "-//W3C//DTD XHTML 1.0 Transitional//EN"
2        "http://www.w3.org/TR/xhtml1/DTD/xhtml1-transitional.dtd">
3    <html xmlns="http://www.w3.org/1999/xhtml" xml:lang="en" lang="en">
4    <head>
5        <meta http-equiv="content-type" content="text/html; charset=utf-8" />
6        <title>Add A Quotation</title>
7    </head>
8    <body>
9    <?php // Script 11.1 - add_quote.php
10   /* This script displays and handles an HTML form. This script takes text input and stores it in
     a text file. */
11
12   // Check for a form submission:
13   if (isset($_POST['submitted'])) { // Handle form.
14
15       if ( !empty($_POST['quote']) && ($_POST['quote'] != 'Enter your quotation here.') ) { //
         Need some thing to write.
16
17          if ($fp = fopen ('../quotes.txt', 'ab')) { // Try to open the file.
18
19              // Set the encoding:
20              stream_encoding($fp, 'utf-8');
21
22              fwrite($fp, "{$_POST['quote']}\n"); // Write the data. Use \r\n on Windows.
23              fclose($fp); // Close the file.
24
```

(script continues on next page)

2. Create a section of PHP code:

```php
<?php // Script 11.1 - add_quote.php
```

3. See if the form has been submitted:

```php
if (isset($_POST['submitted'])) {
```

This page both displays and handles the HTML form. This conditional checks to see if the form has been submitted, in which case the quotation should be written to the text file.

4. Check that a quotation was entered:

```php
if ( !empty($_POST['quote']) &&
→ ($_POST['quote'] != 'Enter your
→ quotation here.') ) {
```

This simple conditional validates the user-supplied data. The first part confirms that the `$_POST['quote']` variable isn't empty. The second part confirms that the variable doesn't still have the default value (as shown in Figure 11.7).

Script 11.1 *continued*

```
25            // Print a message:
26            print "<p>Your quotation has been stored.</p>";
27
28        } else { // Could not open the file.
29            print '<p style="color: red;">Your quotation could not be stored due to a system
             error.</p>';
30        }
31
32    } else { // Failed to enter a quotation.
33        print '<p style="color: red;">Please enter a quotation!</p>';
34    }
35
36 } // End of submitted IF.
37
38 // Leave PHP and display the form:
39 ?>
40
41 <form action="add_quote.php" method="post">
42    <textarea name="quote" rows="5" cols="30">Enter your quotation here.</textarea>
43    <input type="submit" name="submit" value="Add This Quote!" />
44    <input type="hidden" name="submitted" value="true" />
45 </form>
46
47 </body>
48 </html>
```

File Paths

There are two ways of referring to any file or directory on the computer: using an *absolute* or *relative* path. An absolute path begins at the root of the computer:

- `C:\somedir\somefile.txt` (Windows)

- `/Users/username/somefile.txt` (Mac OS X).

A relative path will not start with the root of the computer—C:\ or /. Instead it might be relative to the current working directory:

- `fileA.txt` (this directory)

- `dirB/fileB.txt` (inside `dirB`)

- `../fileC.txt` (inside parent directory)

- `../dirD/fileD.txt` (inside parallel directory)

Two periods together represent the current directory's parent folder. A single period by itself represents the current directory. If a *file's name* begins with a single period, the file is hidden (on Unix, Linux, and Mac OS X).

It technically doesn't matter whether you use a relative or an absolute path to refer to a file, so long as the reference is accurate.

5. Attempt to open the file for writing:

```
if ($fp = fopen ('../quotes.txt',
→ 'ab')) {
```

By placing the `fopen()` statement in a conditional, you make the PHP script attempt to write to the file only if it could be successfully opened for writing. At the same time, the file pointer is created.

The file opened is `quotes.txt`, which should be located in the directory above this script (which is presumably in the Web directory root, see Figure 11.2). See the sidebar "File Paths" for more on this syntax.

The mode being used is *ab*, meaning that the file should be opened for writing and the data being written should be appended to any existing data. The *b* flag is added so that the file is opened in a binary safe mode. That may not be necessary, but it can't hurt.

6. Set the encoding:

```
stream_encoding($fp, 'utf-8');
```

As already explained, since the HTML page is encoded in UTF-8, the submitted data will also be UTF-8 encoded. This line indicates the string's encoding, prior to writing that string to a file.

7. Write the data to the file, close the file, and then print a message:

```
fwrite($fp, "{$_POST['quote']}\n");
fclose($fp);
```

```
print "<p>Your quotation has been
→ stored.</p>";
```

The first line writes the user-submitted data to the file. In this example, you use the \n newline character to mark the end of the line. If you're using Windows, replace \n with \r\n.

After that, the file is closed by referring to the same file pointer, and a simple message is displayed to the user.

continues on next page

8. Complete the conditionals:

```
    } else {
        print '<p style="color:
        → red;">Your quotation
        → could not be stored due
        → to a system error.</p>';
    }
} else {
    print '<p style="color:
    → red;">Please enter a
    → quotation!</p>';
}
} // End of submitted IF.
```

The first else completes the conditional that checks if PHP could open the file for writing. If you see this message, there's likely a permissions issue or the file reference is incorrect. The second else completes the conditional that checks whether no quotation was entered. The final closing curly brace marks the end of the main submission conditional.

Because this page handles the form and then displays it again (so that the user may keep entering quotations), the form isn't displayed as part of an else statement as it has been in other examples in this book.

9. Complete the PHP section:

```
?>
```

Because the rest of this script is standard HTML, exit out of the PHP code by closing the PHP tag.

10. Create the HTML form:

```
<form action="add_quote.php"
→ method="post">
    <textarea name="quote" rows="5"
    → cols="30">Enter your quotation
    → here.</textarea>
    <input type="submit" name=
    → "submit" value="Add This
    → Quote!" />
    <input type="hidden" name=
    → "submitted" value="true" />
</form>
```

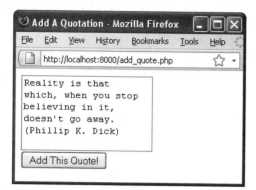

Figure 11.8 Filling out the form...

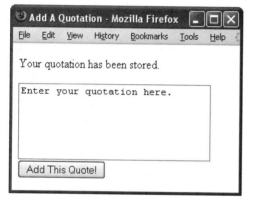

Figure 11.9 ...and the result if all went well.

This HTML form presents a text box where the user can enter a quotation. The text box has a preset value of *Enter your quotation here.*, created by putting that text between the textarea tags.

As you must with any script that both handles and displays a form, be certain that the name of your hidden input matches the $_POST array index being used in the `if (isset($_POST['submitted']))` conditional. Also, the form's action attribute should be the name of this same script.

11. Complete the HTML page:

    ```
    </body>
    </html>
    ```

12. Save the file as `add_quote.php` and place it in the proper directory for your PHP-enabled server.

    Again, refer back to Figure 11.2 for how the `add_quote.php` and `quotes.txt` should be placed on your server relative to each other. If this arrangement isn't possible for you, or if it's just too confusing, then place both documents within the same directory (the one from which you can execute PHP scripts) and change the `fopen()` line to:

    ```
    if ($fp = fopen ('quotes.txt',
    → 'ab')) {
    ```

13. Run the script several times in your Web browser (**Figures 11.8** and **11.9**).

14. If you want, open the `quotes.txt` file in a text editor to confirm that the data has been written to it.

WRITING TO FILES

✔ Tips

■ If you receive a permissions error when you run this script (see Figure 11.1), either the permissions aren't set properly or the PHP script couldn't access the data file. This can happen if you misspell the filename or incorrectly reference the file's path on the server.

■ Having a writable file on your server can be a bit of a security risk. See the sidebar "A More Secure File Structure" earlier in this chapter for ways to improve on the security of a script like `add_quote.php`.

■ PHP 5 added a `file_put_contents()` function to the language. It replicates the `fopen()`, `fwrite()`, `fclose()` process in one step.

■ If your version of PHP is running in safe mode or has the `open_basedir` directive set, you may be limited in using PHP to access files and directories. Check your `phpinfo()` script to see these settings for your server.

■ If a script or Web application will be accessing the same file multiple times, it may make sense to assign the filename and path (where it is on the server) to a variable, for the sake of convenience. Then you can feed this variable to the `fopen()` function.

■ As an extra step of safe-checking, you can use the `is_writable()` function to determine whether the server will allow you to write data to the file before you attempt to open it. Here is how you'd begin to incorporate it (this is only a part of the script):

```
if (is_writable('../quotes.txt')) {
    // Attempt to open...
} else {
    print '<p style="color: red;">The
    → file is not writable!</p>';
}
```

Table 11.2

flock( ) Lock Types	
LOCK	**MEANING**
LOCK_SH	Shared lock for reading purposes
LOCK_EX	Exclusive lock for writing purposes
LOCK_UN	Release of a lock
LOCK_NB	Non-blocking lock

Locking Files

Although the last example worked fine (hopefully), it could be improved on. If only a single user was submitting the form at one time, there would be no problems. But what if two or more users submitted different quotations simultaneously? In such a case, there could be problems.

The solution is to temporarily lock the file while PHP is writing to it. You can do so using the flock() function:

```
$fp = fopen('filename.txt', 'a+b');
flock($fp, locktype)
```

The different lock types are represented by the constants listed in **Table 11.2**.

As an example, to temporarily lock a file during a write, use this code:

```
$fp = fopen('filename.txt', 'a+b');
flock ($fp, LOCK_EX);
fwrite ($fp, 'data to be written');
flock ($fp, LOCK_UN);
```

To demonstrate, let's rewrite add_quote.php to lock the file during the writing process.

To use file locks:

1. Open add_quote.php (Script 11.1) in your text editor or IDE, if it isn't already open.

2. Before the fwrite( ) line, add the following (**Script 11.2**):

   flock($fp, LOCK_EX);

   This command places an exclusive lock on the file so that other scripts can't write to it at the same time.

3. After the fwrite( ) line, add:

   flock($fp, LOCK_UN);

   This command unlocks the file so that it can be accessed again.

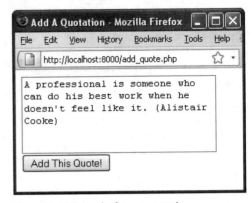

Figure 11.10 Using the form once again...

Script 11.2 The modified version of the add_quote.php script locks the data file for better security and reliability.

```
1   <!DOCTYPE html PUBLIC "-//W3C//DTD XHTML 1.0 Transitional//EN"
2       "http://www.w3.org/TR/xhtml1/DTD/xhtml1-transitional.dtd">
3   <html xmlns="http://www.w3.org/1999/xhtml" xml:lang="en" lang="en">
4   <head>
5       <meta http-equiv="content-type" content="text/html; charset=utf-8" />
6       <title>Add A Quotation</title>
7   </head>
8   <body>
9   <?php // Script 11.2 - add_quote.php #2
10  /* This script displays and handles an HTML form. This script takes text input and stores it in
    a text file. */
11
12  // Check for a form submission:
13  if (isset($_POST['submitted'])) { // Handle form.
14
15      if ( !empty($_POST['quote']) && ($_POST['quote'] != 'Enter your quotation here.') ) { //
        Need some thing to write.
16
17          if ($fp = fopen ('../quotes.txt', 'ab')) { // Try to open the file.
18
19              // Set the encoding:
20              stream_encoding($fp, 'utf-8');
21
22              // Lock the file:
23              flock($fp, LOCK_EX);
24
25              fwrite($fp, "{$_POST['quote']}\n"); // Write the data. Use \r\n on Windows.
26              flock($fp, LOCK_UN); // Unlock.
27              fclose($fp); // Close the file.
28
29              // Print a message:
30              print "<p>Your quotation has been stored.</p>";
31
```

(script continues on next page)

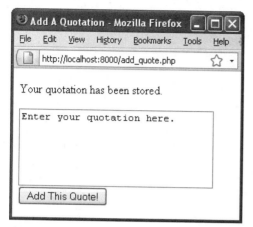

Figure 11.11 ...the quotation is still stored without a problem.

4. Save the file, place it in the proper directory for your PHP-enabled server, and test it again in your Web browser (**Figures 11.10** and **11.11**).

✔ Tips

- The file will automatically be unlocked when its closed, but it's still not a bad idea to specifically unlock it once the file writing is complete.

- Technically, if a file is opened in an appending mode, as in this example, not locking it probably won't be a problem even if multiple scripts are writing to the file simultaneously. That said, better safe than sorry!

- For locking to work, every script that writes to a file needs to use locking.

- In truth, the benefit added by locking a file is only marginal (but every little bit helps). A more secure and reliable method of storing data is to use a database. You'll learn more about this in the next chapter.

LOCKING FILES

Script 11.2 *continued*

```
32        } else { // Could not open the file.
33            print '<p style="color: red;">Your quotation could not be stored due to a system
              error.</p>';
34        }
35
36    } else { // Failed to enter a quotation.
37        print '<p style="color: red;">Please enter a quotation!</p>';
38    }
39
40    } // End of submitted IF.
41
42    // Leave PHP and display the form:
43    ?>
44
45    <form action="add_quote.php" method="post">
46        <textarea name="quote" rows="5" cols="30">Enter your quotation here.</textarea>
47        <input type="submit" name="submit" value="Add This Quote!" />
48        <input type="hidden" name="submitted" value="true" />
49    </form>
50
51    </body>
52    </html>
```

Reading from Files

Now that you've created a script that writes data to a file, it's time to create one that can read the information. Reading data from a file can be much easier than writing to it. Instead of creating a file pointer and using the fopen() function, you can read the file in one fell swoop:

```
$data = file('filename.txt');
```

The file() function is a valuable built-in tool in PHP. It reads everything from a file and places that information into an array. Each array element contains one line from the file, where each line is terminated by a newline (\n or \r\n).

If filename.txt contains two lines of information, each of which ends with a newline, the corresponding array will contain two elements. The first element will be equal to the first line of filename.txt, and the second element will be equal to the second line. Once the data is stored into an array, you can easily manipulate or print it, as you learned in Chapter 7, "Using Arrays."

Now you'll use this knowledge to create a script that randomly displays one of the stored quotations.

To read from a file:

1. Create a new PHP document in your text editor or IDE (**Script 11.3**):

```
<!DOCTYPE html PUBLIC "-//W3C//DTD
→ XHTML 1.0 Transitional//EN"
   "http://www.w3.org/TR/xhtml1/DTD/
   → xhtml1-transitional.dtd">
<html xmlns="http://www.w3.org/1999/
→ xhtml" xml:lang="en" lang="en">
<head>
   <meta http-equiv="content-type"
   → content="text/html;
charset=utf-8" />
   <title>View A Quotation</title>
</head>
<body>
```

2. Open a PHP code section:

```
<?php // Script 11.3 - view_quote.php
```

3. Read the file contents and store them in an array:

```
$data = file('../quotes.txt');
```

The function reads the file data into an array called $data. Each element of $data is a string, which is the submitted quotation.

If the quotes file is not in the parent directory of this script, change the reference here accordingly.

continues on next page

Script 11.3 The `view_quote.php` file retrieves all the quotations from the text file and displays one at random.

```
1    <!DOCTYPE html PUBLIC "-//W3C//DTD XHTML 1.0 Transitional//EN"
2        "http://www.w3.org/TR/xhtml1/DTD/xhtml1-transitional.dtd">
3    <html xmlns="http://www.w3.org/1999/xhtml" xml:lang="en" lang="en">
4    <head>
5        <meta http-equiv="content-type" content="text/html; charset=utf-8" />
6        <title>View A Quotation</title>
7    </head>
8    <body>
9    <?php // Script 11.3 - view_quote.php
10   /* This script displays and handles an HTML form. This script reads in a file and prints a
     random line from it. */
11
12   // Read the file's contents into an array:
13   $data = file('../quotes.txt');
14
15   // Count the number of items in the array:
16   $n = count($data);
17
18   // Pick a random item:
19   $rand = rand(0, ($n - 1));
20
21   // Print the quotation:
22   print '<p>' . trim($data[$rand]) . '</p>';
23
24   ?>
25
26   </body>
27   </html>
```

4. Pick a random number based on the number of elements in $data:

```
$n = count($data);

$rand = rand(0, ($n - 1));
```

In the first step, you count how many elements (which is to say, how many quotations) are in the $data array. Then you use the rand() function to select a random number.

If $data has ten elements, they're indexed between 0 and 9, so that's the range you want to use for rand(). To calculate this range for a variable number of lines in the text file, use 0 and one less than the number of elements in $data.

5. Print out the quotation:

```
print '<p>' . trim($data[$rand])
→ . '</p>';
```

A simple print() statement involving concatenation is used to print the random quotation. To retrieve the quotation, you refer to the $data array and use the generated $rand number as the index. The retrieved quotation is then trimmed to cut off the newline characters from the end of the quotation.

6. Complete the PHP code and the HTML page:

```
?>

</body>

</html>
```

7. Save the file as view_quote.php, place it on your Web server (in the same directory as add_quote.php), and test it in your Web browser (**Figure 11.12**).

8. Reload the page in your Web browser to view another random quote (**Figure 11.13**).

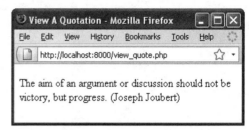

Figure 11.12 A random quotation is displayed each time the page is viewed.

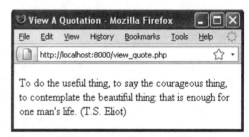

Figure 11.13 Subsequent viewings of the view_quote.php script display different quotations from the text file.

✔ Tips

- If you want to be extra careful, you can use the is_readable() function to test that PHP can read a file before you call the file() function.

- The file_get_contents() function works exactly like file() but returns the entire file as one long string, rather than as an array.

- The readfile() function reads through a file and sends the contents to the Web browser window.

- Later in the chapter, you'll learn a more complex method of reading a file using fgets() and fgetcsv().

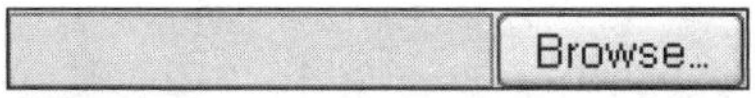

Figure 11.14 This is how Firefox interprets the file input type.

Choose File no file selected

Figure 11.15 This is how the Safari Web browser interprets the file input type (prior to selecting a file).

Handling File Uploads

As this book has demonstrated, handling HTML forms using PHP is a remarkably easy achievement. Regardless of the data being submitted, PHP can handle it easily and directly. The same is true when the user uploads a file via an HTML form.

In order to give the user the option of uploading a file, you must make three changes to the standard HTML form. First, the initial form tag must include the code enctype="multipart/form-data", which lets the browser know to expect different types of form data:

```
<form action="upload_file.php" enctype=
→ "multipart/form-data" method="post">
```

The form must also use the POST method.

Second, a special hidden input type should be added:

```
<input type="hidden" name="MAX_FILE_
→ SIZE" value="1000" />
```

This is a recommendation to the browser of how large a file, in bytes, can be uploaded.

Third, the <input type="file" name="my_file" /> element is used to create the necessary form field (**Figures 11.14** and **11.15**).

The file type of form input allows the user to select a file on their computer, which, upon submission, will be uploaded to the server. Once this has occurred, you can then use PHP to handle the file.

In the PHP script, you refer to the $_FILES variable (think of it as the file equivalent of $_POST) to reference the uploaded file. The $_FILES array contains five elements:

◆ name, the name of the file as it was on the user's computer

◆ type, the mime type of the file (for example, *image/jpg*)

continues on next page

HANDLING FILE UPLOADS

- `size`, the size of the file in bytes

- `tmp_name`, the temporary name of the file as it's stored on the server

- `error`, an error code if something goes wrong (**Table 11.3**)

When a file is uploaded, the server places it in a temporary directory. You can then use the `move_uploaded_file()` function to store the file in its final destination:

```
move_uploaded_file($_FILES['thefile']
→ ['tmp_name'], "/path/to/dest/
→ filename");
```

For PHP to be able to take these steps, you must set several configurations in the `php.ini` file (see the sidebar), and the Web server needs write access to both the temporary and final destination directories.

You'll write a basic script that uploads a file and stores it on the server. Like the `add_quote.php` script, this example also both creates the HTML form (**Figure 11.16**) and processes it, all in one page. First, though, you'll create a writable directory as the destination point.

To create a writable directory:

1. Create a new folder called `uploads`, located outside of the Web directory root (**Figure 11.17**).

2. Using the steps outlined in the first section of this chapter, set the permissions so that everyone can write to, read from, and search (0777 in Unix terms) the directory.

   Again, if you're running Windows, you likely don't need to do anything (try the next script to see for sure). If you're running another operating system, check the list of bullet points for the suggestion that works for your situation.

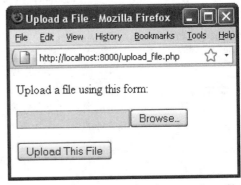

Figure 11.16 This HTML form lets the user select a file on their computer to upload to the server.

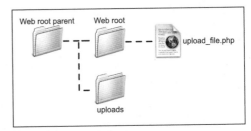

Figure 11.17 For this example, a writable `uploads` directory must exist. Here, it's placed in the same directory as the Web root folder. Thus `uploads` is in the directory above the one in which the `upload_file.php` script resides and is not accessible via the Internet.

Table 11.3

\$_FILES Error Codes	
CODE	**MEANING**
0	No error has occurred.
1	The file exceeds the `upload_max_filesize` setting in `php.ini`.
2	The file exceeds the `MAX_FILE_SIZE` setting in the HTML form.
3	The file was only partially uploaded.
4	No file was uploaded.
6	No temporary directory exists.
7	Failed write to disk.
8	Upload prevented by an extension.

To use PHP for file uploads:

1. Create a new PHP document in your text editor or IDE (**Script 11.4**):

```
<!DOCTYPE html PUBLIC "-//W3C//DTD
→ XHTML 1.0 Transitional//EN"
    "http://www.w3.org/TR/xhtml1/DTD/
    → xhtml1-transitional.dtd">
<html xmlns="http://www.w3.org/1999/
→ xhtml" xml:lang="en" lang="en">
<head>
    <meta http-equiv="content-type"
    → content="text/html;
    → charset=utf-8" />
    <title>Upload a File</title>
</head>
<body>
```

continues on page 321

Script 11.4 This script handles a file upload by first defining the proper HTML form and, second, invoking move_uploaded_file( ) to move the file to the desired location.

```
                               Script
1   <!DOCTYPE html PUBLIC "-//W3C//DTD XHTML 1.0 Transitional//EN"
2       "http://www.w3.org/TR/xhtml1/DTD/xhtml1-transitional.dtd">
3   <html xmlns="http://www.w3.org/1999/xhtml" xml:lang="en" lang="en">
4   <head>
5       <meta http-equiv="content-type" content="text/html; charset=utf-8" />
6       <title>Upload a File</title>
7   </head>
8   <body>
9   <?php // Script 11.4 - upload_file.php
10  /* This script displays and handles an HTML form. This script takes a file upload and stores it
    on the server. */
11
12  if (isset($_POST['submitted'])) { // Handle the form.
13
14      // Try to move the uploaded file:
15      if (move_uploaded_file ($_FILES['thefile']['tmp_name'], "../uploads/{$_FILES['thefile']
        ['name']}")) {
16
17          print '<p>Your file has been uploaded.</p>';
18
19      } else { // Problem!
20
21          print '<p style="color: red;">Your file could not be uploaded because: ';
22
```

(script continues on next page)

319

Script 11.4 *continued*

```
23        // Print a message based upon the error:
24        switch ($_FILES['thefile']['error']) {
25            case 1:
26                print 'The file exceeds the upload_max_filesize setting in php.ini';
27                break;
28            case 2:
29                print 'The file exceeds the MAX_FILE_SIZE setting in the HTML form';
30                break;
31            case 3:
32                print 'The file was only partially uploaded';
33                break;
34            case 4:
35                print 'No file was uploaded';
36                break;
37            case 6:
38                print 'The temporary folder does not exist.';
39                break;
40            default:
41                print 'Something unforeseen happened.';
42                break;
43        }
44
45        print '.</p>'; // Complete the paragraph.
46
47    } // End of move_uploaded_file() IF.
48
49  } // End of submission IF.
50
51  // Leave PHP and display the form:
52  ?>
53
54  <form action="upload_file.php" enctype="multipart/form-data" method="post">
55      <p>Upload a file using this form:</p>
56      <input type="hidden" name="MAX_FILE_SIZE" value="30000" />
57      <p><input type="file" name="thefile" /></p>
58      <p><input type="submit" name="submit" value="Upload This File" /></p>
59      <input type="hidden" name="submitted" value="true" />
60  </form>
61
62  </body>
63  </html>
```

2. Create a section of PHP code:

```
<?php // Script 11.4 - upload_file.
→ php
```

3. Check whether the form has been submitted:

```
if (isset($_POST['submitted'])) {
```

Once again, this script both displays and handles the HTML form. If it has been submitted, the uploaded file should be addressed.

4. Attempt to move the uploaded file to its final destination:

```
if (move_uploaded_file ($_FILES
→ ['thefile']['tmp_name'],
→ "../uploads/{$_FILES['thefile']
→ ['name']}")) {
```

The move_uploaded_file() function attempts to move the uploaded file (identified by $_FILES['thefile'] ['tmp_name']) to its new location (../uploads/{$_FILES['thefile'] ['name']}). The location is the uploads directory, which is located in the folder above the one this script is in. The file's name will be the same as it was on the user's computer.

Placing this function as a condition in an if statement makes it easy to respond based on whether the move worked.

5. Print messages indicating the success of the operation:

```
print '<p>Your file has been
→ uploaded.</p>';
} else { // Problem!
print '<p style="color: red;">Your
→ file could not be uploaded
→ because: ';
```

The first print() statement is executed if the move worked. The else applies if it didn't work, in which case an error message is begun. This message will be made more explicit in Step 6.

continues on next page

6. Print out the error message if the move didn't work:

```
switch ($_FILES['thefile']['error']) {
    case 1:
        print 'The file exceeds the
        → upload_max_filesize setting
        → in php.ini';
        break;
    case 2:
        print 'The file exceeds the
        → MAX_FILE_SIZE setting in the
        → HTML form';
        break;
    case 3:
        print 'The file was only
        → partially uploaded';
        break;
    case 4:
        print 'No file was uploaded';
        break;
    case 6:
        print 'The temporary folder
        → does not exist.';
        break;
    default:
        print 'Something unforeseen
        → happened.';
        break;
}
```

If a move doesn't work, the $_FILES ['thefile']['error'] variable contains a number indicating the appropriate error message. By using this in a switch conditional, the PHP script can print out the appropriate error message.

You wouldn't normally place something like this is a public site (it's a little too much information), but it's exceptionally good for helping you to debug a problem.

7. Complete the error message, and close both conditionals:

```
print '.</p>'; // Complete the
→ paragraph.
} // End of move_uploaded_file()
→ IF.
} // End of submission IF.
```

8. Exit out of PHP and create the HTML form:

```
?>
<form action="upload_file.php"
→ enctype="multipart/form-data"
→ method="post">
  <p>Upload a file using this
  → form:</p>
  <input type="hidden" name="MAX_
  → FILE_SIZE" value="30000" />
  <p><input type="file" name=
  → "thefile" /></p>
  <p><input type="submit" name=
  → "submit" value="Upload This
  → File" /></p>
  <input type="hidden" name=
  → "submitted" value="true" />
</form>
```

The HTML form is simple (Figure 11.16), containing only two visible elements: a file input type and a submit button. It differs from other HTML forms in this book in that it uses the enctype attribute and a MAX_FILE_SIZE hidden input type. The other hidden input is used to trigger the handling of the form.

Be careful when giving your file input a name, because this value must exactly match the index used in the $_FILES variable. Here, you use a generic *thefile*.

9. Complete the HTML page:

```
</body>
</html>
```

continues on next page

Configuring PHP for File Uploads

In order for file uploading to work, a number of settings in your php.ini configuration file must be set. These may or may not be enabled in your configuration, so you should check them by viewing the php.ini file or running a phpinfo() script.

For starters, file_uploads must be on. Second, the upload_tmp_dir value must be set to a directory on the server where PHP can place files (in other words, it must exist and be modifiable by the Web server). If this setting has no value, that's probably fine (meaning that a hidden directory created expressly for purposes such as these will be used).

The upload_max_filesize and post_max_size settings dictate how large a file can be sent. Whereas the MAX_FILE_SIZE hidden form input is a recommendation to the Web browser, these two settings control whether the file is uploaded.

Finally, if really large files will be uploaded (many megabytes or larger), you may need to increase the memory_limit and max_execution_time settings to give PHP the time and the resources to do what it needs to do.

HANDLING FILE UPLOADS

10. Save the page as `upload_file.php`, place it in the proper directory for your PHP-enabled server relative to the `uploads` directory (see Figure 11.17), and test it in your Web browser (**Figures 11.18**, **11.19**, and **11.20**).

Only files smaller than about 30 KB should be allowed, thanks to the `MAX_FILE_SIZE` restriction.

11. Check the `uploads` directory to ensure that the file was placed there.

✔ Tips

■ If the file couldn't be moved and a permissions denied error is shown, check the permissions on the `uploads` directory. Then check that the path to the directory used in the script is correct and that there are no spelling errors.

■ As you might discover, files uploaded through the Web browser are owned (in terms of permissions) by the Web server application.

■ From a security standpoint, it's better to rename an uploaded file. To do so, you'll need to devise a system that generates a new, unique filename and stores both the original and new filenames in a text file or a database.

■ A script can handle multiple file uploads as long as they have different names. In such a case, you need only one `MAX_FILE_SIZE` hidden input. In the PHP script, you'd apply the `move_uploaded_file()` function to `$_FILES['filename1']`, `$_FILES['filename2']`, and so on.

■ You can limit a file upload to a specific size or type by referencing the appropriate index (for example, `$_FILES['thefile']['size']`) in your PHP script (after the file has been uploaded).

■ Use `unlink()` to delete a file without moving or copying it.

■ You can use the `copy()` function to make a copy of a file on the server.

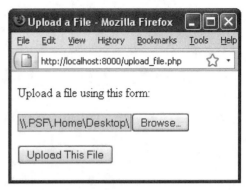

Figure 11.18 Select a file on your computer to upload.

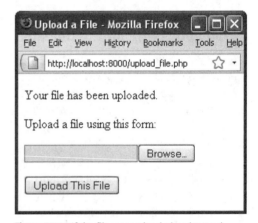

Figure 11.19 If the file was uploaded and moved successfully, a message is printed and the form is displayed again.

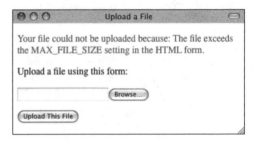

Figure 11.20 If a problem occurred, the script indicates the cause.

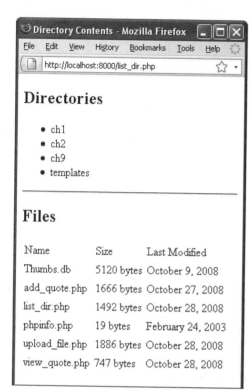

Figure 11.21 The `list_dir.php` script shows the contents of a directory. The top part lists the subfolders, and the bottom table lists the files.

Navigating Directories

The previous PHP scripts worked with files, but you can also do many things with directories using PHP. In this example, you'll write a script that lists a directory's contents, but first you'll need to understand the usage and syntax of many of the functions you'll use.

To find all of the contents of a directory, the easiest option is to use the `scandir()` function:

`$stuff = scandir('dirname');`

This function, added in PHP 5, returns an array of every item—directory or file—found within the given directory.

While you're working with files, you'll use the `filesize()` function in this example; it determines how large a file is in bytes. This value can be assigned to a variable or be printed:

`$number = filesize('filename');`

Similarly, the `filemtime()` function retrieves the modification time of a file. It returns a timestamp, which can be formatted using the `date()` function.

Finally, PHP includes several functions that identify attributes. This chapter has already mentioned `is_writable()` and `is_readable()`, but there are also `is_dir()` and `is_file()`. They return TRUE if the item in question is a directory or a file, respectively.

You'll put all of these capabilities together into one page, which will constitute a Web-based control panel for viewing a directory's contents (**Figure 11.21**).

To create the directory control panel:

1. Create a new PHP document in your text editor or IDE (**Script 11.5**):

```
<!DOCTYPE html PUBLIC "-//W3C//DTD
→ XHTML 1.0 Transitional//EN"
  "http://www.w3.org/TR/xhtml1/DTD/
  → xhtml1-transitional.dtd">
<html xmlns="http://www.w3.org/1999/
→ xhtml" xml:lang="en" lang="en">
<head>
  <meta http-equiv="content-type"
  → content="text/html;
→ charset=utf-8" />
  <title>Directory Contents</title>
</head>
<body>
```

Script 11.5 This script displays the contents of a directory. First the subdirectories are listed, followed by the files (with their sizes and modification dates) in a table.

```
1   <!DOCTYPE html PUBLIC "-//W3C//DTD XHTML 1.0 Transitional//EN"
2       "http://www.w3.org/TR/xhtml1/DTD/xhtml1-transitional.dtd">
3   <html xmlns="http://www.w3.org/1999/xhtml" xml:lang="en" lang="en">
4   <head>
5       <meta http-equiv="content-type" content="text/html; charset=utf-8" />
6       <title>Directory Contents</title>
7   </head>
8   <body>
9   <?php // Script 11.5 - list_dir.php
10  /* This script lists the directories and files in a directory. */
11
12  // Set the time zone:
13  date_default_timezone_set('America/New_York');
14
15  // Set the directory name and scan it:
16  $search_dir = '.';
17  $contents = scandir($search_dir);
18
19  // List the directories first...
20  // Print a caption and start a list:
21  print '<h2>Directories</h2>
22  <ul>';
23  foreach ($contents as $item) {
24      if ( (is_dir($item)) AND (substr($item, 0, 1) != '.') ) {
25          print "<li>$item</li>\n";
26      }
27  }
28
```

(script continues on next page)

2. Begin the PHP code and set the time zone:

```php
<?php // Script 11.5 - list_dir.php
date_default_timezone_set('America/
→ New_York');
```

Because this script will make use of the `date()` function, it needs to establish the time zone once. See Chapter 8, "Creating Web Applications," for more and for the reference in the PHP manual where you can find your time zone.

continues on next page

Script 11.5 *continued*

```
29   print '</ul>'; // Close the list.
30
31   // Create a table header:
32   print '<hr /><h2>Files</h2>
33   <table cellpadding="2" cellspacing="2" align="left">
34   <tr>
35   <td>Name</td>
36   <td>Size</td>
37   <td>Last Modified</td>
38   </tr>';
39
40   // List the files:
41   foreach ($contents as $item) {
42      if ( (is_file($item)) AND (substr($item, 0, 1) != '.') ) {
43
44         // Get the file size:
45         $fs = filesize($item);
46
47         // Get the file's modification date:
48         $lm = date('F j, Y', filemtime($item));
49
50         // Print the information:
51         print "<tr>
52         <td>$item</td>
53         <td>$fs bytes</td>
54         <td>$lm</td>
55         </tr>\n";
56
57      } // Close the IF.
58
59   } // Close the FOREACH.
60
61   print '</table>'; // Close the HTML table.
62
63   ?>
64   </body>
65   </html>
```

3. Identify the directory to be opened, and scan in its contents:

```
$search_dir = '.';
$contents = scandir($search_dir);
```

By establishing this value as a variable at the top of the PHP script, it will be easy to find and change as needed. Here you use the period to refer to the current directory. You could also use an absolute path to another directory (`/Users/larry/Documents` or `C:\\myfiles\\directory`) or a relative path (`../myfiles`), as long as PHP has permission to read the named directory.

The second line scans in the directory's contents and assigns them as an array to the variable `$contents`.

4. List the subdirectories of this directory:

```
print '<h2>Directories</h2>
<ul>';
foreach ($contents as $item) {
  if ( (is_dir($item)) AND
→ (substr($item, 0, 1) != '.') ) {
      print "<li>$item</li>\n";
  }
}
```

This `foreach` loop accesses every item in the array, assigning each one to the `$item` variable. You first want to list every directory, so you use the `is_dir()` function to confirm the item's type. Then you check that it isn't the current directory (marked by a single period on Unix systems) or the parent directory (marked by a double period on Unix systems). If this conditional is TRUE, then the item's name is printed out, within list item tags, followed by a newline (to make for neater HTML source code).

5. Close the list:

```
print '</ul>';
```

6. Create a new heading, and start a table for the files:

```
print '<hr /><h2>Files</h2>
<table cellpadding="2" cellspacing=
→ "2" align="left">
<tr>
<td>Name</td>
<td>Size</td>
<td>Last Modified</td>
</tr>';
```

The script also displays the files' sizes and modification dates. To make this look nicer, the results are placed in an HTML table.

7. Begin looping through the files in this directory:

```
foreach ($contents as $item) {
    if ( (is_file($item)) AND
    → (substr($item, 0, 1) != '.') ) {
```

Another foreach loop is used to go through the directory contents again. This time, the conditional only wants items that are files (but not hidden files that begin with a single period).

8. Calculate the file's size and modification date, and then print out the information:

```
$fs = filesize($item);
$lm = date('F j, Y', filemtime
→ ($item));
print "<tr>
<td>$item</td>
<td>$fs bytes</td>
<td>$lm</td>
</tr>\n";
```

The first line calls the filesize() function to retrieve the file's size in bytes. The second line calls the filemtime() function, which returns a timestamp of the file's modification time. This is then fed

continues on next page

NAVIGATING DIRECTORIES

into the date() function, along with the proper formatting, to return a string like *November 24, 2008*. Finally, these two items and the file's name are printed in the appropriate columns of the table.

9. Complete the conditional and the loop:

```
    }

}
```

10. Close the table:

```
print '</table>';
```

11. Complete the PHP code and the HTML page:

```
?>
</body>
</html>
```

12. Save the file as list_dir.php, place it in the proper directory for your PHP-enabled server, and test it in your Web browser (Figure 11.21).

✔ Tips

■ Notice that you need to use double backslashes to create absolute path names on a Windows server. This is necessary because the single backslash, used in Windows path names, is the escape character. So, it must be escaped to be taken literally.

■ The glob() function lets you search a directory for files whose name matches a pattern (like *.jpg or *filename*.doc).

■ Other file functions you might appreciate include fileperms(), which returns the file's permissions; fileatime(), which returns the last time a file was accessed; and fileowner(), which returns the user who owns the file.

■ To find out about other file and directory functions, look in the PHP manual under *Directories* and *Filesystem*.

Creating Directories

Understanding how to read from and write to files on the server is only part of the data storage process. It's likely you'll also want to use directories for this purpose as well.

The command for creating a directory in PHP is

```
mkdir('directory_name', permissions);
```

The directory name is the name of the directory to be created. This can also be a path:

```
mkdir('C:\\inetpub\\users\\eleanor');
```

On Windows servers, the permissions are ignored and therefore not required (as in the preceding example). On other servers, the permissions are 0777 by default (see the section "File Permissions" of this chapter to learn what those numbers mean).

With this in mind, let's create a script that makes a new directory for a user when the user registers. This script also records the username and password to a text file, so that the user can be validated when logging in. You'll begin by creating the parent directory (which must be writable so that PHP can create subdirectories in it) and the users.txt data file.

To create the directory and the data file:

1. Create a new folder called users, located outside of the Web directory root.

   It could be created in the same location as the uploads folder made earlier (see Figure 11.17).

2. Using the steps outlined in the first section of this chapter, set the permissions so that everyone can write to, read from, and search (0777 in Unix terms) the directory.

   If you're running Windows, this step will most likely not be necessary.

continues on next page

3. In your text editor, create a new, blank document.

4. Save this file in the users directory with the name users.txt.

5. Again using the steps outlined earlier in the chapter, set the permissions on users.txt so that everyone can write to and read from the file (0666 in Unix terms).

   Again, this will probably not be necessary if you're running Windows on your PHP server.

To create the registration script:

1. Begin a new PHP document in your text editor or IDE (**Script 11.6**):

   ```
   <!DOCTYPE html PUBLIC "-//W3C//DTD
   → XHTML 1.0 Transitional//EN"
      "http://www.w3.org/TR/xhtml1/DTD/
      → xhtml1-transitional.dtd">
   <html xmlns="http://www.w3.org/1999/
   → xhtml" xml:lang="en" lang="en">
   <head>
      <meta http-equiv="content-type"
      → content="text/html;
      → charset=utf-8" />
      <title>Register</title>
      <style type="text/css"
      → media="screen">
         .error { color: red; }
      </style>
   </head>
   <body>
   ```

   In the page's head, a CSS class is defined that will be used to format errors.

2. Begin the PHP code:

   ```
   <?php // Script 11.6 - register.php
   ```

continues on page 334

Script 11.6 The register.php script serves two purposes: it records the user's information in a text file and creates a new directory for that user's stuff.

```
1    <!DOCTYPE html PUBLIC "-//W3C//DTD XHTML 1.0 Transitional//EN"
2        "http://www.w3.org/TR/xhtml1/DTD/xhtml1-transitional.dtd">
3    <html xmlns="http://www.w3.org/1999/xhtml" xml:lang="en" lang="en">
4    <head>
5      <meta http-equiv="content-type" content="text/html; charset=utf-8" />
6      <title>Register</title>
7      <style type="text/css" media="screen">
8          .error { color: red; }
9      </style>
10   </head>
11   <body>
12   <?php // Script 11.6 - register.php
13   /* This script registers a user by storing their information in a text file and creating a
     directory for them. */
14
15   if (isset($_POST['submitted'])) { // Handle the form.
16
17       $problem = FALSE; // No problems so far.
18
19       // Check for each value...
20       if (empty($_POST['username'])) {
21           $problem = TRUE;
22           print '<p class="error">Please enter a username!</p>';
23       }
24
25       if (empty($_POST['password1'])) {
26           $problem = TRUE;
27           print '<p class="error">Please enter a password!</p>';
28       }
29
30       if ($_POST['password1'] != $_POST['password2']) {
31           $problem = TRUE;
32           print '<p class="error">Your password did not match your confirmed password!</p>';
33       }
34
35       if (!$problem) { // If there weren't any problems...
36
37           if ($fp = fopen ('../users/users.txt', 'ab')) { // Open the file.
38
39               // Set the encoding:
40               stream_encoding($fp, 'utf-8');
41
42               // Create the data to be written:
43               $dir = time() . rand(0, 4596);
44               $data = $_POST['username'] . "\t" . md5(trim($_POST['password1'])) . "\t" . $dir .
                 "\n"; // \r\n on Windows
45
```

(script continues on next page)

CREATING DIRECTORIES

333

3. Check whether the form has been submitted:

```
if (isset($_POST['submitted'])) {
```

Once again, this page both displays and handles the HTML form. This is accomplished using a conditional that checks for the value of the $_POST['submitted'] variable.

4. Validate the registration information:

```
$problem = FALSE;
if (empty($_POST['username'])) {
    $problem = TRUE;
```

Script 11.6 *continued*

```
46      // Write the data and close the file:
47      fwrite ($fp, $data);
48      fclose ($fp);
49
50      // Create the directory:
51      mkdir ("../users/$dir");
52
53      // Print a message:
54      print '<p>You are now registered!</p>';
55
56      } else { // Couldn't write to the file.
57          print '<p class="error">You could not be registered due to a system error.</p>';
58      }
59
60      } else { // Forgot a field.
61          print '<p class="error">Please go back and try again!</p>';
62      }
63
64  } else { // Display the form.
65
66  // Leave PHP and display the form:
67  ?>
68
69  <form action="register.php" method="post">
70      <p>Username: <input type="text" name="username" size="20" /></p>
71      <p>Password: <input type="password" name="password1" size="20" /></p>
72      <p>Confirm Password: <input type="password" name="password2" size="20" /></p><br />
73      <input type="submit" name="submit" value="Register" />
74      <input type="hidden" name="submitted" value="true" />
75  </form>
76  <?php } // End of submission IF. ?>
77  </body>
78  </html>
```

```
print '<p class="error">Please
→ enter a username!</p>';
}
if (empty($_POST['password1'])) {
    $problem = TRUE;
    print '<p class="error">Please
→ enter a password!</p>';
}
if ($_POST['password1'] !=
→ $_POST['password2']) {
    $problem = TRUE;
    print '<p class="error">Your
→ password did not match your
→ confirmed password!</p>';
}
```

The registration form is a simpler version of earlier registration forms developed in this book. The same validation process you previously developed is used to check the submitted username and passwords. The $problem variable is used as a flag to indicate whether a problem occurred.

5. Check for problems:

```
if (!$problem) {
```

Again, the $problem variable lets you know if it's okay to register the user. If no problems occurred, it's safe to continue.

6. Attempt to open the users.txt file and set the encoding:

```
if ($fp = fopen ('../users/users.
→ txt', 'ab')) {
    stream_encoding($fp, 'utf-8');
```

Like before, the data file is opened as part of a conditional, so that the script can respond to its success. The file being opened is in the users directory, which is in the directory above this script. The file is opened using the ab mode, appending data to the file.

Next, the encoding is set as this page uses UTF-8.

continues on next page

CREATING DIRECTORIES

7. Create the data to be written to the file, and then write it:

```
$dir = time() . rand(0, 4596);
$data = $_POST['username'] . "\t"
→ . md5(trim($_POST['password1']))
→ . "\t" . $dir . "\n";
fwrite ($fp, $data);
fclose ($fp);
```

The name of the directory being created is a number based on the time the user registered and a random value. This system helps to guarantee that the directory created is both unique and has a valid name.

Instead of storing a single string as you previously have, this script stores three separate pieces of information: the user's name; an encrypted version of the password (using the md5() function, see the first tip); and the directory name, created in the preceding line. The password is trimmed first, to get rid of any extraneous spaces.

To distinguish between the pieces of information, you insert a tab (created using the \t code). A newline is used to mark the end of the line (Windows users should use \r\n instead).

8. Create the user's directory, and print a message:

```
mkdir ("../users/$dir");
print '<p>You are now registered!
→ </p>';
```

The mkdir() function creates the directory in the users directory. The directory is named whatever random number was generated earlier and has open permissions.

9. Complete the conditionals:

```
    } else {
        print '<p class="error">You
        → could not be registered due
        → to a system error.</p>';
    }
```

```
} else {
    print '<p class="error">Please go
→ back and try again!</p>';
}
```

The first `else` completes the conditional if the script couldn't open the `users.txt` file for writing. The second `else` completes the conditional if the user failed to complete the form properly.

10. Add an `else` clause to the main conditional, and exit out of PHP:

```
} else {
?>
```

Unlike the previous examples in this chapter, this PHP script first displays the form and then handles it. Whereas the other scripts would then display the form again, this one does not, as the form creation is part of an `else` statement. Because the rest of the page is just HTML, you exit out of PHP to create the form.

11. Display the HTML form:

```
<form action="register.php"
→ method="post">
    <p>Username: <input type="text"
    → name="username" size="20" />
    → </p>
    <p>Password: <input type=
    → "password" name="password1"
    → size="20" /></p>
    <p>Confirm Password: <input
    → type="password" name=
    → "password2" size="20" />
    → </p><br />
    <input type="submit" name=
    → "submit" value="Register" />
    <input type="hidden" name=
    → "submitted" value="true" />
</form>
```

continues on next page

12. Complete the main conditional:

`<?php } // End of submission IF. ?>`

This final closing curly brace closes the main submit conditional. For it to work, a new PHP section must be created first.

13. Complete the HTML page:

`</body>`

`</html>`

14. Save the file as `register.php`, place it in the proper directory for your PHP-enabled server, and test it in your Web browser (**Figures 11.22** and **11.23**).

15. If you want, open the `users.txt` file in your text editor to see its contents (**Figure 11.24**).

✔ Tips

■ The `md5()` function creates a *hash*: a mathematically calculated representation of a string. So this script doesn't actually store the password but a representation of that password (in theory, no two strings would have the same `md5()` value). You'll soon see how this is used by a login script.

■ You can also ensure that the page worked as it should by looking in the `users` directory for the new subdirectories.

■ The `rmdir()` function deletes an existing directory, assuming PHP has permission to do so.

■ At some point, you may want to create a system to guarantee unique usernames. The process for doing so is simple enough: Before you attempt to create the directory, use PHP to check your list of existing usernames for a match to the just-registered name. If no match is found, the new name is acceptable. If the username is already in use, then PHP can create an error message requesting a new username.

Figure 11.22 The registration form is quite basic but serves its purpose.

Figure 11.23 This is what the user sees if the registration process worked.

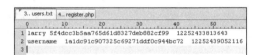

Figure 11.24 The `users.txt` file lists three tab-delineated fields of information: the username, a scrambled version of the user's password, and their associated directory name.

Reading Files Incrementally

In the `view_quote.php` script (Script 11.3), an entire file was read into an array using the `file()` function. But what if you want to read in only a little of the file at a time? Then you need to use the `fgets()` function.

The `fgets()` function returns a string of a certain length. It's most often placed in a `while` loop that uses the `feof()` function to make sure the end of the file hasn't been reached. For example:

```
$fp = fopen('filename', 'rb');
while (!feof($fp)) {
    $string = fgets($fp, 1024);
}
fclose ($fp);
```

In this example, the `fgets()` function returns 1023 bytes of data at a time (the 1024 indicated length minus 1) until it reaches the end of the file. The length argument is optional, but if present, it should be a number larger than a single line of text in the file.

In an example where the data is stored in a delineated format (commonly using a comma, hence a CSV—comma-separated values—format), you can use the `fgetcsv()` function instead. It breaks the string into parts, using the marked separator, and returns an array:

```
$array = fgetcsv($fp, length, delimiter);
$array = fgetcsv($fp, 1024);
```

Again, the preceding function call returns 1023 bytes of data, but it breaks the string into an array using the default delimiter—a comma—as an indicator of where to make elements. This function is the equivalent of using the `fgets()` and `explode()` functions together.

continues on next page

Finally, because these functions rely upon identifying the end of a line, it's a good extra precaution to enable PHP's `auto_detect_line_endings` setting. You can do so using the `ini_set()` function:

```
ini_set('auto_detect_line_endings', 1);
```

As an example, let's create a login script that uses the `users.txt` file created in the preceding example. It will continue to read a file until a matching username/password combination has been found.

To read a file incrementally:

1. Begin a new PHP document in your text editor or IDE (**Script 11.7**):

```
<!DOCTYPE html PUBLIC "-//W3C//DTD
 XHTML 1.0 Transitional//EN"
   "http://www.w3.org/TR/xhtml1/DTD/
    xhtml1-transitional.dtd">
<html xmlns="http://www.w3.org/1999/
 xhtml" xml:lang="en" lang="en">
<head>
   <meta http-equiv="content-type"
    content="text/html;
    charset=utf-8" />
   <title>Login</title>
</head>
<body>
```

2. Create the PHP section:

```
<?php // Script 11.7 - login.php
```

3. Check whether the form has been submitted:

```
if (isset($_POST['submitted'])) {
```

4. Create a dummy variable to use as a flag:

```
$loggedin = FALSE;
```

The `$loggedin` variable is used to indicate whether the user entered the correct username/password combination. When the script first starts, it's assumed that they have not.

5. Open the file for reading:

```
ini_set('auto_detect_line_endings', 1);
$fp = fopen('../users/users.txt',
→ 'rb');
```

Unlike the file() function, the fgetcsv() function requires a file pointer. Therefore, the users.txt file must be opened with the fopen() function, using the appropriate mode. Here, that mode is rb, meaning the file should be opened for reading in a binary safe mode.

First, though, just to be safe, PHP's auto_detect_line_encodings setting is enabled.

continues on next page

Script 11.7 The login.php script uses the information stored in users.txt (created by Script 11.6) to validate a user.

```
1    <!DOCTYPE html PUBLIC "-//W3C//DTD XHTML 1.0 Transitional//EN"
2        "http://www.w3.org/TR/xhtml1/DTD/xhtml1-transitional.dtd">
3    <html xmlns="http://www.w3.org/1999/xhtml" xml:lang="en" lang="en">
4    <head>
5        <meta http-equiv="content-type" content="text/html; charset=utf-8" />
6        <title>Login</title>
7    </head>
8    <body>
9    <?php // Script 11.7 - login.php
10   /* This script logs a user in by check the stored values in text file. */
11
12   if (isset($_POST['submitted'])) { // Handle the form.
13
14       $loggedin = FALSE; // Not currently logged in.
15
16       // Enable auto_detect_line_settings:
17       ini_set('auto_detect_line_endings', 1);
18
19       // Open the file:
20       $fp = fopen('../users/users.txt', 'rb');
21
22       // Loop through the file:
23       while ( $line = fgetcsv($fp, 100, "\t") ) {
24
25           // Check the file data against the submitted data:
26           if ( ($line[0] == $_POST['username']) AND ($line[1] == md5(trim($_POST['password']))) ) {
27
28               $loggedin = TRUE; // Correct username/password combination.
29
```

(script continues on next page)

6. Loop through each line of the file:

```
while ( $line = fgetcsv($fp, 100,
→ "\t") ) {
```

This while loop reads another 100 bytes or one line of the file—whichever comes first—with each iteration. The data being read is broken into an array, using the tab to indicate the separate elements.

Because the users.txt file stores its data in the format *username tab password tab directory newline*, the $line array contains three elements indexed at 0 (*username*), 1 (*password*), and 2 (*directory*).

Script 11.7 *continued*

```
30          // Stop looping through the file:
31          break;
32
33      } // End of IF.
34
35    } // End of WHILE.
36
37    fclose($fp); // Close the file.
38
39    // Print a message:
40    if ($loggedin) {
41        print '<p>You are now logged in.</p>';
42    } else {
43        print '<p style="color: red;">The username and password you entered do not match those on
          file.</p>';
44    }
45
46  } else { // Display the form.
47
48  // Leave PHP and display the form:
49  ?>
50
51  <form action="login.php" method="post">
52      <p>Username: <input type="text" name="username" size="20" /></p>
53      <p>Password: <input type="password" name="password1" size="20" /></p>
54      <input type="submit" name="submit" value="Login" />
55      <input type="hidden" name="submitted" value="true" />
56  </form>
57  <?php } // End of submission IF. ?>
58  </body>
59  </html>
```

7. Check the submitted values against the retrieved values:

```
if ( ($line[0] == $_POST
→['username']) AND ($line[1] ==
→md5(trim($_POST['password']))) ) {
```

This two-part conditional checks the submitted username against the stored username ($line[0]) and checks the submitted password against the stored password ($line[1]). However, because the stored password was scrambled using md5( ), apply md5( ) to the submitted value and then make the comparison.

8. If a match was found, set $loggedin to TRUE and exit the while loop:

```
$loggedin = TRUE;
break;
```

If the conditional is TRUE, the submitted username and password match those on file. In this case, the $loggedin flag is set to TRUE, and the break statement is used to exit the while loop. The benefit of this system is that only as much of the file is read as is required to find a match.

9. Close the conditional, the while loop, and the file:

```
    }
}
fclose ($fp);
```

10. Print a message to the user:

```
if ($loggedin) {
    print '<p>You are now logged
in.</p>';
} else {
    print '<p style="color: red;">The
username and password you entered
do not match those on file.</p>';
}
```

continues on next page

Using the $loggedin flag, the script can now say whether the user is "logged in." You could add some functionality to this process by storing the user's directory in a session and then sending them to a file-upload page.

11. Continue the main submit conditional, and exit PHP:

```
} else {
?>
```

12. Create the HTML form:

```
<form action="login.php"
→ method="post">
    <p>Username: <input type="text"
    → name="username" size="20" />
    → </p>
    <p>Password: <input type=
    → "password" name="password1"
    → size="20" /></p>
    <input type="submit" name=
    → "submit" value="Login" />
    <input type="hidden" name=
    → "submitted" value="true" />
</form>
```

13. Return to PHP to complete the main conditional:

```
<?php } // End of submission IF. ?>
```

14. Finish the HTML page:

```
</body>
</html>
```

15. Save the file as login.php, place it in the proper directory for your PHP-enabled server, and test it in your Web browser (**Figures 11.25**, **11.26**, and **11.27**).

✔ Tips

■ As of PHP 4.2, the length argument in fgets() is optional and defaults to 1 KB (1024 bytes). As of PHP 4.3, the length argument defaults so that it automatically returns all the data until the end of the line.

Figure 11.25 The login form takes a username and password.

Figure 11.26 If the submitted username and password match those previously recorded, the user sees this message.

Figure 11.27 The result if the user submits a username and password combination that doesn't match the values previously recorded.

■ As of PHP 4.3, the fgetcsv() function takes another optional argument: the string being used to enclose the elements.

■ If a line is blank, fgetcsv() returns an array containing a single null value.

Intro to Databases

Strange as it may sound, the Internet wouldn't be where it is today if not for the existence of databases. In fact, PHP probably wouldn't be as popular or as useful if not for its built-in support for numerous types of databases.

There are currently many existing database applications or Database Management Systems (DBMSs), which function on different platforms. On the high end there's Oracle, generally considered one of the best DBMSs, but its price puts it out of the running for all but the largest and best-financed applications. For Windows and Windows NT, you'll often encounter Access or SQL Server, both of which are fine but not cross-platform compliant. For basic needs, there's the open-source SQLite, which is an excellent product.

This chapter will use MySQL as the example DBMS. Although MySQL—which is available for most platforms—may not be as powerful as other database servers, it has enough speed and functionality for most purposes. And its price—free for most uses—makes it the most common choice for Web development.

This chapter shows you how to develop a simple database that creates a *blog* (a Web-based journal). Although you'll learn enough here to get started, you may want to visit Appendix B, "Resources and Next Steps," once you've finished this chapter to find some references where you can learn more about the topic.

Introduction to SQL

A *database* is a collection of tables (tables being made up of columns and rows) that stores information. Databases are created, updated, and read using SQL (Structured Query Language). There are surprisingly few commands in SQL (**Table 12.1** lists the six most important), which is both a blessing and a curse.

SQL was designed to be written a lot like the English language, which makes it very user friendly; but it does take some thought to create more elaborate SQL statements with only the handful of available terms. In this chapter you'll learn how to define all of the fundamental SQL statements (also called *queries*).

For people new to PHP, confusion can stem from PHP's relationship to HTML (i.e., PHP can be used to generate HTML but PHP code is never executed in the Web browser). When you incorporate a database, the relationships can become even fuzzier. The process is actually quite simple: PHP is used to send SQL statements to the database application, where they are executed. The result of the execution—the creation of a table, the insertion of a record, the retrieval of some records, or even an error—is then returned by the database to the PHP script (**Figure 12.1**).

With that in mind, PHP's `mysql_query()` function will be the most-used tool in this chapter. It sends an SQL command to MySQL:

`$result = mysql_query(SQL statement);`

I start this chapter with all this prologue because the addition of SQL and MySQL to the Web development process will complicate things. When problems occur—and undoubtedly they will—you'll need to know how best to debug them.

The best way to debug problems that occur is to execute the SQL command using another

Table 12.1

Common SQL Commands

COMMAND	PURPOSE
CREATE	Creates a database or table
DELETE	Deletes records from a table
DROP	Deletes a database or table
INSERT	Adds records to a table
SELECT	Retrieves records from a table
UPDATE	Updates records in a table

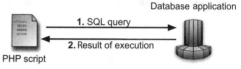

Figure 12.1 PHP will be used to send an SQL statement to MySQL. MySQL will execute the statement and return the result to the PHP script.

MySQL Support in PHP

Support for the MySQL database server has to be built into PHP in order for you to use PHP's MySQL-specific functions. In earlier versions of PHP, support for MySQL was part of the software by default. As of PHP 5, that's no longer the case.

For users of any version of PHP, if you see an error message saying *...undefined function mysql_...*, this means the version of PHP you're using doesn't have support for MySQL. (Or, you misspelled the function name, which you should also check.)

Enabling support for MySQL takes a little effort, but it can be done if you have administrative-level control over your server. For more information, see the PHP manual.

Introduction to SQL

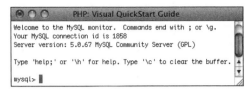

Figure 12.2 The MySQL monitor comes with the MySQL database software and can be used to execute queries without the need for a PHP script.

application. By doing so, you can see if the problem is an SQL/MySQL one or a PHP one. Your two best tools in this cause are

◆ The MySQL client (**Figure 12.2**), a command-line tool for interacting with MySQL

◆ phpMyAdmin (**Figure 12.3**), a PHP-based MySQL interface

For a demonstration of using the MySQL monitor, see Appendix A. For information on phpMyAdmin, see `www.phpmyadmin.net`.

✔ Tips

■ Technically, a DBMS, or database application, is the software that interfaces with the database proper. However, most people use the terms *database* and *DBMS* synonymously.

■ Lots other applications are available for interacting with MySQL aside from the MySQL client and phpMyAdmin. Some are free, and others cost. A quick search using Google for *MySQL*, *admin*, and your operating system should turn up some results.

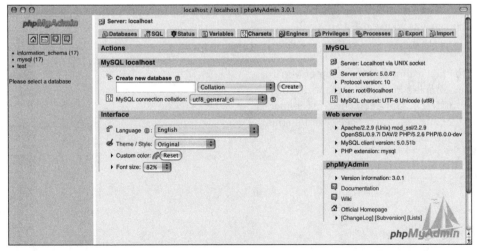

Figure 12.3 phpMyAdmin is perhaps the most popular software written in PHP. It provides a Web-based interface for a MySQL database.

INTRODUCTION TO SQL

Connecting to MySQL

When you worked with text files in Chapter 11, "Files and Directories," you saw that you first had to create a file pointer while opening the file. This pointer then acts as a reference point to that open file. You use a similar process when working with databases. First, you have to establish a connection to the database server (in this case, MySQL). This connection is then used as the access point for any future commands. The syntax for connecting to a database is

```
$dbc = mysql_connect(hostname, username,
→ password);
```

The database connection (**$dbc**) is established using at least three arguments: the host, which is almost always *localhost*; the username; and the password for that username.

If you're using a database through a hosting company, the company will most likely provide you with the username and password to use. If you're running MySQL on your own computer, see Appendix A to learn how you create a user.

Once you're done working with a database, it's considered good form to close the connection, just as you'd close an open file:

```
mysql_close();
```

For the first example of this chapter, you'll write a simple script that attempts to connect to MySQL. Once you have this connection working, you can proceed through the rest of the chapter.

Script 12.1 Being able to connect to the MySQL server is the most important step. This script tests that process.

```
1    <!DOCTYPE html PUBLIC "-//W3C//DTD XHTML
     1.0 Transitional//EN"
2         "http://www.w3.org/TR/xhtml1/DTD/
     xhtml1-transitional.dtd">
3    <html xmlns="http://www.w3.org/1999/
     xhtml" xml:lang="en" lang="en">
4    <head>
5         <meta http-equiv="content-type"
     content="text/html; charset=utf-8" />
6         <title>Connect to MySQL</title>
7    </head>
8    <body>
9    <?php // Script 12.1 - mysql_connect.php
10   /* This script connects to the MySQL
     server. */
11
12   // Attempt to connect to MySQL and print
     out messages:
13   if ($dbc = mysql_connect('localhost',
     'username', 'password')) {
14
15       print '<p>Successfully connected to
     MySQL!</p>';
16
17       mysql_close(); // Close the connection.
18
19   } else {
20
21       print '<p style="color: red;">Could
     not connect to MySQL.</p>';
22
23   }
24
25   ?>
26   </body>
27   </html>
```

To connect to MySQL:

1. Begin a new PHP document in your text editor or IDE (**Script 12.1**).

   ```
   <!DOCTYPE html PUBLIC "-//W3C//DTD
   → XHTML 1.0 Transitional//EN"
       "http://www.w3.org/TR/xhtml1/DTD/
       → xhtml1-transitional.dtd">
   <html xmlns="http://www.w3.org/1999/
   → xhtml" xml:lang="en" lang="en">
   <head>
       <meta http-equiv="content-type"
       → content="text/html;
       → charset=utf-8" />
       <title>Connect to MySQL</title>
   </head>
   <body>
   ```

2. Start the section of PHP code:

   ```
   <?php // Script 12.1 -
   → mysql_connect.php
   ```

3. Connect to MySQL, and report on the results:

   ```
   if ($dbc = mysql_connect('localhost',
   → 'username', 'password')) {
       print '<p>Successfully connected
       → to MySQL!</p>';
       mysql_close();
   } else {
       print '<p style="color: red;">
       → Could not connect to MySQL.</p>';
   }
   ```

   By placing the connection attempt as the condition in an if-else statement, you make it easy to report on whether the connection worked.

   continues on next page

This chapter will continue to use *username* and *password* as values. For your scripts, you'll need to replace these with the values provided by your Web host or set them when you add a user using the steps outlined in Appendix A.

If a connection was established, a positive message is printed and then the connection is closed. Otherwise, an opposite message is printed, and there is no need to close the database connection (because it wasn't opened).

4. Complete the PHP code and the HTML page:

```
?>
</body>
</html>
```

5. Save the file as mysql_connect.php, place it in the proper directory of your PHP-enabled computer, and test it in your Web browser (**Figure 12.4**).

If you see results like those in **Figure 12.5**, double-check the username and password values. They should match up with those provided to you by your Web host or those you used to create the user. You can always test your connection username and password by using them in the MySQL client (again, see Appendix A).

If you see *call to undefined function mysql_connect...*, your version of PHP doesn't support MySQL (see the sidebar).

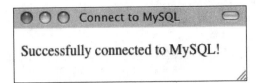

Figure 12.4 If PHP has support for MySQL and the username/password/host combination you used was correct, you should see this simple message.

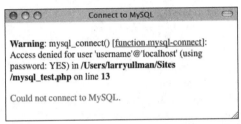

Figure 12.5 If PHP couldn't connect to MySQL, you'll probably see something like this. The warning message may or may not appear, depending upon your error management settings.

✔ Tips

- Most of the MySQL-related PHP functions take an optional argument that is the database connection ($dbc in this case). All the examples in this chapter omit this argument, but you'll frequently see the functions used with or without it.

- The *localhost* value is used as the host name when both the PHP script and the MySQL database reside on the same computer. You can use PHP to connect to a MySQL database running on a remote server by changing the host name in the PHP script and creating the proper permissions in MySQL.

- PHP has built-in support for most databases, including dBase, FilePro, mSQL, MySQL, Oracle, PostgreSQL, and Sybase. If you're using a type of database that doesn't have direct support—for example, Access or SQL Server—you'll need to use PHP's ODBC (Open Database Connectivity) functions along with that database's ODBC drivers to interface with the database.

- The combination of using PHP and MySQL is so common now that you may run across terms that identify servers configured with both PHP and MySQL: *LAMP*, *MAMP*, and *WAMP*. These stand for the operating system—*Linux*, *Mac OS X*, or *Windows*—plus the *Apache* Web server, the *MySQL* DBMS, and *PHP*.

- You'll be working with MySQL, so all the functions you use in this chapter are MySQL specific. For example, to connect to a database in MySQL, the proper function is mysql_connect( ), but if you're using PostgreSQL, you'd instead write pg_connect( ). If you aren't using a MySQL DBMS, use the PHP manual (available through www.PHP.net) to find the appropriate function names.

MySQL Extensions

PHP can communicate with MySQL using two different extensions. The first, used in this chapter, is the standard MySQL extension. It has been around for years and works with all versions of PHP and MySQL. All of the standard MySQL extension functions begin with *mysql_*.

The second extension is called *MySQLi* (Improved MySQL Extension). This extension was added in PHP 5 and can be used with MySQL 4.1 or greater. These functions all begin with *mysqli_* and take advantage of some of the added features in MySQL. If possible, it's preferable to use the MySQLi functions, but as the older extension is more universally enabled, this book uses it exclusively. See the PHP manual or my book *PHP 6 and MySQL 5 for Dynamic Web Sites: Visual QuickPro Guide* (Peachpit Press, 2007) for details on the MySQLi extension.

CONNECTING TO MySQL

MySQL Error Handling

Before this chapter gets too deep into working with MySQL, it would be best to discuss some error-handling techniques up front. Common errors you'll encounter are

◆ Failure to connect to MySQL

◆ Failure in selecting a database

◆ Inability to run a query

◆ No results being returned by a query

◆ Data not being inserted into a table

Experience will teach you why these errors normally occur, but immediately seeing what the problem is when running your scripts can save you much debugging time. To have your scripts give informative reports about errors that occur, use the `mysql_error()` function. This function returns a textual version of the error that the MySQL server returned.

Along with this function, you may want to use some PHP tools for handling errors. Specifically, the error suppression operator (@), when used preceding a function name, suppresses any error messages or warnings the function might invoke:

```
@function_name();
```

Note that this operator doesn't stop the error from happening, it just prevents the message from begin immediately displayed. You'd use it in situations where you intend to handle the error yourself, should one occur.

Script 12.2 By adding error control to the script (the @ symbol and the `mysql_error()` function), you can more purposefully address problems that occur.

```
1    <!DOCTYPE html PUBLIC "-//W3C//DTD XHTML
     1.0 Transitional//EN"
2        "http://www.w3.org/TR/xhtml1/DTD/
     xhtml1-transitional.dtd">
3    <html xmlns="http://www.w3.org/1999/
     xhtml" xml:lang="en" lang="en">
4    <head>
5        <meta http-equiv="content-type"
     content="text/html; charset=utf-8" />
6        <title>Connect to MySQL</title>
7    </head>
8    <body>
9    <?php // Script 12.2 - mysql_connect.php #2
10   /* This script connects to the MySQL
     server. */
11
12   // Attempt to connect to MySQL and print
     out messages:
13   if ($dbc = @mysql_connect('localhost',
     'username', 'password')) {
14
15       print '<p>Successfully connected to
     MySQL!</p>';
16
17       mysql_close(); // Close the connection.
18
19   } else {
20
21       print '<p style="color: red;">Could
     not connect to MySQL:<br />' . mysql_
     error() . '.</p>';
22
23   }
24
25   ?>
26   </body>
27   </html>
```

To use error handling:

1. Open `mysql_connect.php` (Script 12.1) in your text editor or IDE.

2. Suppress any PHP errors created by the `mysql_connect()` function by changing the `if` conditional as follows (**Script 12.2**):

   ```
   if ($dbc = @mysql_connect
   → ('localhost', 'username',
   → 'password')) {
   ```

   Rather than have PHP print out an error message when the `mysql_connect()` function backfires (Figure 12.5), the message will be suppressed here using the @ symbol. The errors still occur, but they're handled by the change made in the next step.

3. Add the `mysql_error()` function to the `print()` statement in the `else` section:

   ```
   print '<p style="color: red;">Could
   → not connect to MySQL:<br />'
   → . mysql_error() . '.</p>';
   ```

   Instead of printing a message or relying on whatever error PHP kicks out (see Figure 12.5), the script now prints the MySQL error within this context. You accomplish this by printing some HTML concatenated with the `mysql_error()` function.

continues on next page

MySQL Error Handling

4. Save the file and test it again in your Web browser (**Figure 12.6**).

If there was a problem, this result now looks better than Figure 12.5. If the script connected, the result is like that in Figure 12.4, because neither of the error-management tools is involved.

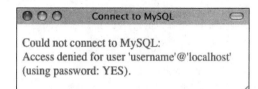

Figure 12.6 Using PHP's error-control functions, you can adjust how errors are handled.

✔ Tips

■ In this chapter, error messages are revealed to assist in the debugging process. Live Web sites should not have this level of explicit error messages being shown to the user.

■ You can use the @ symbol to suppress errors, notices, or warnings stemming from any function, not just a MySQL-related one. For example:

```
@include('./filename.php');
```

■ In previous editions of this book, I've also called `die()`, which is an alias for `exit()`, when a connection error occurs. The thinking is that since a database connection cannot be made, there's no point in continuing. I've omitted its use in this chapter because it's just too heavy-handed and is often misused.

Creating and Selecting a Database

Before a PHP script can interact with a database, the database must first be selected. Of course, in order to select a database, it must exist. You can create a database using PHP, the MySQL client, phpMyAdmin, or any number of tools, so long as the MySQL hostname/username/password combination you are using has permission to do so.

Database permissions are a bit more complicated than file permissions, but you need to understand this fact: Different types of users can be assigned different database capabilities. For example, one DBMS user may be able to create new databases and delete existing ones (you may have dozens of databases in your DBMS), but a lower-level user may only be able to create and modify tables within a single database. The most basic user may just be able to read from, but not modify, tables.

If you're using PHP and MySQL for a live, hosted site, the hosting company will most likely give you the second type of access—control over a single database but not the DBMS itself—and establish the initial database for you. If you're working on your own server or have administrative access, you should have the capability to create new users and databases.

To create a database with PHP, you use the `mysql_query()` function with the CREATE DATABASE *databasename* SQL command:

```
mysql_query('CREATE DATABASE somedb');
```

Once you've done this, you can select the database using `mysql_select_db()`:

```
mysql_select_db('somedb');
```

continues on next page

Note that you only ever need to create a database once, but it must always be selected before any other queries are run on it. In other words, some developers need to perform this first step, but everyone must take the second step with every PHP script.

In this example, you'll create a new database and then select it. To repeat, creating a database requires that you have administrator access. If your Web host restricts your access, it should create the initial database for you upon request; you can just write the second part of this script, which selects the database.

To create and select a database:

1. Open mysql_connect.php (Script 12.2) in your text editor or IDE.

2. After the first print() statement, create the new database, if necessary (**Script 12.3**):

```
if (@mysql_query('CREATE DATABASE
→ myblog')) {
    print '<p>The database has been
    → created!</p>';
} else {
    print '<p style="color: red;">
    → Could not create the database
    → because:<br />' . mysql_error()
→ . '.</p>';
}
```

If you need to create the database, use this construct to handle the task cleanly and effectively. The query—CREATE DATABASE myblog—is run using the mysql_query() function. The @ symbol is used to suppress any error messages, which are instead handled by print() in conjunction with the mysql_error() function in the else clause.

If the database has already been created for you, skip this step.

Script 12.3 Creating a new database consists of three steps: connecting to the database, running a CREATE DATABASE query using the mysql_query() function, and then closing the connection.

```
1   <!DOCTYPE html PUBLIC "-//W3C//DTD XHTML
    1.0 Transitional//EN"
2       "http://www.w3.org/TR/xhtml1/DTD/
        xhtml1-transitional.dtd">
3   <html xmlns="http://www.w3.org/1999/
    xhtml" xml:lang="en" lang="en">
4   <head>
5       <meta http-equiv="content-type"
        content="text/html; charset=utf-8" />
6       <title>Create the Database</title>
7   </head>
8   <body>
9   <?php // Script 12.3 - create_db.php
10  /* This script connects to the MySQL
    server. It also creates and selects the
    database. */
11
12  // Attempt to connect to MySQL and print
    out messages:
13  if ($dbc = @mysql_connect('localhost',
    'username', 'password')) {
14
15      print '<p>Successfully connected to
        MySQL!</p>';
16
17      // Try to create the database:
18      if (@mysql_query('CREATE DATABASE
        myblog')) {
19
20          print '<p>The database has been
            created!</p>';
21
22      } else { // Could not create it.
23          print '<p style="color: red;">Could
            not create the database because:
            <br />' . mysql_error() . '.</p>';
24      }
25
26      // Try to select the database:
27      if (@mysql_select_db('myblog')) {
28          print '<p>The database has been
            selected.</p>';
29      } else {
30          print '<p style="color: red;">Could
            not select the database because:<br
            />' . mysql_error() . '.</p>';
31      }
32
```

(script continues on next page)

Script 12.3 *continued*

```
33     mysql_close(); // Close the connection.
34
35   } else {
36
37     print '<p style="color: red;">Could
       not connect to MySQL:<br />' . mysql_
       error() . '.</p>';
38
39   }
40
41   ?>
42   </body>
43   </html>
```

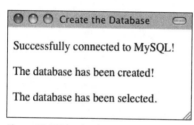

Figure 12.7 If the database could be created and selected, you'll see this result in the Web browser.

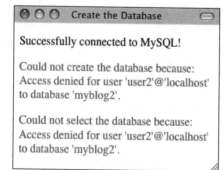

Figure 12.8 If the user doesn't have the authority to create a database, you'll see a message like this. A similar result will occur if the user doesn't have permission to select the database.

3. Attempt to select the database:

```
if (@mysql_select_db('myblog')) {
    print '<p>The database has been
    → selected.</p>';
} else {
    print '<p style="color: red;">
    → Could not select the database
    → because:<br />' . mysql_error()
    → . '.</p>';
}
```

This conditional has the same structure as that in Step 2. If PHP can select the database, a message is printed. If it can't select the database, the specific MySQL error will be displayed instead.

Every PHP script that runs queries on a database must connect to MySQL and select the database in order to work.

4. If you want, change the page title to reflect this script's new purpose:

```
<title>Create the Database</title>
```

5. Save your script as `create_db.php`, place it in the proper directory for your PHP-enabled server, and test it in your Web browser (**Figures 12.7** and **12.8**).

✔ Tips

■ You probably won't create databases with any frequency and may not normally do so using a PHP script. Still, this example demonstrates both how you execute simple queries using PHP as well as the SQL command needed to create a database.

■ You haven't done so in these examples, but in general it's a good idea to set your database information—host name, username, password, and database name—as variables or constants. Then you can plug them into the appropriate functions. By doing so, you can separate the database specifics from the functionality of the script, allowing you to easily port that code to other applications.

Creating a Table

Once the initial database has been created and selected, you can begin to create individual tables in it. A database can consist of multiple tables, but in this simple example you'll create one table in which data will be stored.

To create a table in the database, you'll use SQL—the language that databases understand. Because SQL is a lot like spoken English, the proper query to create a new table reads like so:

```
CREATE TABLE tablename (column1
→ definition, column2 definition, etc.)
```

For each column, separated by commas, you first indicate the column name and then the column type. Common types are TEXT, VARCHAR (a variable number of characters), DATETIME, and INT (integer). Because it's highly recommended that you create a first column that acts as the *primary key* (a column used to refer to each row), a simple CREATE statement could be

```
CREATE TABLE my_table (id INT PRIMARY
→ KEY, information TEXT)
```

A table's primary key is a special column of unique values that is used to refer to the table's rows. The database makes an index of this column in order to more quickly navigate through the table. A table can have only one primary key, which you normally set up as an automatically incremented column of integers. The first row has a key of 1, the second has a key of 2, and so forth. Referring back to the key always retrieves the values for that row.

Table 12.2

entries Table	
COLUMN NAME	**COLUMN TYPE**
entry_id	Positive, non-null, automatically incrementing integer
title	Text up to 100 characters in length
entry	Text of any length
date_entered	A timestamp including both the date and the time the row was added

Script 12.4 To create a database table, define the appropriate SQL statement and then invoke the `mysql_query()` function.

```
1   <!DOCTYPE html PUBLIC "-//W3C//DTD XHTML
    1.0 Transitional//EN"
2       "http://www.w3.org/TR/xhtml1/DTD/
    xhtml1-transitional.dtd">
3   <html xmlns="http://www.w3.org/1999/
    xhtml" xml:lang="en" lang="en">
4   <head>
5       <meta http-equiv="content-type"
    content="text/html; charset=utf-8" />
6       <title>Create a Table</title>
7   </head>
8   <body>
9   <?php // Script 12.4 - create_table.php
10  /* This script connects to the MySQL
    server, selects the database, and creates
    a table. */
11
12  // Connect and select:
13  if ($dbc = @mysql_connect('localhost',
    'username', 'password')) {
14
15      // Handle the error if the database
    couldn't be selected:
16      if (!@mysql_select_db('myblog')) {
17          print '<p style="color: red;">Could
    not select the database because:<br
    />' . mysql_error() . '.</p>';
18          mysql_close();
19          $dbc = FALSE;
20      }
21
22  } else { // Connection failure.
23      print '<p style="color: red;">Could
    not connect to MySQL:<br />' . mysql_
    error() . '.</p>';
24  }
25
26  if ($dbc) {
27
28      // Define the query:
29      $query = 'CREATE TABLE entries (
30  entry_id INT UNSIGNED NOT NULL AUTO_
    INCREMENT PRIMARY KEY,
31  title VARCHAR(100) NOT NULL,
32  entry TEXT NOT NULL,
33  date_entered DATETIME NOT NULL
34  )';
35
```

(script continues on next page)

You can visit the MySQL Web site for more information on SQL. By following the directions in this section, though, you should be able to accomplish some basic database tasks. The table that you'll create in this example is described in **Table 12.2**.

In this example, you'll create a table that stores information submitted via an HTML form. In the next section of the chapter, you'll write the script that inserts the submitted data into the table created here.

To create a new table:

1. Begin a new PHP document in your text editor or IDE (**Script 12.4**):

   ```
   <!DOCTYPE html PUBLIC "-//W3C//DTD
   → XHTML 1.0 Transitional//EN"
       "http://www.w3.org/TR/xhtml1/DTD/
       → xhtml1-transitional.dtd">
   <html xmlns="http://www.w3.org/1999/
   → xhtml" xml:lang="en" lang="en">
   <head>
       <meta http-equiv="content-type"
       → content="text/html;
       → charset=utf-8" />
       <title>Create a Table</title>
   </head>
   <body>
   ```

2. Begin a section of PHP code:

   ```
   <?php // Script 12.4 - create_table.
   → php
   ```

   continues on next page

3. Connect to the MySQL server, and select the database:

```
if ($dbc = @mysql_connect
→('localhost', 'username',
→'password')) {
  if (!@mysql_select_db('myblog')) {
    print '<p style="color:
    →red;">Could not select the
    →database because:<br />'
    →. mysql_error() . '.</p>';
    mysql_close();
    $dbc = FALSE;
  }
} else {
  print '<p style="color: red;">
  →Could not connect to MySQL:<br
  →/>' . mysql_error() . '.</p>';
}
```

This is a alternative version of the code used in the preceding script. The main difference is that no messages are printed if each step was successful (we'll assume everything's working by this point).

If, for some reason, the database could not be selected, then an error is printed and the connection is closed. It makes sense to do this because if the database cannot be selected, there's no point in trying to create the table in it. The $dbc variable, which had represented the connection, is set to FALSE then, as an indication that its assigned CREATE query shouldn't be executed (see Step 4).

4. Create the query for making the table:

```
if ($dbc) {
  $query = 'CREATE TABLE entries (
entry_id INT UNSIGNED NOT NULL
→AUTO_INCREMENT PRIMARY KEY,
title VARCHAR(100) NOT NULL,
entry TEXT NOT NULL,
date_entered DATETIME NOT NULL
)';
```

Script 12.4 *continued*

```
36    // Execute the query:
37    if (@mysql_query($query)) {
38        print '<p>The table has been
          created.</p>';
39    } else {
40        print '<p style="color: red;">
          Could not create the table
          because:<br />' . mysql_error() .
          '.</p><p>The query being run was: '
          . $query . '</p>';
41    }
42
43    mysql_close(); // Close the connection.
44
45  }
46  ?>
47  </body>
48  </html>
```

First, if $dbc still has a value, the table should be created. If not, meaning that no connection could be made or the database couldn't be selected, then none of the following code will be executed.

As for the query itself, let's break that into more recognizable parts. First, to create a new table, you write CREATE TABLE *tablename* (where *tablename* is replaced by the actual, desired table name). Then, within parentheses, you list every column you want with each column separated by a comma. Your table and column names should be alphanumeric, with no spaces.

The first column in the table is called entry_id; it's an unsigned integer (INT UNSIGNED—which means that it can only be a positive whole number). By including the words NOT NULL, you indicate that this column must have a value for each row. The values automatically increase by one for each row added (AUTO INCREMENT) and stand as the primary key.

The next two columns consist of text. One, called title, is limited to 100 characters. The second, entry, can be nearly limitless in size. Each of these fields is also marked as NOT NULL, making them required fields.

Finally, the date_entered column is a timestamp that marks when each record was added to the table.

5. Execute the query:

```
if (@mysql_query($query)) {
    print '<p>The table has been
    → created.</p>';
} else {
    print '<p style="color: red;">
    → Could not create the table
    → because:<br />' . mysql_error()
    → . '.</p><p>The query being run
    → was: ' . $query . '</p>';
}
```

continues on next page

To create the table, you call the `mysql_query()` function using the `$query` variable as the argument. If a problem occurred, the MySQL error is printed, along with the value of the `$query` variable. This last step is a particularly useful debugging technique.

6. Close the database connection and complete the `$dbc` conditional:

```
mysql_close();
}
```

7. Complete the PHP code and the HTML page:

```
?>
</body>
</html>
```

8. Save the script as `create_table.php`, place it in the proper directory for your PHP-enabled server, and test it in your Web browser (**Figures 12.9** and **12.10**).

✔ Tips

■ It's not necessary to write your SQL queries partially in all capital letters as you have here, but doing so helps to distinguish your SQL keywords from the table and column names.

■ On larger Web applications, it's highly recommended that you place the database connection and selection code (lines 13 through 24 here) in a separate file, located outside of the Web directory. Then, each page that requires the database can include this external file.

■ The `mysql_query()` function returns TRUE if a query was successfully run on a database. That result doesn't necessarily mean the desired result occurred.

■ This chapter presents the basics of MySQL and SQL-related knowledge (including column types). You'll want to check out other resources—listed in Appendix B—once you're comfortable with the fundamentals.

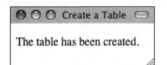

Figure 12.9 If all went well, all you'll see is this message.

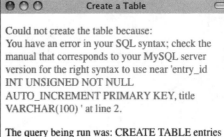

Figure 12.10 Between the MySQL error message and printing out the query being executed, you should be able to figure out what the problem is if the script does not work properly.

Inserting Data into a Database

As mentioned, this database will be used as a blog, an online journal. Blog entries—consisting of a title and text—will be added to the database using one page and then displayed on another page. It's a simple but relevant use of a database.

In the last section, you created the table, which consists of four columns: `entry_id`, `title`, `entry`, and `date_entered`. The process of adding information to a table is similar to creating the table itself in terms of which functions you use, but the SQL query is different. To insert records, you use the INSERT SQL command using either of the following models:

```
INSERT INTO tablename VALUES (value1,
→ value2, value3, etc.)
```

```
INSERT INTO tablename (column1_name,
→ column2_name) VALUES (value1, value2)
```

The query begins with INSERT INTO *table-name*. Then you can either specify which columns you're inserting values for or not. The latter is more specific and is therefore preferred, but it can be tedious if you're populating a slew of columns. In either case, you must be certain to list the right number and type of values for each column in the table.

The values are placed within parentheses, with each value separated by a comma. Non-numeric values—strings and dates—need to be quoted, numbers do not:

```
INSERT INTO example (name, age) VALUES
→ ('Jonah', 1)
```

You run this query on the database using the `mysql_query()` function. Because these queries are often complex, it often makes sense to assign each query to a variable and send that variable to the `mysql_query()` function (as in the previous example).

To demonstrate, let's create a page that adds blog entries to the database. Like many of the examples in the preceding chapter, this one will both display and handle the HTML form. Before getting into the example, though, I'll say that this script knowingly has a security hole in it; it'll be explained and fixed in the next section of the chapter.

To enter data into a database from an HTML form:

1. Begin a new PHP document in your text editor or IDE (**Script 12.5**):

```
<!DOCTYPE html PUBLIC "-//W3C//DTD
→ XHTML 1.0 Transitional//EN"
    "http://www.w3.org/TR/xhtml1/DTD/
→ xhtml1-transitional.dtd">
<html xmlns="http://www.w3.org/1999/
→ xhtml" xml:lang="en" lang="en">
<head>
    <meta http-equiv="content-type"
→ content="text/html;
→ charset=utf-8" />
    <title>Add a Blog Entry</title>
</head>
<body>
```

2. Create the initial PHP section and check for the form submission:

```
<?php // Script 12.5 - add_entry.php
if (isset($_POST['submitted'])) {
```

3. Connect to and select the database:

```
$dbc = mysql_connect('localhost',
→ 'username', 'password');
mysql_select_db('myblog');
```

At this point, if you're running these examples in order, I'll assume you have a working connection and selection process down, so I'll dispense with all the conditionals and error reporting (mostly to shorten the script). If you have problems connecting to and selecting the database, apply the code already outlined in the chapter.

Script 12.5 The query statement for adding information to a database is straightforward enough, but be sure to match the number of values in parentheses to the number of columns in the database table.

```
1   <!DOCTYPE html PUBLIC "-//W3C//DTD XHTML
    1.0 Transitional//EN"
2       "http://www.w3.org/TR/xhtml1/DTD/
        xhtml1-transitional.dtd">
3   <html xmlns="http://www.w3.org/1999/
    xhtml" xml:lang="en" lang="en">
4   <head>
5       <meta http-equiv="content-type"
        content="text/html; charset=utf-8" />
6       <title>Add a Blog Entry</title>
7   </head>
8   <body>
9   <?php // Script 12.5 - add_entry.php
10  /* This script adds a blog entry to
    the database. */
11
12  if (isset($_POST['submitted'])) {
    // Handle the form.
13
14      // Connect and select:
15      $dbc = mysql_connect('localhost',
        'username', 'password');
16      mysql_select_db('myblog');
17
18      // Validate the form data:
19      $problem = FALSE;
20      if (!empty($_POST['title']) &&
        !empty($_POST['entry'])) {
21          $title = trim($_POST['title']);
22          $entry = trim($_POST['entry']);
23      } else {
24          print '<p style="color:
            red;">Please submit both a title
            and an entry.</p>';
25          $problem = TRUE;
26      }
27
28      if (!$problem) {
29
30          // Define the query:
31          $query = "INSERT INTO entries
            (entry_id, title, entry, date_
            entered) VALUES (0, '$title',
            '$entry', NOW())";
32
```

(script continues on next page)

Script 12.5 *continued*

```
33        // Execute the query:
34        if (@mysql_query($query)) {
35            print '<p>The blog entry has
              been added!</p>';
36        } else {
37            print '<p style="color:
              red;">Could not add the entry
              because:<br />' . mysql_error()
              . '.</p><p>The query being run
              was: ' . $query . '</p>';
38        }
39
40        } // No problem!
41
42        mysql_close();
43
44    } // End of form submission IF.
45
46    // Display the form:
47    ?>
48    <form action="add_entry.php"
      method="post">
49        <p>Entry Title: <input type="text"
          name="title" size="40" maxsize="100"
          /></p>
50        <p>Entry Text: <textarea name="entry"
          cols="40" rows="5"></textarea></p>
51        <input type="submit" name="submit"
          value="Post This Entry!" />
52        <input type="hidden" name="submitted"
          value="true" />
53    </form>
54    </body>
55    </html>
```

Figure 12.11 PHP still performs some basic form validation so that empty records are not inserted into the database.

4. Validate the form data:

```
$problem = FALSE;
if (!empty($_POST['title']) &&
→ !empty($_POST['entry'])) {
    $title = trim($_POST['title']);
    $entry = trim($_POST['entry']);
} else {
    print '<p style="color: red;">
    → Please submit both a title and
    → an entry.</p>';
    $problem = TRUE;
}
```

Before using the form data in an INSERT query, it ought to be validated. Here just a minimum of validation is used, guaranteeing that some values are provided. If so, new variables are assigned those values, after trimming away extraneous spaces. If not, an error message is printed (**Figure 12.11**) and the $problem flag variable is set to TRUE (because there is a problem).

5. Define the INSERT query:

```
if (!$problem) {
    $query = "INSERT INTO entries
    → (entry_id, title, entry,
    → date_entered) VALUES (0,
    → '$title', '$entry', NOW())";
```

The query begins with the necessary INSERT INTO *tablename* code. Then it lists the columns for which values will be submitted. After that is the word VALUES, followed by four values (one for each column, in order) within single quotation marks and separated by commas. When you assign this query to the $query variable, you use double quotation marks both to access the $title and $entry variable values and to avoid conflicts with the single quotation marks used to demarcate the values.

continues on next page

Because the entry_id column has been set to AUTO_INCREMENT, you can use 0 as the value and MySQL will automatically use the next logical value for that column. To set the value of the date_entered column, you use the MySQL NOW() function. It inserts the current time as that value.

6. Run the query on the database:

```
if (@mysql_query($query)) {
    print '<p>The blog entry has been
    → added!</p>';
} else {
    print '<p style="color: red;">
    → Could not add the entry
    → because:<br />' . mysql_error()
    → . '.</p><p>The query being run
    → was: ' . $query . '</p>';
}
```

The query, once defined, is run using the mysql_query() function. By calling this function as the condition of an if-else statement, you can print simple messages indicating the result of the query execution.

As an essential debugging tool, if the query didn't run properly, the MySQL error and the query being run are both printed to the Web browser (**Figure 12.12**).

7. Close the $problem conditional, the database connection, and complete the main conditional and the PHP section:

```
    } // No problem!
    mysql_close();
} // End of form submission IF.
?>
```

From here on out, the form will be displayed.

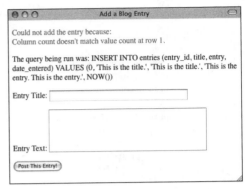

Figure 12.12 If the INSERT query didn't work, the MySQL error is printed along with the query that was run.

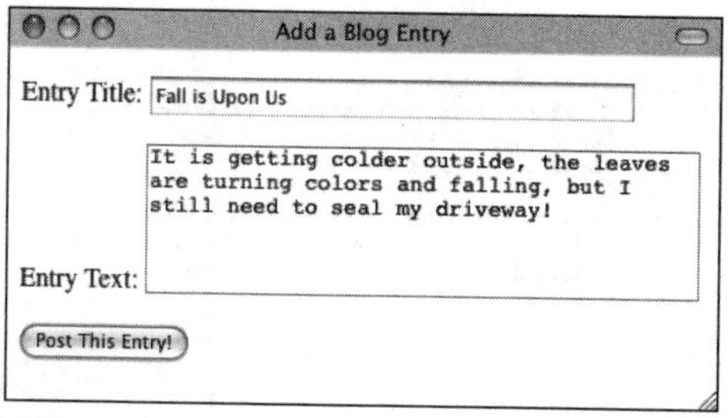

Figure 12.13 This is the form for adding an entry to the database.

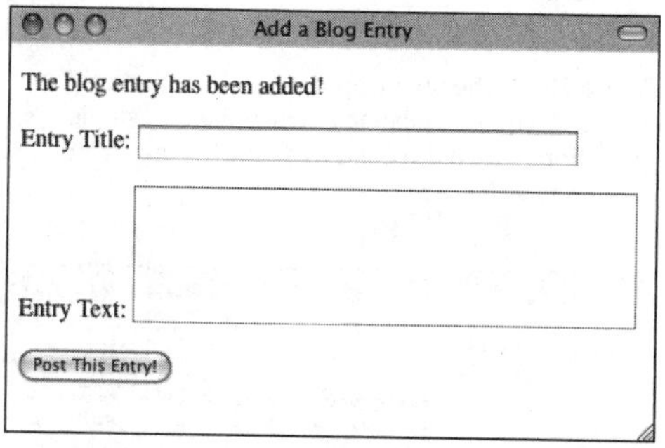

Figure 12.14 If the INSERT query ran properly, a message is printed and the form is displayed again.

8. Create the form:

```
<form action="add_entry.php"
→ method="post">
    <p>Entry Title: <input type="text"
    → name="title" size="40"
    → maxsize="100" /></p>
    <p>Entry Text: <textarea
    → name="entry" cols="40"
    → rows="5"></textarea></p>
    <input type="submit" name="submit"
    → value="Post This Entry!" />
    <input type="hidden" name=
    → "submitted" value="true" />
</form>
```

The HTML form is very simple, requiring only a title for the blog entry and the entry itself. As a good rule of thumb, use the same name for your form inputs as the corresponding column names in the database. Doing so makes errors less likely.

9. Finish the HTML page:

```
</body>
</html>
```

10. Save the script as add_entry.php, place it in the proper directory for your PHP-enabled server, and test it in your Web browser (**Figures 12.13** and **12.14**).

✔ Tips

- MySQL allows you to insert several records at once, using this format:
  ```
  INSERT INTO tablename VALUES
  → (value1, value2), (value3, value4);
  ```
  Most other database applications don't support this construct, though.

- To retrieve the automatically incremented number created for an AUTO_INCREMENT column, use the mysql_insert_id() function.

Securing Query Data

As I mentioned in the introduction to the preceding sequence of steps, the code as written has a pretty bad security hole in it. As it stands, if someone submits text that contains an apostrophe, that data will break the SQL query (**Figure 12.15**). The result is obviously undesirable, but why is it insecure?

If a malicious user knows they can break a query by typing an apostrophe, they may try to run their own queries using this hole. If someone submitted *'DROP TABLE entries;* as the blog post title, the resulting query would be:

```
INSERT INTO entries (entry_id, title,
→ entry, date_entered) VALUES (0,
→ ''DROP TABLE entries;', '<entry
→ text>', NOW())
```

The initial provided apostrophe completes that part of the query, making the whole query syntactically incorrect. The hope there is that the newly provided query—DROP TABLE entries—will be run when the original INSERT query fails. This is called an *SQL injection attack*, but fortunately it's easy to prevent.

To do so, send potentially insecure data to be used in a query through the mysql_real_escape_string() function. This function will escape—preface with a backslash—any potentially harmful characters, making the data safe to use in a query:

```
$var = mysql_real_escape_string($var);
```

Let's apply this function to the preceding script.

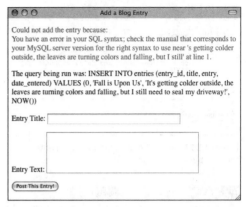

Figure 12.15 The apostrophe in the conjunction *It's* breaks the query because apostrophes (or single quotation marks) are used to delimit strings used in queries.

Figure 12.16 Now apostrophes in form data...

Figure 12.17 ...will not cause problems.

Script 12.6 To better secure the Web application and the database, the `mysql_real_escape_string()` function is applied to the form data used in the query.

```
1    <!DOCTYPE html PUBLIC "-//W3C//DTD XHTML
     1.0 Transitional//EN"
2        "http://www.w3.org/TR/xhtml1/DTD/
     xhtml1-transitional.dtd">
3    <html xmlns="http://www.w3.org/1999/
     xhtml" xml:lang="en" lang="en">
4    <head>
5        <meta http-equiv="content-type"
     content="text/html; charset=utf-8" />
6        <title>Add a Blog Entry</title>
7    </head>
8    <body>
9    <?php // Script 12.6 - add_entry.php #2
10   /* This script adds a blog entry to the
     database. It now does so securely! */
11
12   if (isset($_POST['submitted'])) { //
     Handle the form.
13
14       // Connect and select:
15       $dbc = mysql_connect('localhost',
     'username', 'password');
16       mysql_select_db('myblog');
17
18       // Validate and secure the form data:
19       $problem = FALSE;
20       if (!empty($_POST['title']) &&
     !empty($_POST['entry'])) {
21           $title = mysql_real_escape_
     string(trim($_POST['title']));
22           $entry = mysql_real_escape_
     string(trim($_POST['entry']));
23       } else {
24           print '<p style="color: red;">
     Please submit both a title and an
     entry.</p>';
25           $problem = TRUE;
26       }
27
28       if (!$problem) {
29
30           // Define the query:
31           $query = "INSERT INTO entries
     (entry_id, title, entry, date_
     entered) VALUES (0, '$title',
     '$entry', NOW())";
32
```

(script continues on next page)

To secure query data:

1. Open `add_entry.php` (Script 12.5) in your text editor or IDE, if it is not already.

2. Update the assignment of the `$title` and `$entry` variables to read (**Script 12.6**):

   `$title = mysql_real_escape_string` → `(trim($_POST['title']));`

   `$entry = mysql_real_escape_string` → `(trim($_POST['entry']));`

   These two lines will greatly improve the security and functionality of the script. For both posted variables, their values are first trimmed, then sent through `mysql_real_escape_string()`. The result will be safe to use in the query.

3. Save the script, place it on your PHP-enabled server, and test it in your Web browser (**Figures 12.16** and **12.17**).

✔ Tips

- The `mysql_real_escape_string()` function requires the database connection, so it can only be called if it has access to a live connection.

- If you see (later in the chapter) that the displayed blog posts have extra backslashes before apostrophes, this is likely because you're using a version of PHP prior to version 6 and Magic Quotes is enabled. (Magic Quotes automatically escapes problematic characters in form data, although not as well `mysql_real_escape_string()`.) If that's the case, you'll need to apply the `stripslashes()` function to remove the extraneous slashes from the submitted values:

```
$title = mysql_real_escape_string
→ (stripslashes(trim($_POST
→ ['title'])));
```

Script 12.6 *continued*

```
33      // Execute the query:
34      if (@mysql_query($query)) {
35          print '<p>The blog entry has
            been added!</p>';
36      } else {
37          print '<p style="color:
            red;">Could not add the entry
            because:<br />' . mysql_error()
            . '.</p><p>The query being run
            was: ' . $query . '</p>';
38      }
39
40      } // No problem!
41
42      mysql_close();
43
44  } // End of form submission IF.
45
46  // Display the form:
47  ?>
48  <form action="add_entry.php"
    method="post">
49      <p>Entry Title: <input type="text"
        name="title" size="40" maxsize="100"
        /></p>
50      <p>Entry Text: <textarea name="entry"
        cols="40" rows="5"></textarea></p>
51      <input type="submit" name="submit"
        value="Post This Entry!" />
52      <input type="hidden" name="submitted"
        value="true" />
53  </form>
54  </body>
55  </html>
```

Retrieving Data from a Database

The next process this chapter demonstrates for working with databases is retrieving data from a populated table. You still use the `mysql_query()` function, but retrieving data is slightly different than inserting data—you have to assign the retrieved information to a variable in order to use it. This section goes through this process one step at a time.

The basic syntax for retrieving data is the `SELECT` query:

`SELECT what_columns FROM what_table`

The easiest query for reading data from a table is

`SELECT * FROM tablename`

The asterisk is the equivalent of saying *every column*. If you only require certain columns to be returned, you can limit your query, like so:

`SELECT title, entry FROM entries`

This query requests that only the information from two columns (`title` and `entry`) be gathered. Keep in mind that this structure doesn't limit what rows (or records) are returned, just what columns for those rows.

Another way to alter your query is to add a conditional restricting which rows are returned, accomplished using a `WHERE` clause:

`SELECT * FROM users WHERE (first_name=`
`→ 'Larry')`

Here you want the information from every column in the table, but only from the rows where the `first_name` column is equal to *Larry*. This is a good example of how SQL uses only a few terms effectively and flexibly.

continues on next page

The main difference in retrieving data from a database as opposed to inserting data into a database is that you need to handle the query differently. You may want to assign the results of the query to a variable:

```
$result = mysql_query($query);
```

In layman's terms, this variable now knows what the result of the query is (technically, it points to the returned rows in the MySQL server). To access multiple rows of information retrieved, you should run the $result variable through a loop:

```
while ($row = mysql_fetch_array
→ ($result)) {
    // Do something with $row.
}
```

With each iteration of the loop, the next row of information from the query (referenced by $result) is turned into an array called $row. This process continues until no more rows of information are found.

As with any array, when you retrieve records from the database, you must refer to the columns exactly as they're defined in the database (the keys are case-sensitive). So, in this example, you must use $row['entry'] instead of $row['Entry']. For this reason, it's recommended that you use entirely lower-case column names when you create a table.

The best way to comprehend this system is to try it. You'll write a script that retrieves the posts stored in the entries table and displays them (**Figure 12.18**). You may want to run through add_entry.php a couple more times to build up the table, first.

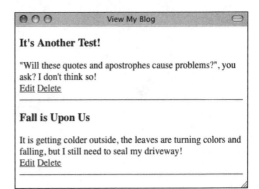

Figure 12.18 This dynamic Web page uses PHP to pull out data from a database.

To retrieve data from a table:

1. Begin a new PHP document in your text editor or IDE (**Script 12.7**):

```
<!DOCTYPE html PUBLIC "-//W3C//DTD
→ XHTML 1.0 Transitional//EN"
  "http://www.w3.org/TR/xhtml1/DTD/
  → xhtml1-transitional.dtd">
<html xmlns="http://www.w3.org/1999/
→ xhtml" xml:lang="en" lang="en">
<head>
  <meta http-equiv="content-type"
  → content="text/html;
  → charset=utf-8" />
  <title>View My Blog</title>
</head>
<body>
```

continues on next page

Script 12.7 The SQL query for retrieving all data from a table is quite simple; but in order for PHP to access every returned record, you must loop through the results one row at a time.

```
1    <!DOCTYPE html PUBLIC "-//W3C//DTD XHTML 1.0 Transitional//EN"
2        "http://www.w3.org/TR/xhtml1/DTD/xhtml1-transitional.dtd">
3    <html xmlns="http://www.w3.org/1999/xhtml" xml:lang="en" lang="en">
4    <head>
5      <meta http-equiv="content-type" content="text/html; charset=utf-8" />
6      <title>View My Blog</title>
7    </head>
8    <body>
9    <?php // Script 12.7 - view_blog.php
10   /* This script retrieves blog entries from the database. */
11
12   // Connect and select:
13   $dbc = mysql_connect('localhost', 'username', 'password');
14   mysql_select_db('myblog');
15
16   // Define the query:
17   $query = 'SELECT * FROM entries ORDER BY date_entered DESC';
18
19   if ($r = mysql_query($query)) { // Run the query.
20
```

(script continues on next page)

2. Define your PHP section and connect to the database:

```php
<?php // Script 12.7 - view_blog.php
$dbc = mysql_connect('localhost',
→ 'username', 'password');
mysql_select_db('myblog');
```

3. Define the SELECT query:

```php
$query = 'SELECT * FROM entries ORDER
→ BY date_entered DESC';
```

This basic query tells the database that you'd like to see every column of every row in the entries table. The returned records should be sorted, as indicated by the ORDER BY clause, by the order in which they were entered (recorded in the date_entered column), starting with the most recent first. This last option is indicated by DESC, which is short for *descending*. If the query was ORDER BY date_entered ASC, the most recent addition would be retrieved last.

Script 12.7 *continued*

```
21    // Retrieve and print every record:
22    while ($row = mysql_fetch_array($r)) {
23        print "<p><h3>{$row['title']}</h3>
24        {$row['entry']}<br />
25        <a href=\"edit_entry.php?id={$row['entry_id']}\">Edit</a>
26        <a href=\"delete_entry.php?id={$row['entry_id']}\">Delete</a>
27        </p><hr />\n";
28    }
29
30    } else { // Query didn't run.
31        print '<p style="color: red;">Could not retrieve the data because:<br />' . mysql_error() .
          '.</p><p>The query being run was: ' . $query . '</p>';
32    } // End of query IF.
33
34    mysql_close(); // Close the database connection.
35
36    ?>
37    </body>
38    </html>
```

4. Run the query:

```
if ($r = mysql_query($query)) {
```

The SELECT query is run like any other. However, the result of the query is assigned to a $result (or, more tersely, $r) variable, which will be referenced later.

5. Print out the returned results:

```
while ($row = mysql_fetch_array($r)) {
    print "<p><h3>{$row['title']}</h3>
    {$row['entry']}<br />
    <a href=\"edit_entry.php?id=
→ {$row['entry_id']}\">Edit</a>
    <a href=\"delete_entry.php?id=
→ {$row[entry_id']}\">Delete</a>
    </p><hr />\n";

}
```

This loop sets the variable $row to an array containing the first record returned in $r. The loop then executes the following commands (the print( ) statement). Once the loop gets back to the beginning, it assigns the next row, if it exists. It continues to do this until there are no more rows of information to be obtained.

Because the mysql_fetch_array( ) function was used, you can refer to each individual column in the row as you would any other array. The array's keys are the names of the columns from the table—hence, entry_id, title, and entry (there's no need to print out the date_entered).

At the bottom of each post, two links are created: to edit_entry.php and delete_entry.php. These will be written in the rest of the chapter. Each link passes the posting's database ID value along in the URL. That information will be necessary for those other two pages to edit and delete the blog posting.

continues on next page

RETRIEVING DATA FROM A DATABASE

6. Handle the errors if the query didn't run:

```
} else {
    print '<p style="color: red;">
    →Could not retrieve the data
    →because:<br />' . mysql_error()
    → . '.</p><p>The query being run
    →was: ' . $query . '</p>';
}
```

If the query couldn't run on the database, it should be printed out, along with the MySQL error (for debugging purposes).

7. Close the database connection:

```
mysql_close();
```

8. Complete the PHP section and the HTML page:

```
?>
</body>
</html>
```

9. Save the script as view_blog.php, place it in the proper directory for your PHP-enabled server, and test it in your Web browser (Figure 12.18).

10. If you want, add another record to the blog using the add_entry.php page (Script 12.6), and run this page again (**Figure 12.19**).

11. If you want, check the source code of the page to see the dynamically generated links (**Figure 12.20**).

✔ Tips

■ The mysql_fetch_array( ) function takes another argument, which is a constant indicating what kind of array should be returned. MYSQL_ASSOC returns an associative array, whereas MYSQL_NUM returns a numerically indexed array.

■ The mysql_num_rows( ) function returns the number of records returned by a SELECT query.

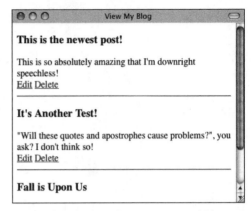

Figure 12.19 Thanks to the SELECT query, which orders the returned records by the date they were entered, the most recently added entry is always listed first.

Figure 12.20 Part of the HTML source of the page. Note that the two links have *?id=X* appended to each URL.

■ It's possible to paginate returned records so that 10 or 20 appear on each page (like the way Google works). Doing so requires more advanced coding than can be taught in this book, though. See one of the author's other, more advanced books, or look online for code examples and tutorials.

■ You might want to apply the nl2br( ) function to the blog entry ($row['entry']) to turn new lines in the entry into HTML <br /> tags. You can do so either prior to storing the data or when displaying it.

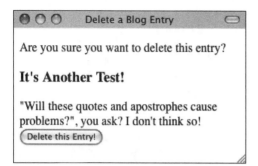

Figure 12.21 When the user arrives at this page, the blog entry is revealed and the user must confirm that they want to delete it.

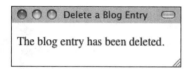

Figure 12.22 If the delete query worked properly, the user sees this result.

Deleting Data in a Database

Sometimes you might also want to run a DELETE query on a database. Such a query removes records from the database. The syntax for a delete query is

DELETE FROM *tablename* WHERE *column=value*

The WHERE clause isn't required, but if it's omitted, you'll remove every record from the table. You should also understand that once you delete a record, there's no way to recover it (unless you have a backup of the database).

As a safeguard, if you want to delete only a single record from a table, add the LIMIT clause to the query:

DELETE FROM *tablename* WHERE *column=value*
→ LIMIT 1

This clause ensures that only one record is deleted at most. Once you've defined your query, it's again executed using the mysql_query( ) function, like any other query.

To see if a DELETE query worked, you can use the mysql_affected_rows( ) function. This function returns the number of rows affected by an INSERT, DELETE, or UPDATE query.

As an example, let's write the delete_entry. php script, which is linked from the view_blog.php page. This page receives the database record ID in the URL. It then displays the entry to confirm that the user wants to delete it (**Figure 12.21**). If the user clicks the button, the record will be deleted (**Figure 12.22**).

To delete data from a database:

1. Begin a new PHP document in your text
editor or IDE (**Script 12.8**):

```
<!DOCTYPE html PUBLIC "-//W3C//DTD
→ XHTML 1.0 Transitional//EN"
   "http://www.w3.org/TR/xhtml1/DTD/
   → xhtml1-transitional.dtd">
<html xmlns="http://www.w3.org/1999/
→ xhtml" xml:lang="en" lang="en">
<head>
   <meta http-equiv="content-type"
   → content="text/html;
   → charset=utf-8" />
   <title>Delete a Blog Entry</title>
</head>
<body>
```

Script 12.8 The DELETE SQL command permanently removes a record (or records) from a table.

```
1    <!DOCTYPE html PUBLIC "-//W3C//DTD XHTML 1.0 Transitional//EN"
2        "http://www.w3.org/TR/xhtml1/DTD/xhtml1-transitional.dtd">
3    <html xmlns="http://www.w3.org/1999/xhtml" xml:lang="en" lang="en">
4    <head>
5        <meta http-equiv="content-type" content="text/html; charset=utf-8" />
6        <title>Delete a Blog Entry</title>
7    </head>
8    <body>
9    <?php // Script 12.8 - delete_entry.php
10   /* This script deletes a blog entry. */
11
12   // Connect and select:
13   $dbc = mysql_connect('localhost', 'username', 'password');
14   mysql_select_db('myblog');
15
16   if (isset($_GET['id']) && is_numeric($_GET['id']) ) { // Display the entry in a form:
17
18       // Define the query:
19       $query = "SELECT title, entry FROM entries WHERE entry_id={$_GET['id']}";
20       if ($r = mysql_query($query)) { // Run the query.
21
22           $row = mysql_fetch_array($r); // Retrieve the information.
23
```

(script continues on next page)

2. Start the PHP code and connect to the database:

```php
<?php // Script 12.8 -
→ delete_entry.php
$dbc = mysql_connect('localhost',
→ 'username', 'password');
mysql_select_db('myblog');
```

continues on next page

Script 12.8 *continued*

```php
24       // Make the form:
25       print '<form action="delete_entry.php" method="post">
26       <p>Are you sure you want to delete this entry?</p>
27       <p><h3>' . $row['title'] . '</h3>' .
28       $row['entry'] . '<br />
29       <input type="hidden" name="id" value="' . $_GET['id'] . '" />
30       <input type="submit" name="submit" value="Delete this Entry!" /></p>
31       </form>';
32
33       } else { // Couldn't get the information.
34           print '<p style="color: red;">Could not retrieve the blog entry because:<br />' . mysql_
             error() . '.</p><p>The query being run was: ' . $query . '</p>';
35       }
36
37   } elseif (isset($_POST['id']) && is_numeric($_POST['id'])) { // Handle the form.
38
39       // Define the query:
40       $query = "DELETE FROM entries WHERE entry_id={$_POST['id']} LIMIT 1";
41       $r = mysql_query($query); // Execute the query.
42
43       // Report on the result:
44       if (mysql_affected_rows() == 1) {
45           print '<p>The blog entry has been deleted.</p>';
46       } else {
47           print '<p style="color: red;">Could not delete the blog entry because:<br />' . mysql_
             error() . '.</p><p>The query being run was: ' . $query . '</p>';
48       }
49
50   } else { // No ID set.
51       print '<p style="color: red;">This page has been accessed in error.</p>';
52   } // End of main IF.
53
54   mysql_close(); // Close the database connection.
55
56   ?>
57   </body>
58   </html>
```

DELETING DATA IN A DATABASE

3. If the page received a valid entry ID in the URL, define and execute a SELECT query:

```
if (isset($_GET['id']) &&
→ is_numeric($_GET['id']) ) {
    $query = "SELECT title, entry
    → FROM entries WHERE entry_id=
    → {$_GET['id']}";
    if ($r = mysql_query($query)) {
```

To display the blog entry, the page must confirm that a numeric ID is received by the page. Because it should come in the URL (when the user clicks the link in view_blog.php, see Figure 12.20), you reference $_GET['id'].

The query is like the SELECT query used in the preceding example, except that the WHERE clause has been added to retrieve a specific record. Also, because only the two stored values are necessary—the title and the entry itself—only those are being selected.

This query is then run on the database using the mysql_query() function.

4. Retrieve the record, and display the entry in a form:

```
$row = mysql_fetch_array($r);
print '<form action="delete_entry.
→ php" method="post">
<p>Are you sure you want to delete
→ this entry?</p>
<p><h3>' . $row['title'] . '</h3>' .
$row['entry'] . '<br />
<input type="hidden" name="id"
→ value="' . $_GET['id'] . '" />
<input type="submit" name="submit"
→ value="Delete this Entry!" /></p>
</form>';
```

Instead of retrieving all the records using a while loop, as you did in the preceding example, you use one call to the mysql_fetch_array() function to assign the returned record to the $row variable. Using this array, the record to be deleted can be displayed.

The form first shows the blog entry (see Figure 12.21), much as it did in the `view_blog.php` script. When the user clicks the button, the form will be submitted back to this page, at which point the record should be deleted. In order to do so, the blog identification number, which is passed to the script as `$_GET['id']`, must be stored in a hidden input so that it exists in the `$_POST` array upon submission (because `$_GET['id']` won't have a value at that point).

5. Report an error if the query failed:

```
} else {
    print '<p style="color: red;">
→ Could not retrieve the blog
→ entry because:<br />' .
→ mysql_error() . '.</p><p>The
→ query being run was: ' . $query
→ . '</p>';
}
```

If the `SELECT` query failed to run, the MySQL error and the query itself is printed out.

6. Check for the submission of the form:

```
} elseif (isset($_POST['id']) &&
→ is_numeric($_POST['id'])) {
```

This `elseif` clause is part of the conditional begun in Step 3. It corresponds to the second usage of this same script (the form being submitted). If this conditional is TRUE, the record should be deleted.

7. Define and execute the query:

```
$query = "DELETE FROM entries WHERE
→ entry_id={$_POST['id']} LIMIT 1";
$r = mysql_query($query);
```

This query deletes the record whose `entry_id` has a value of `$_POST['id']`. The ID value comes from the form, where it's stored as a hidden input. By adding the `LIMIT 1` clause to the query, you can guarantee that only one record, at most, is removed.

continues on next page

8. Check the result of the query:

```
if (mysql_affected_rows() == 1) {
    print '<p>The blog entry has been
    → deleted.</p>';
} else {
    print '<p style="color: red;">
    → Could not delete the blog entry
    → because:<br />' . mysql_error()
    → . '.</p><p>The query being run
    → was: ' . $query . '</p>';
}
```

The `mysql_affected_rows()` function returns the number of rows altered by the most recent query. If the query ran properly, one row was deleted, so this function should return 1. If so, a message is printed. Otherwise, the MySQL error and query are printed for debugging purposes.

9. Complete the main conditional:

```
} else { // No ID set.
    print '<p style="color: red;">This
    → page has been accessed in
    → error.</p>';
} // End of main IF.
```

If no numeric ID value was passed to this page using either the GET method or the POST method, then this `else` clause takes effect.

10. Close the database connection, and complete the page:

```
mysql_close();
?>
</body>
</html>
```

11. Save the script as `delete_entry.php`, place it in the proper directory for your PHP-enabled server, and test it in your Web browser (Figures 12.21 and 12.22).

To test this script, you must first run `view_blog.php`. Then, click one of the Delete links to access `delete_entry.php`.

✔ Tips

■ You can empty a table completely by running the query `TRUNCATE TABLE tablename`. This approach is preferred over using `DELETE FROM tablename`. `TRUNCATE` will completely drop and rebuild the table, which is better for the database.

■ It's a fairly common error to try to run the query `DELETE * FROM tablename`, like a `SELECT` query. Remember that `DELETE` doesn't use the same syntax as `SELECT`, because you aren't deleting specific columns.

■ Admittedly, you probably don't want to create an application that displays records and lets any user delete them at will. Instead, you'd probably have one version of the `view_blog.php` script without the Edit and Delete links (for the public) and this version for your administration of the blog.

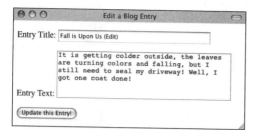

Figure 12.23 When the user arrives at the edit page, the form is shown with the existing values.

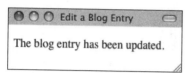

Figure 12.24 Upon submitting the form, the user sees a message like this.

Updating Data in a Database

The final type of query this chapter will cover is UPDATE. It's used to alter the values of a record's columns. The syntax is as follows:

```
UPDATE tablename SET column1_name=value,
→ column2_name=value2 WHERE some_column=
→ value
```

As with any other query, if the values are strings, they should be placed within single quotation marks:

```
UPDATE users SET first_name='Eleanor',
→ age=5 WHERE user_id=142
```

As with a DELETE query, you should use a WHERE clause to limit the rows that are affected. If you don't do this, every record in the database will be updated.

To test that an update worked, you can again use the mysql_affected_rows() function to return the number of records altered.

To demonstrate, let's write a page for editing a blog entry. It will let the user alter an entry's title and text, but not the date entered or the blog ID number (as a primary key, the ID number should never be changed). This script will use a structure like that in delete_entry.php (Script 12.8), first showing the entry (**Figure 12.23**), then handling the submission of that form (**Figure 12.24**).

To update data in a database:

1. Begin a new PHP document in your text editor or IDE (**Script 12.9**).

```
<!DOCTYPE html PUBLIC "-//W3C//DTD
→ XHTML 1.0 Transitional//EN"
  "http://www.w3.org/TR/xhtml1/DTD/
  → xhtml1-transitional.dtd">
<html xmlns="http://www.w3.org/1999/
→ xhtml" xml:lang="en" lang="en">
<head>
  <meta http-equiv="content-type"
  → content="text/html;
  → charset=utf-8" />
  <title>Edit a Blog Entry</title>
</head>
<body>
```

continues on page 386

Script 12.9 You can edit records in a database table by using an UPDATE SQL command.

```
1    <!DOCTYPE html PUBLIC "-//W3C//DTD XHTML 1.0 Transitional//EN"
2        "http://www.w3.org/TR/xhtml1/DTD/xhtml1-transitional.dtd">
3    <html xmlns="http://www.w3.org/1999/xhtml" xml:lang="en" lang="en">
4    <head>
5        <meta http-equiv="content-type" content="text/html; charset=utf-8" />
6        <title>Edit a Blog Entry</title>
7    </head>
8    <body>
9    <?php // Script 12.9 - edit_entry.php
10   /* This script edits a blog entry using an UPDATE query. */
11
12   // Connect and select:
13   $dbc = mysql_connect('localhost', 'username', 'password');
14   mysql_select_db('myblog');
15
16   if (isset($_GET['id']) && is_numeric($_GET['id']) ) { // Display the entry in a form:
17
18       // Define the query.
19       $query = "SELECT title, entry FROM entries WHERE entry_id={$_GET['id']}";
20       if ($r = mysql_query($query)) { // Run the query.
21
22           $row = mysql_fetch_array($r); // Retrieve the information.
23
```

(script continues on next page)

Script 12.9 *continued*

```
24        // Make the form:
25        print '<form action="edit_entry.php" method="post">
26    <p>Entry Title: <input type="text" name="title" size="40" maxsize="100" value="' .
      htmlentities($row['title']) . '" /></p>
27    <p>Entry Text: <textarea name="entry" cols="40" rows="5">' . htmlentities($row['entry']) .
      '</textarea></p>
28    <input type="hidden" name="id" value="' . $_GET['id'] . '" />
29    <input type="submit" name="submit" value="Update this Entry!" />
30    </form>';
31
32    } else { // Couldn't get the information.
33        print '<p style="color: red;">Could not retrieve the blog entry because:<br />' . mysql_
      error() . '.</p><p>The query being run was: ' . $query . '</p>';
34    }
35
36  } elseif (isset($_POST['id']) && is_numeric($_POST['id'])) { // Handle the form.
37
38    // Validate and secure the form data:
39    $problem = FALSE;
40    if (!empty($_POST['title']) && !empty($_POST['entry'])) {
41        $title = mysql_real_escape_string(trim($_POST['title']));
42        $entry = mysql_real_escape_string(trim($_POST['entry']));
43    } else {
44        print '<p style="color: red;">Please submit both a title and an entry.</p>';
45        $problem = TRUE;
46    }
47
48    if (!$problem) {
49
50        // Define the query.
51        $query = "UPDATE entries SET title='$title', entry='$entry' WHERE entry_id={$_
      POST['id']}";
52        $r = mysql_query($query); // Execute the query.
53
54        // Report on the result:
55        if (mysql_affected_rows() == 1) {
56            print '<p>The blog entry has been updated.</p>';
57        } else {
58            print '<p style="color: red;">Could not update the entry because:<br />' . mysql_
      error() . '.</p><p>The query being run was: ' . $query . '</p>';
59        }
60
61    } // No problem!
62
63  } else { // No ID set.
64    print '<p style="color: red;">This page has been accessed in error.</p>';
65  } // End of main IF.
66
67  mysql_close(); // Close the database connection.
68
69  ?>
70  </body>
71  </html>
```

2. Start your PHP code and connect to the database:

```php
<?php // Script 12.9 - edit_entry.php
$dbc = mysql_connect('localhost',
→ 'username', 'password');
mysql_select_db('myblog');
```

3. If the page received a valid entry ID in the URL, define and execute a SELECT query:

```php
if (isset($_GET['id']) &&
→ is_numeric($_GET['id']) ) {
    $query = "SELECT title, entry
    → FROM entries WHERE entry_id=
    → {$_GET['id']}";
    if ($r = mysql_query($query)) {
```

This code is exactly the same as that in the delete page, selecting the two column values from the database for the provided ID value.

4. Retrieve the record, and display the entry in a form:

```php
$row = mysql_fetch_array($r);
print '<form action="edit_entry.php"
→ method="post">
<p>Entry Title: <input type="text"
→ name="title" size="40" maxsize=
→ "100" value="' . htmlentities($row
→ ['title']) . '" /></p>
<p>Entry Text: <textarea name=
→ "entry" cols="40" rows="5">'
→ . htmlentities($row['entry'])
→ . '</textarea></p>
<input type="hidden" name="id"
→ value="' . $_GET['id'] . '" />
<input type="submit" name="submit"
→ value="Update this Entry!" />
</form>';
```

Again, this is almost exactly the same as in the preceding script, including the most important step of storing the ID value in a hidden form input. Here, though, the stored data isn't just printed but is actually used as the values for form elements. For security and to avoid potential conflicts, each value is run through `htmlentities()` first.

5. Report an error if the query failed:

```
} else {
    print '<p style="color: red;">
    → Could not retrieve the blog
    → entry because:<br />' .
    → mysql_error() . '.</p><p>The
    → query being run was: ' . $query
    → . '</p>';
}
```

6. Check for the submission of the form:

```
} elseif (isset($_POST['id']) &&
→ is_numeric($_POST['id'])) {
```

This conditional will be TRUE when the form is submitted.

7. Validate and secure the form data:

```
$problem = FALSE;
if (!empty($_POST['title']) &&
→ !empty($_POST['entry'])) {
    $title = mysql_real_escape_
    → string(trim($_POST['title']));
    $entry = mysql_real_escape_
    → string(trim($_POST['entry']));
} else {
    print '<p style="color: red;">
    → Please submit both a title and
    → an entry.</p>';
    $problem = TRUE;
}
```

continues on next page

UPDATING DATA IN A DATABASE

This code comes from the page used to add blog postings. It performs minimal validation on the submitted data and then runs it through the mysql_real_escape_string() function to be safe. Because the form data can be edited, the form should be validated as if it were a new record being created.

8. Define and execute the query:

```
if (!$problem) {
    $query = "UPDATE entries SET
    → title='$title', entry='$entry'
    → WHERE entry_id={$_POST['id']}";
    $r = mysql_query($query);
```

The UPDATE query sets the title column equal to the value entered in the form's title input and the entry column equal to the value entered in the form's entry textarea. Only the record whose entry_id is equal to $_POST['id'], which comes from a hidden form input, is updated.

9. Report on the success of the query:

```
if (mysql_affected_rows() == 1) {
    print '<p>The blog entry has been
    → updated.</p>';
} else {
    print '<p style="color: red;">
    → Could not update the entry
    → because:<br />' . mysql_error()
    → . '.</p><p>The query being run
    → was: ' . $query . '</p>';
}
```

If one row was affected, then a success message is returned. Otherwise, the MySQL error and the query are sent to the Web browser.

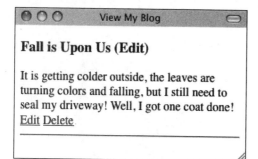

Figure 12.25 Reloading the `view_blog.php` script reflects the changes made to the entries.

10. Complete the conditionals:

```
  } // No problem!
} else { // No ID set.
   print '<p style="color: red;">
   → This page has been accessed in
   → error.</p>';
} // End of main IF.
```

If no numeric ID value was passed to this page using either the GET method or the POST method, then this `else` clause takes effect.

11. Close the database connection, and complete the page:

```
mysql_close();
?>
</body>
</html>
```

12. Save the file as `edit_entry.php`, place it in the proper directory for your PHP-enabled server, and test it in your Web browser (Figures 12.23 and 12.24).

As in the preceding example, to edit an entry, you must click its Edit link in the `view_blog.php` page.

13. Revisit `view_blog.php` to confirm that the changes were made (**Figure 12.25**).

✔ Tips

- The id is a primary key, meaning that its value should never change. By using a primary key in your table, you can change every other value in the record but still refer to the row using that column.

- The mysql_real_escape_string() function does not need to be applied to the ID values used in the queries, as the is_numeric() test confirms they don't contain apostrophes or other problematic characters.

- More thorough edit and delete pages would use the mysql_num_rows() in a conditional to confirm that the SELECT query returned a row prior to fetching it:

  ```
  if (mysql_num_rows($r) == 1) {…
  ```

- If you run an update on a table but don't change a record's values, mysql_affected_rows() will return 0.

- It can't hurt to add a LIMIT 1 clause to an UPDATE query, to ensure that only one row, at most, is affected.

REGULAR EXPRESSIONS

If there were just two things you should understand about regular expressions, they would be that regular expressions are supremely useful in advanced programming and that they're easy to use but taxing to write. However, once you understand the rules for writing regular expressions, that extra knowledge will pay off in spades because regular expressions can vastly improve the quality of your programming.

This chapter will identify what regular expressions are, discuss the rules for constructing them (in great detail), and provide some useful examples demonstrating their capabilities.

Important Compatibility Note

Most of the book has been updated for PHP 6, while still being backward compatible for older versions. The type of regular expressions covered in this chapter—called POSIX Extended—may be disabled in the final version of PHP 6. Because, at the time of this writing, it is not known when PHP 6 will be released or if POSIX Extended regular expressions will be disabled, I've retained this chapter in this edition. If you are running PHP 6 and you find that the functions and code used herein don't work, turn to the book's corresponding Web site (www.DMCInsights.com/phpvqs3/) and support forum (www.DMCInsights.com/phorum/) for assistance.

What Are Regular Expressions?

Think of regular expressions as an elaborate system of matching patterns. For example, a United State zip code is in the format #####-####, where # stands for an integer between 0 and 9 and the last four digits (plus the hyphen) are optional. Therefore, any valid zip code can be identified if it matches this pattern:

^([0-9]{5})(-[0-9]{4})?$

Writing the pattern is the hardest part of using regular expressions, and over the course of this chapter you'll learn what each character means. After you've created a pattern, you then use one of PHP's built-in functions to check a value against the pattern.

PHP supports two types of regular expressions: POSIX Extended and PCRE (Perl compatible). The latter are more powerful and slightly faster, but this chapter covers the former, which are easier to learn, which is why I cover them in this book. Both versions have been supported in PHP for some time now, although POSIX Extended functions may be disabled in PHP 6.

PHP has six POSIX functions for working with regular expressions. These are listed in **Table 13.1** (it's really just three functions plus case-insensitive versions of those three).

In order to explain how patterns are created, this chapter starts by introducing literals and then discusses metacharacters (special symbols) and how to group characters together. Next you'll learn about quantifiers and conclude with classes. The combination of literals, metacharacters, groupings, quantifiers, and classes defines your pattern.

As a formatting rule, this section defines patterns in bold code font (**pattern**) and indicates what the pattern matches in *italics*.

Table 13.1

POSIX Extended Functions

FUNCTION	PURPOSE	CASE SENSITIVE?
ereg()	Match a pattern	Yes
eregi()	Match a pattern	No
ereg_replace()	Match and replace a pattern	Yes
eregi_replace()	Match and replace a pattern	No
split()	Split a string using a pattern	Yes
spliti()	Split a string using a pattern	No

✔ Tips

■ Some text editors, such as BBEdit for Macintosh, TextPad for Windows, and emacs for Unix, among others, allow you to use regular expressions to match and replace patterns within and throughout several documents (**Figure 13.1**). This may be another good reason to learn regular expressions and is something to consider when choosing your text editor.

■ If you learned regular expressions in Unix, Perl, or another technology, you might be able to begin using PHP's PCRE functions with just a little explanation. See the PHP manual for the proper functions to use and their syntax.

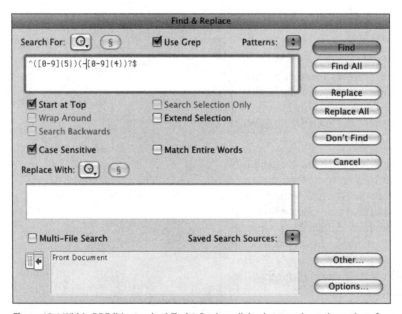

Figure 13.1 Within BBEdit's standard Find & Replace dialog box, you have the option of using regular expressions (even across several files or folders) by checking the Use Grep box. BBEdit can also store regular expression patterns for you and has some built in.

WHAT ARE REGULAR EXPRESSIONS?

Matching Patterns

Two functions are built into PHP expressly for the purpose of matching a pattern within a string: `ereg()` and `eregi()`. The only difference between the two is that `ereg()` treats patterns as case-sensitive, whereas `eregi()` is case-insensitive, making it less particular. The latter is generally recommended for common use, unless you need to be more explicit (perhaps for security purposes, as with passwords). Both functions are evaluated to TRUE if the pattern is matched or FALSE if it isn't.

Here are two different ways to use these functions:

```
eregi('pattern', 'string');
```

or

```
$pattern = 'pattern';
$string = 'string';
eregi($pattern, $string);
```

Throughout the rest of the chapter, you'll assign the pattern to a variable, as in the second example, to draw more attention to the pattern itself—the heart of any regular expression.

The best way to learn and master regular expressions is by practicing. Over the course of this chapter you'll learn how to define a pattern by combining the various building blocks: literals, metacharacters, groupings, and classes. Rather than throw pages of information at you and then apply all of that at once, let's create a simple script that tests a string against a pattern.

This script will display a form that takes two text inputs: the regular expression pattern and the string (or, potentially, number) being checked. The script will then submit these values to itself and report on whether that string matches that pattern. You'll use this script to practice with patterns through most of this chapter.

To match a pattern:

1. Begin a new PHP document in your text editor or IDE (**Script 13.1**):

```
<!DOCTYPE html PUBLIC "-//W3C//DTD
→ XHTML 1.0 Transitional//EN"
    "http://www.w3.org/TR/xhtml1/DTD/
    → xhtml1-transitional.dtd">
<html xmlns="http://www.w3.org/1999/
→ xhtml" xml:lang="en" lang="en">
<head>
  <meta http-equiv="content-type"
  → content="text/html;
  → charset=utf-8" />
  <title>Testing Regular Expression
  → Patterns</title>
</head>
<body>
```

continues on next page

Script 13.1 This simple script lets you enter a pattern and a string or number to test regular expressions.

```
1    <!DOCTYPE html PUBLIC "-//W3C//DTD XHTML 1.0 Transitional//EN"
2        "http://www.w3.org/TR/xhtml1/DTD/xhtml1-transitional.dtd">
3    <html xmlns="http://www.w3.org/1999/xhtml" xml:lang="en" lang="en">
4    <head>
5        <meta http-equiv="content-type" content="text/html; charset=utf-8" />
6        <title>Testing Regular Expression Patterns</title>
7    </head>
8    <body>
9    <?php // Script 13.1 - test_pattern.php
10   /* This script takes a submitted string and checks it against a submitted pattern. */
11
12   // Set the variables to blank values:
13   $string = '';
14   $pattern = '';
15
16   if ( isset($_POST['submitted'])) { // Has the form been submitted?
17
18       // Assign values from the form:
19       $pattern = trim($_POST['pattern']);
20       $string = $_POST['string'];
21
```

(script continues on next page)

2. Create a PHP section and initialize two variables:

```
<?php // Script 13.1 - test_pattern.
→ php
$string = '';
$pattern = '';
```

The HTML form displays the submitted string and pattern as the default values for those inputs (**Figure 13.2**). Because these variables won't have a default value when the page is first loaded (at which point the form hasn't been submitted), they're initially set to an empty value.

3. Check to see whether the form has been submitted:

```
if ( isset($_POST['submitted'])) {
```

Because this page both displays and handles the HTML form, a conditional is used to check for the value of a submit variable.

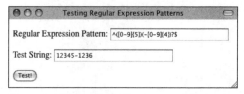

Figure 13.2 The form is *sticky*—it remembers the values that were entered in its previous use.

Script 13.1 *continued*

```
22      // Print the results:
23      print "<p>The result of checking<br /><span style=\"font-style: italic;\">$string</span><br
        />against<br /><span style=\"font-weight: bold;\">$pattern</span><br />is ";
24      if ( eregi($pattern, $string) ) {
25          print 'TRUE!</p>';
26      } else {
27          print 'FALSE!</p>';
28      }
29
30      }
31      // Display the HTML form:
32      ?>
33      <form action="test_pattern.php" method="post">
34          <p>Regular Expression Pattern: <input type="text" name="pattern" value="<?php print
            $pattern; ?>" size="30" /></p>
35          <p>Test String: <input type="text" name="string" value="<?php print $string; ?>" size="30"
            /></p>
36          <input type="submit" name="submit" value="Test!" />
37          <input type="hidden" name="submitted" value="true" />
38      </form>
39      </body>
40      </html>
```

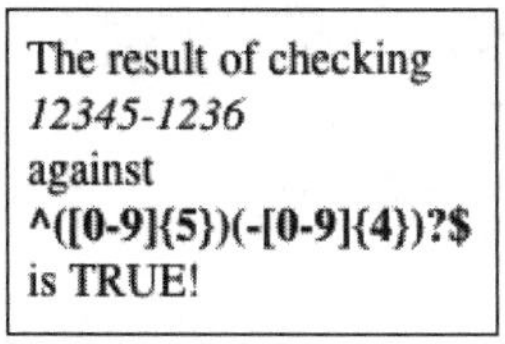

The result of checking
12345-1236
against
^([0-9]{5})(-[0-9]{4})?$
is TRUE!

Figure 13.3 The script reprints the values that were entered in the form.

Adjusting for Magic Quotes

If you're using an older version of PHP and Magic Quotes is enabled, you'll need to add some code to the first script in this chapter. If you don't, the extra backslashes that Magic Quotes adds to form data will throw off the regular expression results. To see if Magic Quotes is enabled, call the `get_magic_quotes_gpc()` function. If it returns TRUE, you would apply the `stripslashes()` function to the form data:

```
if (get_magic_quotes_gpc()) {
    $pattern = stripslashes(trim
    ➝ ($_POST['pattern']));
    $string = stripslashes($_POST
    ➝ ['string']);
} else {
    $pattern = trim($_POST
    ➝ ['pattern']);
    $string = $_POST['string'];
}
```

You would use this code instead of that on lines 19 and 20 of Script 13.1. This change will not be required in the second script, which deals specifically with URLs. If a submitted URL contains quotation marks, it won't be a valid URL anyway, so it would fail the regular expression.

4. Get the submitted values:

```
$pattern = trim($_POST['pattern']);
$string = $_POST['string'];
```

In order to also improve the accuracy of the regular expressions, any extra spaces are removed from the beginning and end of the pattern using `trim()`. This step will be more important once your patterns define the characters a string must begin and end with (in which case a space could make a valid string invalid). For that reason, extraneous spaces are not automatically removed from the string to be matched.

If you're using PHP 4 or 5, see the sidebar for the Magic Quotes adjustment you may need to make in this script.

5. Begin printing out the results:

```
print "<p>The result of checking
➝ <br /><span style=\"font-style:
➝ italic;\">$string</span><br />
➝ against<br /><span style=\"font-
➝ weight: bold;\">$pattern</span>
➝ <br />is ";
```

The main purpose of this script is to run a regular expression using a submitted pattern and a string. While you're reporting on the results, it will be beneficial to see the submitted pattern and string again. These values are printed out here, along with some formatting (and many break tags to make the result flow over several lines; **Figure 13.3**).

6. Check for a match, and report on its success:

```
if ( eregi($pattern, $string) ) {
    print 'TRUE!</p>';
} else {
    print 'FALSE!</p>';
}
```

continues on next page

MATCHING PATTERNS

The `eregi()` function—which is case-insensitive—is the condition for an `if-else` statement. If the string matches the pattern, `eregi()` returns TRUE and that result is printed. Otherwise, the string didn't match the pattern. (Each `print()` statement also closes the paragraph begun in Step 5, in case you were wondering what those closing `</p>` tags were doing.)

7. Complete the form submission conditional and close the PHP section:

   ```
   }
   ?>
   ```

8. Create the HTML form:

   ```
   <form action="test_pattern.php"
   → method="post">
       <p>Regular Expression Pattern:
       → <input type="text" name=
       → "pattern" value="<?php print
       → $pattern; ?>" size="30" /></p>
       <p>Test String: <input type="text"
       → name="string" value="<?php print
       → $string; ?>" size="30" /></p>
       <input type="submit" name="submit"
       → value="Test!" />
       <input type="hidden" name=
       → "submitted" value="true" />
   </form>
   ```

   This is a very simple HTML form containing just two text inputs and a submit button. The text inputs have preset values; they use `print()` statements to print the values of `$pattern` and `$string`.

9. Complete the HTML page:

   ```
   </body>
   </html>
   ```

10. Save the script as `test_pattern.php`, place it in the proper directory for your PHP-enabled server, and load it in your Web browser (**Figure 13.4**).

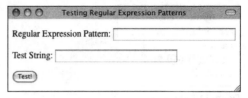

Figure 13.4 This form takes the user input for a regular expression pattern and a string.

✔ Tips

- When it comes time for you to create a script that validates a certain string format—like an email address, a name, or a URL—use this script to test your pattern.

- Remember that regular expressions in PHP are case-sensitive by default. The `eregi()` function used in this example overrules this standard behavior.

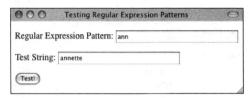

Figure 13.5 The first regular expression test checks a literal (*ann*) against a string.

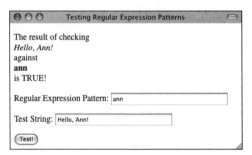

Figure 13.6 A match is made.

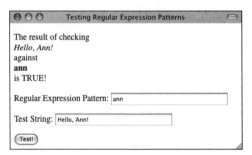

Figure 13.7 Another match is made even though *ann* is in the middle of the string and capitalized.

✔ Tip

■ The examples in this section are purely for demonstration purposes. You should never use a pattern containing just literals in a regular expression. If you need to match specific text, the `strstr()` function is more efficient.

Using Literals

The first type of character you'll use for defining patterns is a *literal*. A literal is a value that is written exactly as it is interpreted. For example, the pattern **a** matches the letter *a*, **ab** matches *ab*, and so forth.

One trick to understanding literals is that they make a match assuming the literal is found anywhere in a string. So, assuming you're using a case-insensitive regular expression function (like `eregi()`), the literal **cat** will match any of the following strings:

◆ *catalog*

◆ *That darn cat*

◆ *My name is Catherine.*

This flexibility with respect to where in a string a pattern is matched applies for all patterns—not just literals—unless you use special characters, as you'll see next. But first, let's use the test script to see literals and `eregi()` in action.

To use literals:

1. Load `test_pattern.php` in your Web browser.

2. Enter **ann** as your pattern and *annette* as your string (**Figure 13.5**).

3. Submit the form to see the results (**Figure 13.6**).

   As you'd expect, a match is made because the string *annette* begins with *ann*.

4. Retest using the same pattern but with *Hello, Ann!* as your string (**Figure 13.7**).

   Again, a match is made because the letters *ann* are found within the string.

5. Continue testing until you're comfortable with the concept of matching literals.

   Any string you submit will make a match as long as it includes *ann* somewhere, regardless of case.

Using Metacharacters

Just one step beyond literals in terms of complexity are metacharacters (**Table 13.2**). These are special symbols that have a meaning beyond their literal value. Whereas **a** simply means *a*, the first metacharacter, the period (.), matches any single character (. matches *a*, *b*, *c*, *1*, *&*, and so on). This is pretty straightforward, although you should note that if you want to refer to a meta-character literally, you must escape it, much as you escape a quotation mark to print it. Hence \. matches the period.

Two metacharacters specify where certain characters must be found. The caret (^)—pronounced like the vegetable and some-times referred to as the *hat*—marks the beginning of a pattern. So, whereas **abc** matches *someabcstring*, **^abc** doesn't (it matches *abcsomestring*).

There is also the dollar sign (**$**). It works like the caret but marks the end of a pattern. Therefore, **a$** matches any string ending with an *a*, like *somestringa*.

You can combine metacharacters and literals to make more demanding patterns. For example, **^a$** only matches *a*; **^a.$** matches any two-character string beginning with *a*, followed by whatever; and **^.a$** corresponds to any two-character string ending with *a*.

Regular expressions also use the pipe (|), which is the equivalent of *or*. Therefore, **^a|b$** matches any string that either begins with *a* or ends with *b*. More practically, **gre|ay** matches both potential spellings of the color.

Using the basic symbols established so far, you can begin to incorporate parentheses to group characters into more involved patterns. Think of parentheses as being used to estab-lish a new literal. Whereas **yes|no** matches many things, including *yeso* or *yeno* (*ye* plus either *s* or *n* plus *o*), **(yes)|(no)**, accepts either of those two words in their entirety, which is certainly what you'd rather look for.

Table 13.2

Metacharacters		
CHARACTER	**NAME**	**MEANING**
.	Period	Any single character
^	Caret	Beginning of a string
$	Dollar sign	End of a string
		Pipe	Alternatives (or)
( )	Parentheses	Group

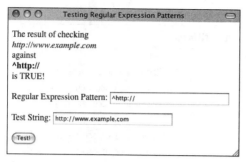

Figure 13.8 This is the beginning of a pattern for matching valid URLs.

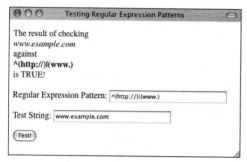

Figure 13.9 A more flexible pattern uses grouping and the pipe.

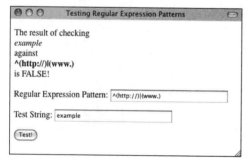

Figure 13.10 Strings that don't begin with either *http://* or *www.* don't pass the regular expression.

To use metacharacters:

1. Load `test_pattern.php` in your Web browser, if it isn't loaded already.

2. Enter **^http://** as your pattern and `http://www.example.com` as your string.

   One way to check for a valid URL is to look for the *http://* start. This pattern insists that the submitted code begin with those characters.

3. Submit the form to see the results (**Figure 13.8**).

   As long as the submitted string begins with *http://*, it will pass the regular expression. This isn't an absolute way to check for a valid URL, but it's a start.

4. Retest using **^(http://)|(www.)** as your pattern and *www.example.com* as your string (**Figure 13.9**).

   If you want, you can broaden the pattern so that the submitted URL begins with either *http://* or *www.*

5. Continue testing until you're comfortable with the concepts of metacharacters and groupings (**Figure 13.10**).

✔ Tips

- To include special characters (^.[]$()|*?{}\) in a pattern, you need to *escape* them (put a backslash before them). This is true for the metacharacters and the grouping symbols (parentheses and brackets). You can also use the backslash to match new lines (\n) and tabs (\t), as you would in a `print()` statement.

- Another benefit of grouping is the ability to use back referencing. This technique is covered in the section "Matching and Replacing Patterns" of this chapter.

- Using the pipe within patterns is referred to as *alternation*.

USING METACHARACTERS

Using Quantifiers

Three special metacharacters called quantifiers allow for multiple occurrences in a pattern (**Table 13.3**). The question mark (?) matches zero or one of a thing, the asterisk (*) is used to match zero or more of a thing, and the plus matches one or more of a thing. (I use this imprecise *thing* in this explanation because quantifiers can be applied to single characters, groupings, or classes.)

So **a?** matches up to one *a* (*a* or no *a*'s match), **a*** matches zero or more *a*'s (*a*, *aa*, *aaa*, and so on), and **a+** matches one or more *a*'s (*a*, *aa*, *aaa*, and so on, but there must be at least one).

To match a certain quantity of a thing, put the quantity between curly braces ({ }), stating either a specific number, a minimum, or a minimum and a maximum. Thus, **a{3}** matches *aaa*; **a{3,}** matches *aaa*, *aaaa*, and so on (three or more *a*'s); and **a{3,5}** matches just *aaa*, *aaaa*, and *aaaaa* (between three and five).

Using parentheses, you can apply quantifiers to groupings. Hence, **a{3}** matches *aaa*, but **(abc){3}** matches *abcabcabc*. As a better example, **bon*** matches a string containing *bon* followed by zero or more *n*'s (say, *bone* or *bonnet*), but **(bon)*** matches a string containing *bon*, followed by zero or more *bon*'s (*bonjour* or *bonbon*).

Table 13.3

Quantifiers

Character	Meaning
?	Zero or one occurrences
*	Zero or more occurrences
+	One or more occurrences
{x}	Exactly x occurrences
{x, y}	Between x and y occurrences (inclusive)
{x,}	At least x occurrences

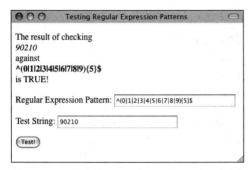

Figure 13.11 This unseemly pattern checks for a valid five-digit zip code.

Figure 13.12 A single letter placed within the zip code causes it to no longer match the pattern.

To use quantifiers:

1. Load `test_pattern.php` in your Web browser, if it isn't loaded already.

2. Enter `^(0|1|2|3|4|5|6|7|8|9){5}$` as your pattern and a five-digit number as your string, and submit the form to see the results (**Figure 13.11**).

   A valid United States zip code is a number five digits long. To check for this, you use the caret to indicate that the submitted string must begin with what follows. In parentheses, you list all the numerals, with the pipe in between them. This grouping says that the characters can be a zero or a one or a two or a three, and so forth. Then the {5} quantifier specifies exactly how many characters must be used out of the grouping. Finally, the dollar sign indicates that this (the five numbers) must be the end of the string.

3. Retest using the same pattern but using a valid or invalid zip code as your string (**Figure 13.12**).

4. Continue testing until you're comfortable using quantifiers.

✔ Tips

- The regular expression used in this example is a complicated way to validate a zip code. When you learn about classes in the next section of this chapter, you'll see a shorthand notation for representing numerals.

- When you use curly braces to specify a number of characters, you must always include the minimum number, but the maximum is optional. Thus $a\{3\}$ and $a\{3,\}$ are acceptable, but $a\{,3\}$ isn't.

Using Classes

As the preceding example demonstrates, trying to factor in a range of possible characters (like every numeral) can make for tedious patterns. This would be even worse if you wanted to check for any ten-letter word (in which case there would be 26 allowable characters). As a shorthand notation for commonly searched characters, you can define and utilize classes (more formally referred to as character classes).

You create classes by placing characters within square brackets ([ ]). For example, you can match any vowel with **[aeoiu]**. Or, you can use the hyphen to indicate a range of characters: **[a-z]** matches any lowercase letter, **[A-Z]** matches any uppercase letter, and **[0-9]** matches any digit.

Classes can also use quantifiers: **^[a-z]{3}$** matches any lowercase word that's three letters long. Or, you can combine multiple ranges within a class: **[A-Za-z]** is any letter, and **[A-Za-z0-9]** is any alphanumeric character.

One odd thing you should remember is that, within the square brackets, the caret symbol—which is normally used to indicate an accepted beginning of a string—is used to exclude a character. So, **[^a]** matches any character that isn't *a*.

PHP defines some classes that will be most useful to you in your programming (**Table 13.4**). These classes have slightly different notations but are used the same way.

By defining your own classes and using those built into PHP, you can make better patterns for regular expressions.

Table 13.4

Character Classes	
CLASS	MEANING
[a-z]	Any lowercase letter
[a-zA-Z]	Any letter
[0-9]	Any numeral
[\f\r\t\n\v]	Any white space
[aeoiu]	Any vowel
[[:alnum:]]	Any letter or number
[[:alpha:]]	Any letter (same as [a-zA-Z])
[[:blank:]]	Any tabs or spaces
[[:digit:]]	Any numeral(same as [0-9])
[[:lower:]]	Any lowercase letter
[[:upper:]]	Any uppercase letter
[[:punct:]]	Any punctuation character (. , ; : -)
[[:space:]]	Any white space

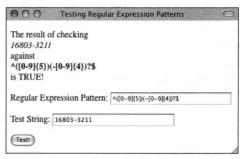

Figure 13.13 This pattern allows for any valid U.S. zip code.

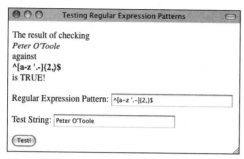

Figure 13.14 The pattern being used here— `^[a-z '-]{2,}$`—checks for a valid name value.

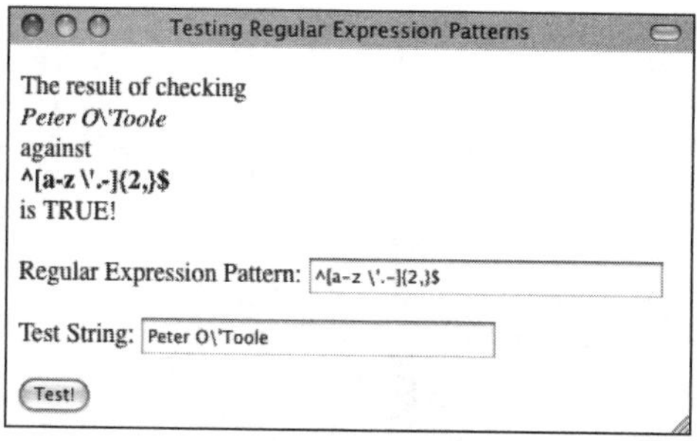

Figure 13.15 If Magic Quotes is enabled, the apostrophe character will be escaped automatically.

✔ Tips

- The biggest problem with using regular expressions is coming up with a pattern that is neither too strict nor too loose. For example, while the pattern for testing a valid name is fairly good, it still wouldn't allow some names (like Danish ones). As a programmer, your goal is to find the pattern that is appropriately strict enough for the task at hand.

- The dollar sign and the period have no special meaning inside of a class.

- Some operating systems throw errors if you use the hyphen in a class without marking a range. In other words, `[a-z]` is okay, but `['.-]` isn't. To work around this, you can escape the hyphen with the backslash: `^[a-z '.\-]{2,}$`.

To use classes:

1. Load `test_pattern.php` in your Web browser, if it isn't loaded already.

2. Enter `^([0-9]{5})(-[0-9]{4})?$` as your pattern and a five- or ten-digit zip code as your string, and submit the form to see the results (**Figure 13.13**).

    This is the zip code pattern mentioned in the first section of this chapter—now you can understand what it means. The caret indicates that the submitted string must begin with what follows. In the first parentheses, it's indicated that five digits are required, using the `[0-9]` class.

    The second parenthetical starts with the hyphen. Then four digits are required. This whole grouping can either exist or not (the question mark indicates that zero or one of this grouping is valid). The dollar sign marks the conclusion of the pattern.

    Using this pattern, zip codes like *12345* and *12345-6789* will match, whereas *123456789* and *12345-* won't.

3. Test the pattern `^[a-z '.-]{2,}$` against common names (**Figure 13.14**).

    To check that someone entered a valid name, use this loose pattern. It has a class that allows for letters, spaces, an apostrophe, a period, and a hyphen. This pattern successfully matches names like *Homer J. Simpson*, *Peter O'Toole*, and *Joe Bagadonuts*.

    If you see results like those in **Figure 13.15**, you're probably using an older version of PHP that has Magic Quotes enabled. See the sidebar earlier in the chapter for the code you'd use to undo the effects of Magic Quotes.

4. Continue testing until you're comfortable working with character classes.

USING CLASSES

Matching and Replacing Patterns

The ereg() and eregi() functions are great for validating strings, but you can take your programming one step further by matching a pattern and then replacing it with a slightly different pattern or with specific text. The syntax for using the two functions is as follows:

```
eregi_replace('pattern', 'replace',
→ 'string');
```

or

```
$pattern = 'pattern';
$replace = 'replace';
$string = 'string';
$new_string = eregi_replace($pattern,
→ $replace, $string);
```

You might want to use this approach to turn a user-entered Web site address (a URL) into a clickable HTML link, by encapsulating it in <a href="url">link</a> tags. Let's write a new script to do just that.

To match and replace a pattern:

1. Begin a new PHP document in your text editor or IDE (**Script 13.2**):

```
<!DOCTYPE html PUBLIC "-//W3C//DTD
→ XHTML 1.0 Transitional//EN"
    "http://www.w3.org/TR/xhtml1/DTD/
    → xhtml1-transitional.dtd">
<html xmlns="http://www.w3.org/1999/
→ xhtml" xml:lang="en" lang="en">
<head>
  <meta http-equiv="content-type"
  → content="text/html;
  → charset=utf-8" />
  <title>Make URL Click-able</title>
</head>
<body>
```

continues on page 408

Script 13.2 The `eregi_replace()` function can be used to turn a user-submitted URL into a hot-clickable link automatically. This is possible due largely to back referencing.

```
1    <!DOCTYPE html PUBLIC "-//W3C//DTD XHTML 1.0 Transitional//EN"
2        "http://www.w3.org/TR/xhtml1/DTD/xhtml1-transitional.dtd">
3    <html xmlns="http://www.w3.org/1999/xhtml" xml:lang="en" lang="en">
4    <head>
5        <meta http-equiv="content-type" content="text/html; charset=utf-8" />
6        <title>Make URL Click-able</title>
7    </head>
8    <body>
9    <?php // Script 13.2 - convert_url.php
10   /* This script turns a valid URL into an HTML link. */
11
12   if ( isset($_POST['submitted'])) { // Has the form been submitted?
13
14       // Trim off extraneous spaces, just in case:
15       $url = trim($_POST['url']);
16
17       // Establish the patterns:
18       $pattern1 = '^((http|https|ftp)://){1}([[:alnum:]-])+(\.)([[:alnum:]-]){2,6}
         ([[:alnum:]/+=%&_.~?-]*)$';
19       $pattern2 = '^([[:alnum:]-])+(\.)([[:alnum:]-]){2,6}([[:alnum:]/+=%&_.~?-]*)$';
20
21       // Test the submitted value against the patterns....
22       if (eregi($pattern1, $url)) { // Check for an existing http/https/ftp.
23
24           $url = eregi_replace($pattern1, '<a href="\\0">\\0</a>', $url);
25           print "<p>Here is the URL: $url<br />The code is now: " . htmlentities ($url) . '</p>';
26
27       } elseif (eregi($pattern2, $url)) { // No http/https/ftp, add http://.
28
29           $url = eregi_replace($pattern2, '<a href="http://\\0">\\0</a>', $url);
30           print "<p>Here is the URL: $url<br />The code is now: " . htmlentities ($url) . '</p>';
31
32       } else { // Invalid URL.
33           print'<p>Please enter a valid URL.</p>';
34       }
35
36   } // End of main conditional.
37   // Display the HTML form:
38   ?>
39   <form action="convert_url.php" method="post">
40       <p>URL: <input type="text" name="url" size="30" /></p>
41       <input type="submit" name="submit" value="Convert" />
42       <input type="hidden" name="submitted" value="true" />
43   </form>
44   </body>
45   </html>
```

MATCHING AND REPLACING PATTERNS

2. Start the PHP section:

```
<?php // Script 13.2 - convert_url.
→ php
```

3. Check that the form has been submitted, and trim spaces from the submitted URL:

```
if ( isset($_POST['submitted'])) {
    $url = trim($_POST['url']);
```

4. Establish the patterns being used:

```
$pattern1 = '^((http|https|ftp)://)
→ {1}([[:alnum:]-])+(\.)
→ ([[:alnum:]-]){2,6}
→ ([[:alnum:]/+=%&_.~?-]*)$';
$pattern2 = '^([[:alnum:]-])+(\.)
→ ([[:alnum:]-]){2,6}
→ ([[:alnum:]/+=%&_.~?-]*)$';
```

These two patterns are essentially the same except that the first tests for the presence of *http://*, *https://*, and *ftp://* whereas the second one doesn't. You'll see why in Steps 6 and 7.

Both patterns are fairly generic. They test for the presence of letters, digits, and the hyphen. Then they check for a single period, followed by a two- to six-letter section (*.com*, *.edu*, *.travel*, and so on). After that can come pretty much anything. This pattern allows for extra domains (*.uk*), pathnames (*/directory*), and so forth.

5. Test the submitted URL against the first pattern:

```
if (eregi($pattern1, $url)) {
```

The if-elseif-else conditional is the heart of the script. It begins by checking for a URL that matches the first pattern (in other words, a URL that begins with *http://*, *https://*, or *ftp://*).

6. Make the code replacement, and print the results:

```
$url = eregi_replace($pattern1,
→ '<a href="\\0">\\0</a>', $url);

print "<p>Here is the URL: $url<br
→ />The code is now: " . htmlentities
→ ($url) . '</p>';
```

If the first pattern is matched, then the URL is turned into the URL enclosed within <a href=""></a> tags. This converted URL is printed so that it appears as a clickable link. It's also printed after being run through the htmlentities() function so that you can see the generated code without looking at the source.

7. Repeat Step 6 using the second pattern:

```
} elseif (eregi($pattern2, $url)) {
    $url = eregi_replace($pattern2,
    → '<a href="http://\\0">\\0</a>',
    → $url);

    print "<p>Here is the URL:
    → $url<br />The code is now: " .
    → htmlentities ($url) . '</p>';
```

If the submitted URL matches the second pattern, then it doesn't begin with *http://,* *https://,* or *ftp://.* In this case, most of the code is the same as in Step 7, except that the URL is preceded with *http://* to make it a valid link.

8. Print a message if the URL is invalid:

```
} else {
    print'<p>Please enter a valid
    → URL.</p>';
}
```

If the submitted URL doesn't match either of the patterns, an error message is printed.

9. Complete the main conditional, and close the PHP code:

```
}
?>
```

continues on next page

10. Create the HTML form:

```
<form action="convert_url.php"
method="post">

    <p>URL: <input type="text"
    → name="url" size="30" /></p>

    <input type="submit" name=
    → "submit" value="Convert" />

    <input type="hidden" name=
    → "submitted" value="true" />

</form>
```

This form just has a URL text input.

11. Complete the HTML page:

```
</body>

</html>
```

12. Save the script as convert_url.php, place it in the proper directory for your PHP-enabled server, and run the page in your Web browser.

13. Test the script using a valid URL (**Figure 13.16**).

✔ Tips

- If eregi_replace() doesn't find a match, the original string is returned.

- The ereg() and eregi() functions can also return matched patterns in an optional third argument, meaning that the code in this example could be replicated using those two functions.

- The split() and spliti() functions work like explode() in that they turn a string into an array. The difference is that these functions let you use regular expressions to define the separator.

- The Perl-compatible version of the ereg_replace() function is preg_replace().

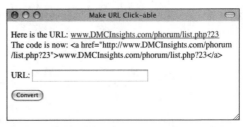

Figure 13.16 Thanks to the eregi_replace() function, a submitted URL, with or without the http:// prefix, is turned into a clickable link.

Back Referencing

There is one more concept to discuss with regard to establishing patterns and making replacements: *back referencing*.

In the zip code matching pattern, ^([0-9]{5})(-[0-9]{4})?$, notice that there are two groupings within parentheses—([0-9]{5}) and (-[0-9]{4}). Within a regular expression pattern, PHP automatically numbers parenthetical groupings beginning at 1. Back referencing allows you to refer to each individual section by using a double backslash (\\) in front of the corresponding number. For example, if you match the zip code *94710-0001* with this pattern, referring back to \\1 will give you *94710*.

This may make more sense once you see the example. It refers to \\0, which represents the entire, matched URL.

INSTALLATION AND CONFIGURATION

There are three technical requirements for executing all of the examples: MySQL (the database application), PHP (the scripting language), and the Web serving application (that PHP runs through). In this appendix I will describe the installation of these tools on two different platforms—Windows and Macintosh. If you are using a hosted Web site, all of this will already be provided for you, but these products are all free and easy enough to install, so putting them on your own computer still makes sense.

After the installation section, this appendix demonstrates some basics for working with MySQL and configuring PHP. The PHP and MySQL manuals cover installation and configuration in a reasonable amount of detail. You may want to also peruse them, particularly if you encounter problems.

Before getting into the particulars, there's one little heads-up: PHP 6 has not been formally released at the time of this writing. I was able to use PHP 6 for all of the examples by building my own installation of PHP 6 for both Windows and Mac. However, in these steps I highly recommend using premade installers, so what you'll see in this appendix are installers and images for PHP 5. When PHP 6 is formally released, these installers will undoubtedly be updated and the steps will likely be the same or very nearly so.

Installation on Windows

In previous versions of this book I've advocated that Windows users take advantage of the available, and free, all-in-one installers. These programs will install and configure the Web server (like Apache, Abyss, or IIS), PHP, and MySQL for you. In past editions, after making that recommendation, I have also demonstrated how to install PHP and MySQL individually yourself. But repeated changes in those installation steps and multiple questions from readers having problems have convinced me to cut to the chase and walk through the all-in-one steps instead.

There are several all-in-one installers out there for Windows. The two that I see mentioned most frequently are XAMPP (www.apachefriends.org) and WAMP (www.wampserver.com). For this appendix, I'll use XAMPP, which runs on Windows 2000, 2003, XP, and Vista.

Along with Apache, PHP, and MySQL, XAMPP also installs:

◆ PEAR, a library of PHP code

◆ phpMyAdmin, the Web-based interface to a MySQL server

◆ A mail server (for sending email)

◆ Several useful extensions

At the time of this writing XAMPP (Version 1.6.8) installs both PHP 5.2.6 and 4.4.9, MySQL 5.0.67, Apache 2.2.9, and phpMyAdmin 2.11.9.2.

I'll run through the installation process in these next steps. Note that if you have any problems, you can use the book's supporting forum (www.DMCInsights.com/phorum/), but you'll probably have more luck turning to the XAMPP site (it is their product, after all). Also, the installer works really well and isn't that hard to use, so rather than detail every single step in the process, I'll highlight the most important considerations.

On Firewalls

A firewall prevents communication over ports (a port being an access point to a computer). Versions of Windows starting with Service Pack 2 of XP include a built-in firewall. You can also download and install third-party firewalls, like ZoneAlarm. Firewalls improve the security of your computer, but they will also interfere with your ability to run Apache, MySQL, and some of the other tools used by XAMPP because these all use ports.

If you see a message like that in Figure A.5, choose Unblock. Otherwise, you can configure your firewall manually (for example, on Windows XP, it's done through Control Panel > Security Center). The ports that need to be open are: 80 (for Apache), 3306 (for MySQL), and 25 (for the Mercury mail server). If you have any problems starting or accessing one of these, disable your firewall and see if it works then. If so, you'll know the firewall is the problem and that it needs to be reconfigured.

Just to be clear, firewalls aren't found just on Windows, but in terms of the instructions in this appendix, the presence of a firewall will more likely trip up a Windows user than any other.

INSTALLATION ON WINDOWS

Figure A.1 From the Apache Friends Web site, grab the latest installer for Windows.

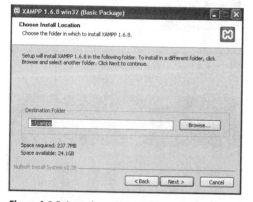

Figure A.2 Select where XAMPP should be installed.

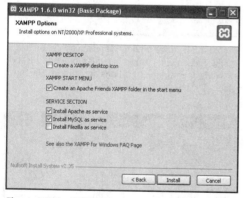

Figure A.3 The XAMPP options I'd recommend using.

To install XAMPP on Windows:

1. Download the latest release of XAMPP for Windows from www.apachefriends.org.

   You'll need to click around a bit to find the download section, but eventually you'll come to an area like that in **Figure A.1**. Then click *Installer*, which is the specific item you want.

2. On your computer, double-click the downloaded file in order to begin the installation process.

3. Click your way through the installation process.

4. When prompted (**Figure A.2**), install XAMPP somewhere other than in the Program Files directory.

   You shouldn't install it in the Program Files directory because of a permissions issue in Windows Vista. I'd recommend installing XAMPP in your root directory (e.g., C:\).

   Wherever you decide to install the program, make note of that location, as you'll need to know it several other times as you work through this appendix.

5. If given the option, install both Apache and MySQL as services (**Figure A.3**).

   Installing them as services just changes how they can be started and stopped, among other things.

   continues on next page

6. After the installation process has done its thing, click Finish (**Figure A.4**).

After you click Finish, a DOS prompt (aka console window) will open up for XAMPP to try a couple of things. If you see a message like that in **Figure A.5**, choose the Unblock option (see the sidebar "On Firewalls" for more on this subject).

7. To start, stop, and configure XAMPP, open the XAMPP Control Panel (**Figure A.6**).

A shortcut to the control panel may be created on your Desktop and in your Start menu, if you checked those options in Figure A.3.

8. Using the control panel, start Mercury (see Figure A.6).

This is the mail server that XAMPP installs. It needs to be running in order to send email using PHP (see Chapter 8, "Creating Web Applications").

9. Immediately set a password for the root MySQL user.

How you do this is explained later in the chapter.

✔ Tips

■ See the configuration section at the end of this chapter to learn how to configure PHP by editing the php.ini file.

■ Your Web root directory—where your PHP scripts should be placed in order to test them—is the htdocs folder in the directory where XAMPP was installed. For my installation (see Figure A.2), this would be C:\xampp\htdocs.

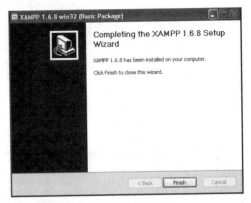

Figure A.4 Installation is complete!

Figure A.5 If you're running a firewall of any kind, you'll see some messages like this when Apache and, possibly, the other applications are started. See the sidebar "On Firewalls" for more.

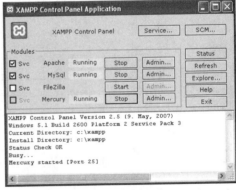

Figure A.6 The XAMPP Control Panel, your gateway to using all of the installed software.

Installation on Mac OS X

Thanks to some ready-made packages, installing MySQL and PHP on Mac OS X used to be surprisingly easy (and may still be). Mac OS X already uses Apache as its Web server and comes with a version of PHP installed but not enabled. Thanks to Marc Liyanage (www.entropy.ch), who does a ton of work supporting the Mac operating system, more current and feature-rich versions of PHP can be easily installed.

I say that installation "used to be" and "may still be" easy because it depends upon the hardware and operating system you're using. The most current Macs at the time of this writing use Intel 64-bit processors. These computers can run 32-bit or 64-bit software. The Apache built into Mac OS X 10.5 (Leopard) is a 64-bit version, meaning that PHP must also be a 64-bit version, as must every library that PHP uses. This is not easily done.

Because of the complications that have arisen from Mac OS X 10.5 using the 64-bit version of Apache (if possible), I've decided to take a more universally foolproof route and recommend that you use the all-in-one MAMP installer (www.mamp.info). It's available in both free and commercial versions, is very easy to use, and won't affect the Apache server built into the operating system.

Along with Apache, PHP, and MySQL, MAMP also installs phpMyAdmin, the Web-based interface to a MySQL server, and lots of useful PHP extensions. At the time of this writing MAMP (Version 1.7.2) installs both PHP 5.2.6 and 4.4.8, MySQL 5.0.41, Apache 2.0.59, and phpMyAdmin 2.11.7.1.

continues on next page

INSTALLATION ON MAC OS X

I'll run through the installation process in these next steps. Note that if you have any problems, you can use the book's supporting forum (www.DMCInsights.com/phorum/), but you'll probably have more luck turning to the MAMP site (it is their product, after all). Also, the installer works really well and isn't that hard to use, so rather than detail every single step in the process, I'll highlight the most important considerations.

To install MAMP on Mac OS X:

1. Download the latest release of MAMP from www.mamp.info.

   From the front page, click *Download*, and then click *MAMP & MAMP PRO 1.7.2*. (**Figure A.7**). The same downloaded file is used for both products. (As new releases of MAMP come out, the link and filename will obviously change accordingly.)

2. On your computer, double-click the downloaded file in order to mount the disk image (**Figure A.8**).

3. Copy the MAMP folder from the disk image to your Applications folder.

   If you think you might prefer the commercial MAMP PRO, copy that folder instead. It comes with a free 14-day trial period.

   Whichever folder you choose, note that you must place it within the Applications folder. It cannot go in a subfolder or another directory on your computer.

4. Open the Applications/MAMP (or Applications/MAMP PRO) folder.

Figure A.7 Download MAMP from this page at www.mamp.info.

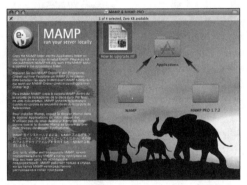

Figure A.8 The contents of the downloaded MAMP disk image.

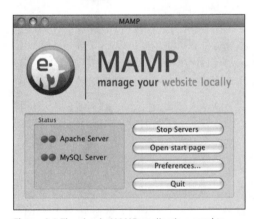

Figure A.9 The simple MAMP application, used to control and configure Apache, PHP, and MySQL.

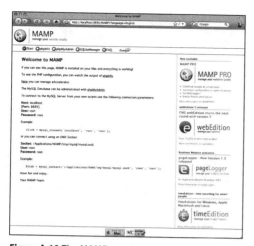

Figure A.10 The MAMP start page.

5. Double-click the MAMP (or MAMP PRO) application to start the program (**Figure A.9**).

It may take just a brief moment to start the servers, but then you'll see a result like that in Figure A.9.

A start page should also open in your default Web browser (**Figure A.10**). Through this page you can view the version of PHP that's running, as well as how it's configured, and interface with the MySQL database using phpMyAdmin.

6. To start, stop, and configure MAMP, use the MAMP application (Figure A.9).

There's not much to the application itself (which is a good thing), but if you click Preferences, you can tweak the application's behavior (**Figure A.11**), set the version of PHP to run (**Figure A.12**), and more.

continues on next page

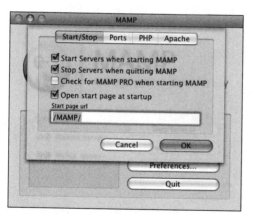

Figure A.11 These five options dictate what happens when you start and stop the MAMP application.

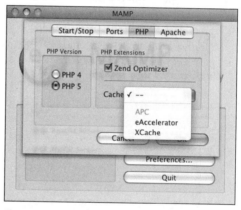

Figure A.12 Because MAMP comes with multiple versions of PHP, you can choose which you'd like to use. You can also enable the Zend Optimizer and a cache for improved performance.

INSTALLATION ON MAC OS X

7. Immediately set a password for the root MySQL user.

How you do this is explained later in the chapter.

✔ Tips

- See the configuration section at the end of this chapter to learn how to configure PHP by editing the `php.ini` file.

- You may want to change the Apache Document Root (**Figure A.13**) to the `Sites` directory in your home folder. By doing so, you assure that your Web documents will backed up along with your other files (and you are performing regular backups, right?).

- MAMP also comes with a Dashboard widget you can use to control the Apache and MySQL servers.

- Your Web root directory—where your PHP scripts should be placed in order to test them—is the `htdocs` folder in the directory where MAMP was installed. For my installation, this would be `Applications/MAMP/htdocs`.

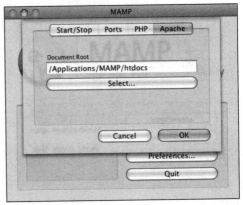

Figure A.13 MAMP allows you to change where the Web documents are placed.

Figure A.14 A command prompt on Windows.

Using the MySQL Client

The MySQL software comes with an important tool called the MySQL client. This application provides an interface for communicating with the MySQL server. It's a command-line tool that must be accessed using the Terminal application on Linux and Mac OS X or through the command (DOS) prompt on Windows.

To use the MySQL client:

1. Make sure the MySQL server is running.

2. Find the MySQL `bin` directory.

   To connect to the client, you'll need to know where it's located. The MySQL client is found within the `bin` directory for your installation. I'll run through the common possibilities...

   If you installed MySQL yourself, the client's location depends on where you installed the software, but it's most likely

   `C:\mysql\bin\mysql` (Windows)

   or

   `/usr/local/mysql/bin/mysql` (Mac OS X and Unix)

   If you used XAMPP on Windows, it's `C:\xampp\mysql\bin\mysql` (assuming you installed XAMPP in `C:\`). If you installed MAMP on Mac OS X, the MySQL directory is `/Applications/MAMP/Library/bin/mysql`.

3. Access a command prompt.

   On Mac OS X and Unix, you can accomplish this by running the Terminal application. On Mac OS X, it's found within the `Applications/Utilities` folder.

   On Windows, click the Start menu, select Run, and then type `cmd` and press Enter at the prompt (**Figure A.14**).

   continues on next page

USING THE MYSQL CLIENT

4. Attempt to connect to the MySQL client.

To connect, enter the pathname identified in Step 2 plus -u *username* -p. So, the
command might be

`c:\mysql\bin\mysql -u` *username* `-p`
(Windows)

or

`/usr/local/mysql/bin/mysql -u` *user-*
name `-p` (Unix and Mac OS X)

or

`C:\xampp\mysql\bin\mysql -u` *username*
`-p` (Windows)

or

`/Applications/MAMP/Library/bin/mysql`
`-u` *username* `-p` (Mac OS X)

Replace *username* with the user name you
want to use. If you haven't yet created any
other users, this will be *root* (root is the
supreme MySQL user). If you haven't yet
established a root user password, you can
omit the -p flag.

5. Enter the password at the prompt
(**Figure A.15**).

The password requested is the MySQL
password for the user named during the
connection. You'll see this prompt only if
you used the -p option in Step 4.

If you installed MAMP on Mac OS X, the
password for the root user will be *root*.

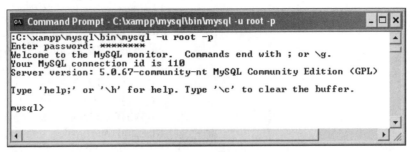

Figure A.15 Successfully accessing the MySQL client on Windows.

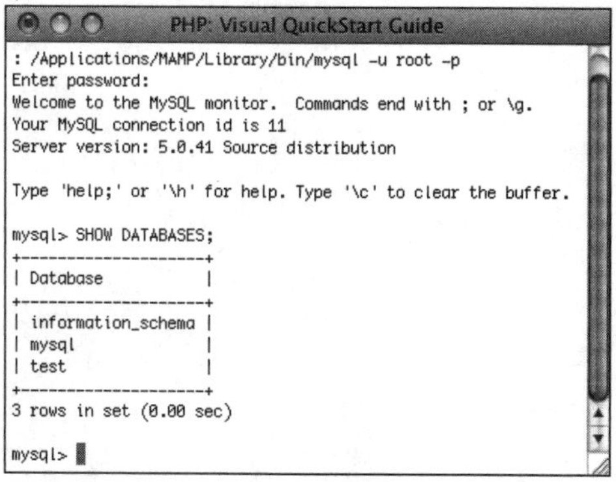

```
   PHP: Visual QuickStart Guide
: /Applications/MAMP/Library/bin/mysql -u root -p
Enter password:
Welcome to the MySQL monitor.  Commands end with ; or \g.
Your MySQL connection id is 11
Server version: 5.0.41 Source distribution

Type 'help;' or '\h' for help. Type '\c' to clear the buffer.

mysql> SHOW DATABASES;
+--------------------+
| Database           |
+--------------------+
| information_schema |
| mysql              |
| test               |
+--------------------+
3 rows in set (0.00 sec)

mysql> 
```

Figure A.16 After a fresh MySQL installation, you'll see only the three default databases.

6. List the available databases (**Figure A.16**):

   SHOW DATABASES;

   The SHOW DATABASES command is an SQL query that lists every database hosted on that MySQL installation that the connected user can see.

7. Exit the MySQL client.

   To do so, type exit or quit.

✔ Tips

- If you see a *Can't connect to local MySQL server through socket...* error message, it normally means MySQL isn't running.

- Remember that the MySQL client is your best tool for debugging PHP scripts that work with MySQL. You can use the MySQL client to check user permissions and to run queries outside of the PHP script.

Creating MySQL Users

Once you've successfully installed MySQL, you need to begin creating users. The initial MySQL installation comes with one user (named *root*) with no password set (except when using MAMP, which sets a default password of *root*). At the very least, you should create a new password for this user.

After that, you can create other users with more limited permissions. As a rule, you shouldn't use the root user for normal, day-to-day operations.

Setting the root user password

One of the first uses of the MySQL client is to assign a password to the root user. When you install MySQL, no value—or no secure password—is established. This is certainly a security risk that should be remedied before you begin to use the server. Just to clarify, your databases can have several users, just as your operating system might. MySQL users are different from operating system users, even if they share a common name. Therefore, the MySQL root user is a different entity than the operating system's root user— it has different powers and even different passwords (preferably but not necessarily).

Most importantly, understand that the MySQL server must be running in order for you to use the MySQL client. If MySQL isn't currently running, start it now using the steps outlined earlier in the appendix.

To assign a password to the root user:

1. Connect to the MySQL client.

See the preceding set of steps for detailed instructions.

2. Enter the following command, replacing *thepassword* with the password you want to use (**Figure A.17**):

```
SET PASSWORD FOR 'root'@'localhost'
→ = PASSWORD('thepassword');
```

Keep in mind that passwords in MySQL are case-sensitive, so *Kazan* and *kazan* aren't interchangeable. The term PASSWORD that precedes the actual quoted password tells MySQL to encrypt that string. And there cannot be a space between *PASSWORD* and the opening parentheses.

3. Exit MySQL:

```
exit
```

4. Test the new password by logging in to the MySQL client again.

Now that a password has been established, you need to add the -p flag to the connection command. You'll see an *Enter password:* prompt, where you enter the just-created password.

Figure A.17 You should establish a secure root user's password immediately after you install the software.

Creating users and privileges

After you have MySQL successfully up and running, and after you've established a password for the root user, it's time to begin adding other users. To improve the security of your databases, you should always create new users to access your databases rather than using the root user at all times.

The MySQL privileges system was designed to ensure proper authority for certain commands on specific databases. This technology is how a Web host, for example, can let several users access several databases without concern. Each user in the MySQL system can have specific capabilities on specific databases from specific hosts (computers). The root user—the MySQL root user, not the system's—has the most power and is used to create sub-users, although sub-users can be given rootlike powers (inadvisably so).

When a user attempts to do something with the MySQL server, MySQL first checks to see if the user has permission to connect to the server at all (based on the user name, the user's password, and the information in the MySQL database's user table). Second, MySQL checks to see if the user has permission to run the specific SQL statement on the specific databases—for example, to select data, insert data, or create a new table. **Table A.1** lists the various privileges you can set on a user-by-user basis.

There are a handful of ways to set users and privileges in MySQL, but it's recommended that you do it manually using the MySQL client and the GRANT command. The syntax goes like this:

```
GRANT privileges ON database.* TO
→ 'username' IDENTIFIED BY 'password';
```

For the *privileges* aspect of this statement, you can list specific privileges from Table A.1, or you can allow for all of them by using ALL

Table A.1

MySQL Privileges	
PRIVILEGE	ALLOWS
SELECT	Read rows from tables.
INSERT	Add new rows of data to tables.
UPDATE	Alter existing data in tables.
DELETE	Remove existing data from tables.
INDEX	Create and drop indexes in tables.
ALTER	Modify the structure of a table.
CREATE	Create new tables or databases.
DROP	Delete existing tables or databases.
RELOAD	Reload the grant tables (and therefore enact user changes).
SHUTDOWN	Stop the MySQL server.
PROCESS	View and stop existing MySQL processes.
FILE	Import data into tables from text files.
GRANT	Create new users.
REVOKE	Remove users' permissions.

(which isn't prudent). The *database.** part of the statement specifies which database and tables the user can work on. You can name specific tables using *database.tablename* syntax or allow for every database with **.** (again, not prudent). Finally, you can specify the user name and a password.

The user name has a maximum length of 16 characters. When you're creating a user name, be sure to avoid spaces (use the underscore instead), and note that user names are case-sensitive.

The password has no length limit but is also case-sensitive. The passwords are encrypted in the MySQL database, meaning they can't be recovered in a plain text format. Omitting the IDENTIFIED BY '*password*' clause results in that user not being required to enter a password (which, once again, should be avoided).

Finally, you have the option of limiting users to particular hostnames. The hostname is either the name of the computer on which the MySQL server is running (*localhost* being the most common value here) or the name of the computer from which the user will be accessing the server. This can even be an IP address, should you choose. To specify a particular host, change your statement to

```
GRANT ALL ON database.* TO
→ 'username'@'hostname' IDENTIFIED
→ BY 'password';
```

To allow for any host, use the hostname wildcard character (%):

```
GRANT ALL ON database.* TO
→ 'username'@'%' IDENTIFIED BY
→ 'password';
```

As an example of this process, you'll create two new users with specific privileges on the temp database. Keep in mind that you can only grant permissions to users on existing databases. This next sequence will also show how to create a database.

To create new users:

1. Log in to the MySQL client as a root user.

   Use the steps already explained to do this. You must be logged in as a user capable of creating databases and other users.

2. Create a new database (**Figure A.18**):

   CREATE DATABASE temp;

   If your MySQL server doesn't yet have a temp database, create one using CREATE DATABASE temp (followed by a semicolon, as is required by the MySQL client).

3. Create a user with administrative-level privileges on the temp database (**Figure A.19**):

   GRANT SELECT, INSERT, UPDATE,
   → DELETE, CREATE, DROP, ALTER, INDEX
   → ON temp.* TO 'llama'@'localhost'
   → IDENTIFIED BY 'camel';

   This user, *llama*, can create tables, alter tables, insert data, update data, and so forth, on the temp database. This essentially includes every administrative-level capability aside from creating new users. Be certain to use a password—perhaps one more clever than used here—and, preferably, specify a particular host.

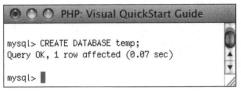

Figure A.18 Creating a new database.

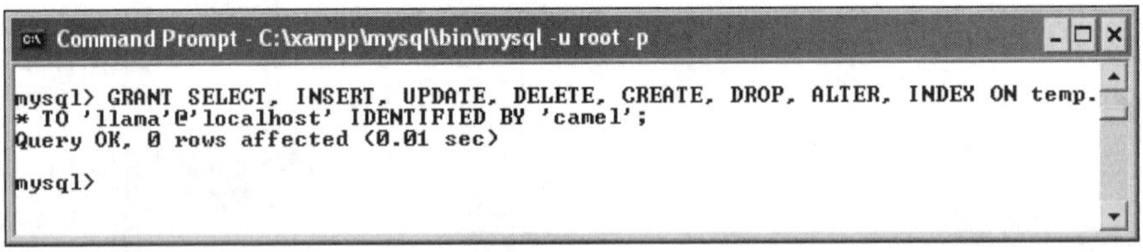

Figure A.19 Creating an administrative-level user for a single database.

Figure A.20 This user has more restricted rights to the same database.

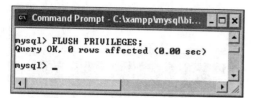

Figure A.21 Don't forget this step before you try to access MySQL using the newly created users.

4. Create a user with basic access to the databases (**Figure A.20**):

   ```
   GRANT SELECT, INSERT, UPDATE, DELETE
   → ON temp.* TO 'webuser'@'localhost'
   → IDENTIFIED BY 'BroWs1ng';
   ```

   Now the generic *webuser* can browse through records (SELECT from tables) as well as add, edit, and delete them, but this user can't alter the structure of the database. When you're establishing users and privileges, work your way from the bottom up, allowing the bare minimum of access at all times.

5. Apply the changes (**Figure A.21**):

   ```
   FLUSH PRIVILEGES;
   ```

   The changes just made won't take effect until you've told MySQL to reset the list of acceptable users and privileges, which is what this command does. Forgetting this step and then being unable to access the database using the newly created users is a common mistake.

✔ Tips

- Any database whose name begins with test_ can be modified by any user who has permission to connect to MySQL. Therefore, be careful not to create a database named this way unless it truly is experimental.

- The REVOKE command removes users and permissions.

PHP Configuration

One of the benefits of installing your own version of PHP is that you can configure it as you prefer. How PHP runs is determined by the php.ini file, which is normally created when PHP is installed.

Two of the most important settings you may want to consider tweaking are display_errors and error_reporting (both are discussed in Chapter 3, "HTML Forms and PHP"). To change any setting, open the PHP configuration file, edit it as needed, then save it, and restart the Web server.

To alter PHP's configuration:

1. Open the php.ini file in any text editor.

   The file's location on your computer depends on many things. The best way to find it is to run a phpinfo() script in your Web browser (**Figure A.22**).

2. Change the settings as you wish.

   Depending on your operating system, you may need authority to make changes to this file.

   Many instructions are included in the file. Lines are commented out (made inactive) by preceding them with a semicolon.

3. Save the php.ini file.

4. Restart your Web server.

   You don't need to restart the entire computer, just the Web server (e.g., Apache).

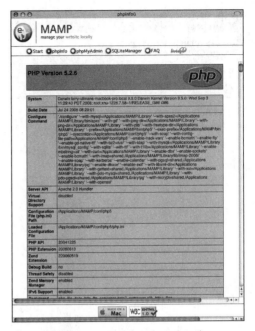

Figure A.22 The phpinfo() function prints the location of the active php.ini file as well as all the configuration information.

✔ Tips

- It's possible that your computer doesn't have a `php.ini` file. In that case, create one from scratch or take one from the downloaded PHP source code.

- You can also use the `phpinfo()` script to check that your configuration changes have taken effect.

- If you edit the `php.ini` file and restart the Web server but your changes don't take effect, make sure you're editing the proper `php.ini` file (you may have more than one on your computer).

Enabling Mail

The `mail()` function works only if the computer running PHP has access to sendmail or another mail server. One way to enable the `mail()` function is to set the `smtp` value in the `php.ini` file (for Windows only). This approach works, for example, if your Internet provider has an SMTP address you can use. Unfortunately, you can't use this value if your ISP's SMTP server requires authentication.

For Windows, there are also a number of free SMTP servers, like Mercury. It's installed along with XAMPP, or you can install it yourself if you're not using XAMPP.

Mac OS X comes with a mail server installed—postfix and/or sendmail—that needs to be enabled. Search Google for instructions on manually enabling your mail server on Mac OS X.

Alternatively, you can search some of the PHP code libraries to learn how to use an SMTP server that requires authentication.

RESOURCES AND NEXT STEPS

This book was written to give beginning PHP programmers a good foundation on which to base their learning. A few topics have been either omitted or glossed over due to this book's more fundamental focus. This appendix lists a number of useful PHP-related Internet resources; briefly discusses where to obtain more information for databases and some uncovered topics; and includes a few tables, both old and new.

Along with those sites included here, you should familiarize yourself with the book's companion Web site, found at www.DMCInsights.com/phpvqs3/. There you'll find:

◆ More Web links

◆ All the scripts used in the book

◆ A support forum for your questions

◆ An errata page, listing printing errors in this book (which do happen, sadly)

When the first edition of this book was written, few good PHP sites were available. Now there are literally dozens (and hundreds of not-so-good ones). The best, most obvious ones are included here, but a quick Internet search will always be a great resource for you.

Online PHP Resources

If you have questions specifically about PHP, you should be able to find the answer with ease. This section of the appendix highlights the best Internet-specific tools for you to use.

The PHP manual

All PHP programmers should familiarize themselves with and possibly acquire some version of the PHP manual before beginning to work with the language. The manual is available from the official PHP site— www.php.net/docs.php—as well as from a number of other locations.

You can download the manual in nearly a dozen languages in different formats. The official Web site also has an annotated version of the manual available at www.php.net/manual/en/ (in English), where users have added helpful notes and comments. If you're having problems with a particular function, reading the manual's page for that function will likely provide an answer.

You can quickly access the documentation page for any specific function by going to www.php.net/*functionname*. For example, the page for the number_format() function is www.php.net/number_format.

General PHP Web sites

This section mentions a few of the many useful Web sites you can turn to when you're programming, but it leaves it up to you to discover the ones you like best. Most of these also contain links to other PHP-related sites. The first, and most obvious, site to bookmark is PHP.net (www.php.net), the official site for PHP.

Secondarily, you should familiarize yourself with Zend (www.zend.com), the home page for the creators of PHP's core. The site contains numerous downloads plus a wealth of other resources—straight from the masters, so to speak.

For information on specific topics, PHPBuilder (`www.phpbuilder.com`) is a good place to turn. The site has dozens of articles explaining how to do particular tasks using PHP. On top of that, PHPBuilder provides support forums and a code library where programmers have uploaded sample scripts.

W3Schools (`www.w3schools.com`) is a good general Web development site, but it also focuses a good portion of its energies on PHP. For a cohesive look at developing dynamic Web sites using PHP, HTML, CSS, and JavaScript, this is an excellent place to turn.

One final Web reference is the PHP Coding Standard, available through `http://www.DMCInsights.com/links/2`. The standard is a document that makes recommendations for programming in PHP in terms of proper format and syntax for variable names, control structures, and so forth. You shouldn't feel obligated to abide by these rules, but they provide some solid and well-thought-out recommendations that can help minimize errors as you program.

Code repositories

There's no shortage of code libraries online these days. Due to the generous (and often showy) nature of PHP programmers, many sites have scores of PHP scripts, organized and available for download. The best online code repositories are as follows:

◆ WeberDev (`www.weberdev.com/maincat.php3?categoryID=106&category=PHP`)

◆ HotScripts (`www.hotscripts.com/PHP/`).

◆ PX: the PHP Code Exchange (`http://px.sklar.com`)

◆ PHP Resource Index (`http://php.resourceindex.com`)

◆ PHP Classes Repository (`www.phpclasses.org`)

ONLINE PHP RESOURCES

You can also find code examples at Zend and PHPBuilder or by searching the Web. There's even a search engine dedicated to finding code: `www.koders.com`.

Newsgroups and mailing lists

If you have access to newsgroups, you can use them as a great sounding board for ideas as well as a place to get your most difficult questions answered. Of course, you can always give back to the group by offering your own expertise to those in need.

The largest English-language PHP newsgroup is `comp.lang.php`. You may be able to access it through your ISP or via a pay-for-use Usenet organization. Newsgroups are also available in languages other than English.

The PHP Web site lists the available mailing lists you can sign up for at `www.php.net/mailing-lists.php`.

Before you post to any newsgroup or mailing list, it will behoove you to read Eric Steven Raymond's "How to Ask Questions the Smart Way" at `www.catb.org/~esr/faqs/smart-questions.html`. The ten minutes spent reading that document will save you hours when you go asking for assistance.

Database Resources

Which database resources will be most useful to you depends, obviously, on which database management system (DBMS) you're using. The most common database used with PHP is probably MySQL, but PHP supports all of the standard databases.

To learn more about using MySQL, begin with the official MySQL Web site (`www.mysql.com`). You can download the MySQL manual to use as a reference while you work. A handful of books are also available specifically on MySQL, including my own *MySQL: Visual QuickStart Guide, 2nd Edition* (Peachpit Press, 2006).

If you're using MySQL, don't forget to download and install phpMyAdmin (`www.phpmyadmin.net`). Written in PHP, this is an invaluable tool for working with a database. If you're using PostgreSQL or even Oracle, you can find similar tools available for interfacing with them. Every database application also has its own mailing lists and newsgroups.

Another area of database resources you should delve into is SQL. Web sites discussing SQL, the language used by every database application, include the following:

◆ SQL Course (`www.sqlcourse.com`)

◆ A Gentle Introduction to SQL (`www.sqlzoo.net`)

◆ W3Schools' SQL Tutorial (`www.w3schools.com/sql`)

◆ SQL.org (`www.sql.org`)

My *PHP 6 and MySQL 5 for Dynamic Web Sites: Visual QuickPro Guide* (Peachpit Press, 2008) also discusses SQL and MySQL in much greater detail than this book.

Top Ten Frequently Asked Questions (or Problems)

Debugging is a valuable skill that takes time and experience to fully develop. But rather than send you off on that journey ill-equipped, I've included the ten most frequently seen problems in PHP scripts, along with the most likely causes. First, though, here are five of my best pieces of advice when it comes to debugging a problem:

1. Know what versions of PHP you're running.

   Some problems are specific to a version of PHP. Use a `phpinfo()` script to test the version in use whenever you go to use a server for the first time. Also make sure you know what version of MySQL you're using, if applicable, the operating system, the Web server (e.g., Apache 2.2), etc.

2. Run all PHP scripts through a URL.

   If you don't run a PHP script through a URL—and this includes the submission of a form to a PHP script, the Web server will not handle the request, meaning that PHP will never execute the code.

3. Trust the error message!

   Many beginners have more difficulty than they should in solving a problem because they don't believe the error message they see. While some of PHP's error messages are cryptic and even a small few can be misleading, if PHP says there's a problem on line 22, the problem is probably on line 22.

4. Avoid "trying" things to fix a problem!

   If you're not sure as to what's causing the problem and what the proper fix is, avoid trying random things as a solution. You'll likely create new issues this way and only further confuse the original problem.

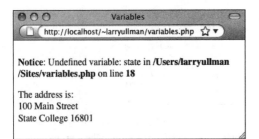

Figure B.1 Errors complaining about undefined variables or indexes often come from spelling or capitalization mistakes.

5. Take a break!

The best piece of advice I can offer is to step away from the computer and take a break. I've solved many, many problems this way. Sometimes a clear head is what you really need.

Moving on, here are the top ten likely problems you'll encounter in PHP:

1. Blank Web pages

If you see a blank screen in your Web browser after submitting a form or loading a PHP script, it's most likely because an error occurred that terminated the execution of the page. First check the HTML source code to see if it's an HTML problem. Then turn on `display_errors` in your `php.ini` configuration file or PHP script to see what PHP problem could be occurring.

2. *Undefined variable* or *undefined index* error (**Figure B.1**)

These errors occur when error reporting is set on its highest level, and they may or may not indicate a problem. Check the spelling of each variable or array index to make sure it's correct. Then, either change the error reporting settings or initialize variables prior to referring to them. Also make sure, of course, that variables that should have a value actually do!

3. Variables don't have a value

Perhaps you referred to a variable by the wrong name. Double-check your capitalization and spelling of variable names, and then be certain to use `$_GET`, `$_POST`, `$_COOKIE`, and `$_SESSION` as appropriate. If need be, use the `print_r()` function to see the name and value of every variable.

continues on next page

4. *Call to undefined function...* error

Such an error message means you're attempting to use a function that PHP doesn't have. This problem can be caused by a misspelling of a function name, failure to define your own function before calling it, or using a function that's not available in your version of PHP. Check your spelling and the PHP manual for a non-user-defined function to find the problem.

5. *Headers already sent* error (**Figure B.2**)

This error message indicates that you've used an HTTP header-related function—`header()`, `setcookie()`, or `session_start()`—after the Web browser has already received HTML or even a blank space. Double-check what occurs in a script before you call any of these functions, or use output buffering to avoid the hassle. You can also make use of output buffering to prevent these errors from occurring.

6. *Access denied* error (**Figure B.3**)

If you see this message while attempting to work with a database, then the user name, password, and host combination you're using doesn't have permission to access the database. This isn't normally a PHP issue. Confirm the values that are being used, and attempt to connect to the database using a different system (such as the MySQL client).

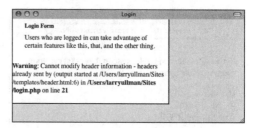

Figure B.2 Some functions create *headers already sent* errors if called at the wrong time.

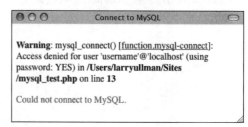

Figure B.3 If the MySQL access information is incorrect, you'll see a message saying that database access has been denied.

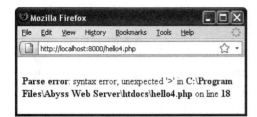

Figure B.4 Parse errors are all too common and prevent scripts from executing.

7. *Supplied argument is not a valid MySQL result resource* error

This is another database-related error message. The message means that a query result is being used inappropriately. Most frequently, this is because you're trying to fetch rows from a query that didn't return any records. To solve this problem, print out the query being run and test it using another tool (such as the MySQL client or phpMyAdmin). Also check that you've been consistent with your variable names.

8. Preset HTML form values are cut off

You must put the value attribute of an HTML form input within double quotation marks. If you fail to do so, only the part of the value up to the first space will be set as that input's value.

9. Conditionals or loops behave unpredictably

These logical errors are quite common. Check that you haven't used the wrong operator (such as = instead of ==) and that you refer to the proper variables. Then use `print()` statements to let you know what the script is doing.

10. Parse errors (**Figure B.4**)

Parse errors are the most ubiquitous problems you'll deal with. Even the most seasoned PHP programmer sees them occasionally. Check that every statement concludes with a semicolon and that all quotation marks, parentheses, square braces, and curly brackets are evenly paired. If you still can't find the parse error, comment out large sections of the script using the /* and */ characters. Uncomment a section at a time until you see the parse error again. Then you'll know where in the script the problem is (or most likely is).

Next Steps

This book will get you started using PHP, but there are a few topics that you may want to investigate further.

Security

Web servers, operating systems, databases, and PHP security are all topics that could merit their own books. Although this book tries to demonstrate writing secure Web applications, there's always room for you to learn more in this area. Start by checking out these sites:

◆ A Study in Scarlet (www.securereality. com.au/studyinscarlet.txt)

◆ W3C Security Resources (www.w3.org/ Security)

The first is an article about writing secure PHP code. The second is the World Wide Web Consortium's resources page for Web-related security issues.

You should also read the relevant sections of the PHP manual and the manual for the database you're using. Searching the Internet for *PHP* and *security* will turn up many interesting articles as well.

Object-Oriented Programming

The subject of objects and object-oriented programming (OOP) is not covered in this book for two reasons:

1. It's well beyond the scope of a beginner's guide.

2. You won't be restricted as to what you can do in PHP by not understanding objects.

When you decide you want to learn the subject, you can search the PHP sites for tutorials, check out a framework (see the next section of the appendix), or read my *PHP 5 Advanced: Visual QuickPro Guide* (Peachpit Press, 2007). I dedicate around 150 pages of that book just to OOP (and there are still aspects of OOP that I didn't get to)!

Frameworks

A framework is an established library of code that you can use to develop sophisticated Web applications. By reusing someone else's proven PHP, you can quickly build parts or all of a Web site.

There are many PHP frameworks available, starting with PEAR. The PEAR library is an immense repository of PHP code, written using objects (classes, technically). Even if you don't use objects yourself or you barely understand the concept, you can still get a lot of value out of the PEAR Web site (http:// pear.php.net). PEAR and its Web site provide free, wonderful code and demonstrate good PHP coding style. PECL (http://pecl. php.net) is PEAR's more powerful sibling.

Another framework to consider is the Zend Framework (http://framework.zend.com). A relative newcomer, this framework has a lot of benefits and is well documented.

Many people love frameworks and what they offer. On the other hand, it does take some time to learn how to use a framework, and customizing the framework's behavior can be daunting.

JavaScript and Ajax

JavaScript is a client-side technology that runs in the Web browser. It can be used to add various dynamic features to a Web site, from simple eye candy like image rollovers to interactive menus and forms. Because it runs within the Web browser, JavaScript provides some functionality that PHP cannot. And, like PHP, JavaScript is relatively easy to learn and use. For more, see:

◆ JavaScript.com (`www.javascript.com`)

◆ W3School's JavaScript pages (`www.w3schools.com/js/`)

Ajax (which either means Asynchronous JavaScript and XML or doesn't, depending upon whom you ask) has been all the rage in the Web development community since around 2005. This technology uses JavaScript to communicate with the server without the user knowing it. The net effect is a Web site that behaves more like a desktop application. For more, see:

◆ Ajaxian (`www.ajaxian.com`)

◆ CrackAjax.net (`www.crackajax.net`)

Other Books

It is my hope that after reading this book you'll be interested in learning more about PHP and Web development in general. While I could recommend books by other writers, there's an inherent conflict there and my opinion as a rival writer would not be the same as yours as a reader. So, instead, I'll just quickly highlight a couple of my other books and how they compare to this one.

The *PHP 6 and MySQL 5 for Dynamic Web Sites: Visual QuickPro Guide* (Peachpit Press, 2008) is kind of a sequel to this one. There is some overlap in content, particularly in the early chapters, but the examples are different and it goes at a faster pace. MySQL and SQL in particular get a lot more coverage, and there are three different example chapters: a multilingual forum, a user registration and login system, and an e-commerce setup.

My *PHP 5 Advanced: Visual QuickPro Guide* (Peachpit Press, 2007) is kind of a sequel to the PHP and MySQL book just mentioned. This book is much more advanced, spending a lot of time on topics such as OOP and PEAR. It's not intended to be read as linearly as this one, but rather each chapter focuses on a specific topic.

The *MySQL: Visual QuickStart Guide, Second Edition* (Peachpit Press, 2006) looks almost exclusively at just MySQL and SQL. Although there are four chapters covering languages used to interact with MySQL—PHP, Perl, and Java, plus a techniques chapter, this book largely addresses things like installation, administration, and maximizing your MySQL knowledge.

Finally, my *Building a Web Site with Ajax: Visual QuickProject Guide* (Peachpit Press, 2008) walks through the process of coding an Ajax-enabled Web site. It also uses PHP and MySQL, but those technologies aren't taught in the same way that JavaScript and Ajax are.

Tables

This book has a handful of tables scattered about, the three most important of which are reprinted here as a convenient reference. You'll also find one new table that lists operator precedence (**Table B.1**). This partial list goes from highest to lowest (for example, multiplication takes precedence over addition).

Table B.2 lists PHP's main operators and their types. It's most important to remember that a single equals sign (=) assigns a value to a variable, whereas two equals signs (==) are used together to check for equality.

Table B.3 indicates the modes you can use when opening a file. Which you choose determines what PHP can do with that file—write to it, read from it, and so forth.

The various formats for the `date( )` function may be one of the hardest things to remember. Keep **Table B.4** nearby when you're using the `date( )` function.

Table B.1

Operator Precedence
! ++ --
* / %
+ - .
< <= > >=
== != ===
&&
||
= += -= *= /= .= %=
and
xor
or

Table B.2

PHP's Operators		
OPERATOR	USAGE	TYPE
+	Addition	Arithmetic
−	Subtraction	Arithmetic
*	Multiplication	Arithmetic
/	Division	Arithmetic
%	Modulus (remainder of a division)	Arithmetic
++	Incrementation	Arithmetic
--	Decrementation	Arithmetic
=	Assigns a value to a variable	Assignment
==	Equality	Comparison
!=	Inequality	Comparison
<	Less than	Comparison
>	Greater than	Comparison
<=	Less than or equal to	Comparison
>=	Greater than or equal to	Comparison
!	Negation	Logical
AND	And	Logical
&&	And	Logical
OR	Or	Logical
||	Or	Logical
.	Concatenation	String
XOR	Or not	Logical
.=	Concatenates to the value of a variable	Combined concatenation and assignment
+=	Adds to the value of a variable	Combined arithmetic and assignment
-=	Subtracts from the value of a variable	Combined arithmetic and assignment

Table B.3

fopen( ) Modes

MODE	MEANING
r	Read only; begin reading at the start of the file.
r+	Read or write; begin at the start of the file.
w	Write only; create the file if it doesn't exist, and overwrite any existing contents.
w+	Read or write; create the file if it doesn't exist, and overwrite any existing contents (when writing).
a	Write only; create the file if it doesn't exist, and append the new data to the end of the file (retain any existing data and add to it).
a+	Read or write; create the file if it doesn't exist, and append the new data to the end of the file (when writing).
x	Write only; create the file if it doesn't exist, but do nothing (and issue a warning) if the file does exist.
x+	Read or write; create the file if it doesn't exist, but do nothing (and issue a warning) if the file already exists (when writing).

Table B.4

date( ) Function Formatting

CHARACTER	MEANING	EXAMPLE
Y	Year as 4 digits	2004
y	Year as 2 digits	04
L	Is it a leap year?	1 (for yes)
n	Month as 1 or 2 digits	2
m	Month as 2 digits	02
F	Month	February
M	Month as 3 letters	Feb
j	Day of the month as 1 or 2 digits	8
d	Day of the month as 2 digits	08
l (lowercase L)	Day of the week	Monday
D	Day of the week as 3 letters	Mon
w	Day of the week as a single digit	0 (Sunday)
z	Day of the year: 0 to 365	189
t	Number of days in the month	31
S	English ordinal suffix for a day, as 2 characters	rd
g	Hour; 12-hour format as 1 or 2 digits	6
G	Hour; 24-hour format as 1 or 2 digits	18
h	Hour; 12-hour format as 2 digits	06
H	Hour; 24-hour format as 2 digits	18
i	Minutes	45
s	Seconds	18
u	Microseconds	1234
a	am or pm	am
A	AM or PM	PM
U	Seconds since the epoch	1048623008
e	Timezone	UTC
I (capital i)	Is it daylight saving?	1 (for yes)
O	Difference from GMT	+0600

TABLES

INDEX